THE YALE EDITION

OF

HORACE WALPOLE'S

CORRESPONDENCE

EDITED BY W. S. LEWIS

VOLUME TWO

HORACE WALPOLE'S
CORRESPONDENCE

WITH

THE REV. WILLIAM COLE

I I

EDITED BY W. S. LEWIS

AND

A. DAYLE WALLACE, Ph.D.
ASSOCIATE PROFESSOR OF ENGLISH IN THE
UNIVERSITY OF OMAHA

NEW HAVEN
YALE UNIVERSITY PRESS
LONDON : HUMPHREY MILFORD : OXFORD UNIVERSITY PRESS
1937

TABLE OF CONTENTS

VOLUME II

LIST OF ILLUSTRATIONS

VOLUME II

*Grateful acknowledgment is made to Lord Ilchester and the
Trustees of the British Museum for permission to repro-
duce the medallion of Benedict XIV and the drawing of
Cole by Kerrich.*

To Cole, Friday 26 January 1776

Add MS 5952, ff. 150–1.

This letter, and the copy of HW's letter to Astle, 19 Dec. 1775 (Add MS 5952, ff. 148–9), are in Kirgate's hand.

Address: [From Cole's copy, Add MS 5824, f. 91v.] To the Rev. Mr Cole at Milton near Cambridge. Free T. Caswall. [Timothy Caswall (d. 1802), of Sacombe Park, Herts; M.P. for Hertford 1761–8, and for Brackley, Northants, 1771–89. He is probably the 'Mr Caswall' mentioned frequently in *Paris Jour.* for 1767.]

[Arlington Street, Jan. 26, 1776.]

I HAVE deferred answering your last letter, dear Sir, till I cannot answer with my own hand. I made a pilgrimage at Christmas[1] to Queen's Cross at Ampthill, was caught there by the snow, imprisoned there for a fortnight, and sent home bound hand and foot by the gout. The pain, I suppose, is quite frozen, for I have had none; nothing but inflammation and swelling, and they abate. In reality, this is owing to the bootikins, which though they do not cure the gout, take out its sting. You, who are still more apt to be an invalid, feel, I fear, this hyperborean season; I should be glad to hear you did not.

I thought I had at once jumped upon a discovery of the subject of the painted room at the Rose Tavern, but shall not plume myself upon my luck till I have seen the chamber, because Mr Gough's account seems to date the style of the painting earlier than will serve my hypothesis. I had no data to go upon but the site having belonged to the family of Tufton (for I do not think the description at all answers to the taking of Francis the First; nor is it at all credible that there should be arms in the painting, and yet neither those of France or Austria) I turned immediately to Lord Thanet's pedigree in Collins's *Peerage*,[2] and found at once an heroic adventure performed by one of the family,[3] that accords remarkably with the principal circumstance. It is the rescue of the Elector Palatine, son of our Queen of Bohemia,[4] from an ambuscade laid for him by the

1. That is, the first week in January (see HW to Lady Ossory 27 Dec. 1775).

2. See Arthur Collins, *Peerage*, 4th edn, 7 vols, 1768, iii. 276–86.

3. Hon. George Tufton (1650–70), 6th son of John Tufton, 2d E. of Thanet. For an account of his heroism, see ibid. 285.

4. Charles Louis (1617–80), Elector Pala-

Duke of Lorrain.[5] The arms, or and gules, I thought were those of Lorrain, which I since find are argent and gules. The argent indeed may be turned yellow by age, as Mr Gough says he does not know whether the crescent is red or black. But the great impediment is, that this achievement of a Tufton was performed in the reign of Charles the Second. Now in that reign, when we were become singularly ignorant of chivalry, anachronisms and blunders might easily be committed by a modern painter, yet I shall not adhere to my discovery, unless I find the painting corresponds with the style of the modern time to which I would assign it; nor will I see through the eyes of my hypothesis, but fairly.

I shall now turn to another subject. Mr Astle,[6] who has left me off ever since the fatal era of Richard the Third, for no reason that I can conceive but my having adopted his discovery;[7] which for aught I know may be a reason with an antiquary, lately[8] sent me the attainder of George Duke of Clarence, which he has found in the Tower and printed;[9] and on it, as rather glad to confute me and himself, than to have found a curiosity, he had written two or three queries which tended to accuse Richard of having forged the instrument, though to the instrument itself is added another which confirms my acquittal of Richard of the murder of Clarence—but, alas, passion is a spying-glass that does but make the eyes of folly more blind. I sent him an answer, a copy of which I enclose.[10] Since that, I have heard no more of him, nor shall I suppose till I see this new proof of Richard's guilt adopted into the annals of the Society,[11] against which I have reserved some other stigmas for it.[12]

tine; son of Frederick V (1596–1632), Elector Palatine and King of Bohemia, by Elizabeth (1596–1662), dau. of James I.

5. Charles IV (1604–75), D. of Lorraine.

6. Thomas Astle (1735–1803), antiquary and paleographer, who furnished HW with an extract from the coronation roll of Richard III for *Historic Doubts*, 'with other useful assistances' (*Works* ii. 146 n), and also helped him to decipher Rous's Roll of the Earls of Warwick (see HW to Gray 26 Feb. [1768]).

7. This passage indicates that Astle was responsible for the discovery of the coronation roll, but it was first mentioned to HW by Bishop Lyttelton (see *Works* ii. 146 n).

8. 18 Dec. 1775 (see HW to Mason 21 Dec. 1775).

9. 'The Attainder of George Duke of Clarence' was printed in *Rotuli Parliamentorum*, 6 vols, 1767–77, vi. 193–5. Astle, one of its editors, probably sent HW only the sheets containing the copy of the attainder, as the last volume of *Rotuli Parliamentorum* did not appear until the following year. The attainder was reprinted in *The Antiquarian Repertory*, 4 vols, 1775–84, iv. 41–7.

10. See HW to Astle 19 Dec. 1775. The original is missing. HW also sent a copy of the letter to Mason (see HW to Mason 21 Dec. 1775).

11. No account of the bill of attainder appeared in *Archaeologia*.

12. See postscript to this letter.

Mr Edmonson has found a confirmation of Isabella Fitz Osbert having married Jernegan after Walpole. I forget where I found my arms of Fitz Osbert. Though they differ from yours of Sir Roger, the colours are the same, and they agree with yours of William Fitzosborne. There was no accuracy in spelling names even till much later ages; and you know that different branches of the same family made little variations in their coats.

I am very sorry for the death of poor Henshaw, of which I had not heard.

I am yours most sincerely,

H. W.

PS. The queries added to the letter to Mr Astle[13] were not sent with it; and as I reserve them for a future answer,[14] I beg you will show them to nobody.

From COLE, Tuesday 30 January 1776

VA, Forster MS 110, ff. 154–5. COLE's copy, Add MS 5824, ff. 93v, 94v.
Address: For the Honourable Horace Walpole in Arlington Street, London.
Postmark: Cambridge 2 FE.

Milton, Tuesday, Jan. 30, 1776.

Dear Sir,

I CONGRATULATE you on the victory the bootikins have had over the pain of the gout, and wish you may continue to find the good effects of them. I hope what I am going to say will not discredit them, as I am fully persuaded, with you, that they are excel-

13. The following 'Queries to be added to this letter,' (all in Kirgate's hand) follow the copy of HW's letter to Astle 19 Dec. 1775:
'If there was no such Parliament held, would Richard have dared to forge an Act for it?
'Would Henry VII never have reproached him with so absurd a forgery?
'Did neither Sir T. More nor Lord Bacon ever hear of that forgery?
'As Richard declared his nephew the Earl of Warwick his successor, would he have done so, if he had forged an Act of Attainder of Warwick's father?
'If it is supposed he forged the Act, when he set aside Warwick, could he pretend

that Act was not known, when he declared him his heir? Would not so recent an Act's being unknown, have proved it a forgery? And if there had been no such Parliament as that which forged it, would not that have proved it a double forgery? The Act, therefore, and the Parliament that passed it, must have been genuine and existed, though no other record appears. The distractions of the times, the evident insufficience or partiality of the historians of that age, and the interest of Henry VII to destroy all records that gave authority to the House of York and their title, account for our wanting evidence of that Parliament.'
14. HW does not seem to have made this.

lent preservatives against the malignity of the distemper, and I shall be sorry to give you any suspicions of their inefficacy, but it is best always to be upon one's guard against an evil time. When I was at Burnham in October and November last, just such a fit of the gout as you describe attacked me. I thought at first that it had been some little strain on my hand, but after two or three days being too weak to use it, I had a little pain one single night, and then my whole hand was violently inflamed, swelled, and red as an apple, and so continued for about ten days, without the least pain, and then went off. I am apt to attribute it to my leaving off entirely small beer, which used to be my only beverage, never drinking ale in my life,[1] and for this last year drinking nothing but skimmed milk and water, but it is so unaccountable a disorder that one is puzzled in endeavouring to account for all its meanders and protean appearances. I am very glad, however, that you are got home through all the snow on the Dunstable road,[2] where I am informed it has been very formidable. The snow we have had here and at Cambridge is a mere trifle, not so much as usual. One is always best, let one be ever so well lodged, accommodated and attended elsewhere, at home, when out of order. I hope the gout will soon unfetter you and let you enjoy the fine, though sharp, weather, which is much wholesomer than rain and damp. For my own part, though tolerably well, I have not been once over my threshold since I came home,[3] now near eight weeks. The weather, or gout, or something which I am unwilling to call age, affects my knee and ankle so that I can hardly stir from one room to another, but so long as I am free from pain I am easy.

I think your explication of the painting[4] very probable. The only doubt, as you observe, is the modernity of the exploit, which will hardly allow for so much chivalry, of knights, damsels, battle-axes, galleys, etc., except we suppose that it was in imitation of ancient manners, which is by no means improbable. But then what shall we do with *Pater noster, quid me vis facere?* <which see>ms to point out the subject of St Paul's conversion.[5] When I answered Mr Gough's

1. 'and rarely tasting a glass of wine, perhaps not one in a month' (addition in Cole's copy). Cf. Cole, *Jour. to Paris* 41, 166–7.

2. Which HW had travelled on his return from Ampthill Park, 'through mountains of snow and quarries of ice' (HW to Mann 28 Jan. 1776).

3. From Burnham (cf. *ante* 24 Dec. 1775).

4. In the Rose Tavern, London.

5. Cole's surmise was correct (see following letter), but it apparently was an afterthought, as he did not mention it to Gough.

<lett>er,[6] I referred him also to Collins,[7] where mention is made of a Sir Lewis de Tufton, temp. Edward III, who was a principal commander at the battle of Cresey, and afterwards at the siege of Calais. Yet if it alludes to any exploit of one of that family, it seems odd that the Tufton eagle should not be on the painting, except they afterwards changed their arms. I told him that I was rather disposed to think it some Spanish and Moorish story: my reason was this: the arms of Arragon (paly, or and gules) are frequent on the picture, and query, whether the barry, or and gules, which he also mentions to be upon the trumpets and banners, should not be paly, or and gules also, but hanging on these instruments may make them appear as barry. Of this you will be able to form a judgment when you examine it. Mr Bryant, whom I often saw while I was at Burnham, both at his[8] and my house, which are nearly in the same parish, often mentioned you and regretted his not of late calling upon you—Mr Bryant, I say, who had seen the painting, much pressed me to go and look at it as I passed through London to this place, but as I was then ill of a cough and cold, and wanted to be in my own elbow-chair, I only slept one night in town, and had no inclination to go out of my way, especially as I then walked with difficulty.

I am delighted with your sensible letter to Mr Astle, who, I am pretty sure, except he is mad, will never suffer his queries to you about the forgery to appear in the *Archaeologia*. His supposition is so absurd, and your answer so convincing, that I think we shall hear no more of it from that quarter. The only reason that can make me wish he would is that I am in hopes it would be a means to knock down at one blow both the President and his associate, for as to the squib, which is too lively a name for the dronish attack from Landbeche,[8a] I reckon that stupid performance as nothing, and indeed, to speak the truth, I look on Dr Milles's attempt to be very little superior. I accidentally but last week read over your *Richard III* (which every time I read, more fully satisfies me in most of your doubts) and afterwards the pieces in the *Archaeologia* against them. Good God! What a difference in every point! I would always have them read together. Mr Astle has all the opportunities of doing so, and does not profit by it. I am sorry he has interfered in a cause that

---

6. For Gough's letter, see *ante* 12 Dec. 1775; Cole's reply is printed in LA i. 674–5.

7. See his *Peerage*, 4th edn, 7 vols, 1768, iii. 278.

8. Cippenham, in Farnham Royal, Bucks.

8a. Masters's *Observations*, etc.

can do him no credit, and, if you take him in hand, must discredit him forever. I am sorry, I say, because I was much prejudiced in favour of him, though very slightly acquainted with him. I am of opinion your fine ironical strokes throughout your letter will hardly draw him to Arlington Street, though I must needs think he deserved them. I dare be bound to say your correspondence is at end,[9] for it is impossible to answer your difficulties, and the irony is too pointed to be retorted. I own I have ill nature enough to wish you would publish your tract against the Dean, who unnecessarily and wantonly and absurdly attacked a person whom he ought on every account to have fostered. Not a soul shall see the queries you warn me about: you may depend on it.

Have you seen an epitaph, lately discovered in a little church[10] near Lewis in Sussex, on Gundreda, daughter of William the Conqueror, and wife of the first Earl Warren.[11] It is to be printed,[12] so will not send it except you desire it. Mr Gough sent it in a letter to Mr Tyson,[13] who sent it to me last week.

I have not seen Mr Lort since the snow has fallen. He wrote me a note on Friday to inform me he was then setting out for London, and that the snow blinded him so that he could not walk over to me.

I can only wish you every happiness, and am, dear Sir,

Your ever faithful and affectionate servant,

WM COLE

Your silence to these answerers has emboldened others[14] who would not have dared to have attacked you had they known as well as I do what store of artillery you have ready to thunder upon them.[15]

9. This proved not to be the case.

10. The parish church of Isfield.

11. William de Warenne (d. 1089), 1st E. of Surrey, m. (before 1078) Gundred or Gundreda (d. 1085), whose parentage is a matter of dispute; for a summary of the theories, see GEC.

12. The inscription on Gundred's monument is printed in John Watson, *Memoirs of the Ancient Earls of Warren and Surrey*, 2 vols, Warrington, 1782, i. 61; in Gough, *Sepulchral Monuments*, vol. 1, pt 1, p. 9; and in later works. Cole probably refers to *Sepulchral Monuments*; or, he may refer to an unfulfilled plan to publish an account of the monument and epitaph in *Archaeologia*.

13. Tyson's reply to Gough 4 Dec. 1775, is in LA viii. 616. Gough's letter to Tyson has not been printed.

14. Not identified.

15. Doubtless Cole refers to HW's spirited 'Supplement to the Historic Doubts . . . with Remarks on some Answers that have been made to that Work,' which was written in 1769, but not published until 1798 (*Works* ii. 185–220).

To Cole, Friday 1 March 1776

Add MS 5952, ff. 152–3.
Address: To the Reverend Mr Cole at Cambridge. *Postmark:* 1 MR.

Arlington Street, March 1, 1776.

I AM sorry to tell you that the curious old painting at the tavern in Fleet Street is addled, by the subject turning out a little too old. Alas! it is not the story of Francis I—but of St Paul. All the coats of arms, that should have been French and Austrian, and that I had a mind to convert into Palatine and Lorrain, are the bearings of Pharisaic nobility. In short, Dr Percy was here yesterday, and tells me that over Mr Gough's imaginary Pavia is written *Damascus* in capital letters. Oh! our antiquaries!

Mr Astle has at last called on me, but I was not well enough to see him. I shall return his visit, when I can go out. I hope this will be in a week; I have no pain left, but have a codicil of nervous fever, for which I am taking the bark. I have nothing new for you in our old way, and therefore will not unnecessarily lengthen my letter, which was only intended to cashier the old painting, though I hear the antiquaries still go on with having a drawing taken from it[1]—Oh! our antiquaries!

From Cole, Tuesday 26 March 1776

VA, Forster MS 110, f. 156. Cole's copy, Add MS 5824, f. 94v.
Address: For the Honourable Mr Horace Walpole in Arlington Street, London.
Postmark: 28 MR.

Milton, March 26, 1776.

Dear Sir,

I AM still confined by the gout, which at last has fixed, with often shifting, in my weak knee, so that I move with a crutch and stick. I hope by this time both that distemper and feverette have left you to your own amusements and excursions.

Domine, quid me vis facere? and the person's falling from his horse, one would have thought might have been pretty clear indications on what subject it was painted. Damascus leaves no room to

1. HW apparently was misinformed; cf. following letter.

doubt. I don't hear the Antiquary Society think of having a drawing, though it is possible they may have talked of it.

I don't hear from Mr Gough, but I lately saw a letter of his to Mr Tyson,[1] informing him of some dissatisfaction among themselves relating to a drawing by Mr Sherwin,[2] a young ingenious engraver, of a picture at Cowdray, representing the attack of the French on Portsmouth at the end of Henry VIII's reign. The members were much agitated and divided about it, and it is now finally determined to have a slight etching of it, and not an engraving.[3]

Mrs Vertue[4] is lately dead, who was a bountiful benefactress to the Society in honour to her husband's memory.[5] His historical prints[6] and an old map of London in 1560 on pewter[7] are to be distributed on St George's Day.

One Mr Reynolds,[8] a dabbler in antiquities, Butler of Caius College, and a great acquaintance as a sportsman and shooter with Lord Orford, has picked up, among many <o>ther curious old pictures,[9] one of Queen Elizabeth of York, wife of Henry VII.[10] It <is> small, about a foot in length, and holding a white rose.

1. Apparently not printed, but Gough's next letter to Tyson 6 March 1776, referring to the incident mentioned in this paragraph, is LA viii. 617–9. See also the letters between Gough and George Steevens, LI v. 434–5.

2. John Keyse Sherwin (1751?–90), engraver and draughtsman; pupil of Bartolozzi.

3. Cole was mistaken. 'The Encampment of the English Forces near Portsmouth, together with a view of the English and French fleets at the commencement of the action between them on the 19th of July, 1545, engraved from a coeval painting at Cowdry in Sussex, the seat of the Right Honourable Anthony Browne, Lord Viscount Montague. Engraved by James Basire,' was published by the Society of Antiquaries 1 June 1778, 'with a description of the letter press.' The name of the artist is not given. A complete description of the picture appears also in Archaeologia iii (1775). 261–7. The original was destroyed on the night of 24 Sept. 1793, when Cowdray House and most of its contents were burned (see Gough's account of Cowdray House in Kippis, Vetusta Monumenta, vol. iii). Cf. post 18 Oct. 1778.

4. Margaret Evans (1700?–76), m. (1720) George Vertue. She died 17 March 1776 (see LA ii. 254; viii. 406).

5. She gave 22 plates of her husband's engraving, all of which were republished by the Society of Antiquaries in 1781 and 1784 (see ibid. vi. 155).

6. A Description of nine historical prints, representing Kings, Queens, Princes, etc. of the Tudor family; selected, drawn and engraved from the original paintings, by G. Vertue. . . . Republished by the Society of Antiquaries [with the prints], 1776. The plates of this series were purchased from Mrs Vertue for £100 (see loc. cit.). For a list of the plates, see Engravers, Works iv. 147.

7. 'A plan of London in Q. Elizabeth's time, copied by Mr Vertue, 1748, in 8 plates' (Archaeologia vi. 421; see also Engravers, Works iv. 148), or 'View of London about 1560' (Engravers, Works iv. 149).

8. 'formerly a waiter at the Mitre Tavern, now' (addition in Cole's copy).

9. 'at Bury, from Felton Hervey's sale' (addition in Cole's copy). Hon. Felton Hervey (1712–75), 10th son of 1st E. of Bristol; M.P. for Bury St Edmunds in two parliaments (see Collins, Peerage, 1812, iv. 154).

By a letter from Mr Lort I find you have a great acquisition from Mr Mariette's sale,[11] which must afford an infinity of curious prints. I am, dear Sir,

Your most faithful and obedient servant,

WM COLE

To COLE, Tuesday 16 April 1776

Add MS 5952, ff. 154–5.

Address: To the Reverend Mr Cole at Milton near Cambridge.
Postmark: MW 16 AP.

[Arlington Street,][1] April 16, 1776.

YOU will be concerned, my good Sir, for what I have this minute heard from his nephew,[2] that poor Mr Granger was seized at the communion table on Sunday with an apoplexy and died yesterday morning at five.[3] I have answered the letter[4] with a word of advice about his MSS, that they may not fall into the hands of booksellers. He had been told by idle people so many gossiping stories, that it would hurt him and living persons, if all his collections were to be printed; for as he was incapable of telling an untruth himself, he suspected nobody else—too great goodness in a biographer!

Yours ever,

H. W.

10. Elizabeth (1465–1503), of York; dau. of Edward IV and Elizabeth Woodville; Queen of Henry VII. This portrait came into the possession of Cole in 1782 (see *post* 27 May 1782).

11. 'A book of portraits in the reigns of Francis I and Henry II, that belonged to Brantôme, who has written the names' (HW to Lady Ossory 20 Dec. 1775). Pierre Jean Mariette (1694–1774), engraver and collector, an occasional correspondent of HW. Cole wrote a note on Mariette, at p. 76 of his copy of HW's *Engravers*[2] (now WSL): 'Mr. Mariette . . . I was in company with at Paris: he is an elderly man, of no profession, inheriting a good patrimony from his father and grandfather, I think both printsellers. Mr Mariette talks English imperfectly, has all our books which have prints in them, of which he has a vast collection. I did not see them, as it was at Mr Walpole's lodgings at Paris that I met him.' For other purchases by HW at Mariette's sale, see *Description of SH, Works* ii. 461, 475, 504.

1. From Cole's copy, Add MS 5825, f. 151v.

2. Not identified. He is also mentioned in *Private Papers of James Boswell* . . . xi. 255.

3. For an account of his death, see GM July 1776, xlvi. 313; *Granger*[5], vol. 1, p. xxvii.

4. Missing.

PS. The whole world is occupied with the Duchess of Kingston's trial.[5] I don't tell you a word of it, for you will not care about it these 200 years.[6]

From Cole, Thursday 30 May 1776

VA, Forster MS 110, ff. 157–8. Cole's copy, Add MS 5824, f. 94v.
Address: For the Honourable Mr Horace Walpole in Arlington Street, London.
Postmark: Cambridge 31 MA.

May 30, 1776, Milton.

Dear Sir,

I AM ashamed when I look at your letter informing me of the death of poor Mr Granger, whose loss to the public and his friends no one can better judge of than yourself. For my own part I lament him as a worthy, honest, good creature, a person calculated for the part he undertook, and which in all probability will be now neglected. I hope his papers are got into your hands, where they will be safe, but the materials got together and possibly compacted for another volume will be an irreparable loss to the public, except you can put them into some inquisitive, stirring person's custody, who may complete what he has began so successfully under your auspices. I shall ever lament his loss, not only on this account, but his own.

I hope the untoward weather we have had has had no ill effect on your health. Mr Lort wrote me word lately that you was not in town, but supposed that you was at Strawberry Hill.[1] No news in general with me is good news, yet I can't say but I shall be glad to hear of your welfare. For my own part, I have never been able to stir out since November, and now am reduced to a crutch and a stick, but so long as I am well, free from pain, and have my books about me, I am contented. My present occupation is making a general index

5. Elizabeth Chudleigh (1720?–88), m. privately (1744) Augustus John Hervey, afterwards (1775) 3d E. of Bristol. In 1769 she obtained a decree from the Consistory Court declaring her a spinster. In the same year she married Evelyn Pierrepont (1711–73), 2d D. of Kingston. She was tried for bigamy, 15–22 April 1776, before the House of Lords, and was found guilty, but, plead-ing her privilege as a peeress, escaped sentence. She lived abroad until her death.

6. HW was mistaken: Cole's interest in the Duchess of Kingston is shown by Add MS 5829, ff. 141–2.

1. Almost all HW's letters for May 1776 are dated from SH.

to all my volumes, which are run ahead so that I am at a loss to recur <to man>y things for want of such an help.

Mr Gough wrote me word lately that a new Biographical volume
is going forward under the inspection of Dr Kippis,[2] a Dissenting
minister who made some figure some two or three years ago when
the clergy were petitioning against their mother.[3] Mr Gough wanted
me to assist him. I told him his worthies were such as had no niche
in any of my temples. A new volume would be very useful and
pleasant, but coming through Dr Kippis's hands must give it a tinge
I cannot relish.

Mr Vertue's historical prints, which are republishing by the Antiquary Society, are ready, Mr Lort writes, to be delivered to the members.

I must tell you a piece of news which, if you did not hear from
me, you probably would never from anyone else. That pickpocket
neighbour of mine, and antagonist to everything liberal and ingenious, Mr Masters, has been two or three times to call on me. It
was in consequence of meeting him twice in the beginning of last
month at his own village, where the University has one manor and
Benet College another: the Commissary[4] held a court and desired
me to dine there, and four or five days after, the Master of Benet[5] did
the same. Masters was there both times and pressing to drink coffee
with him at his house. If I had refused, it would have been particular, so he returned this visit soon after, but we seem to be, however,
on the shy order, and it is impossible for me ever to esteem so dirty
and illiberal a fellow, though it may be proper not to avoid him.
But too much on so ill a subject, and wishing you every blessing, I
am, dear Sir,

Your ever faithful servant,

Wm Cole

2. That is, the second edition of *Biographia Britannica*, ed. Andrew Kippis
(1725–95), nonconformist divine, reviewer
and biographer. Only five volumes and
part of a sixth were published, 1778–95
(see DNB; Boswell, *Johnson* iii. 174).

3. On 6 February 1772, the Dissenting
clergy presented a petition to Parliament
to obtain relief in the matter of subscription to the Thirty-nine Articles, but the
petition was rejected by a large majority
(see GM Feb. 1772, xlii. 61–3). Later in the
year a bill for their relief was passed by the
House of Commons, then thrown out by
the House of Lords. Kippis was active in
this affair, and published *A Vindication
of the Protestant Dissenting Ministers,
with regard to their late Application to
Parliament*, 1772; 2d edn, corrected and
enlarged, 1773.

4. William Greaves.

5. John Barnardiston.

Since I came to Cambridge, from whence I write this, I met a gentleman[6] who tells me that a lady[7] at Bury has a complete set of agate-
handle knives and forks, formerly the property of King Charles I,
and the gentleman thinks they will be sold at about two guineas. If
you have any curiosity to have them, I will procure them.

To COLE, Saturday 1 June 1776

Add MS 5952, ff. 156–7.

Address: To the Reverend Mr Cole at Milton near Cambridge.
Postmark: W 3 IV.

Strawberry Hill, June 1, 1776.

MR Granger's papers have been purchased by Lord Mount
Stewart,[1] who has the portrait-frenzy as well as I; and though
I am the head of the sect, I have no longer the rage of propagating
it; nor would I on any account take the trouble of revising and publishing the MSS. Mr Granger had drowned his taste for portraits in
the ocean of biography; and though he began with elucidating
prints, he at last only sought prints that he might write the lives of
those they represented. His work was grown and growing so voluminous, that an abridgment only could have made it useful to collectors.

I am not surprised that you will not assist Dr Kippis: Bishop Laud
and William Prynne could never agree. You are very justly more
averse to Mr Masters, who is a pragmatic fellow, and at best troublesome.

6. Michael Tyson, as appears from
Cole's note on his copy of HW's letter to
him 1 June 1776: 'I carried my letter to
Mr Walpole to Cambridge last Thursday,
and left it at the post house, but dining
with the Master of Benet, Mr Tyson told
me that Sir John Cullum of Bury had a
set of agate-handle knives and forks, formerly belonging to King Charles I, and
that he would sell them for about two
guineas, and told me Sir John desired me
to mention them to Mr Walpole: so I sent
for my letter, unsealed it, and wrote as
above' (Add MS 5824, f. 95v). Sir John Cullum (1733–85), 6th Bt, of Hawsted Place
and Hardwick House, Suffolk, was an antiquarian, historian and botanist.

7. An error (cf. *post* 9 June 1776, where
Sir John Cullum is mentioned by name).

———

1. Granger's MSS were used by Rev.
Mark Noble in *A Biographical History of
England* [1688–1727], *being a Continuation
of the Rev. J. Granger's Work*, 3 vols, 1806.
A few years before his death, Granger accompanied Lord Mountstuart on a tour to
the Continent, particularly Holland,
where the latter made an extensive collection of portraits. Granger's incomplete
notes are printed in his *Correspondence*
27–92 (second pagination).

If the agate knives you are so good as to recommend to me can be tolerably authenticated, have any royal marks, or at least, old setting of the time, and will be sold for two guineas, I should not dislike having them, though I have scarce room to stick a knife and fork. But if I trouble you to pay for them, you must let me know all I owe you already, for I know I am in your debt for prints and pamphlets, and this new debt will make the whole considerable enough to be remitted. I have lately purchased three apostle spoons[2] to add to the one you was so kind as to give me.[3]

What is become of Mr Essex? Does he never visit London? I wish I could tempt him thither or hither. I am not only thinking of[4] building my offices in a collegiate style, for which I have a good design and wish to consult him, but I am actually wanting assistance at this very moment about a smaller gallery[5] that I wish to add this summer; and which if Mr Essex was here he should build directly. It is scarce worth asking him to take the journey on purpose, though I would pay for his journey hither and back, and would lodge him here for the necessary time.[6] I can only beg you to mention it to him as an idle jaunt, the object is so trifling. I wish more that you could come with him: do you leave your poor parishioners and their souls to themselves; if you do, I hope Dr Kippis will seduce them. Adieu! dear Sir,

Yours ever,
H. W.

From Cole, Sunday 9 June 1776

VA, Forster MS 110, f. 159. Cole kept no copy.
Address: For the Honourable Mr Horace Walpole in Arlington Street, London.
Postmark: Cambridge 10 IV.

Sunday, June 9, 1776, Milton.

Dear Sir,

I AM glad to find by the cheerfulness of your style that nothing is the matter with you. It is now above twenty months that I have totally abstained from small beer, and stuck to milk and water, in

---

2. They were sold SH xvi. 68–9.

3. See *ante* 3 May 1773.

4. MS reads: 'I am not only of thinking of.'

5. That is, the Beauclerc Closet, part of

the Beauclerc Tower, which was completed in 1777 (see *SH Accounts* 165–7).

6. 'I am to have Mr Essex tomorrow from Cambridge' (HW to Lady Ossory 20 June 1776).

order to abate the vehemence of the gout, yet all won't do: it will have its way, and from November to this moment I can't say I have been free from it. Last Sunday, Monday and Tuesday at the worst, and no rest, but thank God! three good nights since have quite refreshed me. I was not confined to my chamber, having the use of one leg to hop up and down with a crutch. This puts a stop to all possibility of my moving, but Mr Essex, to whom I sent on Thursday, called here the next day, and bids me tell you that he is sorry he did not know your design before, as he is lately returned from town and would have called on you. Indeed, on his return I asked him if he had not done so, but he was afraid of being troublesome. He will now wait on you, however, whenever you will please to let him understand that his coming will be suitable. Name your day and he will set off and wait on you to or at Strawberry Hill for two or three days. If you write to me I will inform him.

<Mr> Tyson is gone to Norwich for a week or two, so can give no account of the knives till his return: it was he that mentioned them to me. I wish upon inspection they answer his account, for I can't conceive that Sir John Cullum, if they are worth keeping, would choose to part with them for two guineas. When he returns I will speak to him and pay for them if they answer his description. As to your supposal that you are in my debt, I know not upon [what] grounds you go, for I am utterly ignorant of it myself. You also mention a gift from me of a silver spoon, but I wish I had enough to complete your set, having been more than doubly paid for it by your generosity.

On Wednesday we had the most remarkable hailstorm I ever remember. I don't hear it has done any mischief, yet it lasted a full quarter of an hour, and the ground was white with it above half an hour after its cessation, though deluges of rain attended it.

I am, Sir,

Your most obliged, affectionate and faithful servant,

WM COLE

To Cole, Tuesday 11 June 1776

Add MS 5952, ff. 158–9.

Address: To the Reverend Mr Cole at Milton near Cambridge.
Postmark: 12 IV.

Strawberry Hill, June 11, 1776.

I AM grieved and feel for your gout; I know the vexation and disappointments it occasions, and how often it will return when one thinks it going or gone. It represents life and its vicissitudes. At last I know it makes one content when one does not feel actual pain—and what contents, may be called a blessing: but it is that sort of blessing that extinguishes hopes and views, and is not so luxurious but one can bear to relinquish it. I seek amusements now to amuse me; I used to rush into them, because I had an impulse and wished for what I sought. My want of Mr Essex has a little of both kinds, as it is for an addition to this place,[1] for which my fondness is not worn out. I shall be very glad to see him here either on the 20th or 21st of this present month, and shall have no engagement till the 23d, and will gladly pay his journey. I am sorry I must not hope that you will accompany him.

Yours ever,

H. Walpole

From Cole, Wednesday 17 July 1776

VA, Forster MS 110, f. 160. Cole kept no copy.

Address: For the Hon. Mr Horace Walpole at Strawberry Hill, Middlesex.

Milton, July 17, 1776, Wednesday.

<Dear> Sir,

MR Essex sent me this morning your letter to him,[1] by my servant, who was at Cambridge market, and told him he meant to answer your letter this day, so I scrawl this to answer your query, if no real answer may be called one. Mr Pentycross[2] is so unknown a

1. The Beauclerc Tower.

1. HW's letter and Essex's reply are missing.

2. Thomas Pentycross (1749–1808), a Blue-coat boy; of Pembroke, Cambridge (A.B. 1771); rector of St Mary's, Wallingford, Berks, 1774–1808; author of sermons

bard to me that I never before heard the name. I have put Mr Essex in a way to get information at Cambridge. Otherwise, Mr Lort, who is going to Paris this month, and is now in Bond Street, is as likely to inform you as anyone I know. I have seen Mr Tyson at last, about a week ago. He was to write again to Sir John Cullum and to inform me of particulars.

A true piece of old Dutch porcelain[3] was lately put into my hands as a piece of curiosity. If it is such, I beg your acceptance of it; if it is of no value, please to return it by Mr Essex, as the man[4] asks rather more for it than is proper to throw away. I am no judge of its value, though it seems elegant—the outside especially.

I am still a prisoner with the gout, and had as bad a night last night with pain in my foot as I ever experienced. You said very truly in your last letter that it was an unaccountable disorder, and that when one thought it going or gone, it returned with double violence. I have found it so to my sorrow: I thought it was leaving me last week, but on Sunday night it showed its malevolence. I heartily wish you no returns of it.

Adieu, dear Sir, and I am

Your most obliged and faithful servant,

WM COLE

I wish the package of the Delf vessel may not disgust you. I had nothing better, but it is the stuffing of the chair of the Professor of Divinity,[5] which was sent to me as a relic some years ago, and was too shabby and too rickety and old to set in any place, and took up too much room, so I pulled it to pieces and made fuel of it.

(see John Kirby Hedges, *History of Wallingford,* 2 vols, 1881, ii. 383–4, 387–8). Why HW applied to Essex about him is not clear, in the absence of their letters. Pentycross addressed some verses, 'Through the bosom of yon trees,' to HW which were printed at SH as a 'detached piece.'

3. Cole notes in one of his volumes: 'When Mr Essex went up a second time to Strawberry Hill to set the workmen about the new octagon room [the Beauclerc Tower], I sent Mr Walpole a curious old piece of Delf [*sic*] ware, curiously painted,

with a mermaid on the bottom, and desired him to send it back again by Mr Essex if it was not valuable' (Add MS 5824, f. 95v).

4. 'Mr York the upholsterer' (*post* 28 July 1776). There were two upholsterers of this name in Cambridge in 1792: Edward and J. York (see *Universal British Directory,* 5 vols, 1791–8?, ii. 494).

5. Possibly John Newcome (1683–1765), Dean of Rochester; Master of St John's College; Professor of Divinity at Cambridge 1727–65.

To Cole, Tuesday 23 July 1776

Add MS 5952, ff. 162–3.

Cole endorsed the letter: 'Rec'd July 25, 1776.' The letter is dated from the first sentence of HW's letter to Cole 24 July 1776.

Address: To the Reverend Mr Cole.

[Strawberry Hill, July 23, 1776.]

YOU are so good to me, my dear Sir, that I am quite ashamed. I must not send back your charming present, but wish you would give me leave to pay for it, and I shall have the same obligation to you and still more. It is beautiful in form and colours, and pleases me excessively. In the meantime I have in a great hurry, for I came home but at noon to meet Mr Essex, chosen out a few prints for you such as I think you will like and beg you to accept them: they enter into no one of my sets.

I am heartily grieved at your account of yourself, and know no comfort but submission. I was absent to see General Conway,[1] who is far from well—we must take our lot as it falls! Joy and sorrow is mixed till the scene closes. I am out of spirits, and shall not mend yours; Mr Essex is just setting out and I write in great haste, but am, as I have so long been,

Most truly yours,

H. W.

To Cole, Wednesday 24 July 1776

Add MS 5952, ff. 160–1.

Address: To the Reverend Mr Cole at Milton near Cambridge.
Postmark: Isleworth 25 IY.

Strawberry Hill, July 24, 1776.

I WROTE to you yesterday, dear Sir, not only in great haste, but in great confusion, and did not say half I ought to have done for the pretty vase you sent me and for your constant obliging attention to me. All I can say is, that gratitude attempted even in my haste and concern to put in its word: and I did not mean to pay you

1. General (afterwards Field-Marshal) Hon. Henry Seymour Conway (1721–95), HW's first cousin, frequent correspondent, and most intimate lifelong friend.

(which I hope you will really allow me to do) but to express my sensibility of your kindness.

The fact was, that to avoid disappointing Mr Essex, when I had dragged him hither from Cambridge, I had returned hither precipitately and yet late from Park Place, whither I went the day before to see General Conway, who has had a little attack of the paralytic kind. You who can remember how very long and dearly I have loved so near a relation and particular friend, and who are full of nothing but gentle and friendly sensations, can judge how shocked I was to find him more changed that I expected. I suffered so much in constraining and commanding myself, that I was not sorry, as the house was full of relations, to have the plea of Mr Essex to get away, and come to sigh here by myself. It is perhaps to vent my concern that I write now. Mr Conway is in no manner of danger, is better, his head nor speech are affected, and the physicians, who barely allow the attack to be of the paralytic nature, are clear it is local in the muscles of the face. Still has it operated such a revolution in my mind, as no time, *at my age,* can efface. It has at once damped every pursuit, which my spirits had even now prevented me from being weaned from, I mean of virtù. It is like a mortal distemper in myself, for can amusements amuse, if there is but a glimpse, a vision of outliving one's friends? I have had dreams in which I thought I wished for fame—it was not certainly posthumous fame at any distance; I feel, I feel it was confined to the memory of those I love. It seems to me impossible for a man who has no friends to do anything for fame—and to me the first position in friendship is, to intend one's friends should survive one—but it is not reasonable to oppress you who are suffering gout with my melancholy ideas. Let me know as you mend. What I have said will tell you, what I hope so many years have told you, that I am very constant and sincere—to friends of above forty years.

I doubt Mr Essex perceived that my mind was greatly bewildered. He gave me a direction to Mr Penticross, who I recollect Mr Gray and not you told me was turned a Methodist teacher. He was a bluecoat boy and came hither then to some of my servants,[1] having at that age a poetic turn. As he has reverted to it, I hope the enthusiasm will take a more agreeable ply. I have not heard of him for many years, and thought he was settled somewhere near Cambridge: I

1. For an account of this visit, see HW to Mary Berry 16–17 Aug. 1796.

find it is at Wallingford.[2] I wonder those madmen and knaves[3] do not begin to wear out, as their folly is no longer new, and as knavery can turn its hand to any trade according to the humour of the age, which in countries like this is seldom constant.

Yours most faithfully,

H. W.

From Cole, Sunday 28 July 1776

VA, Forster MS 110, ff. 161–2. Cole kept no copy.
Address: For the Honourable Mr Horace Walpole at Strawberry Hill, Twick-enham, Middlesex. *Postmark:* Cambridge 30 IY.

Milton, July 28, 1776, Sunday.

Dear Sir,

I AM noways surprised that General Conway's disorder has so much affected you. The only time I ever was in company with him was when he paid you a visit at college, and the little I saw of him so long ago made such an impression on me as I shall never for-get. There was something so engaging, pleasing and *prévenant* in his manner as I never observed the like in any other. For both your sakes I hope he will soon get well again. It is a misfortune to have so much sensibility in one's nature as you are endued with: sufficient are one's own distresses without the additional encumbrance of those of one's friends. Your insensibles, therefore, and those who care only for their own dear selves, have vastly the advantage in this respect, however they may miss of it when they would wish for a friend to comfort them.

Many thanks, dear Sir, for the agreeable present of prints, which I had from Mr Essex yesterday. He sets out for Lincoln Cathedral to-morrow. You said well in your former letter that there were some that you guessed I should like. <Ind>eed there is hardly one but I should have jumped <at> and only lament that you did not put up one of your own in mezzotinto, as I have not one. The last I had I sent framed to be hung up in King's College parlour, and I have been teased, as I now serve you, by two or three persons, so that I

2. Berks.   3. The Methodists.

could never preserve one for myself. I am glad the vase pleased you. As for paying for it, you have over and over done so by your last packet. What made me mention the return of it was my doubt of its being worth your acceptance. Mr York the upholsterer asked me half a guinea for it, which, if it had been only common, ordinary Delf, I thought too much to throw away, and I had it home on condition to return it again if, on examination, I did not approve of it. I beg you will not mention any other payment than what is already received.

I am still as lame as ever, and can get about the house with a crutch and stick, and sometimes into the chaise for an airing, but as I am otherways well and have my books about me, my appetite good and spirits as usual, I am quite content, though I am fearful, as it has lasted me so long, I shall never be right again. My foot is but triflingly swelled, and so has been long, which makes me wonder I do not get on, and better.

Adieu, dear Sir, and pray God you and Mr Conway and other friends may enjoy your healths together as long as life is worth having, and I am

Your most obliged and faithful servant,

WM COLE

I have by Mr Ashby's means got into a correspondence with Mr Pennant. Never sure was a word said with so much justice as one in a letter of yours some two or three years ago: I don't exactly remember the whole, but the purport was that he wrote antiquities as he rode on horseback.[1] If you knew all, I am sure you would be confirmed more than ever in your opinion. I am much pleased with his correspondence, as he condescends to deal now and then in my humble way with epitaphs and old tombs. He was so kind to send me his books. I took the liberty to advertise him of what I thought a mistake. Have you seen his last volume,[2] which he sent me? In it is a print of Cardinal Beaton, Archbishop of St Andrews, who lived in our Henry VIII's time.[3] The print is evidently, by many marks, that

1. '[He] picks up his knowledge as he rides' (*ante* 28 May 1774). See also *post* 18 June 1782.

2. *A Tour in Scotland, 1772, Part II,* 1776.

3. A print of David Beaton or Bethune (1494–1546), Cardinal of San Stephano on Mount Celio, and Abp of St Andrews (see DNB), which appears ibid., Plate XXXI, opp. p. 243. Its authenticity is not questioned in EBP. 'No problem in Scottish portraiture is more puzzling than that of

of a cardinal of our Charles II's time. I think I shall have you of my opinion. He writes me word that the habit is like that of Wolsey, except the bands, and says that the people at Edinburgh are all satisfied that it is of Beaton. I shall never be convinced by Edinburgh evidence. On your inspection I may be better satisfied.

To COLE, Monday 19 August 1776

Add MS 5952, ff. 164–5.

Cole received the letter Wednesday 21 August (see his note below).

Address: To the Reverend Mr Cole at Milton near Cambridge.

Postmark: Isleworth 19 AV.

Strawberry Hill, Aug. 19, 1776.

I HAVE time but to write you a line, and it is as usual to beg your help in a sort of literary difficulty. I have received a letter[1] dated *Catherine Hall* from *Ken. Prescot,* whom I doubt I have forgotten, for he begins *Dear Sir,* and I protest I cannot recollect him, though I ought. He says he wants to send me a few Classical Discourses;[2] he speaks with respect of my father, and by his trembling hand, seems an old man. All these are reasons for my treating him with great regard, and being afraid of hurting him, I have written a short and very civil answer,[3] directed to the *Reverend Dr Prescot.* God knows whether he is a clergyman or a doctor—and perhaps I may have betrayed my forgetfulness, but I thought it was best to err on the over-civil side. Tell me something about him: I dread his *Discourses.* Is he the strange man that a few years ago sent me a volume of an uncommon form and of more uncommon matter? I suspect so.[4]

You shall certainly have two or three of my prints by Mr Essex when he returns hither and hence, and anything else you will command. I am just now in great concern for the terrible death of General Conway's son-in-law Mr Damer,[5] of which perhaps you in your

Cardinal Beaton,' etc., etc. (James L. Caw, *Scottish Portraits;* information from the University Librarian, St Andrews, per M.E.J.).

1. Missing.
2. Probably his *Letters Concerning Homer the Sleeper . . . with additional Classic Amusements,* Cambridge, 1773.

HW had a copy, which was sold SH v. 147.
3. Missing.
4. See *ante* 12 Feb. 1773 and n. 9.
5. John Damer (1744–76), eld. son of Joseph Damer (1718–98), Bn Milton of Milton Abbey, afterwards (1792) 1st E. of Dorchester; m. (1767) Anne Seymour Conway (1749–1828), only child of Hon. Henry Seymour Conway by Caroline, Countess of

solitude have not heard. You are happy who take no part but in the past world, for the *mortui non mordent,* nor do any of the extravagant and distressing things, that perhaps they did in their lives. I hope the gout that persecutes even in a hermitage, has left you.

Yours most sincerely,

H. W.

From COLE, Thursday 22 August 1776

VA, Forster MS 110, f. 163. COLE's copy, Add MS 5824, f. 97v.
Address: For the Hon. Mr Horace Walpole at Strawberry Hill in Twickenham, Middlesex. *Postmark:* Cambridge <23?> AV.

Milton, August 22, 1776.

Dear Sir,

YOU suspect very right. Dr Kenrick Prescot, Master of Catharine Hall, is your correspondent, and the person who sent you the book you mention some three or four years ago. I then got you out of the difficulty by calling at the Lodge, and first sending a letter to excuse your no[1] writing, but how you will get clear of his impertinence, poor man, now, I don't well understand, for I have never set eyes on him or any of the family from that time to this. He is now so disordered that I am told they don't suffer him to go out of the Lodge. When he sent the book he was bad enough to have been confined, though they suffered him then to range about and torment all his acquaintance. I suspect he has taken the opportunity of writing to you, now his wife,[1a] a very sensible and prudent woman, is at a

Ailesbury. He committed suicide 15 Aug. 1776. Cole has the following note on this passage: 'Mr Damer, eldest son of Lord Milton, was lately of Trinity College in Cambridge. He was heir to an immense estate, £15,000 per annum, but last week lost at gaming £20,000 in one night, upon which, not knowing which way to turn himself, on Saturday, Aug. 17, 1776 [Thursday 15 Aug.], after dining with some common women at a tavern, he took an opportunity and shot himself through the head. He has left no children by his lady. This is the account Dr Ewin, who drank tea with

me at Milton, Wednesday, August 21, [gave me] when Mr Walpole's letter was brought to me' (Add MS 5824, f. 97v). Cole also copied several paragraphs on Damer's suicide, from the *Cambridge Chronicle,* 24 Aug. 1776, into his MSS, now loc. cit. ff. 97v, 98v. See also HW to Mann 20 Aug. 1776.

———

1. Cole's copy has *not.*
1a. Mary Appleyard (1727–88), only dau. of Robert A., of the Church Plain, Great Yarmouth, Norfolk; m., 5 Aug. 1744, Kenrick Prescot (see *Yorkshire Genealogist,* ed.

distance. I think if she had been at home the letter would not have been sent. But one of his daughters,[2] a most agreeable and amiable young creature, married well about six months ago, died within this month at Scarborough, and another of his daughters,[3] married in that part of the world, now lies dying, to whom Mrs Prescot is gone. I am sorry you wrote to him, and how you could avoid it well, I do not see. I know how it would distress you to have your letters printed, and with such a crazed correspondent one is in great danger. I think his son,[4] a Fellow of Catharine Hall, with whom I have not the least acquaintance, prints his father's books at a private press in his rooms. This shows no great judgment in the son, who has, however, the appearance of a decent kind of man, for the father, by his publications, has made himself ridiculous, and the son, except he is an idiot, can't but see it. I have twenty of his printed cards and verses.[5]

Dr Ewin was with me yesterday and told me the sad accident of Mr Damer. I heartily pity his lady and those who are connected with her. Otherwise, by the Doctor's account of him, the public has no loss. I hope it will have no ill effect on the General, who, by your late account, is in no condition for such shocks.

The gout has left such a weakness in my ailing knee and my foot that I cannot set it to the ground.

I am, dear Sir,

Your ever faithful and most obliged servant,

WM COLE

Joseph Horsfall Turner, Bingley, 1888, i. 124; GM Oct. 1788, lviii. 936b). According to Cole, Prescot, when Prebendary of Norwich, 'ran away with his wife, a lively pretty woman, daughter to an innkeeper [at Yarmouth] . . . who was supposed to be a great fortune; but . . . the money went elsewhere' (quoted in George F. Browne, *St. Catharine's College*, 1902, p. 207).

2. 'Mrs Preston' (addition in Cole's copy). Mary Prescot (1746–76), m., 22 Dec. 1775, Thomas Preston, Vicar of Scawby, Lincs. She d. at Scarborough, Yorks, 15 July 1776. See *Yorkshire Genealogist* ii (1890). 26; GM Jan. 1776, xlvi. 46a.

3. Susanna Prescot (1748–76), m., 30 April 1768, Rev. Anthony Fountayne Eyre (d. 1794), residentiary of York Cathedral 1773–94. She d. at Barnborough [Barmbrough], Yorks, 2 Nov. 1776. Her father and mother erected a mural monument to the memory of her and her sister in the north aisle of the Church of St Botolph, Cambridge (see *Yorkshire Genealogist*, loc. cit.).

4. Charles Prescot (1745–1820), Fellow of St Catharine's Hall (B.A. 1766, B.D. 1776); rector of Stockport, Cheshire 1783–1820 (see *Eton Coll. Reg. 1753–90*).

5. There seems to be no bibliographical record of this press.

To Cole, Monday 9 September 1776

Add MS 5952, ff. 166–7.
Address: To the Reverend Mr Cole at Milton near Cambridge.
Postmark: Isleworth 10 SE.

Strawberry Hill, Sept. 9, 1776.

MAY I trouble you, dear Sir, when you see our friend Mr Essex, to tell him that the tower is covered in, and that whenever he has nothing to do after this week, I shall be very glad to see him here, if he will only send me a line two or three days beforehand. I have carried this little tower higher than the round one, and it has an exceedingly pretty effect, breaking the long line of the house picturesquely, and looking very ancient, thus.[1] I wish this or anything else could tempt you hither.

I must correct a little error in the spelling of a name in the pedigree you was so kind as to make out for me last year; the Derehaughs were not of Colton, but Coulston Hall. This I discovered oddly this morning. On opening a patch-box that belonged to my mother, and which I have not opened for many years, I found an exceedingly small silver collar or ring about this size;[1] but broad and flat. I remember it was in an old satin bag of coins that my mother found in old Houghton when she first married. I call it a collar from the breadth, for it would not be large enough for a fairy's lap dog. It was probably made for an infant's little finger, and must have been for a ring, not a collar, for I believe, though she was an heiress, young ladies did not elope so early in those days. I never knew how it came into the family, but now it is plain, for the inscription on the outside is, *Of Coulston Hall Suff.* and is a confirmation of your pedigree. I have tied it to a piece of paper with a long inscription; and as it is so small, it will not be melted down for the weight;[2] and if not lost from its diminutive person, may remain in the family a long while, and be preserved when some gamester may spend every other bit of silver he has in the world—at least if one would make heirlooms now, one must take care that they have no value in them.

1. See illustration.
2. 'The ring described above, together with the inscription in Walpole's hand-writing, is now in possession of Earl Waldegrave at Chewton Priory' (Toynbee).

May I trouble you, dear Sr, when you see our friend next free, to tell him that the Tower is covered in, & that whenever he has nothing to do after this week, I shall be very glad to see him here, if he will only send me a line two or three days before hand. I have carried this little ver higher than the round one, & it has an exceedingly pretty effect, aking the long line of the House picturesquely, & looking very ancient. I wish this or any thing else coud tempt you hither.

must correct a little error in the spelling of a name in the pedigree you as so kind as to make out for me last year; the Derehaughs were not Colter, but Coulston hall. This I discovered oddly this morning. on ening a patchbox that belonged to my Mother, & which I have not opend r many years, I found an exceedingly small silver collar or ring about is size O, but broad & flat. I remember it was in an old fallen bag of coins that Mother found in old Houghton when she first married. I call it a collar on the breadth, but woud not be large enough for a Fairy's lapdog. It was probably de for an Infant's little finger, & must have been for a ring, not a collar, for elieve, tho she was an Heiress, young Ladies did not elope so early in those days. ever knew how it came into the family, but now it is plain, for the ription on the outside is, Of Coulston hall Suff. & is a confirmation of yr pedigree,

COLE'S COPY OF 9 SEPTEMBER 1776

I fancy Mrs Prescott is returned, for I have heard no more of the Doctor. I wish you may be able to tell me your gout is gone.

Yours ever,

H. W.

PS. I was turning over Edmondson[3] this evening and observed an odd concurrence of circumstances in the present Lord Carmarthen.[4] By his mother[5] he is the representative of the great Duke of Marlborough and of Lord Treasurer Godolphin; by his father[6] of the Lord Treasurer Duke of Leeds, and by his grandmother[7] is descended from the Lord Treasurer Oxford. Few men are so well ancestored in so short a compass of time.

From Cole, Thursday 19 September 1776

VA, Forster MS 110, f. 164. Cole kept no copy.
Address: For the Honourable Mr Horace Walpole at Strawberry Hill in Twickenham, Middlesex. *Postmark:* Cambridge 20 SE.

Milton, Sept. 19, 1776.

Dear Sir,

I SENT Mr Essex the contents of your letter the day after I received it, and saw him a day or two after. He was just then returned with his wife from Margate, where they had both been for the use of bathing. He called at Canterbury in his way back, and has engaged himself to the chapter there to make out a draft for a new

3. See Joseph Edmondson, *Baronagium Genealogicum: or the Pedigrees of the English Peers,* 6 vols, [1764–84] i. 30.
4. Francis Godolphin Osborne (1751–99), 5th D. of Leeds, styled M. of Carmarthen 1761–89. HW also mentions his pedigree in 'Strange Occurrences: being a Continuation of Baker's Chronicle,' dated 'Dec. 28, 1782,' *Works* iv. 363–7 (at pp. 366–7).
5. Mary Godolphin (1723–64), dau. of Francis Godolphin (1678–1766), 2d E. of Godolphin, son of Sidney Godolphin

(1645–1712), 1st E. of Godolphin, Lord High Treasurer 1700–1, 1702–10. Her mother was Henrietta Churchill (1681–1733), *suo jure* Duchess of Marlborough, dau. of John Churchill (1650–1722), 1st D. of Marlborough.
6. Thomas Osborne (1713–89), 4th D. of Leeds, great-grandson of Sir Thomas Osborne (1632–1712), 1st D. of Leeds, Lord High Treasurer 1673–9.
7. Elizabeth Harley (1691–1713), dau. of Robert Harley (1661–1724), 1st E. of Oxford, who was Lord High Treasurer 1711–4.

roof for part of their cathedral, and they want it forthwith. This, with the present elevation of a new chapel at Sidney College, under his direction, takes him up necessarily after an absence of five weeks, for a few days, and he means to be with you in a few days, and will give you due notice. I wonder he did not call when he passed through London about a week ago, as I know by your preceding letter that you expected him. I wish on every account I could attend him, and would do it with pleasure, but am still confined to my crutch and stick, and without them cannot move an inch, and for these last five or six days have had a trifling pain in my knee which wakes me after I have got to sleep an hour or two. Notwithstanding this, I dined yesterday at Sturbridge Fair with the mayor,[1] where Mr Jenyns engaged me to dine with him today, and though it is ten miles, yet the airing and good roads tempt me while I can hobble out, but must return in the evening.

Lord Mount Stewart was at Cambridge last week or a fortnight ago, and purchased of Dr Ewin a volume of prints which I remember he showed to you, and for which he gave five guineas, and which he had the conscience to take twenty-five for. No wonder Dr Ewin grows rich. Mr Gulston was with him, but I saw nothing of them, though they stayed at Cambridge more than a day or two.

I am glad I hear no complaints of gout from Strawberry Hill. Pray God keep you from it long and long and every other complaint, which is the constant prayer of, dear Sir,

Your ever obliged and faithful servant,

WM COLE

To COLE, Monday 9 December 1776

Add MS 5952, f. 168.

Cole notes before his transcript of the letter: 'I have lost or mislaid two or three letters since the last of September 9. The following contained an elegant print of Bp Trevor [Richard Trevor (1707–71), Bp of St David's 1744–52, and of Durham 1752–71], engraved by J. Collyer' [Joseph Collyer (1748–1827), engraver

---

1. John Newling (information from Mr C. H. Kemp, Town Clerk, Cambridge, Oct. 1936).

and book-illustrator] (Add MS 5824, f. 98v). Cole apparently is mistaken about the 'two or three letters' 'lost or mislaid,' as he apologizes in his reply for his tardiness in thanking HW for some prints sent by Lort.

On the back of the original Cole notes: 'Holtofte. Ermines 3 lozenges ermine, quartered by Walpole.'

Address: [From Cole's copy, Add MS 5824, f. 99v.] To the Rev. Mr Cole at Milton near Cambridge.

Strawberry Hill, Dec. 9, 1776.

I KNOW you love an episcopal print, and therefore I send you one of two that have just been given to me.[1] As you have time and patience too, I recommend to you to peruse Sir John Hawkins's new *History of Music*.[2] It is true there are five huge volumes in quarto, and perhaps you may not care for the expense,[3] but surely you can borrow them in the University, and though you may no more than I, delight in the scientific part, there is so much about cathedral service and choirs, and other old matters, that I am sure you will be amused with a great deal, particularly the two last volumes, and the facsimiles of old music in the first. I doubt it is a work that will not sell rapidly, but it must have a place in all great libraries.

Pray tell Mr Essex his ceiling[4] is nearly finished and very well executed.

As we have not had above[5] two or three cold days, I hope the winter agrees with you, and that your complaints are gone off. Adieu, dear Sir

Yours most sincerely,

H. W.

---

1. See introductory note to this letter. The prints were given to HW by George Allan (1736–1800), antiquary and topographer. See HW to Allan 9 Dec. 1776.

2. *A General History of the Science and Practice of Music,* 5 vols, 1776. HW's copy (A.3.2–6), bound in green morocco, with his arms on the sides, was sold SH i. 53. It is now WSL. Vol. 5 contains MS notes in HW's hand. According to Miss Laetitia Matilda Hawkins, HW 'first suggested to my father the idea of the *History of Music*' (*Anecdotes, Biographical Sketches and Memoirs,* 3 vols, 1822–4, i. 101). In his 'Book of Mate-

rials for 1759,' pp. 101–2, appear HW's notes on English musicians, 'collected for Mr Hawkins.' The notes, about twenty-five in number, were not all used by Hawkins; and the author made no acknowledgments to HW.

3. It sold for £6.6.0 in boards. In the first instalment of the review in GM (Jan. 1777, xlvii. 29), it is called 'this most curious, expensive, and elaborate work.'

4. That is, the ceiling of the Beauclerc Closet, designed by Essex.

5. MS reads *about.*

From Cole, Sunday 15 December 1776

VA, Forster MS 110, f. 165. Cole kept no copy.
Address: For the Hon. Mr Horace Walpole at Strawberry Hill in Twickenham, Middlesex. *Postmark:* [Cambridge] 16 DE.

Milton, Dec. 15, 1776.

Dear Sir,

I WONDER you are so good to me and take any sort of notice of me: I ought long ago to have thanked you for three of your own prints by Mr Lort, who smuggled one of them for the carriage. The Bishop of Durham is very acceptable indeed. He was not only a bishop, but the beauty of holiness: a Holiness come near being Pope. The print is elegant and neatly engraved, and I desire you to accept my best thanks for it.

I have not seen Sir John Hawkins's book, but I hear they have it at Emanuel, and I hope I shall be able to borrow it of Dr Farmer. I heard much commendation of it, and your letter gives me great zeal to see it. You say properly, I have patience. If you was to see what I am now about, you would say so with justice: it is a MS of arms[1] of all the nobility and gentry in Edward I, II and III's times, who attended them in their wars. There are two or three thousand coats, and I have undertaken to copy them all. Among them are many other coats at the end of several of the bishops and abbots in Henry VIII's time, and this increased my desire to go through with so operose a work. At the end of one list of warriors in Edward I's time is a second list with this title, which I don't understand, and will beg your assistance: *Ces sont les Noms et les Armes abatues[2] de grants Seignours,* after which follow the arms of the Earls of Chester, Salisbury, Leicester, Ferrers, Kent, Devonshire, Winchester, Cornwaille and le Mareshal. *Abatues* puzzles me. Surely it does not mean those who were taken prisoners? It is no term of heraldry that I know of.

I am still confined to my chair and crutch without pain, only a weakness. The weather has been delightful, and I hope you have enjoyed the benefit of it.

1. Probably an 'Account of the Nobility of England and Wales to 1589' by Robert Cook (d. 1593?), herald. Cole's copy is in Add MS 5851.

2. *Abatues* probably means *discarded* or *former.*

Mr Essex I reckon I shall see in a few days, when I won't fail to deliver your message.

I am in the dark, because I wait for a person to take this up to town, and am, dear Sir,

Your ever faithful and most obliged servant,

WM COLE

To COLE, Thursday 20 February 1777

Add MS 5953, ff. 1–2.

Address: [From COLE's copy, Add MS 5824, f. 99v.] To the Rev. Mr Cole at Milton near Cambridge.

Arlington Street, Feb. 20, 1777.

Dear Sir,

YOU are always my oracle in any antique difficulties. I have bought at Mr Ives's sale[1] (immensely dear[2]) the shutters of the altar at St Edmundsbury:[3] Mr Ives had them from Tom Martin, who married Peter Leneve's widow;[4] so you see no shutters can be better descended on the mother's side. Next to high birth, personal merit is something: in that respect my shutters are far from defective—on the contrary the figures on the inside are so very good as to amaze me who could paint them here in the reign of Henry VI; they are worthy of the Bolognese school—but they have suffered in several places, though not considerably. Bonus[5] is to repair them, under oath

1. 'His coins, medals, ancient paintings, and antiquities, were sold by auction by Mr Langford, February 13 and 14, 1777.' 'His library was sold by auction, by Messrs Baker and Leigh, March 3–6, 1777' (LA iii. 199).

2. According to a priced copy of the *Catalogue . . . of Coins and Medals . . . of John Ives, Esq. . . . sold by auction by Messrs Langford, Covent Garden . . .* in the British Museum Dept of MSS, the shutters were sold 2nd day, lot 75, for £20.

3. HW had the shutters (the folding covers hinged to the altar-piece) sawn into four pieces, and placed them in the Chapel at SH (see *Description of SH, Works* ii. 507–8). At the time of the SH sale, they had been removed into the waiting room. They

were sold to the Duke of Sutherland SH xxi. 44 for £63.10s.

4. Frances Beeston or Berston, dau. of Robert Beeston, a miller, m. (1727), as his 2d wife, Peter LeNeve (1661–1729), Norfolk antiquary; she m. (2), as his 2d wife, in 1731, Thomas ('Honest Tom') Martin (1697–1771) of Palgrave, LeNeve's executor.

5. —— Bonus, a picture-cleaner of Oxford Road. A 'Mr George Bones' died 24 April 1791 'at his apartments in Holborn, in his 90th year' (GM May 1791, lxi. 489b). See also *The Biographical Mirrour*, ii (1798). 70–1. Bonus did not complete the restoration of the shutters until more than three years later (see HW to Lort 4 June 1779; *post* 30 May 1780).

of only filling up the cracks and restoring the peelings off, but without repainting or varnishing.

The possession of these boards, invaluable to me, was essential. They authenticate the sagacity of my guesses, a talent in an antiquary coequal with prophecy in a saint. On the outside is an archbishop, unchristened by the late possessors, but evidently Archbishop Kempe, or the same person with the prelate in my Marriage of Henry VI—and you will allow from the collateral evidence that it must be Kempe, as I have so certainly discovered another personage in my picture. The other outside is a cardinal, called by Mr Ives, Babington;[6] but I believe Cardinal Beaufort,[7] *for* the lion of England stands by him, which a bastardly prince of the blood was more likely to assume than a true one. His face is not very like nor very unlike the same person in my picture; but this is shaven—but now comes the great point. On the inside is Humphrey Duke of Gloucester, kneeling—not only as exactly resembling mine as possible, but with the same almost-bald head, and the precisely same furred robe. An apostle-like personage stands behind him, holding a golden chalice, as his R. Highness's offering, and, which is remarkable, the Duke's velvet cap of estate, with his coronet of strawberry leaves. I used to say, to corroborate my hypothesis, that the skull of Duke Humphrey at St Alban's was very like the form of head in my picture, which argument diverted the late Lord Holland[8] extremely —but I trust now that nobody will dispute any longer my perfect acquaintance with *all Dukes of Gloucester*—by the way did I ever tell you that when I published my *Historic Doubts* on Richard III, my niece's marriage[9] not being then acknowledged, George Selwyn said, he did not think *I* should have *doubted* about the Duke of

---

6. William Babington (d. 1453), Abbot of the Abbey of Bury St Edmunds 1446–53 (*Dictionary of English Church History;* see also second letter following). There was no Cardinal Babington at this time.

7. Henry Beaufort (d. 1447), Bp of Winchester and Cardinal. He was the second illegitimate son of John of Gaunt by Catherine Swynford. His parents were married in 1396 and he was declared legitimate by Richard II in 1397. His arms 'were those of England within a bordure componé argent and azure with a crescent argent for difference (see John Woodward and George

Burnett, *A Treatise on Heraldry,* 1892, ii. 555); so Walpole's suggestion about the lion of England has some heraldic justification' (Mr K. B. McFarlane).

8. Henry Fox (1705–74), 1st Bn Holland, HW's friend and correspondent. Cf. *ante* 9 Jan. 1775.

9. The marriage of Maria Walpole (1736–1807), Dowager Countess Waldegrave (dau. of Sir Edward Walpole), to William Henry, D. of Gloucester, which took place in 1766, was made public in 1772, and was allowed to be valid in 1773.

Gloucester. On the inside of the other shutter is a man unknown; he is in a stable, as Joseph might be, but over him hangs a shield of arms, that are neither Joseph's nor Mary's. The colours are either black and white, or so changed as not to be distinguishable; but they are thus.[10] These are three bulls' heads. These are ducks or martlets, on the argent, but I have blotted them and the middle quarter at bottom, which should be of six pieces, three charged and three plain, or the bearings lost, for this is the most damaged part. I conclude the person, who is in red and white, was the donor of the altar-piece, or a benefactor; and what I want of you is to discover him, and his arms;[11] and to tell me whether Duke Humphrey, Beaufort, Kempe and Babington were connected with St Edmundsbury, or whether this unknown person was not a retainer of Duke Humphrey, at least of the royal family.

At the same sale I bought a curious pane,[12] that I conclude came from Blickling,[13] with Hobart impaling Boleyn, from which latter family the former enjoyed that seat.

How does this third winter of the season agree with you? The wind today is sharper than a razor and blows icicles into one's eyes. I was confined for seven weeks with the gout, yet am so well recovered as to have been abroad today, though it is as mild under the Pole.

Pray, can you tell me the title of the book that Mr Ives dedicated to me.[14] I never saw it, for he was so odd (I cannot call it modest, lest I should seem not so myself) as never to send it to me, and I never could get it.

Yours most truly,

H. W.[15]

10. A rough drawing appears in the MS. See following page for Cole's copy (Add MS 5824, f. 100v).

11. Cole was unable to do this.

12. It is not described in the Sale Catalogue, but it may have been one of the 'curious pieces of painted glass,' mentioned in the description of the Green Closet (*Description of SH, Works* ii. 427).

13. In Norfolk, the seat of the Boleyn family until the death of Sir James Boleyn, 1561, uncle of Anne Boleyn, when it came into possession of Sir John Clere, son and heir of Sir Robert Clere, who had married Alice Boleyn. His descendant, Sir Edward Clere, sold Blickling to Sir Henry Hobart about 1600 (see Blomefield, *Norfolk*[2] vi. 381–409; also *post* 14 Nov. 1779).

14. *Select Papers chiefly relating to English Antiquities, from the Originals in the Possession of John Ives, Esq.*, Numbers I–III, 1773–5. Number I was dedicated to HW.

15. At the end of Cole's copy of this letter is the following note: 'V. a letter of Mr Walpole dated June 4, 1779, to Mr Lort, on the same subject [that is, the shutters] in my vol. 24, pp. 166, 167 [Add MS 5825].'

(Letters &c. from the Honourable Horace Walpole. 1777.)

in my Marriage of Henry 6. — & you will allow, from the collateral Evidence, that it must be Kempe, as I so certainly discovered another Personage in my Picture. The other Outside is a Cardinal, called by Mr. Babington; but I believe Cardinal Beaufort: for the Lion of England stands by him, which a Bastard Prince of the Blood was more likely to assume, than a true one. His Face is not very like, nor very unlike, some Person in my Picture: but this is slighter. But now comes the great Bird. On the Inside is Humphrey Duke of Gloucester kneeling, not only as exactly resembling mine as possible, but with the same short-bald Head, & the precisely same furred Robes. An Apostle-like Personage stands behind him, holding a golden Chalice, as his R. Highness's Offering, &, which is remarkable, the Duke's Velvet Cap of Estate, with his Coronet of Strawberry Leaves. I used to say, to corroborate my Hypothesis, that the Skull of Duke Humphrey at St. Albans, was very like the Form of Head in my Picture; which Argument diverted the late Lord Holland extremely. But I trust now, that nobody will dispute any longer my perfect acquaintance with All Dukes of Gloucester. By the Way, did I ever tell you, that when I published Historic Doubts on Richard 3. my Neice's Marriage not being then acknowledged, George Selwyn —, He did not think I should have doubted about the Duke of Gloucester. On the Inside of the other Shutter is a Man unknown: He is in a Stable as Joseph might be; but over him hangs a Shield of Arms, that are neither Joseph's nor Mary's. The Colours are either black & white, or so changed as to be distinguishable: but they are these.

These are Ducks
or Martlets on the
Argent: But I have

added them, & the middle Quarter at Bottom, which should be of six Peices, 3 charged, & 3 or the Bearings lost: for this is the most damaged Part. I conclude the Person, who is in red Ermine, was the Donor of the Altar-Peice, or a Benefactor; & what I want of you is to discover him, by the Arms; & to tell me, whether Duke Humphrey, Beaufort, Kempe & Babington were connected with Edmondsbury; or whether this unknown Person was not a Retainer of Duke Humphrey, at least of the Royal Family.

At the same Sale I bought a curious Pane [of Glass] that I conclude came from Blickling, with part impaling Boleyn: from which latter Family the former enjoyed that Seat.

How does this third Winter of the Season agree with you? The Wind to Day is sharper than a razor, & blows Icicles into ones Eyes. I was confined for 7 Weeks with the Gout, yet am so well recovered, as to have been abroad to Day, tho' it is as mild as under the Pole.

When can you tell me the Title of the Book that Mr. Ives dedicated to me. I never saw it: for he so odd, (I cannot call it modest, lest I should seem not so myself) as never to send it to me; never could get it. Yrs most truly HW.

*v. a Letter of Mr. Walpole dated June 4. 1779, to
Mr. Lort, on the same Subject in my Vol. 24. p. 166.
167.

COLE'S COPY OF 20 FEBRUARY 1777

From COLE, Friday 21 February 1777

The original is missing, but it was seen by Warburton, whose text in *Memoirs of Horace Walpole* ii. 405–6 is given below. The chief variations in COLE's copy, Add MS 5824, f. 99, are given in the notes.

Address: [From COLE's copy.] To the Honourable Horace Walpole in Arlington Street, London.

Milton, February 21, 1777.[1]

I HAVE lately read a little scandalous book against King James I, by Sir Anthony Welden,[2] with an answer to it called *Aulicus Coquinariæ; or a Vindication in answer to a pamphlet intituled The Court and Character of King James,* pretended to be penned by Sir A. W., and published after his death, 1650, London, 1650, supposed to have been chiefly written by Godfrey Goodman, Bishop of Gloucester, who died a Roman Catholic in 1655.[3] In this book, which if you have not met with, you will be pleased to see many curious anecdotes of that time, on the Bishop's[4] own knowledge; in particular, a complete vindication, and pretty long, of the old Countess of Exeter,[5] accused of adultery or fornication with the Lord Ross, her son-in-law.[6] If you have not the book, I will send you mine.

Poor Dr. Dodd,[7] though I never saw his sweet face at the Magdalen or elsewhere, excites my pity. I tremble for him tomorrow, and hardly see a glimmering how he can escape the halter. In alleviation to his crime, the only thing to defend him is the general corruption

---

1. Cole's copy begins: 'Dear Sir, My confinement this twelvemonth has enlarged my volumes and done no service to my eyes, but I cannot sit with my hands before me. I wish I could smoke tobacco, which would amuse the evenings, which injure the eyes more than daylight, but I cannot even go on with British herb tobacco.'

2. *The Court and Character of King James I,* 1650, by Sir Anthony Weldon (d. 1649?), historical writer.

3. Godfrey Goodman (1583–1656), Bp of Gloucester 1625–43, was not the author, as Cole supposed. He answered Weldon's book in *Court of James I,* which was first published by the Rev. J. S. Brewer (1810–79), in 1839, from the MS in the Bodleian Library. *Aulicus Coquinariae* was written by Sir William Sanderson (1586?–1676).

4. That is, Sir William Sanderson's.

5. Elizabeth Drury (1579–1654), dau. of Sir William Drury of Hawsted, Suffolk; m., as his 2d wife, William Cecil (1566–1640), 2d E. of Exeter.

6. That is, her stepson, William Cecil (1590–1618), 17th Bn Ros, or Roos, son of 2d E. of Exeter by his 1st wife, Elizabeth Manners (1676–91), *suo jure* Baroness Ros.

7. William Dodd (1729–77), fashionable preacher and forger; preached (1758) the inaugural sermon at the Magdalen House, and acted as chaplain from that time until Aug. 1774. For forging, early in Feb. 1777, the signature of his patron, the Earl of Chesterfield, he was tried and convicted 22 Feb. (the day after this letter), and, despite the efforts of Dr Johnson and others, was sentenced 26 May and hanged 27 June 1777.

of the times, and that many who ride triumphantly, deserve it full as much. We have an odd affair of the sort just now broke out at Cambridge, where our friend Dr. E[win][8] who is greatly disliked there, is reasonably suspected to be linked in with a parcel of people who constantly advertise to lend money to nobility and gentry; one King of that fraternity this time twelvemonth, sent letters nominative to every fellow-commoner in each college, and to many pensioners who were supposed to have fortunes in reversion, with offers of money. A young man of Trinity[9] applied to Dr E[win] who lent him £800 with a bond of £1300 when he came of age, which was near at hand. This has been discovered, and occasions no small talk, even to degradation, etc. A clergyman, also, in the neighbourhood, to whom I sold my Fen estate, is now breaking, in numbers of people's debt, to the ruin of many.[10] Thank God, I took my money of him early, though much pressed to retain it.[11]

From COLE, Sunday 23 February 1777

Edited from Eliot Warburton, *Memoirs of Horace Walpole* ii. 406–9, and from COLE's copy, Add MS 5824, ff. 100v, 101v. The chief variations in the two texts are recorded in the notes. The original is missing.

Address: [From COLE's copy.] To the Honourable Horace Walpole in Arlington Street, London.

Milton, Sunday, Feb. 23, 1777.

Dear Sir,

I CARRIED a letter with me to Cambridge, where I dined on Friday, and on my return the Ely postman had left yours.[1]

I congratulate you on your fresh acquisition to your Lancastrian portraits, and wish I could decipher the arms, but any attempt to

8. Supplied from Cole's copy.

9. Cole's copy identifies him as William Bird (b. 1755), son of Charles Bird of London (see *Admissions to Trinity College, Cambridge, 1701–1800*, p. 236). Cooper, *Annals*, iv. 389, records that Ewin 'in 1775 and 1776 advanced to Mr Bird, then a minor *in statu pupillari*, partly through the agency of a Portuguese Jew named Silva, but who also went by the name of A. Grove, the sum of £750, for which he took notes to the amount of £1090.'

10. Cole's copy identifies him as Thomas Jones, who died in 1788, rector of Prince George, Winyaw, South Carolina (see *Alumni Cantab.*).

11. Cole's copy concludes: 'I will trouble you no longer, and wishing you well and warm this return of winter weather, I remain Yours most faithfully and affectionately, Wm Cole.'

1. From Cole's copy.

that seems vain, as you say that that part of the picture has suffered most, and that you know not whether the bearings are ducks or martlets. As these birds are totally dissimilar, the one having a large bill and long neck, and the other no bill at all and the shortest of necks, they may possibly be something else. I take it they should be thus blazoned: party per fess argent and sable, a pale counter-charged, on the argent three birds sable impaling argent, three bulls' heads caboshed sable, which last are borne by Walrond. As to the other, I can give no account of it at present, but will have it in my mind. It is most likely that he was a retainer to the court, and giver of the altar-piece. I have hunted in many books for benefactors to the Abbey, but can find none to whom these arms suit.

Your other questions are easier to solve. The King,[2] Humphrey Duke of Gloucester, Bishop or Cardinal Kempe, Cardinal Beaufort and Babington were much connected with Bury Abbey. In the first place, King Henry VI, in the twelfth year of his reign, A° 1433, spent his Christmas in that monastery with his court, staying there four months, to St George's Day following, viz., 23 April. This is un-observed by the historians I have consulted, but in a MS of the late Sir James Burrough, Master of Caius College, a good antiquary, a Bury man, and who had made great collections for that place, some of which I have copied, is a long account of his amusements there during that time. Till you show an inclination to know more, I will only transcribe his leave-taking after he, the Duke of Gloucester, and the rest of the nobility had been received into the confraternity of that Abbey,[3] by which they were made participants of their prayers and good works, etc.:—

Quamobrem Rex præfatus in Recessu suo prostratus coram Deo et B. Martyri S[ancto] E[dmundo], devotas et humiles exsolvit Preces; et tan-dem surgens, sequace D. Gloucesteriae, et aliis nobilibus transiit in Do-mum Capitularem, ubi immediate accersito Abbate (licet ibidem Patronus et Fundator extiterit) voluit tamen, ut asseruit, sicut cæteri nobiles, recipi in dicti monasterii numero fraternali: Quem Abbas in conspectu circum-stantium nobilium predictorum, juxta Petitionem regiam, mox pie et de-vote recipiens datoque. Osculo in Signum fraterni vinculi, in dictum nu-

2. Henry VI.
3. Cole's copy reads, 'Quamobrem Rex &c. V. my vol. 45, p. 32.' The extracts are from the Register of Abbot Curteys of Bury St Edmunds (d. 1446), now Add MS 14,848; they are printed from Cole's transcript, Add MS 5846, f. 32, rather than from War-burton. See Wm Dugdale, *Monasticon*, ed. T. Cayley and others, 1821, iii. 129–30.

merum aggregavit, participem fieri omnium suffragiorum, Missarum et aliorum bonorum in perpetuum inibi complendorum. Et tunc paulo post, astantibus nobilibus saepedictus Dux Glouc' prostratus coram Rege, ipsum viscerabiliter imploravit, quatenus supradicto Abbati, propter Humanitatem, quam ergo se, et suos, in Donariis et Expensis indefessam reddiderat, regratiari dignaretur Regia Celsitudo, quem Rex sine Intervallo per manum hilariter recipiens, ei gratias retulit multiformes, et valedicens omnibus, se et suos, Deo et B. Edmundo dictique Abbatis et confratrum suorum Precibus intime commendavit.

Many years after this, from the same MS, viz., in 1446, on the Feast of St Scholastica, a parliament was holden at Bury in the presence of the King, who sat in his chair of estate within the refectory of the abbey. The Archbishop of Canterbury, John Stafford,[4] opened the session with a discourse, taking for his text, *Qui ineunt Pacis Consilium, sequitur illos gaudium* (Prov. xii. 20). Upon which he showed that between the ambassadors of the King and the French King, order was taken for a personal interview or talk of these Kings, and sufficient assurance had for the King's passage beyond seas, for his safe being there and like return, in which case the King was bent to use their counsel, and therefore had called them together. At this parliament Humphrey Duke of Gloucester was arrested, and on the 23rd of February was found dead in his bed. Hall, p. 152, gives this account of the transaction:

The Duke, the night after his imprisonment, was found dead in his bed; and his body shewed to the lords and commons, as though he had died of a palsy or empostome; but all indifferent persons well knew that he died of no natural death, but of some violent force.[5]

He was carried from St Edmundsbury to St Albans for burial.

In the same MS is this list of nobility and gentry who were received into the fraternity of St Edmund Bury Convent in 1440, which I send you only as a curiosity, and not relating to your queries:

Memorandum, quod Ao Dni, 1440, receperunt Fraternitatem capituli nostri 6 Die Martii.

Humfridus Com. Buck. Hert. Staff. Northampt. et Berchie.

4. (d. 1452), Abp of Canterbury 1443–52.
5. Cole has modernized this quotation from Edward Hall, *The Union of the Two*

Noble and Illustre Famelies of Lancastre & Yorke, 1548, opp. fo. clii.

Anna uxor ejus[6] Humfridus[7] et Henricus Stafford[8] filii ejus.

Anna de Vere[9] filia ipsius Comitis.

Hen. de Bourgchier[10] Com. de Ewe et Dominus de Bourgchier.

Johes. Bourgchier[11] ejusdem filius. Isabella Verney,[12] Eliz. Drury,[13] Eliz. Culpeper,[14] Johes. Salveyn,[15] Hen. Drury,[16] Will. Wistowe,[17] Walt. Percevale.[18]

In the same MS is this, which shows the connection of the Beauforts to the Abbey:

A° 1436, Oct. 4. Litera Fraternitatis concessa Henrico Dei Gratia titulo Sancti Eusebii, S. S. Romanæ Ecclesiæ Presbytero, Cardinali de Anglia vulgariter nuncupato, in qua pater ejus, Johannes Dux Lancastriæ vocatur, 'Alter monasterii Sancti Edmundi Fundator.' Thomas Dux Exoniæ, vir sanctissimus, Cardinalis dicti frater, apud Sanctum Edmundum humatus, &c.

By this you see that the Cardinal and Duke Humphrey were both nearly connected with this abbey. Cardinal John Kempe was Archbishop of York from 1426 to 1452, when he was translated to Canterbury, where he died the year after, and had been a busy man in all the intrigues of King Henry's court. As to Babington, there never was such a Cardinal, nor indeed a bishop of that name but one, who was made so in Queen Elizabeth's reign and died in her successor's.[19] It is probable that Mr Ives meant William Babington who was abbot

6. Humphrey Stafford (1402–60), 1st D. of Buckingham, m. Anne Neville (d. 1482), 10th dau. of Ralph Neville, 1st E. of Westmorland.

7. Humphrey Stafford (d. 1455), styled E. of Stafford, eld. son of 1st D. of Buckingham.

8. Henry Stafford (d. 1481), 2d (?) son of 1st D. of Buckingham.

9. Anne Stafford (d. 1472), eld. dau. of 1st D. of Buckingham, m. (1) Aubrey de Vere (d. 1462), heir-apparent of the E. of Oxford, who was executed with his father; and (2) Sir Thomas Cobham (d. 1471).

10. Henry Bourchier (1404–83), 1st Vct Bourchier, afterwards (1461) E. of Essex.

11. John Bourchier (d. 1495), 4th son of the preceding, m. as her 2d husband, Elizabeth Ferrers (d. 1483), Lady Ferrers of Groby.

12. Mr K. B. McFarlane suggests: 'Perhaps the wife of Walter Verney, who, along with Henry Lord Bourchier, John Salvayn, Henry Drury, and others, was appointed a feofee of Stafford's estates in 1427 (*Calendar of Close Rolls, 1422–9,* pp. 318, 321, 322, 334).'

13. Wife of Henry Drury.

14. Possibly the wife of Sir William Colepeper (Mr McFarlane).

15. Mr McFarlane believes this to be Sir John Salvayn, or Salvin, son of George Salvin, of North Duffield, Yorks, and that he died between 1449 and 1453.

16. Mr McFarlane identifies him positively from the *Calendars of Close Rolls, Fine Rolls,* and *Patent Rolls,* and believes he died in 1443.

17. Not identified.

18. Alive 5 Nov. 1443 (*Calendar of Patent Rolls, 1441–6,* p. 218).

19. Gervase Babington (1550?–1610), Bp of Llandaff 1591, of Exeter 1595, and of Worcester 1597.

of St Edmundsbury in 1447, and who had been President or General of his Benedictine Order in England. *Vide* Batteley's *Antiq. Rutup.,* Appendix, p. 161.[20]

The Duke of Exeter's body, perfect, was lit upon among the ruins of the abbey at Bury about four or five years ago.[21] Mr Cullum[22] the surgeon there cut off one of his hands and has it now in spirits.[23]

I have Mr Ives's[24] book and will send it to you.

I had a gentleman and his lady dined here this day. He is a Scotchman of the name of Cummins, a man of literature, Prebendary of St Patrick's in Dublin, where he married the sister of a Sir Harry Hartstong, Bart.[25] He has a brother, a merchant in Cambridge,[26] who married one of Mr Gray's cousin Antrobus.[27] This Scots-Hibernic clergyman was educated in Oxford, is a civil, sensible, talkative man, has an intense desire to see the beauties of Strawberry Hill, with his wife and a friend or two with him, in March or April. If you will send a ticket for him to me, you will much oblige

Your ever affectionate friend and humble servant,

WM COLE

20. *Joannis Battely . . . Opera Posthuma. Viz., Antiquitates Rutupinae et Antiquitates S. Edmundi Burgi,* Oxford, 1745. Cole refers to the second part.

21. Cole's copy reads: 'The body of Tho. Beaufort Duke of Exeter was found in a coffin in digging among the ruins of the church in 1772, as fresh and entire as if just buried.' For an account of the discovery, see *Philosophical Transactions,* 1772, lxii. 465–8; *Archaeologia* iii. 311–5; *Antiquarian Repertory,* 2d edn, 4 vols, 1807–9, iii. 331–2; LA viii. 585–6. Thomas Beaufort (d. 1426), D. of Exeter, was the 3d and illegitimate son of John of Gaunt by Catherine Swynford. He m. Margaret Neville (d. before 1426), dau. of Sir Thomas Neville.

22. Thomas Gery Cullum (1741–1831), brother of Sir John Cullum, whom he succeeded as 7th Bt in 1785; Bath King-of-Arms 1771–1801; an eminent surgeon and botanist.

23. 'His duchess [see n. 21 above] was also buried in the same abbey' (addition in Cole's copy). The remainder of the letter is not in Warburton, but was in the original (see enclosure of following letter which refers to the Comingses).

24. *Select Papers chiefly relating to English Antiquities.*

25. Fowler Comings (1728–82), son of Richard Comings of Burton, Staffs; Prebendary of Swords, St Patrick's Cathedral, Dublin, 1761–82; m. —— Hartstonge, dau. of Price Hartstonge (d. 1734) by Alice Widenham, and sister of Sir Henry Hartstonge (1725?–97), 3d Bt, of Bruffe, co. Limerick (see *Alumni Oxon;* Hugh Jackson Lawlor, *The Fasti of St Patrick's, Dublin,* Dundalk, 1930, p. 161).

26. Richard Comings.

27. Dorothy Antrobus.

To COLE, Thursday 27 February 1777

Add MS 5953, f. 3.

Address: [From COLE's copy, Add MS 5824, f. 101v.] To the Rev. Mr Cole at Milton near Cambridge. Free H. S. Conway.

[Arlington Street,] Feb. 27, 1777.

YOU see, dear Sir, that we thought on each other just at the same moment; but, as usual, you was thinking of obliging me, and I of giving you trouble. You have fully satisfied me of the connection between the Lancastrian princes and St Edmundsbury. Edmondson, I conclude, will be able to find out the proprietor of the arms impaling Walrond.

I am well acquainted with Sir A. Weldon and the *Aulicus Coquinariae,* and will return them with Mr Ives's tracts, which I intend to buy at the sale of his books. Tell me how I may convey them to you most safely. You say, *till I show an inclination to borrow more of your MSS.* I hope you do not think my appetite for that loan is in the least diminished. I should at all minutes and ever be glad to peruse them all—but I was not sure you wished to lend them to me, though you deny me nothing—and my own fear of their coming to any mischance, made me very modest about asking for them—but now, whenever you can send me any of them with perfect security, I eagerly and impudently ask to see them; you cannot oblige me more, I assure you.

I am sorry Dr E.[1] is got into such a dirty scrape. There is scarce any decent medium observed at present between wasting fortunes and fabricating them; and both by any disreputable manner; for as to saving money by prudent economy, the method is too slow in proportion to consumption: even forgery alas! seems to be the counterpart, or restorative of the ruin by gaming.[2] I hope at least that robbery on the highway will go out of fashion as too piddling a profession for gentlemen.

I enclose a card for your friends, but must advertise them that March is in every respect a wrong month for seeing Strawberry. It not only wants its leaves and beauty then, but most of the small pic-

1. Marked through (so as to be illegible) in MS, but Cole's copy reads as above. The reference is of course to Dr Ewin.   2. Alluding to Dr Dodd.

tures and curiosities, which are taken down and packed up in winter, are not restored to their places, till the weather is fine and I am more there. Unless they are confined in time, your friends had much better wait till May—but however they will be very welcome to go when they please. I am more personally interested in hoping to see you there this summer. You must visit my new tower, diminutive as it is. It adds much to the antique air of the whole in both fronts. You know I shall sympathize with your gout, and you are always master of your own hours.

Yours most sincerely,

H. W.

[Enclosure.]³

To Mr Walpole's Housekeeper at Strawberry Hill.
You may at any time show my house to Mr Cumings and four more, on their delivering this ticket to you.

Hor. Walpole

From COLE, Sunday 2 March 1777

VA, Forster MS 110, ff. 166–7. Cole's copy, Add MS 5824, f. 102v.

Address: For the Honourable Horace Walpole in Arlington Street, London.
Postmark: Cambridge.

Milton, March 2, 1777.

Dear Sir,

I AM glad you are likely to get Mr Ives's tracts. You said in your letter you had tried to get them in vain, or I had not sent them, and as they came,¹ I was willing to put the two little books² in the same parcel, not being certain that one at least had fallen in your way. If you please to send them to the Queen's Head in Gray's Inn Lane to the Cambridge fly, and directed to me at the Rose Tavern in Cambridge, I shall meet with them in a day or two.³

---

3. From Cole's copy, Add MS 5824, f. 101v.

1. Cole's copy reads: 'but as I sent them,' which makes his meaning clearer.
2. See *ante* 21 Feb. 1777, nn. 2, 3.

3. 'for though I am a prisoner, it is a prisoner-at-large, and get often into my chariot and am set down at a door where there is not much walking to get to a chair, for I do not love to walk with crutches in the street' (addition in Cole's copy).

You utterly mistook my meaning, or I wrote what I did not think of in my letter respecting my MSS. I remember I said, or meant to say, that if the extract I sent you relating to King Henry's reception at Bury was sufficient, I would spare myself the trouble of transcribing more till I had your orders to do so, as there was a considerable deal more in the MS relating to that affair. However, as you express such a desire of seeing them (a curiosity that would presently be satisfied if you had them), it would be affectation to refuse it, though no person except Dr Lyne[4] and my old friend Mr John Allen of Trinity ever looked into <them>. Indeed you are the only person in the world that I should think a moment about determining to let them go out of my hands, and in good truth they are generally of such a nature as not fit to be seen, for through life I have never disguised artfully my opinions, and as my books were my trusty friends who had engaged never to speak till twenty years after my departure, I always without guile entrusted them with my most secret thoughts of men and things, so that there is what the world would call a heap of scandalous rubbish collected together.

Our friend Dr Ewin's affair brightens up, and I am informed that much more has been propagated to his disadvantage than he deserves. His general character has led people astray, and they have said what they wished. I hope he will clear himself to his own credit and advantage.

Many thanks for the ticket. I make no doubt they[5] will stay till May before they visit Strawberry Hill. I wish I could with the same ease fix on any month in the year to accept your kind invitation, but I am apt to think I am a prisoner for life. The gout has left such a weakness in every part of my foot and knee, which was ailing before, that now after twelve or thirteen months' uninterrupted inability to walk without crutches, gives me but a bad prospect for the future. Thank God I have no pain, my eyes, books and the use of my fingers.

I had a letter last week from Mr Pennant. He sent me a view of Holt Castle in Denbighshire, neatly engraved, designed for his

4. Richard Lyne (1715–67), contemporary of HW and Cole at Eton and King's (B.A. 1738, D.D. 1764); Fellow of King's 1737–46 and of Eton 1752–67; King's Chaplain 1744–67. Cole says ' 'twas thought his disappointment' at not being made Provost of Eton in 1764 'had a bad effect on his constitution, and was the occasion of his death' (*Blecheley Diary* 241). See also *Eton Coll. Reg. 1698–1752*.

5. Mr and Mrs Fowler Comings.

Welsh Tour,[6] also a draft of a picture of Sir John Owen,[7] mentioned by Clarendon,[8] which is also to be engraved: he died in 1666 and is dressed in a long flowing wig and long cravat. It seems early for either dress. In a former letter he told me that he died before the Restoration. I was then positive it could not be meant for him. He says he has a copy of a bust of Lady Venetia Digby which he is going to have engraved.[9] In my answer to him this day I told him that I thought it was a pity, if he meant to have given a print of that lady, that he had not asked your leave for a copy of your incomparable picture of her.[10]

I am forced to leave off, and assure you of my devoted regards,

WM COLE

From COLE, Sunday 18 May 1777

VA, Forster MS 110, f. 168. COLE's copy, Add MS 5824, ff. 102v, 103v.

Address: To the Honourable Horace Walpole in Arlington Street, Piccadilly, London. *Postmark:* None. [Lort carried the letter to HW; see below.]

Dear Sir,   [Milton,] Whitsunday, May 18, 1777.

SUCH a kind visit as you was so good to pay me at this place this day three weeks[1] deserves my most grateful acknowledgments,[2]

6. Plate XVI, Pennant's *A Tour in Wales, 1773,* 1778, opp. p. 205.

7. The portrait was engraved ibid., Plate XXI, opp. p. 263. Sir John Owen (1600–66), Kt and royalist, was twice imprisoned for his efforts in behalf of Charles I, but was released.

8. Edward Hyde (1609–74), 1st E. of Clarendon. Cole refers to his *History of the Rebellion and Civil Wars in England* (see ed. W. Dunn Macray, 6 vols, 1888, iii. 114; iv. 500, 502, 507).

9. It is plate XXI, *Journey from Chester to London,* 1782, opp. p. 337. Cole had already sent HW a full description of the bust, which was at Gothurst, Bucks, and HW had also seen it (see *ante* 16 May 1762, [September 1762]; *Country Seats* 52).

10. A miniature by Peter Oliver, after Van Dyck, companion to one of Sir Kenelm Digby by the same artist after Van Dyck. They were sold together SH xi. 24–5 for £178.10s. and were resold in the Burdett-Coutts sale, 11 May 1922, lot 361. Pennant

(op. cit. 337) refers to HW's 'matchless' miniatures of Lady Venetia which are described in *Description of SH, Works* ii. 421–2.

1. 'Mr Horace Walpole dining with me at Milton, Sunday, April 27, 1777, whither he came on purpose from Barton Mills [in Suffolk, about five miles NW of Bury St Edmunds], where he had been attending on his nephew, George E. of Orford, for above a week, as guardian and nearest relation, he being then seized with a frenzy for the second time, and had attempted to throw himself out of the window more than once' (Cole, quoted in Brydges, *Restituta* iv. 248). Lord Orford was at Eriswell, near Barton Mills. For HW's account of his attendance on his nephew, see HW to Sir Edward Walpole 21, 22, and 25 April 1777, and to Mason 2 May 1777.

2. 'It was at least fifty miles to and from dinner' (addition in Cole's copy).

and is in the stead of a dozen letters. I hope you saw our Chapel[3] in your return. Dr Glynn was unhappy that he did not hear of you, that he might have <do>ne the honours of the College to such an ornament of it. I assure <y>ou it often stands in need of such a refreshment. I am, as well as the Master of Emanuel, who, I think, you would like, sorry that he did not see you. I drank coffee with him on Friday: his lodge and college must have pleased you. I went principally to see a new acquisition of an old picture that he met with: an altar-piece on which are the Howard arms and several of the family pictures in miniature in a compartment under it, on their knees. I think the painter's name is Bungult or Bangult,[4] and would have been worth your looking at. I ascertained also another picture for him, which a painter at Cambridge, an excellent copier,[5] had procured for him and assured him it was designed for Lord Darnley,[6] who was not above two- or three-and-twenty at his death, if I remember right: this is a person of fifty, with the Order of the Golden Fleece, and I am pretty certain is Count Gondomar,[7] for it is very like a print of him by Passe.[8]

When you was here I could not recover a memorandum I had put down for you. It is this: in your *Anecdotes of Painting*, vol. 1, p. 48,[9] <yo>ur memoir mentions a Mr Cumings, whose true name infallibly was Cannings,[10] the f<oun>der and benefactor of St Mary Radcliffe's Church at Br<istol>.

The reason Mr Essex did not call on you before he left town was

3. King's College Chapel.

4. Cole's mistake for Baldung: Hans Baldung (1480?–1545), commonly called Grün or Grien, a well-known German painter of the school of Dürer. In the catalogue of Farmer's sale (7 May 1798 etc.) the picture is described: 'A Dead Christ, School of Albert Durer, by H. B. Baldwig [*sic*], 1512, painted for a branch of the Howard family, who are depicted kneeling in the lower compartment.' It was sold (last day, lot 58 of the pictures) to —— Farmer, who, according to a note in Thomas Park's copy of the catalogue in the Yale University Library, sold it to the D. of Norfolk. It is now in the National Portrait Gallery.

5. Possibly Charles or Joseph Freeman (see *post* 9 June 1779).

6. Henry Stewart or Stuart (1545–67),
Lord Darnley, husband of Mary Q. of Scots.

7. Diego Sarmiento de Acuña (1567–1626), Count of Gondomar, Spanish diplomatist and ambassador in the reign of James I (see *Encyclopaedia Britannica*). This portrait mentioned by Cole is probably the one sold with four other portraits in Farmer's sale (36th day, lot 6 of the pictures) to —— Durousset (?) for 4s. 6d.

8. Both William and Simon Passe engraved portraits of Gondomar (see *Granger*[s] ii. 222–3).

9. Cole refers to the second edition. The mistake remains in *Works* iii. 46, and in later editions.

10. William Canynges (1399?–1474), merchant, sheriff and mayor of Bristol. He rebuilt the Church of St Mary Redcliff. His name is familiar in connection with the Rowley Poems.

that he heard that you was gone into Norfolk. I should be glad in your next favour to know how poor Lord O. does.

I lately read over, on your recommendation, the four first volumes of Sir John Hawkins's *History of Music,* which are in our University Library. In the course of my reading I made a few observations which I put down, and am tempted to have them put into the *Gentleman's Magazine,*[11] but will not do so except you approve of the paper, which I have sent to Mr Lort with this letter, in a packet, and beg the favour of your looking at them, as the paper is short, and correcting anything you find amiss, which will much oblige me. I know you are acquainted with Sir John,[12] who, I suppose, will not be offended at them. If you think he would, I will suppress them. As you pointed out the book, you have a right to the fruits it produced. I will not give you the trouble to seal and send my letter to the *Magazine,* though it will be as much trouble, perhaps, to send it back to Mr Lort, whom I had desired to do it for me.

Adieu, dear Sir, and believe me to be, with the greatest esteem and regard,

Your ever faithful and obedient servant,

Wm Cole

To Cole, Thursday 22 May 1777

Add MS 5953, ff. 4–5.

Address: To the Reverend Mr Cole at Milton near Cambridge.
Postmark: 22 MA.

Arlington Street, May 22, 1777.

IT is not owing to forgetfulness, negligence or idleness, to none of which I am subject, that you have not heard from me since I saw you, dear Sir, but to my miserable occupation with my poor nephew, who engrosses my whole attention, and will, I doubt, destroy my health, if he does not recover his. I have got him within fourteen miles of town with difficulty. He is rather worse than better, may recover in an instant, as he did last time, or remain in his present sullenness. I am far from expecting he should ever be perfectly in

---

11. Cole's observations were printed in GM May 1777, xlvii. 219–21, dated 19 May.   12. 'whom I have met at your house' (addition in Cole's copy).

his senses, which in my opinion, he scarce ever was. His intervals expose him to the worst people, his relapses overwhelm me.

I have put together some trifles I promised you, and will beg Mr Lort to be the bearer when he goes to Cambridge, if I know of it. At present I have time for nothing I like. My age and inclination call for retirement: I envied your happy hermitage and leisure to follow your inclination. I have always *lived post,*[1] and shall now die before I can bait—yet it is not my wish to be unemployed, could I but choose my occupations. I wish I could think of the pictures you mention, or had had time to see Dr Glynn and the Master of Emanuel. I dote on Cambridge and could like to be often there—the beauty of King's College Chapel, now it is restored,[2] penetrated me with a visionary longing to be a monk in it—though my life has been passed in turbulent scenes, in pleasures—or rather pastimes, and in much fashionable dissipation, still books, antiquity and virtu kept hold of a corner of my heart, and since necessity has forced me of late years to be a man of business, my disposition tends to be a recluse for what remains—but it will not be my lot, and though there is some excuse for the young doing what they like, I doubt an old man should do nothing but what he ought, and I hope doing one's duty is the best preparation for death. Sitting with one's arms folded to think about it is a very lazy way of preparing for it. If Charles V had resolved to make some amends for his abominable ambition, by doing good, his duty as a King, there would have been infinitely more merit than in going to doze in a convent. One may avoid active guilt in a sequestered life, but the virtue of it is merely negative, though innocence is beautiful.

I approve much of your corrections on Sir J. Hawkins and send them to the Magazine.[3]

I want the exact blazon of William of Hatfield his arms—I mean the prince buried at York: Mr Mason and I are going to restore his monument,[4] and I have not time to look for them. I know you will be so good as to assist,

Yours most sincerely,

H. W.

1. That is, rapidly.
2. See *ante* 3 Jan. 1771 n. 3.
3. HW's letter enclosing them to Nichols is missing.

4. Cf. *ante* 25 Aug. 1772 n. 5 and Mason to HW 26 May 1777.

To Cole, Wednesday 28 May 1777

Cole's copy, Add MS 5824, f. 103v. The original is missing.
Address: [From Cole's copy.] To the Rev. Mr Cole at Milton near Cambridge.

[Arlington Street,] May 28, 1777.

I HAVE but time for a word. Mr Lort has just been here, and does not return to Cambridge this month. He has advised me to send the box by the wagon: and it goes tomorrow by Burley's from the Bull.[1] It is a large box, and yet contains very little, and less worth sending you; but the glass required bran, which makes the bulk. I found most of the pieces I bought at Mr Ives's had suffered so much, by being brought to London, and carried to Twickenham, that they were too broken to offer you. You will find indeed but one good piece, that in this shape ◯. The strange old ivory carving[2] was given to me by the Dowager Duchess of Aiguillon.[3] There are a few proofs of views of Strawberry:[4] but some time or other you shall have a new and complete set. There is Strawberry's pedigree[5] too; but I can find no print of Ganginelli.[6] I am ashamed so large a box should contain only such rubbish. Adieu!

1. 'Burleigh's wagons, set out from the Bull Inn, Bishopsgate Street every Wednesday, Thursday, and Friday, before noon, and carry goods for Cambridge, Ely [etc.]' (*Cantabrigia Depicta*, Cambridge, [1776], p. 114). James Burleigh is listed as a Cambridge 'carrier' in *Universal British Directory*, 5 vols, 1791–8?, ii. 490. Another James Burleigh (d. 1786), alderman of Cambridge and Justice of the Peace, may have been the owner of the wagons at this time (see GM Jan. 1786, lvi. 84a).

2. From Cole the carving passed to Richard Farmer, who probably bought it after Cole's death. In Farmer's sale catalogue, 1798, it is described as 'a curious piece of antiquity in carved ivory, framed, a present to Mr Cole from the late Lord Orford' and was sold (36th day, lot 66 of the pictures), with a print of Magna Charta by Pine, to —— Dent and —— Douce, for £2.5.0.

3. Anne-Charlotte de Crussol de Florensac (1700–72), Dsse d'Aiguillon.

4. Which HW was having engraved for the 1784 edition of the *Description of SH*.

5. The 'Pedigree of Walpole to explain the Portraits and Coats of Arms at Strawberry Hill, Anno 1776.' HW's annotated, trimmed copy (see *ante* 23 Dec. 1762) measures 25½" × 19". The pedigree is engraved and was almost certainly not done at the SH Press. Cole records in his account of Richard Bentley, the younger, in his *Athenae Cantabrigienses* that Bentley told him it was drawn up by HW and Chute, 'but that he [Bentley] was convinced that many parts did not belong to him [HW]' (Brydges, *Restituta* iv. 385).

6. Pope Clement XIV (Lorenzo Ganganelli) (1705–74), who was Pope from 1769 until his death, and was responsible for the suppression of the Jesuits, 1773 (see *Encyclopaedia Britannica*). HW is rallying Cole on his attachment to the Church of Rome (see following letter n. 4).

From COLE, Sunday 1 June 1777

VA, Forster MS 110, f. 169. COLE's copy, Add MS 5824, ff. 103v, 104v.
Address: For the Honourable Horace Walpole in Arlington Street, London.
Postmark: 2 IV.

Milton, June 1, 1777.

Dear Sir,

A THOUSAND thanks for your bounty. Such rubbish, as you are pleased to call it, is a treasure to me, and doubly enhanced from whence it comes. There are many good pieces of glass,[1] and which I should have been extremely thankful for separately: that of Ananias and Sapphira[2] is very beautiful. The *memento mori*[3] is a most suitable piece of furniture for my cell or hermitage, and though the inhabitant is not a Carthusian, yet he wishes to be as like one as his frailty and profession allows of. I have all my life from a boy experienced your kindness, goodness and friendship. It is a truth that I value and pride myself more in this advantage than all and every other circumstance of my life. When a young man at college,[4] I remember your railleries for my inclination to Popery, and I find your kindness is still on the watch that my old age may not be seduced to idolize Pope Ganganelli. Many thanks for the pretty views of Strawberry; and the pedigree I am quite happy in. From the many figures

1. Besides the pieces mentioned by Cole later in the letter, the box included a cipher J.C. tied together with a noose, which Cole gave in 1780 to Sir John Cotton, 'who placed it in the east window of Madingley Church.' It is still in the southwest window of the chancel at Madingley. Another piece was 'a sundial with holes perforated in the glass to fix the gnomon into. A fly is very well done on it.' Cole 'gave this to Mr Freeman the painter, 1779' (see Palmer, *Monumental Inscriptions* 279, and Plate XLVII).

2. This piece, showing the death of Ananias and Sapphira, is now in the window at the east end of the north aisle of Milton Church (Palmer, *William Cole* 22). It is one of the few pieces in Cole's extensive collection of painted glass whose whereabouts is known.

3. Cole placed this in the bow window of his bedroom. Cole's drawing of it is re-

produced in Palmer, *Monumental Inscriptions*, Plate XLVII. It shows a white death's head on a scroll of, apparently, black leather, at the bottom of which is I.B. Cole adds, 'It is neatly painted on white glass, and has a border of yellow glass all round it. On the top of this yellow border is written in black letters "Memento mori." At the bottom "Disce mori, 1553." . . . This I meant to have given to Alderman J. Bentham.' But he put it into a window in Milton Church, 1779 or 1780 (Palmer, *William Cole* 40).

4. Cole's copy reads: 'When a youth at college, I shall never forget your jocular railleries on my inclination to Popery, and hatred of fanaticism: a disposition that has been predominant through life invariably, and I find your kindness is still on the watch that my old age may not be seduced to idolize Ganganelli.'

in the Duchess of Aiguillon's picture, of persons being sprouting into trees,[5] as they seem to me, and the figure of a stag, twice repeated, it looks as if it had an allusion to Acteon. It is a great curiosity and I am much pleased with it and thank you heartily for it. They all came safe. I was so impatient to have the box that I went to Cambridge myself in the evening of yesterday to fetch it, and think myself more obliged to you, as I see by the care and exactitude of the packing that other hands than servants' had a share in it.

It grieves me extremely to consider your present situation, which is much worse than that of poor Lord Orford, who is insensible of his misfortune, and yours is too much sensibility. I will not dwell on a subject I am sure too much engrosses your attention either to be pleasing or healthful.

In Sandford's *Genealogical History* is a print at p. 177 of King Edward III's tomb in Westminster Abbey. The figure of William of Hatfield is still perfect on it, but unluckily his arms, immediately under his statue, is[6] lost, so that what distinction he bore as second son I know not. No doubt his father's arms, viz., quarterly France semée, and England, are allowable to him, but the common distinction of a second son, viz., a crescent, is what I have not observed for the royal family, who have generally labels charged with some distinctions, but what that is for the young prince in question is more than my heraldry reaches. Mr Edmundson, no doubt, will resolve this difficulty.

I will detain you no longer, and thanking you again for this and every other favour, and sincerely, most sincerely, wishing you not to indulge a too reasonable concern for what it is out of your power to prevent or help, I beg leave to subscribe myself, dear Sir,

Your most faithful and obliged servant,

WM COLE

5. Cole's copy reads 'persons sprouting out into trees.'

6. Cole's copy reads 'are.'

From Cole, Sunday 15 June 1777

VA, Forster MS 110, ff. 170–1. Cole's copy, Add MS 5824, f. 104v.
Address: For the Honourable Horace Walpole in Arlington Street, London.
Postmark: Cambridge 18 IV.

Milton, June 15, 1777.

Dear Sir,

I HAVE two reasons for troubling you with this letter. Since my last, looking accidentally for another purpose into Drake's *Eboracum, or History of York,*[1] I lit upon the old figure in stone, supposed to be designed for William de Hatfield. It is at p. 491, and at the preceding page is a description of it. He was called so from his being born at Hatfield near Doncaster in Yorkshire, and not from Hatfield in Hertfordshire. It is probable you have the book[2] and may be aware of it. However, at all events, I would let you know it, and will transcribe the passage if you have it not.

Reading this day the *Monthly Review* of last month, there is a passage at p. 323 which may by an unobserving reader be construed into an accusation of homicide against you. As it is possible you may not take that *Review,* or meet with it, I will transcribe the whole passage. It is in a disquisition concerning the authenticity of Rowley's *Poems.*[3]

In 1770, Chatterton went to London, and carried all this treasure with him, in hopes, as we may very reasonably suppose, of disposing of it to his advantage; he accordingly applied, as I have been informed, to that learned antiquary [observe the degradation and familiarity. W.C.], Mr Horace Walpole, but met with little or no encouragement from him; soon after *which,* in a fit of despair, as it is supposed, he put an end to his unhappy life, having first cut to pieces and destroyed all the MSS he had in his possession.

Some time ago Dr Glynn, who is Rowley-mad on the side of their authenticity, desired me to request of you to tell me what were the poems he showed to you, whether originals or transcripts. This I

1. Francis Drake (1696–1771), antiquary and surgeon, author of *Eboracum: or the History and Antiquities of the City of York,* 1736.

2. MS reads *probably.* HW's copy of the book (E.1.21) was sold SH ii. 108.

3. The 'disquisition' was written by John Langhorne (1735–79), poet and reviewer (Benjamin Christie Nangle, *The Monthly Review . . . 1749–1789,* Oxford, 1934, p. 176). The passage quoted by Cole was communicated to Langhorne by George Catcott, who figures prominently in the Rowley controversy.

should not, however, have troubled you with, had not this passage in the *Review* struck

Your most faithful and obliged servant,

WM COLE

Since I wrote my letter, Dr Gooch, son to the late Bishop of Ely,[4] drank tea here in his way to the Chapter at Ely. The old Bishop, it seems, had been a great means to push on his present Lordship,[5] with other friends, to the height he has obtained. Dr Gooch, though he has acted as his chaplain on various occasions, and never from him received any favour, on the vacancy of the chancellorship last month by the death of Dr Peck at Norwich,[6] thought he had some pretensions to a favour of this sort, as [did] Dr Ewin, to whom it had been promised at the request and solicitation of Lord Hardwick, but on the usurious affair breaking out, that promise was dissolved with the approbation of Lord Hardwick. However, to most people's surprise, it was given to a man whose face his Lordship never saw,[7] and looks like a design to insult Dr G., who, happily, is independent, and really wants it not. I mention this as a counterpart to a story you told me some two years ago.[8]

To Cole, Thursday 19 June 1777

Add MS 5953, ff. 6–7.

Address: To the Reverend Mr Cole at Milton near Cambridge.
Postmark: 19 IV.

Strawberry Hill, June 19, 1777.

I THANK you for your notices, dear Sir, and shall remember that on Prince William.[1] I did see the *Monthly Review*, but hope one

4. John Gooch (1730?–1804), Prebendary of Ely, son of Sir Thomas Gooch (1674–1754), 2d Bt, and Bp of Ely.

5. Edmund Keene.

6. Wharton Peck (d. 1777), Fellow of Trinity Hall (1718–31, LL.D. 1722), Chancellor of Ely 1728–77. He died 18 May 1777 (see *Alumni Cantab.*).

7. William Compton (1733–1824), of Caius College (LL.D. 1763); Chancellor of Ely 1777–1824 (see *Alumni Cantab.*).

8. The story of Bishop Keene and Mrs Day (Sir Robert's natural daughter), which HW told Cole at SH 29 Oct. 1774, and which was discreditable to Keene (see Cole's account, Add MS 5847, ff. 205v, 206; HW to Mann 11 Dec. 1752).

---

1. Of Hatfield.

is not guilty of the death of every man who does not make one the dupe of a forgery. I believe Macpherson's success with Ossian[1a] was more the ruin of Chatterton than I. Two years passed between my doubting the authenticity of Rowley's poems and his death. I never knew he had been in London till some time after he had undone and poisoned himself there. The poems he sent me were transcripts in his own hand, and even in that circumstance he told a lie; he said he had them from the very person at Bristol to whom he had given them. If any man was to tell you that monkish rhymes had been dug up in Herculaneum which was destroyed several centuries before there was any such poetry, should you believe it? Just the reverse is the case of Rowley's pretended poems. They have all the elegance of Waller and Prior, and more than Lord Surry—but I have no objection to anybody believing what he pleases. I think poor Chatterton was an astonishing genius—but I cannot think that Rowley foresaw metres that were invented long after he was dead, or that our language was more refined at Bristol in the reign of Henry V than it was at court under Henry VIII. One of the chaplains[2] of the Bishop of Exeter[3] has found a line of Rowley in *Hudibras*[4]—the monk might foresee that too! The prematurity of Chatterton's genius is however full as wonderful, as that such a prodigy of Rowley should never have been heard of till the eighteenth century. The youth and industry of the former are miracles too, yet still more credible. There is not a symptom in the poems but the old words that savours of Rowley's age. Change the old words for modern, and the whole construction is of yesterday.[5]

1a. James Macpherson (1736–96), the alleged translator of the Ossianic poems *Fingal* (1762) and *Temora* (1763), was Chatterton's 'model, as an impostor' (Edward H. W. Meyerstein, *A Life of Thomas Chatterton*, 1930, p. 54 *et passim*).

2. Not identified.

3. Frederick Keppel (1729–77), son of William Anne Keppel, 2d E. of Albemarle; Bp of Exeter 1762–77, d. 27 Dec. 1777.

4. HW wrote in his *Letter to the Editor of the Miscellanies of Thomas Chatterton:* 'He [Rowley] was . . . well acquainted with Butler, or Butler with him, for a chaplain of the late Bp of Exeter has found in Rowley a line of *Hudibras*' (*Works* iv. 223). It is said in the *European Magazine*, Jan. 1782, i. 4 n, that 'the line here alluded

to is probably the following:
"A man ascaunse upponn a piece maye looke,
"And *shake hys hedde to styrre his rede aboute;*

P. 72. Mr. Tyrwhit's edition.

"For having three times *shook his head*
"*To stir his wit up*, thus he said.

Hudibras, pt. 2, c. 3, l. 795.'

The passage from 'Rowley' is in the 'Letter to the Dygne Mastre Canynge,' ll. 17–18.

5. In this connection, see HW's 'Ode modernized from Chatterton,' *Works* iv. 235. There were numerous modernizations of the Rowley poems (see, for example, Meyerstein, *Chatterton*, 287, and GM Nov. 1778, xlviii. 534).

The other story you tell me, is very credible, and perfectly in character.

Yours ever,

H. W.

From Cole, Thursday 28 August 1777

VA, Forster MS 110, f. 172. Cole's copy, Add MS 5824, f. 105v, is misdated 8 Aug. 1777.

Address: For the Honourable Horace Walpole at Strawberry Hill in Twickenham, Middlesex. *Postmark:* Cambridge 29 AV.

Milton, Aug. 28, 1777.

Dear Sir,

I HOPE this will find you free from gout and all gouty and other complaints.[1] I am, and have continued so all the summer, too great an invalid to stir from home, though I have been extremely busy with my pen. I have transcribed a whole folio volume of 441 pages within these two months, being Mr Baker's *History of St John's College,*[2] which the Master, the present Vice-Chancellor, was so kind to trust to me.[3] If you are desirous to see it, I will send it to you. You will read it in much less time. I have been deep also in Dr Richardson's MSS,[4] *Catalogues of Fellows of Colleges,* etc. Thank God, the gout has given me leave to do all this with my right hand, though two fingers in my left are, and have been for months, fast bound in flannel.

I dined last week at Bottesham[5] with Mr Jenyns, who has had a mezzotinto print of himself, well executed but by no means like him,

1. 'What a ridiculous thing it is that two such water-drinking people as we have been all our lives should be such sufferers by this disorder! Poor Mr Gray is another deplorable instance that temperance alone will not secure one from its attacks' (addition in Cole's copy).

2. *History of the College of St John the Evangelist,* first published in 1869, ed. John E. B. Mayor, 2 vols, Cambridge. Cole's notes and continuation of the history are included.

3. John Chevallier (1730–89), Master of

St John's College 1775–89. As Cole was not acquainted with Chevallier at this time, his friend Richard Beadon procured the MS for him. Cole later became acquainted with Chevallier and liked him (see *Alumni Cantab.;* Baker, op. cit. ii. 555, 1080–1).

4. William Richardson (1698–1775), antiquary; Master of Emmanuel, 1736–75; chaplain to George II and III. Cole's copies of his MSS mentioned here are in Add MSS 5851 and 5885.

5. Bottisham Hall, the seat of Soame Jenyns, about six miles NE of Cambridge.

scraped by Richardson[6] from a [picture by][7] Sir Joshua Reynolds. I begged two of him. One I mean for you, and will send it by the first proper conveyance I meet with, except you forbid it by saying you have it already.

I am, dear Sir,

Your ever faithful and affectionate servant,

WM COLE

I will also send you at the same time the receipt for William of Worcester,[8] which, if it comes not out by April, you will have your half-guinea again. I know the man,[9] and he will be ashamed to keep it if the book is not printed.

To COLE, Sunday 31 August 1777

Add MS 5953, ff. 8–9.

Address: To the Reverend Mr Cole at Milton near Cambridge.
Postmark: EK 1 SE.

Strawberry Hill, Aug. 31, 1777.

YOU are very kind, dear Sir, in giving me an account of your health and occupations, and inquiring after mine. I am very sorry you are not as free from gout as I have been ever since February; but I trust it will only keep you from other complaints, and never prevent your amusing yourself, which you are one of those few happy beings that can always do: and your temper is so good, and your mind so naturally philosophic, composed and contented, that you neither want the world, care about it, nor are affected by anything that happens in it. This is true wisdom, but wisdom which nothing can give but constitution. Detached amusements have always made a great part of my own delight, and have sown my life

---

6. Cole's mistake: the print is by William Dickinson (1746–1823), mezzotint engraver, most of whose works are after Reynolds. The inscription reads in part, 'Engrav'd by W Dickinson Septr 24th 1776.' See John Chaloner Smith, *British Mezzotinto Portraits* i (1883). p. 185.

7. Missing in original; supplied from Cole's copy.

8. 'which you was so kind to subscribe for at my house' (addition in Cole's copy). This was a book, *Itineraria Simonis Simeonis et Willelmi de Worcestre*, ed. James Nasmith, Cambridge, 1778. HW subscribed for it at Milton 27 April 1777.

9. James Nasmith (see preceding note).

with most of its best moments. My intention was that they should
be the employment of my latter years, but fate seems to have chalked
out a very different scene for me! The misfortune of my nephew
has involved me in business, and consequently care, and opens a
scene of disputes, with which I shall not molest your tranquillity.
The dangerous situation in which his R. H. the Duke of Gloucester
has been,[1] and out of which I doubt he is scarce yet emerged, though
better, has added more thorns to my uneasy mind. The Duchess's
daughters[2] are at Hampton Court, and partly under my care. In one
word my whole summer has been engrossed by duties, which have
confined me at home, without indulging myself in a single pursuit
to my taste. In short, as I have told you before, I often wish myself
a monk at Cambridge. Writers on government condemn very properly a recluse life, as contrary to Nature's intent, who loves pro-
creation. But as Nature seems not very desirous that we should
propagate to threescore years and ten, I think convents very suitable
retreats for those whom our Alma Mater does not emphatically call
to her *opus magnum*. And though to be sure grey hairs are fittest to
conduct state-affairs, yet as the Rehoboams[3] of the world (Louis XVI
excepted) do not always trust the rudder of government to ancient
hands, old gentlemen methinks are very ill placed (when not at the
council-board) anywhere but in a cloister. As I have no more voca-
tion to the ministry than to carrying on my family, I sigh after a
dormitory; and as in six weeks my clock will strike sixty, I wish I had
nothing more to do with the world. I am not tired of living, but—
but what signifies sketching visions? One must take one's lot as it
comes: bitter and sweet are poured into every cup. Tomorrow may
be pleasanter than today. Nothing lasts of one colour. One must embrace the cloister, or take the chances of the world as they present
themselves; and since uninterrupted happiness would but embitter

1. The Duke and Duchess of Gloucester
had been in Italy, where the Duke fell ill.
They started to return to England, but at
Trent the Duke lay dangerously ill for
several weeks. For a full account of this
illness, see *Last Journals* ii. 51–9.

2. They were (1) Lady Elizabeth Laura
Waldegrave (1760–1816), who m. (1782),
George Waldegrave (1751–89), 4th E.
Waldegrave; (2) Lady Charlotte Maria
Waldegrave (1761–1808), who m. (1784)
George Henry Fitzroy (1760–1844), E. of

Euston, afterwards 4th D. of Grafton; (3)
Lady Anna Horatia Waldegrave (1762–
1801), who m. (1785) Lord Hugh Seymour
(1759–1801). They are 'the Ladies Waldegrave' of Reynolds's picture.

3. 'And King Rehoboam took counsel
with the old men, that had stood before
Solomon his father. . . . But he forsook
the counsel of the old men and took counsel with the young men that were grown
up with him, that stood before him' (II
Chronicles 10:6–8).

the certainty that even that must end, rubs and crosses should be softened by the same consideration.

I am not so busied, but I shall be very glad of a sight of your MS[4] and will return it carefully. I will thank you too for the print of Mr Jenyns which I have not, nor have seen. Adieu! Dear Sir.

Yours most cordially,

H. W.

From COLE, Friday 12 September 1777

VA, Forster MS 110, f. 173. COLE's copy, Add MS 5824, ff. 106v, 107v.
Address: To the Honourable Horace Walpole, Strawberry Hill, Twickenham, Middlesex. *Postmark:* [Cambridge] 13 [SE].

Friday, 12 Sept. 1777, Milton.

Dear Sir,

THOUGH I know I shall suffer by my folly, and that my book[1] will forever ruin my reputation and credit of philosophy and moderation which you too hastily bestow upon me, yet I send it to you by the Cambridge fly, which sets out tomorrow, and orders with it to deliver it carefully. To you only will it be seen while I am alive and for many years after that period. You will be astonished at the rapidity of my pen when you observe that this folio of 400 pages,[2] with above an hundred coats of arms and other silly ornaments, was completed in six weeks, for I was called off for above a week to another MS which I expected would be demanded of me every day,[3] and which is part of another book now under hand and greatly advanced, being lists of persons and degrees, etc., but very useful to me. I know I hazard little with your candour, philanthropy and real philosophy in displaying my political opinions, derived to me from old Anthony Wood, Tom Hearne, etc., and which you know I very early embraced, but on no consideration would I trust the book with anyone but yourself.

What I have added to Mr Baker's book, either as annotations or

4. Baker's *History of St John's College.*

1. Baker's *History of St John's College.*
2. Really 441 pages (see preceding letter; Baker, op. cit. ii. 555).

3. This was Dr William Richardson's lists of graduates of Cambridge, mentioned *ante* 28 Aug. 1777; cf. *post* 30 Oct. 1777.

continuation, was done in an extreme hurry. The vacant coats I could have filled up chiefly, but I left them till I had seen a MS in the College and another authority which will ascertain them, and I expect them in a short time. If you discover any blunders, especially in the Latin, which I don't pretend to be well versed in, and in the few Greek words, which I know less of, I will take it as a favour to correct me, or in anything besides. Keep it as long as you like it, and when you have sufficiently wondered at my expedition and nonsense, please to return it <by> the Cambridge fly at the Queen's Head in Gray's Inn Lane, to be left for me at the Rose Tavern in Cambridge till called for.

With it I have sent Mr Jenyns's print. On second thoughts I had better keep the receipt for Mr Nasmith's book, which I had from Mr Lort and to whom I paid the money three months ago, who will deliver the book when printed, or the Cambridge booksellers.

I am extremely concerned at your avocations, as well as for the occasions of them. The public will suffer by them and will feel it. I am glad to hear the Duke of Gloucester is better, though since your letter the papers have given a despairing account of him.

I dined last week at the Palace at Ely, where I had not been these two years. His Lordship received me graciously, but not a word of a proposal I had made to him by a friend[4] near three years ago to accommodate me with an exchange with Burnham for a living in this neighbourhood, as the distance to Burnham makes it grievous to me that I cannot without hazard of my life now and then reside at it. The Bishop repeated to me once or twice that out of regard to your family, and father in particular,[5] he had commissioned his son[6] to buy your father's full-length picture by Vanloo,[7] and sold among Lord Montfort's pictures by Christie.[8] Mr Keene bid as far as twenty-six guineas, but as he found Lord Hertford was determined to have it, he stopped there. I told the Bishop that I knew the late Lord Montfort gave sixty guineas to Vanloo for it.

I will trouble you no more. I am not well, and feverish, but always

Most sincerely and faithfully yours,

WM COLE

4. Unidentified.
5. In this connection, see also HW to Mason 11 March 1776.
6. Benjamin Keene (1753–1837), of Westoe Lodge, Cambs; M.P. for Town of Cambridge 1776–84 (see GM Jan. 1838, ix (n.s.). 107b; DNB, sub Edmund Keene; Burke, Landed Gentry, 1879).
7. Jean Baptiste Vanloo (1684–1746), portrait painter, born in Aix in Provence;

To Cole, Tuesday 16 September 1777

Add MS 5953, ff. 10–11.

Address: To the Reverend Mr Cole at Milton near Cambridge.
Postmark: 16 SE.

Strawberry Hill, Sept. 16, 1777.

I HAVE received your volume safely, dear Sir, and hurry to thank you before I have read a page, that you may be in no pain about its arrival. I will return it with the greatest care, as soon as I have finished it; and at the same time will send Mr Essex the bills,[1] as I beg you will let him know.

I have no less reason for writing immediately, to thank you for the great confidence you place in me. You talk of *nonsense;* alas! what are all our opinions else? If we search for truth before we fix our principles, what do we find but doubt? And which of us begins the search a *tabula rasa?* Nay, where can we hunt but in volumes of error or purposed delusion? Have not we too a bias in our own minds; our passions? They will turn the scale in favour of the doctrines most agreeable to them. Yet let us be a little vain: you and I differ radically in our principles, and yet in forty years they have never cast a gloom over our friendship. We could give the world a reason that it would not like: we have both been sincere, have both been consistent, and neither adapted our principles nor have varied them for our interest.

Your labour, as well as I am acquainted with it, astonishes me. It shows what can be achieved by a man that does not lose a moment: and which is still better, how happy the man is who can always employ himself. I do not believe that the proud prelate,[2] who would not make you a little happier, is half so much to be envied.

Thank you for the print of Soame Jennyns. It is a proof of Sir Joshua's art, who could give a strong resemblance of so uncouth a countenance without leaving it disagreeable.

The Duke of Gloucester is miraculously revived. For two whole

painted in England 1737–42 (see Redgrave, *Dict. of Artists; Works* iii. 448–9).

8. Lord Montfort's pictures were sold at auction in 1776, by James Christie (1730–1803).

———

1. The workmen's bills, for work done on the Beauclerc Tower at SH. They came to £225.14.11½ (*SH Accounts* 16).

2. The words 'proud prelate' have been scratched out in the MS, but the passage reads as above in Cole's copy, Add MS 5824, f. 108v. The reference is to Bishop Keene (see preceding letter).

days I doubted whether he was not dead. I hope fatalists and omen-mongers will be confuted, and that as his grandfather[3] broke the charm of the *second* of the name being an unfortunate prince, the Duke will baffle that which has made the title of Gloucester unpropitious. Adieu! dear Sir,

Yours most gratefully,

H. WALPOLE

To Cole, Monday 22 September 1777

Add MS 5953, ff. 12–13.

Address and Postmark: None. [The letter was sent with Cole's MS (see introductory note to HW's letter 2 Oct. 1777).]

Strawberry Hill, Sept. 22, 1777.

I RETURN you your MS dear Sir, with a thousand thanks, and shall be impatient to hear that you receive it safe. It has amused me much, and I admire Mr Baker for having been able to show so much sense on so dry a subject. I wish, as you say you have materials for it, that you would write his life. He deserved it much more than most of those he has recorded. His book on the Deficiencies of Learning[1] is most excellent, and far too little known. I admire his moderation too, which was extraordinary in a man that had suffered so much for his principles. Yet they warped even him, for he rejects Bishop Burnet's character of Bishop Gunning in p. 200, and yet in the very next page gives the same character of him.[2] Burnet's words

---

3. George II.

1. *Reflections upon Learning, wherein is shewn the Insufficiency thereof, in its several Particulars: In Order to evince the Usefulness and Necessity of Revelation,* published anonymously in 1699. It reached the eighth edition in 1756. HW's copy, 5th edn, 1714, with MS notes, was sold SH vii. 37. It is now in the possession of Lord Walpole, Wolterton Park, Norwich. It has several MS notes in HW's hand, mostly derogatory.

2. Baker rejects the character of Bishop Peter Gunning (1614–84), Bp of Ely and Master of St John's College, by 'a certain prelate' (Burnet) who has been 'slurring enough' in his account (*History of St John's College,* ed. Mayor, i. 238). In the next paragraph he says: 'Papers and MSS he [Gunning] has left in heaps, many of which I have seen, and have perused some of them, and if the rest be like these, I will venture to absolve his trustees that nothing has been published since his death. . . . but what was wanting in his method, was made up by his looks, the most graceful and venerable I ever saw' (ibid. 239). For Bishop Burnet's character of Gunning, see his *History of his Own Time,* 2 vols, 1724–34, i. 181, 590, and Baker, op. cit. ii. 657, 660–1. Cole replies to HW's criticism 4 Oct. 1777.

are,[3] *he had a great confusion of things in his head, but*[4] *could bring nothing into method.* Pray compare this with p. 201. I see nothing in which they differ, except that Burnet does not talk so much of his comeliness as Mr Baker.

I shall not commend *your* moderation when you excuse such a man as Bishop Watson.[5] Nor ought you to be angry with Burnet but with the witnesses on whose evidence Watson was convicted. To tell you the truth, I am glad when such faults are found with Burnet, for it shows his enemies are not angry at his telling falsehoods but the truth. Must not an historian say a bishop was convicted of simony, if he was? I will tell you what I have heard was said on the appearance of Burnet's history by one whose testimony you yourself will not dispute—at least you would not in anything else. That confessor said, 'Damn him, he has told a great deal of truth, but where the devil did he learn it?' This was Saint Atterbury's[6] testimony.

I shall take the liberty of reproving you too, dear Sir, for defending that abominable murderess Queen Christina[7]—and how can you doubt her conversation with Burnet?[8] You must know there are a thousand evidences of her laughing at the religion she embraced. If you approve her, I will allow you to condemn Lord Russel[9] and Algernon Sidney.[10] Well, as we shall never have the same heroes, we will not dispute about them—nor shall I find fault, when you have given me so much entertainment: it would be very ungrateful, and I have a thousand obligations to you, and want to have more. I want to see more of your MSS. They are full of curiosities, and I love

3. See Burnet, op. cit. i. 590. HW's copy was of this edition (G.1.27–8), and was sold SH iv. 80.

4. Burnet, loc. cit. reads *and*.

5. Thomas Watson (1637–1717), Bp of St David's 1687–99; accused of simony, 1695, found guilty and deprived of his see, 1699 (see DNB). Cole says Watson's 'political principles have laid him open to the prejudices of most people, who have more attended to the exaggerations of Burnet than perhaps he deserved. . . . The acquaintance and good word of such a man as Mr Baker will go a great way to counterpoise the malevolence of such a partisan as Burnet' (Baker, *History of St John's College*, ed. Mayor, ii. 698).

6. Francis Atterbury (1662–1732), Bp of Rochester.

7. For Cole's defense of Queen Christina (1626–89) of Sweden, see Baker, op. cit. ii. 678.

8. Burnet tells of his conversation with Queen Christina at Rome, in his *Some Letters. Containing an Account of what seemed most remarkable in Switzerland, Italy, &c.* Rotterdam, 1686, pp. 236–7. For Cole's opinion of the truth of his account, see Baker, loc. cit.

9. William Russell (1639–83), Lord Russell; executed for alleged complicity in Rye House Plot, 1683.

10. (1622–83), executed for complicity in the same plot and, therefore, a Whig hero.

some of your heroes too. I honour Bishop Fisher[11] and love Mr Baker.

I have found very few errata indeed, and have corrected a few with a pencil: all are very trifling. In p. 2, last line but one *originial* is written for *original,* and in p. 6, line 7, of the copy of verses *lyest* for *lyes;* in p. 10, line 17, *authentic* probably for *unauthentic.*

In p. 200, you are a little mistaken. The late King of France was not silent from rule but shyness: he could scarce ever be persuaded to speak to entire strangers.

If I might choose, I should like to see your account of the persons educated at King's—but as you may have objections, I insist if you have, that you make me no word of answer. It is perhaps impertinent to ask it, and silence will lay neither of us under any difficulty. I have no right to make such a request, nor do now, but on the foot of its proving totally indifferent to you. You will make me blame myself, if it should a moment distress you, and I am sure you are too good-natured to put me out of humour with myself, which your making no answer would not do.

I inclose my bills for Mr Essex,[12] and will trouble you to send them to him. I again thank you, and trust you will be as friendlily free with me, as I have been with you. You know I am a brother-monk in everything but in religious and political opinions. I only laugh at the 39 articles, but abhor Calvin as much as I do the Queen of Sweden, for he was as thorough an assassin.

Yours ever,

H. W.   (turn over)

PS. As I have a great mind, and indeed ought when I require it, to show moderation, and when I have not, ought to confess it, which I do, for I own I am not moderate on certain points; if you are busy yourself, and will send me the materials, I will draw up the life of Mr Baker; and if you are not content with it, you shall burn it in Smithfield.[13] In good truth I revere conscientious martyrs of all sects,

11. John Fisher (1459–1535), Bp of Rochester, who was beheaded for refusing to acknowledge the King as supreme head of the Church.

12. See *ante* 16 Sept. 1777 n. 1.

13. Where condemned books (as well as heretics) were burned (see Charles Ripley Gillett, *Burned Books,* 2 vols, N.Y., 1932, *passim*).

communions and parties—I heartily pity them, if they are weak men. When they are as sensible as Mr Baker, I doubt my own understanding more than his. I know I have not his virtues, but should delight in doing justice to them; and perhaps from a man of a different party, the testimony would be the more to his honour. I do not call myself of different principles, because a man that thinks himself bound by his oath, can be a man of no principle, if he violates it. I do not mean to deny that many men might think King James's breach of his oath[14] a dispensation with theirs; but if they did not think so, or did not think their duty to their country obliged them to renounce their king, I should never defend those who took the new oaths from interest.

To Cole, Thursday 2 October 1777

Add MS 5953, ff. 14–15.
Address: To the Reverend Mr Cole at Milton near Cambridge.
Postmark: Isleworth 2 OC.

Strawberry Hill, Oct. 2, 1777.

I AM a little uneasy, dear Sir, at not hearing that you have received your precious volume. I sent it as you ordered to the Queen's Head in Gray's Inn Lane yesterday was sevennight, and my own servant carried it, and they assured him you would receive it the next day. With it I troubled you with a little parcel for Mr Essex. As he promised me to come hither the beginning of this month, I am in hopes he is coming, and will bring me word of your having received your book. I should be out out of my wits if you had not.

Yours ever,

H. W.[1]

14. James II, 'who had violated his coronation oath' to support the Church of England (HW's 'Life of Baker,' *Works* ii. 347).

1. Cole notes on his transcript of HW's letter (Add MS 5824, f. 108v): 'On receiving this by the Ely post on Friday [3 Oct.] about five or [MS reads &] six in eve-

ning, I immediately dispatched my servant to the Rose Tavern, where I had given particular orders to Mr Hart not to send me the book when it returned, but to keep it safely till I called for it, or sent for it. With the book came this letter' [*ante* 22 Sept. 1777].

From COLE, Saturday 4 October 1777

VA, Forster MS 110, ff. 174–5. COLE's copy, Add MS 5824, ff. 109v, 110v.
Address: For the Honourable Horace Walpole at Strawberry Hill, Twickenham, Middlesex. *Postmark:* Cambridge 6 OC.

Dear Sir,   Saturday, Milton, Oct. 4, 1777.

I WAS well aware how much my moderation would suffer by ex-
posing my book to your censure, yet I am so entirely devoted to
you that I care little about it, and believe I shall send you my four
folio volumes of King's College to complete my disgrace, and in order to expiate my saying so many foolish things, by this purgatory I
shall undergo. You will please to observe, and I would inculcate it,
that I have not wrote a line in that work these twenty-five years, except adding occasionally to what has been entered before, yet I have
on loose papers materials to go on with it. You will soon be tired of
names, guessings at preferments and such trash, which makes up the
chief part of that work.

I thought it probable that you would give me notice when you
sent the book, so I neglected calling at the Rose, where it was kept
for me by my own direction. The moment I received your letter last
night, too late to write to you, I dispatched a servant to Cambridge
for the parcel, and what makes it unlucky, though I write today, yet
it won't set off from Cambridge till tomorrow evening, so that you
will not be satisfied that I have my book safe till Monday or Tuesday.

Nothing could please me more than your proposal in the PS. The
materials I have, I am afraid will be scanty towards Mr Baker's life.
The chief are innumerable references to books where he is mentioned, and many others lying scattered in my different volumes. If
I see they will be worth transmitting or will answer your purpose, I
will send them. Dr Gray (Zachary) put some materials together with
such a design, which his daughters gave to my neighbour Masters,
and I have heard him more than once hint that he meant to write a
life of Mr Baker from these materials.[1] I am upon so ticklish a foot-

1. Masters did so: *Memoirs of the Life
and Writings of Thomas Baker, B.D., of
St John's College in Cambridge, from the
papers of Dr Zachary Grey, with a Catalogue of his MS Collections,* Cambridge,
1783. A scathing review of the book appeared in GM March 1784, liv. 194. See LA
ii. 545; v. 116. Masters's Catalogue of Baker's MSS, together with Baker's 'Advice to a
Student,' was Phillips MS 10,980 and is
now WSL.

ing with him that I dare not ask him for them, and if I did, knowing the nature of the beast, I know he would refuse me. Dr Gray knew more of Mr Baker's private life than most people, so no doubt the materials, could they be got out of the clumsy hands they are in, would be most useful. I think I once saw them in Dr Gray's hands: they seemed only to be extracts from what authors had said of him in acknowledgments. His life drawn up by you would be the thing in the world I most wish for, and hope we shall compass it. I will do my endeavour. It will be an honour to him, and credit to St John's. I was reading his *Reflections upon Learning* when your letter came, and am glad you approve what pleases me so much.

If Bishop Burnet had said no more than the line you quote, relating to Bishop Gunning, certainly Mr Baker and he differ not in opinion about him, but no doubt Mr Baker alluded to many other things than his want of method, which Burnet, from Silvester's *Life of Baxter*[2] chiefly, says of him. There are three different places[3] where Burnet takes occasion to mention him, and it is my opinion that Mr Baker referred to them in the gross when he says that Burnet's account of him 'is slurring enough.' His confusion and want of method are slight in respect to his other observations. I have no great opinion of Bishop Watson, yet I must own that I have much the better for his being so grossly abused by the historian, and when I endeavour to excuse him, it is with a perhaps. Upon the whole, I think if he was so vile a character as that bishop represents, a person of Mr Baker's known virtue would not have kept up the <corres>pondence with him, which I have evidence he did. The printed book[4] I enclose is sent as a curiosity which perhaps may not have fallen in your way, for as to the vanity of thinking that you will alter your opinion of the writer of that dedication, just two years before he appeared in evidence[5] point-blank before the House of Lords against him, is as far from my expectations as it [is][6] from my inten-

2. Matthew Sylvester (1636?–1708), nonconformist divine. Richard Baxter (1615–91), the author of *Saint's Everlasting Rest,* was his unpaid assistant. Sylvester edited *Reliquiae Baxterianae,* 1696.

3. See Burnet, *History of his Own Time,* 2 vols, 1724–34, i. 181, 436, 590.

4. Burnet's *A Vindication of the . . . Church and State of Scotland,* Glasgow, 1673 (see introductory note *post* 15 Oct. 1777).

5. 'against the Duke' (addition in Cole's copy). 'The Duke' is John Maitland (1616–82), 1st D. of Lauderdale, whose hatred Burnet incurred after having enjoyed his favour for a number of years. Burnet's *Vindication of the . . . Church and State of Scotland* is dedicated to him.

6. Supplied from Cole's copy.

tion. The reflections upon so versatile a man will occur without anything further said about him. No doubt you have your reasons for patronizing him, and if I have said more about him than became me, it is from a thorough conviction within myself. We have never before had the least altercation, and I am sorry it should be upon such a subject, which I should not unnecessarily have brought before you. I shall dislike him the more, if that is possible, for having been the occasion of so much debate.

I am forced to hurry in order to get my letter ready for my servant carrying it with the parcel to Mr Essex, so conclude in haste, dear Sir,

Your ever affectionate servant,

WM COLE

From COLE, Tuesday 7 October 1777

VA, Forster MS 110, f. 176. Cole kept no copy.
Address and Postmark: None. Essex conveyed the letter to HW.

Milton, Tuesday evening, Oct. 7, 1777.

Dear Sir,

I HAVE just time to write this note to give to Mr Essex, who calls on me in his way from Ely to Cambridge. I have sent a book[1] because I mentioned it, otherwise had rather it had been forgotten. I am extremely busy in collecting my materials about Mr Baker, which you shall have in all convenient speed, though it puts a stop to some necessary writing which I want to have done, as I expect the MSS[2] will be called for every day.

I am, dear Sir,

Your ever faithful servant,

WM COLE

---

1. Burnet's *Vindication of the . . . Church . . . of Scotland.*   2. Richardson's MSS (see *post* 30 Oct. 1777).

To Cole, Wednesday 15 October 1777

Add MS 5953, ff. 16–17.

The letter is endorsed by Cole: 'Received by Mr Essex, Tuesday, Oct. 28, 1777.'

Cole notes at the head of his copy (Add MS 5824, f. 113v): 'Mr Essex going to Strawberry Hill to examine the workmen's bills, I sent Bishop Burnet's *Vindication of the Church of Scotland*, with the dedication in it to Duke Lauderdale. When he returned to Cambridge he brought me the book, and in it the following letter.'

Strawberry Hill, Oct. 15, 1777.

I THANK you much, dear Sir, for the sight of the book, which I return by Mr Essex. It is not new to me that Burnet paid his court to the other side in the former part of his life: nor will I insist that he changed on conviction, which might be said, and generally is for all converts, even those who shift their principles the most glaringly from interest. Duke Lauderdale indeed was such a dog, that the honestest man must have been driven to detest him, however connected with him. I doubt Burnet could not be blind to his character when he wrote the dedication. In truth I have given up many of my saints, though not on the accusations of such wretches as Dalrymple and Macpherson:[1] nor can men so much their opposites shake my

---

1. HW refers to *Memoirs of Great Britain and Ireland*, 2 vols in 3 parts, Edinburgh, 1771–88, by Sir John Dalrymple (1726–1810), 4th Bt; and to *A History of Great Britain from the Restoration to the Accession of the House of Hannover*, 1775, by James Macpherson, the 'translator' of Ossian. Neither of these historians was in sympathy with the Whigs, nor with HW's heroes, Lord Russell and Algernon Sidney. In May 1778, Cole added the following note on this passage (Add MS 5824, f. 124v): 'Mr Walpole . . . calls Dalrymple and Macpherson *wretches,* yet the more candid and moderate, though of a Presbyterian family and ideas, the Earl of Hardwicke, in his *State Papers* [*Miscellaneous State Papers,* 2 vols, 1778], vol. 2, p. 304, speaks in quite a different strain of them, in his introduction to the papers relative to Monmouth's rebellion, thus: "The Editor chooses to pass over the reign of Charles II, as his collection would not add materially to the anecdotes which have appeared in some [Dalrymple's and Macpherson's.— *Hardwicke's note*] late histories, and which

in the main deserve great credit, being derived from very authentic sources." When I read this passage, I was astonished that Whiggism and patriotism could have been so honest and candid: it seems the evidence is too clear to be resisted. But wonders have not ceased: this last week [that is, on 14 May 1778] the great patriot Sir George Saville [Sir George Savile (1726–84), 8th Bt] brought in a bill to repeal the sanguinary laws against the papists, which have been a disgrace to this country, if anything can disgrace it, for these two centuries and more. Lord Lauderdale, also, whom the zeal of Mr Walpole and Burnet have debased to a dog, is represented in different colours to King Charles I by the Marquis of Hamilton [James Hamilton (1606–49), 3d M. and 1st D. of Hamilton in Scottish peerage, and 2d E. of Cambridge in English peerage] in a letter of characters of the Scotch nobility to that King, dated 27 Nov. 1638: "As for Lauderdale, he is a man of no great power; but he is truly honest, and most rightly set in all that concerneth your service" [Hardwicke, *State*

faith in Lord Russel and Algernon Sidney. I do not relinquish those that sealed their integrity with their blood, but such as have taken thirty pieces of silver.

I was sorry you said we had had any variance. We have differed in sentiments, but not in friendship. Two men, however unlike in principles, may be perfect friends, when both are sincere in their opinions, as we are. Much less shall we quarrel about those of our separate parties, since very few on either side have been so invariably consistent as you and I have been; and therefore we are more sure of each other's integrity, than of that of men whom we know less, and who did vary from themselves. As too you and I are only speculative persons and no actors, it would be very idle to squabble now about those that do not exist. In short, we are I trust in as perfect good humour with each other as we have been these forty years.

Pray do not hurry yourself about the anecdotes of Mr Baker, nor neglect other occupations on that account. I shall certainly not have time to do anything this year. I expect the Duke and Duchess of Gloucester in very few days,[2] must go to town as soon as they arrive, and shall probably have not much idle leisure before next summer. It is not very discreet to look even so far forward, nor am I apt any longer to lay distant plans. A little sedentary literary amusement is indeed no very lofty castle in the air, if I do lay the foundation in idea seven or eight months beforehand.

Whatever MSS you lend me, I shall be very grateful for. They entertain me exceedingly, and I promise you we will not have a shadow of an argument about them. I do not love disputation even with those most indifferent to me. *Your* pardon I most sincerely beg for having contested a single point with you. I am sure it was not with a grain of ill humour towards you: on the contrary, it was from wishing at that moment that you did not approve those I disliked— but even that I give up as unreasonable.

You are in the right, dear Sir, not to apply to Masters[3] for any papers he may have relating to Mr Baker. It is a trumpery fellow from whom one would rather receive a refusal than an obligation.

I am sorry to hear Mr Lort has the gout, and still more concerned

Papers ii. 116]. Indeed this was many years before the time of his power, and to which Mr Walpole alludes.'

2. They did not reach London until 24 Oct. (see *Last Journals* ii. 59; cf. *Lloyd's*

Evening Post 22–4 Oct. 1777).

3. Scratched out in MS, but reads as above in Cole's copy (Add MS 5824, f. 114v).

that you still suffer from it. Such patience and temper as yours are the only palliatives. As the bootikins have so much abridged and softened my fits, I do not expect their return with the alarm and horror I used to do; and that is being cured of half the complaint. I had scarce any pain last time, did not keep my bed a day, and had no gout at all in either foot. May not I ask you if this is not some merit in the bootikins? To have cured me of my apprehensions is to me a vast deal, for now the intervals do not connect the fits. You will understand that I mean to speak a word to you in favour of the bootikins, for can one feel benefit and not wish to impart it to a suffering friend. Indeed I am,

Yours most sincerely,

Hor. Walpole

From Cole, Thursday 30 October 1777

VA, Forster MS 110, ff. 177–8. Cole's copy, Add MS 5824, ff. 114v, 115v.
Address: For the Honourable Horace Walpole in Arlington Street, Piccadilly, London. *Postmark:* Cambridge 31 OC.

Milton, Thursday, Oct. 30, 1777.

Dear Sir,

MY servant brought me your letter dated 15th from Cambridge only yesterday, together with the hateful book.[1] I do not know whether I shall not talk Jacobite politics to you in my next, that I may have the pleasure of being confuted so politely and agreeably. At all times you write like no one else: when a little warm, you are charming. I thank you for your candid opinion of me in respect to my principles. They may be wrong, but was it worth while, I think you will do me the justice to believe that I am not one of the thirty-pieces-of-silver gentry.

You do me justice also when you say that you trust we are in perfect good humour with one another. To convince you of it, the moment I received your last, I set about collecting my materials for Mr Baker's life, and finished nineteen quarto pages in about two days. Not caring to consult my old sour neighbour[2] at Landbeche,

1. Burnet's *Vindication of the . . . Church . . . of Scotland.*   2. Robert Masters.

I wrote to Dr Heberden,[3] who knew him well and personally, who
was so obliging to send me some account of his death. I sent his letter to my friend Dr Pennington,[4] an ingenious young physician of
St John's College, with many queries from their register. He wrote
me a short answer that I might expect a longer soon, but have not
yet heard from him, though a fortnight has elapsed. I imagine the
Master, Dr Chevallier, who is now going out of office as Vice-Chancellor, is pretty <mu>ch taken up, and can't attend to my inquiries
at present. To not a soul have I mentioned your name in this affair,
nor has anyone the least idea of it.[5] I thought you might not care to
have it talked of at present. When my notes arrive, you shall have
them, but I would not defer writing and acknowledging the politeness of your last kind letter. Indeed you would wonder how I could
amuse <myself> as I do with old registers. My time is taken up en-
<tirely wi>th them, even so as to grudge myself my time for meals.
The reason for this hurry and intemperance in writing is that the
present Master of Emanuel has been so kind to lend me several MS
volumes of his predecessor's[6] collecting, most of them catalogues and
lists of Cambridge graduates. His son Dr Richardson,[7] many years
chaplain to Sir Joseph Yorke at the Hague, married last year and
has called for the MSS to town, where he resides, but I have reason
to believe that what cost his father most of his life will be made
waste paper of. I have three months ago,[8] by the advice of Dr Farmer,
wrote for leave to retain three or four, but have not had the com-

3. Cole kept a copy of his letter, dated 7
Oct. 1777, and Heberden's reply of 13 Oct.
1777, in his MSS, now Add MS 5824, ff.
111v, 112v.

4. Isaac Pennington (1745–1817), Professor of Chemistry at Cambridge, 1773, and
Regius Professor of Physic, 1793; knighted,
1796. Cole's copy of his letter to Pennington, dated 16 Oct. 1777, is in Add MS 5824,
ff. 112v, 113v, and Pennington's reply,
which Cole received 14 Nov. 1777, at ff.
117v, 123v.

5. Cole made the following note at the
end of his copy of this letter: 'Mr Beadon,
the Orator, called upon me Nov. 6, when I
just showed him my transcript of the MS
he had lent me: and as he was procurer of
it for me, I thought it just to mention the
design of Mr Walpole's writing Mr Baker's
life, but told him that I had mentioned it
to no one, and begged that he would be as

secret, which he promised; and offered me
his copy of Mr Baker's edition of Cardinal
Fisher's sermon on the foundress [Margaret
Beaufort, Countess of Richmond], which
had belonged to Mr Baker, and was full of
his MS notes. I lent him my notes and materials for Mr Baker's life, and desired him
to add anything to them that he knew relating to him, but on Nov. 11 he returned
them by his servant, without any additions.' Beadon also suggested that Cole
write the life if HW refused.

6. William Richardson.

7. Robert Richardson (1732–81), only
son of William Richardson; prebendary of
Lincoln Cathedral, chaplain-in-ordinary to
the King, rector of St Anne's, Westminster,
and of Wallington, Herts.

8. 'when I began the *History of St
John's College* by Mr Baker' (addition in
Cole's copy).

mon civility of an answer, but have kept writing, and am now got to the last volume, containing 702 pages of lists of Bachelors of Arts. I was very loath so much good industry should perish, so labour like an horse to get through these MSS before a summons to return them. The worst of the story is to come. Two days after Dr Farmer lent me these treasures, he and some company dined with me. The books were all on a table in my study, and in the afternoon two or three of the company went out of the parlour to the study to look at it, having not been here before. I did not attend them by reason of my gout. But next morning I missed an octavo volume, and after hunting in every corner and among my books, which have been all removed on purpose, I can find nothing of it. I am pretty clear who took it, and indeed I have wrote to him to know if, among other books he has occasionally lent me, I did not return *that* by mistake with them. The Master is too honourable to take such a step, so I cannot be far from the person,[9] but the book is irrecoverably gone, and what to say or do, I know not. I mean to return them all in the lump, and hope it will not be missed, though in the first parcel sent to me, in which is included the MS in question, I wrote a list myself and sent it to Dr Farmer. I hope he will not recur to it. If he does, I am undone.

My opinion of the bootikins I hope will never reach you. But there is no getting them on one's stomach. The gout I take to be a pestilent humour in the blood which will fix somewhere: if in the extremities, bad enough, but better than in the head or stomach; if driven from the feet, it will go elsewhere. This is my notion of the gout and the bootikins. Thank God I have [had][10] no pain these eighteen months, but foot tender, and flying about. I congratulate you heartily on the arrival of the Duke and Duchess of Gloucester. I hope and pray he will get better and better, and that you will meet with no interruption from that or any other quarter to stop you in your plan of Mr Baker's life, which I have set my heart on. Excuse a hard-nibbed pen and cold fingers from, dear Sir,

Your ever faithful and obliged servant,

Wm Cole

9. 'Dr Barnardiston and Dr Hallifax were also there, but neither of them do I conceive would take it' (addition in Cole's copy).

10. Supplied from Cole's copy.

From Cole, Sunday 29 March 1778

VA, Forster MS 110, f. 179. Cole's copy, Add MS 5824, f. 116v.
The word 'Chandler' has been written, in an unidentified hand, on the cover.
Address: The Honourable Horace Walpole, Arlington Street, London.
Postmark: Penny Post Paid [in a triangle] W[estminster] TU[esday, 31 March 1778].

Milton, March 29, 1778.

\<Dea\>r Sir,

ONE principal reason for my long silence is the constant ill state of health that I have been in since I wrote last. Not once for near seven months have I been able to go out of my house, and I was flattering myself that I should at last get to Cambridge when a fresh fit of the gout seized me in one foot, with more pain than usual, last Thursday. I had good rest last night, but yet my foot and heel put me in mind that I am not to escape so.

However, all this time I have been employed in my way: in transcribing registers and other old papers. But before I began them, I finished my collections relating to Mr Baker, which are ready to be sent to you whenever you are disposed to have them. I did not choose to send you any notice sooner, as you said it was to be summer's work, and that you should be otherwise employed in the winter.

In December Mr Robinson,[1] the Dissenting minister at Cambridge, an ingenious man, as his publications prove, called upon me, though unknown to either, with a civil message from a Dr Kippis, an independent teacher in or about London, that hearing I had made collections in the biographical way, he would be obliged to me for my assistance in a new edition, with additions, of the *Biographical Dictionary*,[2] and particularly for materials for the life of Mr Baker. Having never seen Mr Robinson, and not knowing who he was, I took the liberty to tell him that I should make him the same answer that I did to Mr Gough a year before when he wrote to me on the same subject, and with the same request, though I knew Mr Gough to be a Dissenter, though bred [in] Benet College, viz., that as Dr Kippis had taken the lead in the Clerical Petition against the Church of England, and that his writings tended that way, there was a great

1. Robert Robinson (1735–90), pastor of Stone Yard Baptist Chapel at Cambridge; author of religious works and hymns. His published works in 1778 numbered about six.

2. That is, the *Biographia Britannica*.

prospect of the work's taking a tinge from the writer of it, and that it would be replenished with lives out of Baxter and Calamy,[3] and as I had no niches for heroes of that stamp, I begged to be noways concerned in the work. This was my answer to Mr Gough, from whom I have never heard since. Yet I told Mr Robinson that if he made any collections for Mr Baker's life in the University, I would look it over, though I chose not to part with what I had on that subject. I have not neither [sic] heard from or seen him since. What I foresaw did really happen, for a gentleman of Benet, beneficed in Dorsetshire,[4] brought me about the same time a list of such new lives as Mr Kippis means to add, half of which are of the Dissenting order —reason sufficient to me to be noways concerned. If you are curious to see the list, I will send it, having taken a copy of it.

I will say no more at present, than that I am, dear Sir,

Your most obliged and faithful servant,

WM COLE

Having never been at Cambridge since October, and not seeing Dr Pennington since, to whom I lent Dr Heberden's letter and account of Mr Baker, I have not that memoir, but hope to have it on sending for it.

I was informed by the same gentleman who lent me the list that, being with a friend at the Antiquary Society about two months ago, Mr Gough introduced Dr Kippis and proposed him to be one of the members, and I suppose he is actually so at present.[5] I never mentioned to Mr Robinson that my collections were designed for quite another hand.

3. Edmund Calamy (1671–1732), nonconformist divine, published an abridgment of Baxter's *Reliquiae Baxterianae*, 1702 (republished, with additions, 2 vols, 1713), and *A Continuation of the Account*, 2 vols, 1727.

4. Doubtless William Colman, who was rector of Stalbridge, Dorset, and an intimate friend of Cole. He was elected a member of the Society of Antiquaries 18 June 1778, and was chosen Master of Corpus Christi College a week later (see Masters, *History of the College of Corpus Christi*, ed. John Lamb, 1831, p. 253; John Nichols, *A List of the Members of the Society of Antiquaries . . . to . . . 1796*, 1798, p. 32).

5. Kippis was elected a member of the Society of Antiquaries, 12 March 1778 (see John Nichols, loc. cit.).

To Cole, Tuesday 31 March 1778

Add MS 5953, ff. 18–19.
Address: To the Reverend Mr Cole at Milton near Cambridge.
Postmark: 31 MR.

Arlington Street, March[1] 31, 1778.

I DID think it long indeed, dear Sir, since I heard from you, and I am very sorry the gout was the cause. I hope after such long persecution you will have less now than you apprehend.

I should not have been silent myself, had I had anything to tell you that you would have cared to hear. Politics have been the only language, and abuse the only expression of the winter, neither of which are, or deserve to be, inmates of your peaceable hermitage. I wish however that they may not have grown so serious as to threaten every retreat with intrusion.

I will let you know when I am settled at Strawberry Hill, and can look over your kind collections relating to Mr Baker. He certainly deserves his place in the *Biographia,* but I am not surprised that *you* would not submit to *his* being instituted and inducted by a Presbyterian. In truth, I, who have not the same zeal against Dissenters, do not at all desire to peruse the history of their apostles, which are generally very uninteresting.

You must excuse the shortness of this, in which too I have been interrupted. My nephew is as suddenly recovered as he did last time; and though I am far from thinking him perfectly in his senses, a great deal of his disorder is removed, which though it will save me a great deal of trouble, hurries me at present, and forces me to conclude.

Yours most sincerely,

HOR. WALPOLE

From Cole, Thursday 16 April 1778

VA, Forster MS 110, ff. 180–1. Cole kept no copy.
Address: Hon. Horace Walpole, Arlington Street, Piccadilly, London.
Postmark: Penny Post Paid.

Dear Sir,   April 16, 1778, Milton.

A FRIEND calling here yesterday, who came the day before out of Suffolk from Mr Nasmith, informed me that his book,[1] which

1. MS reads *May,* but Cole has substituted the correct date, March 31. Cf. postmark.

1. See enclosure below.

you was so kind to subscribe for in the summer on my recommendation, is already printed, and that the copies for London will be sent thither and published next week.[2] I therefore take the opportunity of Mr Tyson's going to town on Saturday to send you the receipt.

I was to have dined today with Mr Essex at Cambridge, but am forced to send this letter to Mr Tyson, who is to be there, as I am so much out of order with an hoarseness and sore throat.

Whenever you will be pleased to send for the other papers,[3] they shall be ready and at your service, as is, dear Sir,

Your ever faithful and obliged servant,

WM COLE

[Enclosure.][4]

No. 76.   April 23, 1776.

Received of *the hon:ble Horace Walpole* the Sum of *half a Guinea* for *one* Copy of Itineraria Willelmi de Worcestre & Simonis Simeonis, which I promise to deliver to the Bearer on or before 23 April, 1778, or to return the Money subscribed.

James Nasmith

To COLE, Thursday 23 April 1778

Add MS 5953, ff. 20–1.

Cole made several notes at the end of HW's letter, for his reply of 10 May 1778. They are printed in the introduction to that letter.

Address: To the Reverend Mr Cole at Milton near Cambridge.
Postmark: Isleworth 24 AP.

Strawberry Hill, April 23, 1778.

I THANK you, dear Sir, for the notice of William de Worcestre's appearance, and will send for my book, as soon as I go to town, which will not be till next week. I have been here since Friday as much a hermit as yourself. I wanted air and quiet, having been

2. 'The subscribers to Mr Nasmith's edition of the Itineraries of Simon Simeonis and William of Worcester, may have their copies delivered on Thursday, the 23d of this instant April, and afterwards by sending or bringing their receipts to Mr B.

White, Bookseller, in Fleet Street' (*Lloyd's Evening Post* 20–2 April 1778).
3. Cole's materials for Baker's life.
4. The words in the receipt here printed in italics are in MS. Nasmith's signature differs from the rest of the MS.

much fatigued on my nephew's amendment, trying to dissuade him from making the campaign with his militia; but in vain! I now dread hearing of some eccentric freak.

I am sorry Mr Tyson has quite dropped me, though he sometimes comes to town. I am still more concerned at your frequent disorders —I hope their chief seat is unwillingness to move.

Your Bakeriana will be very welcome about June: I shall not be completely resident here till then; at least not have leisure, as May is the month in which I have most visits from town.

As few spare hours as I have, I have contrived to go through Mr Pennant's Welsh tour[1] and Mr Warton's second volume;[2] both which come within the circle of your pursuits. I have far advanced too in Lord Hardwicke's first volume of *State Papers*.[3] I have yet found nothing that opens a new scene, or sets the old in a new light, yet they are rather amusing, though not in proportion to the bulk of the volumes. One likes to hear actors speak for themselves—but on the other hand they use a great many more words than are necessary; and when one knows the events from history, it is a little tiresome to go back to the details and the delays.

I should be glad to employ Mr Essex on my offices, but the impending war with France deters me. It is not a season for expense! I could like to leave my little castle complete; but though I am only a spectator, I cannot be as indifferent to the melancholy aspect of the times, as the country gentleman was, who was going out with his hounds, as the two armies at Edgehill were going to engage![4] I wish for peace and tranquillity, and should be glad to pass my remaining hours in the idle and retired amusements I love, and without any solicitude for my country. Adieu!

Yours most sincerely,

H. Walpole

1. *Tour in Wales, 1773*, published 23 March 1778 (see *London Chronicle* 5–7, 7–10 March 1778). HW's copy (D.5) was sold SH iv. 6.

2. Of his *History of English Poetry*. It was published 6 April 1778 (see *London Chronicle, passim* 24 March–18 April 1778. HW's copy of the work, 3 vols, 1774–81, was sold SH v. 63.

3. *Miscellaneous State Papers, from 1501 to 1726*, 2 vols, 1778, published Saturday,

11 April (see *London Chronicle* 28–31 March, 2–4, 9–11, 11–14 April 1778). HW's copy was sold SH v. 76, and is now WSL. The pressmarks have been lost in rebinding, but both volumes have numerous annotations by HW.

4. 'As King Charles the first marched to Edgcot near Banbury, on 22 Oct. 1642, he saw him [Sir Richard Shukburgh (1596–1656)] hunting in the fields not far from Shuckborough, with a very good pack of

From COLE, Sunday 10 May 1778

VA, Forster MS 110, f. 182. COLE's copy, Add MS 5824, ff. 123v, 124v.

At the end of the preceding letter, Cole wrote the following notes for use in this letter:

'New history of Norfolk with Houghton and Walpole Church.

'Dr Kippis, first volume of *Biographia* and F. A. S.

'Mr Tyson near London.

'Dr Middleton's letters to Lord Hervey by Dr Knowles.

'Warton, vol. 2, p. 142, repeats what I have mentioned.

'Mr Tyson means to engrave a print of Theodore Haveus, whom you mention.

'Blunders in the last *Gentleman's Magazine*, p. 175, relating to your inscription under Pope Benedict XIV. In the same magazine at p. 183 is a copy of verses on seeing Strawberry Hill.'

Address: Hon. Horace Walpole at Strawberry Hill in Twickenham, Middlesex.
Postmark: None. [Essex probably carried the letter to HW; see following letter.]

Milton, May 10, 1778.

Dear Sir,

I HOPE William of Worcester, and more especially Simon Sime-onis, pleases you. I am convinced you would have been more so, had Mr Nasmith most unaccountably not omitted several very curious little anecdotes in the former, and which I had an opportunity of finding out, for in 1772 he lent me his copy of the MS of William de Worcester before he had thoughts of publishing it, and

hounds, upon which it is reported that he fetched a deep sigh and asked who that gentleman was that hunted so merrily that morning, when he was going to fight for his crown and dignity. And being told that it was . . . Richard Shuckburgh, he was ordered to be called to him, and was by him very graciously received. Upon which he went immediately home, armed all his tenants, and the next day attended on him in the field, where he was knighted, and was present at the battle of Edghill. After the taking in of Banbury Castle and his Majesty's retreat from those parts, he went to his own seat and fortified himself on the top of Shuckborough Hill, where, being attacked by some of the Parliamentary forces, he defended himself till he fell . . . but being taken up, and life perceived in him, he was carried away prisoner to Kenilworth Castle . . . and was forced to purchase his liberty at a dear rate' (Sir Wm

Dugdale, *Antiquities of Warwickshire*, 2d edn, revised, augmented, and continued by Wm Thomas, 2 vols, 1730, i. 309). HW's copy of this edition (E.1.18–19) was sold SH ii. 103. This anecdote, a favourite with HW, is mentioned in at least four other letters: to Hertford 5 May 1765; to Montagu 15 April 1769; to Conway 22 Jan. 1775; and to Mason 14 June 1781. In his 'Book of Materials, 1786' (now Folger Library), p. 51, HW wrote: 'The story of the country gentleman who was going out with his hounds as Charles Ist was going to fight the battle of Naseby, is in no history, but was related by Daniel Earl of Nottingham, who had it from a gentleman present. If true, it was one of the strangest instances of insensibility ever recorded. I have heard that on the King's reproof, the gentleman entered into and was killed in his service.' For a discussion of the historical value of this story, see N&Q, Fourth Series, iv. 329.

as I thought it would never see the light, and esteemed it very curious, I transcribed it with his leave as far as he then had proceeded, which was about half way. The reason, it seems, why he made these omissions was because they were neither historical or topographical. But many of them were historical, and lets one into the manners of the times. It is too late now to say anything to him about it, but the book is much depreciated in my eye for want of these particulars, which would have enlived a book which much wants something of that sort, though a true genuine antiquary must still be pleased with many parts of it, but I pronounce Mr Nasmith to be no true brother. Perhaps he may like it as well not to be thought one.

I am truly sorry Lord O. will go where, of all parties in the world, he could not have chosen a worse. I hope he will weather it and give you pleasure by a propriety of manners which he has judgment sufficient to be master of, if he so pleases.

Mr Tyson is lately in possession of a good living in Essex[1] near Chigwell, about thirteen miles from London. When he gets thither he will be often in town and will have opportunities of paying his respects to you. He bids me tell you that[2] he has taken a drawing of Theodore Haveus, whom you mention as the architect of Caius College, and means to make an etching of it, and bringing [sic] one to you. He was the architect also of the tomb of Anne of Cleves, lately discovered in Westminster Abbey.[3]

I have not yet seen Mr Pennant's *Welsh Tour,* though he sent me the prints of Serjeant Glynn and Sir John Owen.[4] I have neither seen Lord Hardwicke's volumes to look into them. I am not so eager about them, as his Lordship's selections are not like to suit my palate. Warton's second volume I have gone through: I do not like it so much as I did the former volume. There are not so many pretty anecdotes in it, for as to the poetry, it is out of my reach. One thing I

1. The rectory at Lambourne, to which he was presented by Corpus Christi College, Cambridge.

2. 'Mr Kerrich of Magdalen has taken a drawing of Theodore Haveus' (variation in Cole's copy). Thomas Kerrich (1748–1828), antiquarian, painter, draughtsman and lithographer, became in 1797 the principal librarian of Cambridge University. Theodore Haveus (fl. 1576) was an architect, sculptor and painter (see *Anecdotes, Works* iii. 142–3).

3. The tomb of Anne of Cleves (1515–57) was discovered in the sanctuary of Westminster Abbey in the summer of 1775. For a full account of the discovery see Sir Joseph Ayloffe, *An Account of some ancient Monuments in Westminster Abbey . . . read at the Society of Antiquaries March 12, 1778,* 1780, especially p. 15 and Plate VII. This account also appeared in Kippis, *Vetusta Monumenta,* vol. 2, 1789.

4. See Pennant's *Tour in Wales, 1773,* pp. 102, 263.

could not help observing, and which I before took notice of to you: I mean the wording of Chaterton's death as owing to your censure of the poems.[5]

There is a new *History of Norfolk* publishing by numbers.[6] The first promises a view of Walpole Church and Houghton Hall. I have not seen it or heard further of it than the advertisement.

Dr Kippis, I see, has advertised the first volume of the new edition of the *Biographia*, with F.A.S. at the end of his name.[7] I should guess Mr Baker's life is included,[8] but I have neither seen or heard anything of it.

Dr Middleton's correspondence with Lord Hervey about the Roman Senate is now in the press by Dr Knowles of Bury.[9]

It is worth while to see what blunders are made in the last *Gentleman's Magazine*, p. 175, in relation to the inscription you placed under the head of Pope Benedict XIV.[10] In the same magazine at p. 183 is a copy of verses on seeing Strawberry Hill.[11]

Since I wrote this, a letter from Mr Essex informs me of his setting out for town on Tuesday. I have had no opportunity of seeing him this month, as I have been confined to my room wholly that space.

I am, dear Sir,

Your ever faithful and most obliged servant,

WM COLE

5. Warton's words are: 'falling into a dissipated course of life, which ill suited with his narrow circumstances, and finding that a writer of the most distinguished taste and judgment, Mr Walpole, had pronounced the poems to be suspicious, in a fit of despair, arising from distress and disappointment, he destroyed all his papers, and poisoned himself' (*History of English Poetry* ii. 142).

6. *A New and Complete History of Norfolk, collected from the most celebrated Historians . . . illustrated with copperplates*. It 'was begun in 1778, in octavo, by W. Whittingham, the bookseller at Lynn, to appear in sixpenny numbers, two volumes of which were completed' (William Upcott, *A Bibliographical Account of . . . English Topography*, 3 vols, 1818, ii. 957 n. See also Gough, *British Topography*² ii. *38). See *post* 3 Sept. 1778 n. 5.

7. An advertisement, 'Speedily will be published, the first volume of the second

edition of the *Biographia Britannica*. . . . Prepared for the press . . . by Andrew Kippis, D.D. and F.A.S.,' appeared in the *London Chronicle* 17–19 and 21–4 March 1778. Cole probably refers to this or a similar advertisement, as the volume in question was not published until Saturday, 23 May (see *London Chronicle* 16–26 May 1778). Kippis had become F.S.A. 12 March 1778 (see *ante* 29 March 1778 n. 5).

8. It appears at pp. 518–25.

9. *Letters between Lord Hervey and Dr Middleton concerning the Roman Senate. Published from the Original Manuscripts by Thomas Knowles* [1723–1802], *D.D. Rector of Ickworth, in Suffolk*, 1778. It appears from advertisements in the *London Chronicle* (23–5, 25–8 April 1778) that the work was published about a fortnight before the date of Cole's letter.

10. In a review of Caraccioli's *Life of Pope Clement XIV*, it is said that 'a nephew of the minister Walpole, having

BENEDICT XIV AND WALPOLE'S INSCRIPTION

To Cole, Thursday 21 May 1778

Add MS 5953, ff. 22–3.
Address: To the Reverend Mr Cole at Milton near Cambridge.
Postmark: EK 21 MA.

Arlington Street, May 21, 1778.

I WILL not flatter you; I was not in the least amused with either Simon Simeon or William of Wyrcestre.[1] If there was anything tolerable in either, it was the part omitted, or the part I did not read, which was the journey to Jerusalem, about which I have not the smallest curiosity. I thank you for mentioning the *Gentleman's Magazine,* which I sent for.

Mr Essex has called on me and left a drawing of a bridge[2] with which I am perfectly pleased—but I was unluckily out of town, he left no direction, and I know not where to seek him in this overgrown pottle of hay. I still hope he will call again before his return.

May not I, should not I wish you joy on the restoration of popery?[3] I expect soon to see Capucins tramping about the streets, and Jesuits *in high places.* We are relapsing fast to our pristine state, and have nothing but our island and our old religion.

Mr Nasmith's publication[4] directed me to his catalogue of the

procured a bust of Lambertini [Pope Benedict XIV (1675–1758)] to be made, ordered the following inscription to be engraved on the pedestal: "A man, who never spoke a good word of any priest of the church of Rome, caused this monument to be erected in honour of Benedict XIV, Sovereign Pontiff." ' The reviewer concludes, however, that the person meant is HW, 'well known for his genius and virtu.' The inaccuracies of this account may be seen from a comparison of HW's 'Inscription on a Picture of the late Pope,' in *Fugitive Pieces, Works* i. 218. The bust, in wax, with the inscription in HW's hand behind it, was in the Green Closet at SH (see *Description of SH, Works* ii. 430, where there is a misprint of 'Benedict XIII' for 'XIV'). It was sold SH xviii. 115, and is now in the possession of Lord Ilchester at Holland House (see his *The House of the Hollands,* 1937, pp. 56–7).

11. 'When Walpole's genius watch'd Britannia's fate,' etc. The verses (36 lines) are signed 'Y.' A copy of them in Kirgate's

hand is pasted into HW's extra-illustrated copy of his 1784 *Description of SH,* now wsl.

---

1. *Itineraria Simonis Simeonis et Willelmi de Worcestre,* ed. James Nasmith, Cambridge, 1778.

2. This was the bridge, not built until 1792, 'which spanned,' as HW has written on the back of the original drawing, 'the rivulet at Twickenham which runs by Mr Walpole's flower-garden and crosses the road between that and Mr Briscoe's garden.' The drawing is pasted into HW's extra-illustrated copy of his *Description of SH,* 1784, now wsl (see 'Genesis of SH' 86, and Fig. 32).

3. An act relieving Roman Catholics from 'certain penalties and disabilities' was passed in the House of Commons 21 May 1778, the date of HW's letter (see *Commons Journals*). Sir George Savile brought in the bill, and in consequence was attacked by the Gordon rioters in 1780.

4. See n. 1.

MSS in Bennet Library,[5] which I did not know was printed. I found two or three from which I should be glad to have transcripts, and would willingly pay for; but I left the book at Strawberry, and must trouble you another time with that commission.[6]

The City wants to bury Lord Chatham in St Paul's,[7] which as a person[8] said to me this morning, would literally be *robbing Peter to pay Paul.*[9] I wish it could be so, that there might be some decoration in that nudity, *en attendant* the re-establishment of various altars.

It is not my design to purchase the new edition of the *Biographia.* I trust they will give the old purchasers the additions as a supplement.[10] I had corrected the errata of the press throughout my copy; but I could not take the trouble of transcribing them, nor could lend them the original, as I am apt to scribble notes in the margins of all my books, that interest me at all.

Pray let me know if Baker's life is among the additions, and whether you are satisfied with it, as there could not be events enough in his retired life to justify two accounts of it.

There are no new *old news,* and you care for nothing within the memory of man. I am always intending to draw up an account of my intercourse with Chatterton,[11] which I take very kindly your reminding me of, but some avocation or other has still prevented it. My perfect innocence of having even indirectly been an ingredient in his dismal fate, which happened two years after our correspondence, and after he had exhausted both his resources and constitution, have made me more easy to prove that I never saw him, knew nothing of his ever being in London, and was the first person instead of

5. *Catalogus Librorum Manuscriptorum quos Collegio Corporis Christi et B. Mariae Virginis in Academia Cantabrigiensi legavit . . . Matthaeus Parker,* Cambridge, 1777.

6. HW apparently never asked Cole for a copy of the MSS to which he refers.

7. William Pitt, 1st E. of Chatham, d. 11 May and was buried 9 June in Westminster Abbey (see *Last Journals* ii. 173–4, 176, 186).

8. Not identified.

9. Westminster Abbey is the Collegiate Church of St Peter in Westminster. Burke is credited with a similar *bon mot* after the death of Dr Johnson, when there was a discussion as to whether a monument to his memory should be erected in St Paul's or Westminster Abbey (see James Prior, *Life of . . . Edmund Burke,* 5th edn, 1854, p. 240).

10. HW's copy of the first edition of *Biographia Britannica,* 7 vols, 1747–66 (L.1. 15–21) was sold SH iii. 195. As no supplementary volume containing the additions in the second edition was issued, HW bought the second edition, 5 vols (D.2), which was sold SH i. 136.

11. HW's letter to Bewley, which he incorporated into his *Letter to the Editor of the Miscellanies of Thomas Chatterton,* is dated 23 May 1778—two days after HW wrote this letter to Cole.

the last, on whom he had practised his impositions, and founded his chimeric hopes of promotion. My very first, or at least second letter, undeceived him in those views, and our correspondence was broken off before he quitted his master, business and Bristol—so that his disappointment with me was but his first ill success; and he resented my incredulity so much, that he never condescended to let me see him. Indeed what I have said now to you, and which cannot be controverted by a shadow of doubt, would be sufficient vindication. I could only add to the proofs a vain regret of never having known his distresses, which his amazing genius would have tempted me to relieve, though I fear he had no other claim to compassion. Mr Warton[12] has said enough to open the eyes of everyone that is not greatly prejudiced to his forgeries. Dr Milles is one, who will not make a bow to Dr Percy for not being as wilfully blind as himself— but when he gets a beam in his eye that he takes for an antique truth, there is no persuading him to submit to be couched. Adieu! Dear Sir,

Yours most sincerely,

Hor. Walpole

From Cole, Saturday 23 May 1778

VA, Forster MS 110, ff. 183–4. Cole's copy, Add MS 5824, ff. 125v, 126v.
Address: Honourable Horace Walpole, Arlington Street, Piccadilly, London.
Postmark: Cambridge 25 MA.

Milton, May 23, 1778, Saturday.

<Dear> Sir,

THIS is to inform you, if Mr Essex has not yet called or is not already gone out of town, where certainly you will meet with him or hear of him. If he is not at the Queen's Head in Gray's Inn Lane, where he often lodges when in town, he is at Mr Beacroft's[1] in Paternoster Row. I am sorry we are going to lose him at Cambridge. He is trying to get an house on Epping Forest. He has acquired a

---

12. In his *History of English Poetry,* vol. 2, sect. VIII, pp. 139–64.

---

1. John Beecroft (d. 1779), a wholesale bookseller, 'and many years Agent to the University of Cambridge, was Master of the Stationers' Company in 1773' (LA iii. 422).

good fortune and wants to be nearer town.[2] The last time I saw him he seemed much pleased with your generosity to him.[3]

I am sorry Simon Fitz-Simon and William of Wyrcester are so low in your estimation. I suppose I may, without fear of being saucy, pronounce upon you as I did on their editor, *that you are no true, genuine antiquary*. You are better, and have availed yourself of it.

The liberal bill which lately passed to take away all sanguinary and penal laws from the papists really gives me joy, and I accept your gratulation, but I must needs say I don't like the quarter it comes from: it puts me in mind of the unnatural junction of the Presbyterians and them in King James II's time, against the Church of England. Indeed I never suspected such a favour from patriotism. Even that won't reconcile me to their tricks. I know a little of them, which makes me dread even their favours.

Whenever you are pleased to send your commission for transcripts out of Benet College Library, I will endeavour to get them executed. The poor Master,[4] my most particular friend, is now dying.[5] The last visit I paid at Cambridge seven weeks ago was to him. I had then no notion of his living a week. Had he been well, I had free liberty, had I been in a condition, to have had any books to his lodge, for they must not go out of College, and would have transcribed them for you. My situation at present won't let me imagine it, yet I have friends there sufficient to get it done for you.

I wish with you, as Lord Chatham is to have a public funeral, that his bones may lie at St Paul's. Such a beginning would put it in fashion and ornament the bare walls that want covering. I hope the livery[6] will seize Wilkes's body also in due time: altars to two such patriotic worthies as these will bring the Lord Mayor and Aldermen to that church, which they seem to have neglected of late.

I will inquire after the new edition of *Biographia*. I hope nothing, or nothing to the purpose, will be found therein, that I may not be frustrated of a life of Mr Baker by the hand of a master.

I was told t'other day that Mr Terwhit, who published an edition of Chaucer, and who was originally an advocate for the authenticity

2. 'having one only daughter' (addition in Cole's copy).

3. Cole presumably means HW's employment of him at SH.

4. John Barnardiston. He did not die until 17 June 1778 (see Robert Masters, *History of Corpus Christi College,* ed. John Lamb, 1831, p. 252).

5. 'I heard from him this morning' (addition in Cole's copy).

6. That is, the city companies.

THE REVEREND WILLIAM COLE
BY THOMAS KERRICH

of Rowley, but is now convinced of the forgery of Chatterton, is going to print an account of that matter.[7]

I have a favour to beg of you. A friend of mine, Mr Kerrich of Magdalen, who is a most ingenious painter, and whom I mentioned in my last as taking the draft of Theodore Haveus in Caius College Lodge, begged me to beg for him a few of the duplicates, if you have any, of the artists and painters which were done for your *Anecdotes*.[8] You was so kind to give me some formerly, and he, seeing them in my collection, was eager to have a few: he only collects artists. He was at Rome four years on a travelling fellowship. If you should happen to have any undisposed of, you will much oblige, dear Sir,

Your ever faithful and most obliged servant,

Wm Cole

Perhaps Mr Essex may be at the White Horse in Fetter Lane. I think he has left going to the Queen's Head.

To Cole, Wednesday 3 June 1778

Add MS 5953, ff. 24–5.
Address: To the Reverend Mr Cole at Milton near Cambridge.
Postmark: Isleworth 4 IV.

Strawberry Hill, June 3, 1778.

I WILL not dispute with you, dear Sir, on patriots and politics. One point is past controversy, that the ministers have ruined this country; and if the Church of England is satisfied with being recon-

7. Thomas Tyrwhitt (1730–86), classical commentator and master of English literature, edited Chaucer's *Canterbury Tales*, 5 vols, 1775–8, and *Poems supposed to have been written at Bristol, by Thomas Rowley and Others, in the Fifteenth Century* (1st and 2d edns, 1777), to the 3d edn (1778) of which he added *An Appendix . . . tending to prove, that they were written . . . entirely by Thomas Chatterton*. The appendix was also issued separately, price sixpence, paged to bind in with the earlier editions. For an account of Tyrwhitt's position in the Rowley controversy, see Meyerstein, *Chatterton* 461–2 nn, 463 and n.

8. 'He was at Rome three or four years [1771–5] on a [Drury] travelling fellowship, has a small living [the vicarage of Dersingham] in Norfolk of £60 per annum, held by a Mr Hey of his college for him, as the tenure of his by-fellowship won't allow his taking it himself. As his fortunes are very small and his genius very great, I took the liberty, when I sat to him for my picture at his room in college last autumn, to tell him that I thought he had better give up his design of going into orders, for which also he has no inclination, and take up with the better profession of a face painter, for which he seems admirably calculated' (addition in Cole's

ciled to the Church of Rome, and thinks it a compensation for the loss of America, and all credit in Europe, she is as silly an old woman as any granny in an almshouse. France is very glad we are grown such fools, and soon saw that the Presbyterian Dr Franklyn[1] had more sense than all our ministers together. She has got over all her prejudices, has expelled the Jesuits,[2] and made the Protestant Swiss, Necker, her Comptroller General.[3] It is a little woeful, that we are relapsing into the nonsense that[4] the rest of Europe is shaking off! and it is the more deplorable, as we know by repeated experience that this country has always been disgraced by Tory administrations. The rubric is the only gainer by them in a few martyrs.[5]

I do not know yet what is settled about the spot of Lord Chatham's interment. I am no more an enthusiast to his memory than you. I knew his faults and his defects—yet one great fact cannot only not be controverted, but I doubt more remarkable every day—I mean, that under him we attained not only our highest elevation, but the most solid authority in Europe. When the names of Marlborough and Chatham are still pronounced with awe in France, our little cavils make a puny sound. Nations that are beaten, cannot be mistaken.

I have been looking out for your friend[6] a set of my heads of painters, and find I want six or seven. I think I have some odd ones in town. If I have not, I will have deficiencies supplied from the plates, though I fear they will not be good, as so many have been taken off. I should be very ungrateful for all your kindnesses, if I neglected any opportunity of obliging you, dear Sir. Indeed our old and unalterable friendship is creditable to us both, and very uncommon between two men who differ so very much in their opinions relative to church and state—I believe the reason is, that we are both sincere, and never meant to make advantage by our principles, which I allow is too common on both sides, and I own too fairly,

copy). 'Mr Hey' was Samuel Hey (d. 1828), brother of John, William and Richard Hey, who are noticed in DNB; of Magdalene College (B.A. 1771). He apparently held the vicarage of Dersingham from 1775 to 1784, when Kerrich became vicar (see *Wiltshire: the Topographical Collections of John Aubrey . . . corrected and enlarged by John Edward Jackson. . . .* Devizes, 1862, p. 354; Edward Kelly Purnell, *Magdalene College*, 1904, pp. 168–9).

1. Benjamin Franklin.

2. See *ante* 5 Sept. 1765 n. 4. The order of Jesuits was abolished by Pope Clement XIV, 21 July 1773.

3. Jacques Necker (1732–1804) was appointed director-general of the finances of France, 29 June 1777.

4. MS reads *than*.

5. This paragraph and the next are a rejoinder to Cole's fling at Chatham and Wilkes in his last letter. It is a rare instance of 'warmth' in this correspondence.

6. Thomas Kerrich.

more common on my side of the question than on yours. There is a reason too for that: the honours and emoluments are in the gift of the Crown: the nation has no separate treasury to reward its friends.

If Mr Tyrwhit has opened his eyes to Chatterton's forgeries, there is an instance of conviction against strong prejudice! I have drawn up an account of my transaction with that marvellous young man. You shall see it one day or other, but I do not intend to print it.[7] I have taken a thorough dislike to being an author; and if it would not look like begging you to compliment me by contradicting me, I would tell you what I am most seriously convinced of, that I find what small share of parts I had, grown dulled—and when I perceive it myself, I may well believe that others would not be less sharp-sighted. It is very natural; mine were spirits rather than parts; and as time has rebated the one, it must surely destroy their resemblance to the other—pray don't say a syllable in reply on this head, or I shall have done exactly what I said I would not do. Besides, as you have always been too partial to me, I am on my guard—and when I will not expose myself to my enemies, I must not listen to the prejudice of my friends; and as nobody is more partial to me, than you; there is nobody I must trust less in that respect.

Yours most sincerely,

H. W.

From Cole, Sunday 7 June 1778

VA, Forster MS 110, ff. 185–6. Cole's copy, Add MS 5824, ff. 126v, 127v, 128v.
Address: The Honourable Horace Walpole at Strawberry Hill in Twicken-ham, Middlesex. *Postmark:* Cambridge 8 IV.

Milton, Whitsunday, June 7, 1778.

Dear Sir,

I HURRY to answer your most obliging letter in order to prevent your trouble in having any prints taken off for Mr Kerrich. He

---

7. HW refers to his letter to William Bewley 23 May 1778, which he printed with his *Letter to the Editor of the Miscellanies of Chatterton,* SH [Jan. —] 1779, in an edition of 200 copies (*Jour. Print. Off.* 19, 63). The *Letter to the Editor* was not written until 23 July 1778 (see HW to Mason 24 July 1778), and it was afterward enlarged (see 'Short Notes'). William Bewley (d. 1783), apothecary and scientist, was an intimate friend of Dr Charles Burney.

would be satisfied with half a dozen or more of them, and I never meant, and beg you will not trouble yourself for, more.

As to politics, I never will say one word more about them on any occasion. My principles, as you may remember, were imbibed very early. I never saw occasion to alter them, and what is more, I have all my life lived and acted with the Whigs, who were my friends, though perhaps might not always wish them success, and yet in no part of my life ever caballed with the contrary party, with whom to this day I have little or no connection. I never solicited Whig or Tory to get preferment, and the only time I ever asked a favour of that sort is this very post, when for the first time in my life I solicit a living. My reasons are: I am tired of not being able to reside at Burnham, which I wish to resign, yet I can't with prudence do it without getting another, and as our Bishop[1] has these seven years made a merit to himself by saying to others, before I had Burnham, that he wished to serve me, I have taken the resolution to put him in mind of what he has said of that sort to Lord Montfort, Mr Stevenson,[2] etc. But this has carried me the Lord knows whither. I meant to say that as I had been so disinterested all my days and kept my politics to myself and my books, I was in hopes I should have passed through life as easy as such outside moderation would promise me. We never were serious till Mr Baker's history disclosed my politics. I was in hopes you would have indulged an old friend in his whimsies, and have as easily passed over the foibles of my age as you used agreeably to rally my early prejudices in college. I don't forget that you laughingly used to say that[3] I used to pinch old Mother Oliver the fruitwoman for her being a Presbyterian. Thus much and no more forever for politics, <but> before I conclude forever I will do you the justice to say that you are a most fair antagonist and make more concessions than I really expected from one of your side.

Come we now to a much more agreeable argument.

You say you mean not to print any more, but that you will let me

---

1. Edmund Keene, Bp of Ely. Nothing came of Cole's request for an exchange of livings.

2. Probably one of the sons of Cole's friend, John Stevenson (1699–1749), of Newton, Cambs: Robert (1734–92), William (1736–1815) or John (1737–1829). The first presumably inherited his father's property, and might have been on friendly terms with Bishop Keene; the third was chaplain of Trinity College 1764–1829 (see *Eton Coll. Reg. 1698–1752*; Palmer, *Monumental Inscriptions*, pp. xiii, 258; Add MS 5808, f. 59).

3. 'I never bought apples of old Mother Oliver . . . but that' (addition in Cole's copy).

see what you have said of Chatterton.[4] I must see it here or nowhere, for I am afraid I never shall go far from hence again. Your writings give me pleasure always, even though against my will, and if you say the word, not a soul shall see a letter of it. But this is as you judge proper. What concerns me more is the inference I draw from your distaste to be any further an author. I wish it has not an evil aspect to Mr Baker's life. I have all my materials together that I mean to search after, and if this is meant as an order not to send them, though it mortifies me extremely, yet I am a passive-obedience man and submit to the decision of my superiors. You forbid me to say anything on your last paragraph. It is very hard to have one's mouth closed when I could contradict every word of it, nor do I believe a single syllable of it. What is it to me whether I am pleased and enraptured by parts or spirits? The world will be satisfied, so that they are amused, and never enter into those nice distinctions and refinements to know how it comes to pass that your writings please more than anyone's else. I am afraid almost to tell you my surmises on this subject. Since you have seen my vehemence in some particulars, and may guess that the materials I shall furnish you with to compose this life may be in the same style, you are unwilling to undertake a task which you have a right to finish in your own way, and which I am sure will be the right one, and care not to run counter to what you judge will not be pleasant to me. I assure you I shall be thoroughly satisfied, do it in what way you please. I defy you not to make even so dry a subject palatable to everyone's taste. But I entreat you to use your own pleasure herein, and if you are really set against it, I freely, though reluctantly, give up your promise.

I have seen for two or three hours the new *Biographia*. The life[5] there I am satisfied will not interfere with anything that may be said in <your> work. I have selected out of that life the only passage that I had not before and <which> is new, but unfortunately a falsehood, viz., that Mr Prior allowed Mr Baker the profits of his fellowship during his life.[6] Now it is well known Mr Prior, though a

---

4. In HW's letter to Bewley 23 May 1778.

5. Of Thomas Baker.

6. Though Baker 'lost his fellowship, it appears that this was in part made up to him by the generosity of a friend. The celebrated Matthew Prior, not scrupling the oaths, or needing the profits of a fellowship, took the oaths, kept his fellowship, and gave Mr Baker the profits of it' (*Biographia Britannica*[2] i. 520). The note on this passage says that 'this curious fact was communicated to the Rev. Mr R. Robinson, of Chesterton, by the Rev. Dr Goddard, Master of Clare Hall, Cambridge.'

plenipotentiary, yet was a beggar, and had it not in his power to be
so generous. I have drawn up a paper to prove it. I wish you would
send for that and its fellows, and not leave them in my hands, who
will make sorry work of them.

There is one thing in the *Biographia nova* that will oblige you to
send for it, and then you may judge of Mr Baker's article. It is at
p. 203, where is a note by the Independent Dr Kippis,[7] very impertinent in respect to your father and yourself. In his new preface
he says he is impartial, neither Whig nor Tory, etc., etc., but is a
friend to the liberties of mankind.[8] It provokes me to see these constant insinuations from these sort of people (who, I will venture to
say and prove, are, when in power, the most arbitrary and tyrannical)
in complimenting one another at the expense of their opposites.

I am, dear Sir,

Your ever faithful and obliged servant,

WM COLE

Poor Mr Bentham[9] dined here this day sennight and was well as
usual, but died next day of an apoplexy. On Friday I dined at the
Rose where was a meeting of the deputy lieutenants and justices
about the militia: Mr Wortham,[10] a man of fortune and nothing else,
was one of them. Just before our dinner he dropped down in the
same way and died before evening.

To COLE, Wednesday 10 June 1778

Add MS 5953, ff. 26–7.
Address: To the Reverend Mr Cole at Milton near Cambridge.

Strawberry Hill, June 10, 1778.

I AM as impatient and in as much hurry as you was, dear Sir, to
clear myself from the slightest intention of censuring your poli-

7. For this passage, see *post* 14 June
1778.

8. 'It is our wish, and will be our aim, to
conduct this publication with real impartiality. We mean to rise above narrow
prejudices, and to record, with fidelity and
freedom, the virtues and vices, the excellencies and defects of men of every profession and party. . . . We scruple not to
declare our attachment to the great interests of mankind, and our enmity to big-
otry, superstition, and tyranny, whether
found in Papist or Protestant, Whig or
Tory, Churchman or Dissenter' (*Biographia Britannica*[2], vol. 1, p. xxi).

9. Joseph Bentham, alderman of Cambridge and Printer to the University.

10. Hale Wortham of Shepreth, Cambs.

tics. I know the sincerity and disinterested goodness of your heart, and when I must be convinced how little certain we all are of what is truth, it would be very presumptuous to condemn the opinions of any good man, and still less an old and unalterable friend, as I have ever found you. The destruction that violent and arbitrary principles have drawn on this blinded country, has moved my indignation. We never were a great and happy country till the Revolution. The system of these days tended to overturn and has overturned that establishment, and brought on the disgraces that ever attended the foolish and wicked councils of the house of Stuart. If man is a rational being, he has a right to make use of his reason, and to enjoy his liberty. We, we alone almost, had a constitution that every other nation upon earth envied or ought to envy. This is all I contend for. I will give you up whatever descriptions of men you please, that is, the leaders of parties, not the principles. These cannot change, those generally do, when power falls into the hands of them or their party, because men are corruptible, which truth is not. But the more the leaders of a party dedicated to liberty are apt to change, the more I adore the principle, because it shows that extent of power is not to be trusted even with those that are the most sensible of the blessing of liberty. Man is a domineering animal; and it has been not only my principle but practice too, to quit everybody at the gate of the palace. I trust we shall not much differ on these outlines—but we will bid adieu to the subject; it is never an agreeable one to those who do not mean to make a trade of it.

I heartily wish you may not find the pontiff, what I think the order,[1] and what I know him, if you mean the high priest of Ely. He is all I have been describing and worse: and I have too good an opinion of you, to believe that he will ever serve you.

What I said of disclaiming authorship, by no means alluded to Mr Baker's life. It would be enough that you desire it, for me to undertake it. Indeed I am inclined to it, because he was what you and I are, a party man from principle, not from interest: and he who was so candid, surely is entitled to the strictest candour. You shall send me your papers whenever you please. If I can succeed to your satisfaction, I shall be content; though I do assure you there was no

The occasion of the meeting was 'to ballot for the militia of that county' (*London Chronicle* 6–9 June 1778).

1. That is, 'what I think the order of bishops generally is.'

affectation in my saying that I find my small talent decline. I shall write the life to oblige you, without any thoughts of publication, unless I am better pleased than I expect to be; and even then, not in my own life. I had rather show that I am sensible of my own defects, and that I have acquired judgment enough not to hope praise for my writings; for surely when they are not obnoxious, and one only leaves them behind one, it is a mark that one is not very vain of them.

I have found the whole set of my *Painters*[1] and will send them the first time I go to town; and I will have my paper on Chatterton[2] transcribed for you, though I am much chagrined at your giving me no hope of seeing you again here. I will not say more of it, for while it is in my power, I will certainly make you a visit now and then, if there is no other way of our meeting. Mr Tyrrwhit, I hear, has actually published an appendix in which he gives up Rowley. I have not seen it, but will. Shall I beg you to transcribe the passage in which Dr Kippis abuses my father and me, for I shall not buy the new edition, only to purchase abuse on me and mine. I may be angry at liberties he takes with Sir Robert; but not with myself: I shall rather take it as flattery to be ranked with him; though there can be nothing worse said of my father, than to place us together. Oh! that great, that good man!—Dr Kippis may as well throw a stone at the sun!

I am sorry you have lost poor Mr Bentham. Will you say a civil thing for me to his widow, if she is living, and you think it not improper? I have not forgotten their great kindness to me. Pray send me your paper on Mr Prior's generosity to Mr Baker. I am sorry it was not so. Prior is much a favourite with me, *though a Tory,* nor did I ever hear anything ill of him. He left his party, but not his friends, and seems to me to have been very amiable. Do you know I pretend to be very impartial sometimes. Mr Hollis wrote against me for not being Whig enough. I am offended at Mrs Macaulay for being too much a Whig[3]—In short, we are all silly animals, and scarce ever more so, than when we affect sense.

Yours ever,

H. W.

1. The prints in *Anecdotes,* which Cole had requested for his friend Thomas Kerrich (see *ante* 23 May 1778).

2. That is, his letter to Bewley 23 May

1778. Cole's copy of it, which he transcribed 31 July 1778, is in Add MS 5852, ff. 51–3.

3. Cole's note on this passage is as follows: 'I am surprised at Mr Hollis's objec-

From Cole, Sunday 14 June 1778

VA, Forster MS 110, ff. 187–8. Cole's copy, Add MS 5824, ff. 129v, 130v.
Address: The Honourable Horace Walpole, Strawberry Hill in Twickenham, Middlesex. *Postmark:* Cambridge 17 IV.

Trinity Sunday, June 14, 1778, Milton.

Dear Sir,

I RECEIVED with great pleasure your most agreeable and condescending letter. That you will undertake Mr Baker's life gives me great pleasure, and I hope it will so far please you as to print it. However that be, I shall be greatly obliged to you for portraying a character which, it is my belief, you will not dislike the worse upon a nearer inspection of it. I shall send you all my materials, most of which were drawn up before Christmas. Indeed I have done little since that time. At present you will find them all confusion, and if you find some of my party spirit in the notes, you will please to observe that they were placed there before our political debates. I could not take the trouble to copy them over again. I have sent Dr Heberden<'s> letter, with some others and my own, which I meant to have sent to you on May 28.[1] You will have a deal of reading, but from the whole confusion you will strike out the light that is wanting. As I have made no memoranda of this matter, I shall be obliged to you, after you have done with them, to let me have them again, for there may and will be much dross that you will throw aside, and which a genuine dull antiquary and biographer would retain by choice. The paper about Prior is among them. I sent to Dr Goddard[2] to know on what authority he had told the Dissenting minister Mr Robinson that anecdote: he had no other than tradition, but it is a tradition I never heard, and I think I should of Dr Middleton had it been founded.

tion, as well as at Mr Walpole's to Mrs Macaulay: they are both in their writings determined republicans, and if I greatly do not mistake, this can be no offense at Strawberry Hill' (Add MS 5824, f. 129v). Hollis wrote against HW in the newspapers (see *post* 5 Feb. 1780). Mrs Catherine Macaulay (1731–91), afterwards Graham, was the author of *A History of England*, 8 vols, 1763–83, five volumes of which had ap-

peared at this time. HW's copy (C.5.33–40) was sold SH v. 51.

———

1. Cole did not send his own, as appears from his copy of it. See Appendix 1, where it is given.

2. Peter Stephen Goddard (1705–81), Master of Clare Hall, 1762–81 (see *Alumni Cantab.*). See also *ante* 7 June 1778 n. 6.

I long to see your account of Chatterton. The day which brought
your favour I received one from Mr Lort. This passage was in it:

Our President[3] has been at Bristol to procure proofs to support the
authenticity of Rowley's poems, but I believe he had not seen Mr Tyrwhit's appendix when he left London. It was rumoured that he had fallen
down the stairs of the tower in Redcliffe Church, and hurt his other leg,
but I hope this will prove a joke only. Dr Glynne has busied himself
much in the same pursuit. When I called on him in London, he refused
to open his lips to me on the subject, assigning as a reason what I will
venture to say is a very false one, that I had treated him in the same
manner at Cambridge.

By this you will perceive that people are as alert about it as if it was
a new discovery, and that it was a certainty. Dr Glynne is a perfect
enthusiast on the subject, and Mr Lort not far from it. I did not
know before that Dr Milles was lame. However that may be, it is
but a dull joke to take advantage of sneering at that which he can't
help.

I hope I did not say in my last that the biographers had abused
your father and you. The most they can be taxed with is impertinence to both. I sent yesterday to Cambridge for the volume,[4] and
this is the transcript, at p. 203, and at the conclusion of the life of
Arthur Earl of Anglesey:[5]

The ingenious Mr. Walpole, in his usual lively manner, hath made
several remarks on the character of Lord Anglesey, and upon the account
of him in the preceding article, which merit attention (*Cat. of Roy. &
Nob. Auth.*, vol. 2, pp. 65–77).[6] We agree with Mr. Walpole, that it is not
probable that the Earl of Anglesey should decline being Prime Minister
to avoid envy. Indeed, it is not at all likely that any such offer should have
been made to him at or a little after the Restoration; since no person
could at that time stand in competition, in this respect, with Lord Clarendon. We farther agree with Mr. Walpole, that the Earl of Anglesey's sitting in judgment upon the regicides, is not so honourable to him as hath
been represented, though he certainly had no concern in the King's death;
and that his being employed for 22 years by King Charles II is but an
insufficient proof of his not having been a bad man. It is certainly an

3. Jeremiah Milles, P.S.A.
4. *Biographia Britannica*[2] vol. 1.
5. Arthur Annesley (1614–86), 1st E. of
Anglesey; statesman and author.

6. This reference is to the 2d edn, 2 vols,
1759; the passage is in *Works* i. 411–6.

improbable supposition, as Mr. Walpole justly remarks, that the Earl should be thought of for Lord Chancellor by King James II when he had a Chancellor so moulded to his purposes as Jefferies.[7] If the fact were true, instead of being an honour to Lord Anglesey, it would reflect the greatest disgrace on his character.

It is from the preceding account of the Earl of Anglesey in particular, that Mr. Walpole hath taken occasion to make a severe stricture on our work, by saying, that notwithstanding its singular merit, he cannot help calling it Vindicatio Britannica, or a Defence of every body. But in answer to this remark, it may be observed, 1st, That the censure, so far as it is just, can only be applied to a few articles. 2dly, That in an undertaking of this kind, which is not intended to be the vehicle of scandal, or of petulant criticism, but to do justice to ability and merit, of whatever religious or political principle, party and profession, it is safest to err on the candid side. 3dly, That the removal of particular charges which have been hastily or groundlessly brought against eminent men, falls, with peculiar propriety, within the compass of our design. And 4thly, That if we have been guilty of an excess of gentleness, we must guard, for the future, against this amiable error. It will behove us, for instance, when we come to the Life of Sir Robert Walpole, to take care that we be not too *milky*. However, we hope it will be the glory of this work, to treat every character with all the candour which is consistent with truth. . . .

K.

This is the passage. I think this Mr Impartial has run counter to his *safety of erring on the candid side* when he renews Dr Jortin's illiberal attack on Mr Baker, even though the former Biographers had censured Jortin for it.[8] This proves my reason to be good (in regard to my own opinions) why I would not be concerned in lending materials to such colourers, whose classical historians are Baxter, Calamy, Neal,[9] etc., with eternal fightings against the prejudices of Anthony Wood, mostly taken from Calamy.

Before I have my answer from the pontiff, of whose real worth I

7. George Jeffreys (1648–89), 1st Bn Jeffreys of Wem.

8. John Jortin (1698–1770), ecclesiastical historian, was the author of a *Life of Erasmus*, 1758, in which he attacked Baker for his defense of Erasmus at the expense of LeClerc (Jortin's 'guide and master') in *Reflections on Learning*. According to Jortin, Baker 'attacked LeClerc with a virulence which one would not have expected from a man, who, as I remember, was accounted, and who desired to be accounted, a candid, genteel, and polite person. But party zeal guided his pen' (Jortin, ibid. 550, quoted in *Biographia Britannica*[2] i. 518–9 n). A writer in *Biographia Britannica*[1] (1747) vi. 3726 n. quotes Baker's passage, and asks whether the last sentence should not be applied to Jortin as well.

9. Daniel Neal (1678–1743), author of the *History of the Puritans*, 4 vols, 1732–8.

have long been assured, I am of your opinion entirely, that he will do nothing for me, yet I was entitled to ask him, as for these six or seven years he has been talking of it to others, and always reserved to myself.

Your very kind expression of meaning to see me here if I can't remove from my spot, of which I have no hopes, is so friendly and good that I have not words to express my obligation. Here is always a clean spare bed, but a note would be proper, as I have but two to spare, for fear, by accident, they may be occupied. I will soon send the papers[10] by some friend going to town, and am, dear Sir,

Your ever faithful and obliged servant,

WM COLE

From COLE, Thursday 2 July 1778

VA, Forster MS 110, ff. 189–90. COLE's copy, Add MS 5824, f. 156v.

Cole dated this letter *July 3, 1778. Thursday,* in the original and in his copy, but Thursday fell on 2 July in 1778. Furthermore, Cole states in his letter, 'I will go to Cambridge tomorrow [i.e., 3 July] and put this letter into the post,' and in his letter, Saturday, 4 July, he says, 'I went to Cambridge yesterday.' The postmark indicates, however, that the letter did not leave Cambridge until Saturday, 4 July.

Address: Honourable Horace Walpole at Strawberry Hill in Twickenham, Middlesex. *Postmark:* Cambridge 4 IY.

Milton, July 3 [2], 1778, Thursday.

Dear Sir,

I AM out of all patience that I have not yet sent the papers. All the beginning of last month I was inquiring for some friend to take and leave them in Arlington Street, and could meet with none. I was the less solicitous as I thought it certain that Mr Lort would be here for a day or two about the middle of the month, as I heard he meant it, at the election of a new Principal Librarian.[1] However, he did not come, and I was then disappointed. My servant was at St Mary's this day, being the grand music for the Hospital,[2] when he

10. Relating to Baker.

1. On the death of John Barnardiston,

Richard Farmer was elected Principal Librarian, 27 June 1778.

2. An annual concert (as well as an

told me he saw him in the church. I shall see him in a day or two, probably on Sunday, though it is Commencement Sunday. For fear I should not, I will go to Cambridge tomorrow and put this letter into the post and see after Mr Lort, who, I make no doubt, will go to town immediately after Commencement Tuesday, and I hope will deliver my packet to you safely. Though the oratorio of *Judas Maccabeus*[3] is to be performed at St Mary's tomorrow by the best hands and voices from town, and I have a longing to hear it, yet I dare not venture, from the heat and the cold. If Mr Lort does not go on Wednesday, I will send it by the fly to the Queen's Head in Grey's Inn Lane. I know the carriage thither will be safe, but I don't love to employ a porter to carry it to you, who will demand double of its conveyance to London. I wish I had sent it by that conveyance at first.

Since I wrote last I have given a cu<rso>ry view to the new articles in the new *Biographia*,[4] and find your name mentioned in two other places slightly. The one is at p. 62, in Mr Addison's life, where the editor has added in a note that 'Mr Walpole's censure of Mr Addison's character of Lord Somers is by no means to be justified.'[5]

The other is at p. 5 in Abbot's life,[6] where Dr Kippis observes that Archbishop Abbot was as great a flatterer of King James as any other court chaplain, and gives an instance of such gross and fulsome flattery as one could scarcely believe. The passage is this, in a preface by Abbot before a pamphlet entitled *The Examinations, Arraignment and Conviction of George Sprot*, etc., 1608, where, speaking of King James, Abbot says thus:

. . . whose life hath been so immaculate and unspotted in the world, so free from all touch of viciousness and staining imputation, that even malice itself, which leaveth nothing unsearched, could never find true blemish in it, nor cast probable aspersion on it. Zealous as David; learned

oratorio mentioned below) was performed at Great St Mary's Church for the benefit of Addenbrooke's Hospital. Cf. *ante* 9 July 1772 n. 1.

3. By Handel; it was first performed in 1747.

4. *Biographia Britannica*[2] vol. 1.

5. Cole's quotation is not exact. The passage reads: 'Mr Walpole censures Mr Addison's character of Lord Somers, in the *Freeholder* (No. 39, May 4, 1716), as diffuse

and feeble; and says, that in truth he was sometimes as weak a writer, when he wrote seriously, as he was admirable in touching the delicacies of natural humour (*Royal and Noble Authors*, vol. ii, pp. 107–10 [2d edn, 1759]). But a few passages, which may be thought exceptionable, can by no means justify so severe a charge.'

6. The life of George Abbot (1562–1633), Abp of Canterbury.

and wise, the Solomon of our age; religious as Josias; careful of spreading Christ's faith as Constantine the Great; just as Moses; undefiled in all his ways as a Jehosaphat or Hesekias; full of clemency as another Theodosius.

The editor then adds:

If Mr Walpole had seen this passage, he certainly would not have said that 'honest Abbot could not flatter.'[7]

When these hypercritics thus make it their business to pick holes in other people's works, how careful ought they not to be to let anything slip from their pens of the same kind? Yet I thi<nk th>e blunder in relation to Mr Prior, which they might easily have known, <as I th>ink they cite Swift's *Letters*, from whence I recollected the circumstance,[8] shows that they are not infallible, and that if a person was to make it his business to sit down and examine their own new articles, an abundant crop of things to be found fault with might be met there. In half a day's perusal I made a few memoranda of the sort.

I will trouble you no longer than to subscribe myself, dear Sir,

Your ever faithful and most obliged servant,

WM COLE

I hope for the future all admirers of Abbot will forget the blasphemous exclamation, as it has been called, of Whitgift at the Hampton Court Conference,[9] or at least acknowledge that the Puritans were as apt scholars in court idolatry as the clergy who had more exalted notions of church matters.

---

7. Kippis's note: '*Noble Authors*, vol. i, p. 174.' He refers to the second edition.

8. For Cole's quotation from Swift's *Letters*, see Appendix I, Cole to HW 28 May 1778, which was never sent to HW. The writers in the *Biographia Britannica* used a later edition of Swift's works (see ibid. 45, 54, 625, etc.).

9. Cole probably refers to the report that was circulated by Patrick Galloway, that 'the Archbishop [John Whitgift, (1530?–1604), Abp of Canterbury] and Bishops of London and Winchester fell down on their knees to the King, and desired

that all things might remain as they were, lest the Papists might think they had been in an error hitherto, and might say, they would persuade them to come to a Church having errors in it: and lest the Puritans should allege, they had been long persecuted unjustly. . . . And that at last the Archbishop and Bishop of London (as almost despairing of their cause) besought his Majesty to take their cause into his own hands, and to make some good end of it, as might stand with their credit' (John Strype, *The Life and Acts of John Whitgift*, 3 vols, Oxford, 1822, ii. 492).

From COLE, Saturday 4 July 1778

VA, Forster MS 110, f. 191. Cole kept no copy.
Address: For the Honourable Horace Walpole at Strawberry Hill in Twickenham, Middlesex. *Postmark:* Cambridge 5 IY.

Saturday, July 4, 1778, Milton.

Dear Sir,

I WENT to Cambridge yesterday and saw Mr Lort, who returns to town on Tuesday and engages to deliver my packet[1] into your own hands either in Arlington Street or at Strawberry Hill, for it seems he is to preach at Twickenham on Sunday. He does the same at Ely tomorrow for the Dean,[2] who is not well, and will take the parcel in his pocket either going or coming back.

Poor Mr Tyson had like to have made a fatal exchange on Tuesday for a coffin instead of a marriage bed. He and the lady[3] dined with me on Sunday last and was to have been married on Tuesday and set off immediately for Essex, but a sudden putrid sore throat seized him that morning and prevented the nuptials. He was thought to have been in danger for some hours. I sent yesterday to hear after him, for I cannot walk, and found him got tolerably well again.

Miss Harrop[4] and other sirens have enchanted our academics beyond measure. Their performances are much extolled. I did not venture to church and the Senate House to hear them.

A person calling, gives me this opportunity of sending my letter to the post, though it won't set off from Cambridge till tomorrow evening.

I am, dear Sir, with the greatest esteem,

Your ever faithful servant,

WM COLE

1. Containing Cole's materials for the life of Baker.

2. Hugh Thomas, Dean of Ely.

3. Margaret Wale (fl. 1760–85), dau. of Hitch Wale of Shelford, and 'one of the prettiest and most amiable women' Cole ever met. She and Tyson were married 4 July 1778, the date of this letter (see Brydges, *Restituta* iv. 238–9). She m. (2) in

1784, J. Crouch, 'assistant clerk of the minutes of the custom house' (see GM Oct. 1784, liv. 796).

4. Sarah Harrop (d. 1811), soprano; m. (1780) Joah Bates (1741–99); a successful concert singer, especially of sacred music. Cole refers to her performance in the oratorio *Judas Maccabeus* (see preceding letter).

To Cole, Sunday 12 July 1778

Add MS 5953, ff. 28–9.
Address: To the Reverend Mr Cole at Milton near Cambridge.
Postmark: Isleworth 13 IY.

[Strawberry Hill,] July 12, 1778.

MR Lort has delivered your papers to me, dear Sir; and I have already gone through them. I will try if I can make anything of them, but fear I have not art enough, as I perceive there is absolutely but one fact, the expulsion. You have certainly very clearly proved that Mr Baker was neither supported by Mr Prior nor Bishop Burnet—but these are mere negatives. So is the question whether he intended to compile an *Athenae Cantabrigienses* or not; and on that you say but little, as you have not seen his papers in the Museum. I will examine the printed catalogue and try if I can discover the truth thence. When I go to town, I will also borrow the new *Biographia,* as I wish to know more of the expulsion. As it is our only fact, one would not be too dry on it. Upon the whole I am inclined to think that it would be preferable to draw up an ample character of Mr Baker, rather than a life.[1] The one was most beautiful, amiable, conscientious: the other totally barren of more than one event; and though you have taken excellent pains to discover all that was possible; yet there is an obscurity hangs over even the circumstances that did attend him; as his connection with Bishop Crewe[2] and his living. His own modesty comes out the brighter; but then it composes a character, not a life.

As to Mr Kippis and his censures, I am perfectly indifferent to them. He betrays a pert malignity in hinting an intention of being severe on my father, for the pleasure of exerting a right I allowed and do allow to be a just one—though it is not just to do it for *that* reason—however, let him say his pleasure. The truth will not hurt my father; falsehood will recoil on the author.

His asserting that my censure of Mr Addison's character of Lord Somers is not to be justified, is a silly *ipse dixit,* as he does not, in truth cannot, show why it is not to be justified. The passage I objected to is the argument of an old woman; and Mr Addison having

---

1. HW adhered to this plan, and his 'Life of Baker' is properly a character study.
2. Nathaniel Crew (1633–1721), 3d Bn

Crew of Stene, and Bp of Durham. For his connection with Baker, see Appendix I.

been a writer of true humour is not a justification of his reasoning like a superstitious gossip.

In the other passage you have sent me, Mr Kippis is perfectly in the right, and corrects me very justly. Had I ever seen Archbishop Abbot's preface with the outrageous mass of flattery on and lies of James I, I should certainly never have said, *Honest Abbot could not flatter*. I should have said, and do say, I never saw grosser perversion of truth. One can almost excuse the faults of James when his bishops were such base sycophants. What can a King think of human nature, when it produces such wretches? I am too impartial to prefer Puritans to clergy, or *vice versa*, when Whitgift and Abbot only ran a race of servility and adulation: the result is

That priests of all religions are the same.[3]

James and his Levites were worthy of each other; the golden calf and the idolaters were well coupled; and it is pity they ever came out of the wilderness.

I am very glad Mr Tyson has escaped death and disappointment; pray wish him joy of both from me. Has not this Indian summer dispersed your complaints? We are told we are to be invaded. Our Abbots and Whitgifts now see with what success and consequences their preaching up a crusade against America has been crowned! Archbishop Markham may have an opportunity of exercising his martial prowess.[4] I doubt he would resemble Bishop Crewe more than good Mr Baker. Let us respect only those that are Israelites indeed. I surrender Dr Abbot to you. Church and presbytery are human nonsense invented by knaves to govern fools. Church and kirk are terms for monopolies. *Exalted notions of church matters* are contradictions in terms to the lowliness and humility of the gospel. There is nothing sublime but the Divinity. Nothing is sacred but as His work. A tree or a brute stone is more respectable as such, than

3. 'For priests of all religions are the same.'—Dryden, *Absalom and Achitophel*, pt I, l. 99.
4. William Markham (1719–1807), Abp of York, was the author of *A Sermon* [on Daniel vii. 14] *preached before the . . . Society for the Propagation of the Gospel in Foreign Parts . . . February 21, 1777*, 1777, in which he spoke strongly in favour of submission from the American colonies,

and criticized the opposition. On 30 May 1777, in the House of Lords, he was answered particularly by the D. of Grafton and Lord Shelburne. Markham 'rose with most intemperate pride and fury, and said, that though, as a Christian and bishop, he ought to bear wrongs, there were injuries that would provoke any patience, and that he, if insulted, *should know how to chastise any petulance*' (*Last Journals* ii. 29).

a mortal called an archbishop, or an edifice called a church, which are the puny and perishable productions of men. Calvin and Wesley had just the same views as the Popes; power and wealth, their objects. I abhor both, and admire Mr Baker.

PS. I like Popery, as well as you, and have shown I do. I like it as I do chivalry and romance. They all furnish one with ideas and visions, which Presbyterianism does not. A Gothic church or convent fill one with romantic dreams—but for the mysterious, the Church in the abstract, it is a jargon that means nothing or a great deal too much, and I reject it and its apostles from Athanasius to Bishop Keene.[5]

From Cole, Sunday 19 July 1778

VA, Forster MS 110, f. 192. Cole kept no copy.

Address: For the Honourable Horace Walpole at Strawberry Hill in Twickenham, Middlesex. *Postmark:* Cambridge 20 IY.

Sunday, Milton, July 19, 1778.

Dear Sir,

I HAVE only to thank you for yours of the 12th instant, and to say that I am sorry the materials are not sufficient to the design of a life of Mr Baker. As that is the case, I shall be glad to have his char-

---

5. Cole has the following note at the end of his copy of HW's letter (Add MS 5824, f. 157v): 'I make no doubt but Mr Walpole is sincere in what he writes: that he thinks himself impartial too I am as clear of, but my notions of men and things are as utterly different as light and darkness, yet I am as sincere. So that what can be said on a subject so perplexing, when two persons equally sincere see the same object through a medium so different!—except that Mr Walpole, with more wit, vivacity, learning and judgment, can penetrate more nicely into religion, history and politics than one of a more confined and obtuse understanding. Yet his abilities do not convince, nor even perplex me. Mr Walpole is piqued, I can see, at my reflections on Abbot's flattery, and is even driven to Quaker arguments to oppose an expression I made use

of. When the nobility and great people, who are to set examples to the clergy and lower class, will lead the way to the humility prescribed in the Gospel, it will then be a shame for any set of clergy or laity to entertain exalted notions of church matters. But the true state of the case is this: the nobility are willing enough to see the clergy low and humble, however loath they are to be so themselves, and take my word for it, whatever is the practice of the higher order will, in a degree, be that of the inferior part of the world.

Regis ad exemplum totus componitur orbis. [Cf. Claudian, *De Quarto Consulatu Honorii Augusti Panegyris* ll. 299–300.]

But, as I hinted in my letter, I do believe King James's character to have been most

acter by a pencil like yours, and quite satisfied that you model them into what form will please you best. I am certain I shall be pleased in whatever way it is done.

Mr Tyson has left college this fortnight, and married. He is settled at Chigwell within two or three miles of his living[1] in Essex, till his own house can be ready to receive him. I have sent him your civil message.

This Indian weather, as you aptly term it, has put leathern <shoes> on both my feet, which had not had them on for two years before. The gouty complaints are not so prevalent, yet I cannot be well, and believe I never shall again. I rejoice at your spirits, and may you long enjoy them, with health and every other blessing.

I had two young men of Queen's College to dinner here yesterday: one of them, Mr Bridges,[2] who, I think, though am not clear about it, knows you. He is a native of Kent. I am not much acquainted with him, but as he is a lover and collector of prints, that has drawn us together. This gentleman yesterday told me that Mr Gray was going to have a monument erected for him in Westminster Abbey, and that there were only four verses to be put under his bust.[3] Perhaps you may know more of this matter than I do. I understood that Mr Mason has the management of it.

I am, dear Sir,

Your ever faithful and obedient servant,

WM COLE

vilely outraged and abused by the patriots, republicans and puritans in his time, and their malicious impressions and invectives abundantly heightened and improved by their successors in our time, and my reason for saying so is what Fuller, no prejudiced writer in favour of high churchmen, has said of Dr Townson in his [*Worthies of England,* 1662] *Worthies of Cambridgeshire* 154.'

1. Lambourne.
2. Edward Tymewell Brydges (1749–1807), elder brother of Sir Samuel Egerton Brydges (1762–1837), Queens' College (B.A. 1771). On the death of the D. of Chandos in 1789, he, at his brother's suggestion, preferred his claim to the barony of Chandos,

but it was not allowed (see DNB, *sub* Brydges, Sir Samuel Egerton). Cole was mistaken in supposing that he was acquainted with HW (see following letter).

3. The monument was executed by John Bacon (1740–99) at the joint expense of Mason, Brown and Stonehewer, and is placed immediately under the monument to Milton. The following epitaph by Mason appears on it:

No more the Grecian Muse unrivall'd
   reigns,
  To Britain let the nations homage pay;
She felt a Homer's fire in Milton's strains,
  A Pindar's rapture from the lyre of Gray.

(See *The Works of William Mason,* 4 vols, 1811, i. 141.)

To Cole, Friday 24 July 1778

Add MS 5953, ff. 30–1.

Cole has made the following notes on the cover for his letters of 4 and 17 Aug. 1778:

'Bishop Ralph de Walpole's monument in the cloister and inscription.

'In *Gentleman's Magazine*, p. 321, for July, is K[ippis]'s note relating to your charge against the old *Biographia Britannica,* and the hinting of not being too milky in respect to your father. I suspect the whole article is a puff of the work from the editors, to recommend it and make it known.

'At pp. 324–5 [of the same number of the *Gentleman's Magazine*], a sort of critique upon *The Castle of Otranto.*

'In the *Critical Review* for last month, p. 9, is an advertisement from Lord Hardwick apologizing for his printing the letter about Jane Shore. It looks as if his Lordship was very familiar with these Critics.'

The notes were used and marked through (see *post* 4 and 17 Aug. 1778).

Address: To the Reverend Mr Cole at Milton near Cambridge.

Postmark: 25 IY.

Strawberry Hill, July 24, 1778.

UPON reviewing your papers, dear Sir, I think I can make more of them than I at first conceived. I have even commenced the life, and do not dislike my ideas for it, if the execution does but answer. At present I am interrupted by another task, which you too have wished me to undertake. In a word, somebody has published Chatterton's works, and charged me heavily for having discountenanced him. He even calls for the indignation of the public against me.[1] It is somewhat singular that I am to be offered up as a victim at the altar of a notorious impostor! but as many saints have been impostors, so many innocent persons have been sacrificed to them. However, I shall not be patient under this attack, but shall publish an answer, and the narrative I mentioned to you. I would, as you

1. Chatterton's *Miscellanies in Prose and Verse,* 1778, was edited by John Broughton, whose remarks in the preface have haunted HW's reputation ever since: 'One of his [Chatterton's] first efforts, to emerge from a situation so irksome to him, was an application to a gentleman well known in the republic of letters; which unfortunately for the public, and himself, met with a very cold reception; and which the disappointed author always spoke of with a high degree of acrimony, whenever it was mentioned to him' (pp. xviii–xix).

'. . . perhaps he ['the reader'] may feel some indignation against the person to whom his first application was made, and by whom he was treated with neglect and contempt. It were to be wished that the public was fully informed of all the circumstances attending that unhappy application; the event of which deprived the world of works which might have contributed to the honour of the nation, as well as the comfort and happiness of their unfortunate author' (pp. xx–xxi).

know, have avoided entering into this affair, if I could; but as I do not despise public esteem, it is necessary to show how groundless the accusation is. Do not speak of my intention, as perhaps I shall not execute it immediately.

I am not in the least acquainted with the Mr Bridges you mention, nor know that I ever saw him.

The tomb for Mr Gray is actually erected, and at the generous expense of Mr Mason, and with an epitaph of four lines, as you heard, and written by him²—but the scaffolds are not yet removed. I was in town yesterday and intended to visit it,³ but there is digging a vault for the family of Northumberland, which obstructs the removal of the boards.

I rejoice in your amendment, and reckon it among my obligations to the fine weather, and hope it will be the most lasting of them.

Yours ever,

H. W.

From Cole, Tuesday 4 August 1778

VA, Forster MS 110, ff. 193–4. Cole's copy, Add MS 5824, f. 158v.

In connection with this letter, see introductory note to HW's letter to Cole 24 July 1778.

Address: The Honourable Mr Horace Walpole at Strawberry Hill in Twickenham, Middlesex. *Postmark:* Cambridge 5 AV.

Milton, Aug. 4, 1778.

Dear Sir,

I KNOW I sent you my papers in sad confusion, but I was not, nor have I been for some time in a mood or disposition to do anything but collect, and never to combine. You would be able to judge upon sight whether from such a rude mass you could erect a sightly edifice. I knew your powers and abilities, and never for a moment doubted of them, so that the lime, mortar, bricks and other materials were worthy to be worked with, and the subject approved of. Of the last I have not the least doubt, as in frequent dispatches I have dis-

---

2. See preceding letter. Mason bore only one-third of the expense.

3. See HW to Charles Bedford 22 July 1778.

covered your value for the amiable and virtuous qualities of Mr
Baker. It delights me that you have began [*sic*] his life. I wanted only
that, for as to the execution, I am quite satisfied about it; let it be
done in what manner you please, I shall be thoroughly satisfied: it
cannot but be complete if it comes from Strawberry Hill. I am only
concerned for the interruption, but as Mr Lort[1] communicated to
me your narrative,[2] I presume you have finished, in a manner, what
you have to say on that subject, which will convince the world both
of your humanity and tenderness for the young man, of your innocence in respect to his exit, and the impracticability of his making
you a dupe to his forgeries.

I never pretend to more than I know: poetry and criticism are as
much out of my element as to dissert about the excellencies of De-
mosthenes or the divinity of Plato; yet, dabbling into Rowley's *Poems*
when they[3] first appeared, I had no opinion of their genuineness. I
always objected to Dr Glynn and Mr Lort, the enthusiasts in their
favour, the name of Sir Charles Baldwin: the Christian name Charles
was rarely in use in England till the Stuarts put it in fashion, and
though Sir Charles Brandon[4] and a very small number of instances
to the contrary, probably from Charles V,[5] may be met with among
us, yet they are so few that that alone staggered my faith about them,
besides the utter improbability of such a poet as Rowley, coeval with
Lidgate and Gower,[6] being unnoticed and unheard of, insomuch
that we are yet to learn whether he was a regular or secular priest.
In William of Worcester,[7] lately printed, a native of Bristol as well
as Rowley, one who talks so much of Canning and the city of Bristol,
can we suppose that he would not have mentioned a poet who would
have added such lustre to the place of his nativity had such a person
existed in reality? I desired Dr Glynn and mentioned it to Lort, both
of whom I think have made two journeys to Bristol on this sole occasion, two years ago, that since they spared no pains or trouble
about it, to search Bishop Carpenter[8] of Worcester's register or the
registers there, in order to find his name entered, which it would

---

1. 'this last week has been at Cambridge,
and . . .' (addition in Cole's copy).

2. The 'narrative' as Cole saw and transcribed it was merely HW's letter to Bewley 23 May 1778. See *ante* 3 June 1778.

3. MS reads *the*.

4. (ca 1484–1545), Kt, Vct Lisle and 1st
D. of Suffolk; soldier and statesman.

5. King of France, 1364–80.

6. John Lydgate (1370?–1451?) and John
Gower (1325?–1408).

7. His *Itineraria*; see *ante* 16 Apr. 1778.

8. John Carpenter (d. 1476), Bp of
Worcester 1444–76.

RALPH WALPOLE, BISHOP OF ELY

probably be although a regular, and certainly if a secular and beneficed in the diocese. I know not whether they followed my direction.

I was in hopes of getting a MS life of a contemporary of Mr Baker
at the College,⁹ in which I did not despair <of m>eeting something
to the purpose, but as a wedding is in the family, and al<l in a
hu>rry, I question whether they have time to think of anything else.

In writing some account of the Bishops of Ely, I have occasionally
mentioned Ralph de Walpole¹⁰ and your effigies of him in the cloister. If you have a draft of it, and the inscription, I shall be glad of
them.

I am, dear Sir,

Your most obliged and affectionate servant,

WM COLE

To Cole, Saturday 15 August 1778

Add MS 5953, ff. 32–3.
Address: To the Reverend Mr Cole at Milton near Cambridge.
Postmark: Isleworth 15 AV.

Strawberry Hill, Aug. 15, 1778.

YOUR observation of Rowley not being mentioned by William
of Wyrcestre is very strong indeed, dear Sir, and I shall certainly take notice of it.¹ It has suggested to me too that he is not
named by Bale or Pitts, is he? Will you trouble yourself to look? I
conclude he is not, or we should have heard of it. Rowley is the reverse of King Arthur and all those heroes that have been expected
a second time; he is to come again for the first time—I mean, as a
great poet.

My defense² amounts to thirty pages of the size of this paper; yet

9. Presumably St John's College.

10. (d. 1302), Bp of Ely 1299–1302. 'In
the winding cloisters on the right hand,' as
one entered SH through 'the great north
gate,' was 'a brass plate with the effigies of
Ralph Walpole, Bishop of Norwich and
Ely, engraven by Müntz (a Swiss painter
who lived some time with Mr Walpole)'
(*Description of SH, Works* ii. 400 n). See illustration. This drawing was made, prob-

ably by G. P. Harding, for one of Kirgate's
extra-illustrated copies of the *Description
of SH*. It is now WSL.

1. For HW's use of Cole's information,
see his *Letter to the Editor* 31–2 nn
(*Works* iv. 221 n).

2. *Letter to the Editor.* At this time it
apparently was in or very near its final
form.

I believe I shall not publish it. I abhor a controversy, and what is it to me whether people believe in an impostor or not? Nay, shall I convince everybody of my innocence, though there is not a shadow of reason for thinking I was to blame? If I met a beggar in the street, and refused him sixpence, thinking him strong enough to work, and two years afterwards he should die of drinking, might not I be told I had deprived the world of a capital rope-dancer? In short, to show oneself sensible to such accusations, would only invite more; and since they accuse me of contempt, I will have it for my accusers.

My brass plate for Bishop Walpole was copied exactly from the print in Dart's *Westminster* of the tomb of Robert Dalby Bishop of Durham, with the sole alteration of the name.[3]

I shall return, as soon as I have time, to Mr Baker's Life; but I shall want to consult you, or at least the account of him in the new *Biographia,* as your notes want some dates. I am not satisfied yet with what I have sketched; but I shall correct it. My small talent was grown very dull. This attack about Chatterton has a little revived it; but it warns me to have done, for if one comes to want provocatives, the produce will soon be feeble. Adieu!

Yours most sincerely,
H. W.

From Cole, Monday 17 August 1778

VA, Forster MS 110, ff. 195–6. Cole's copy, Add MS 5824, f. 159v.

In connection with this letter, see introductory note to HW to Cole 24 July 1778.

Address: The Honourable Horace Walpole, Strawberry Hill in Twickenham, Middlesex. *Postmark:* Cambridge 20 AV.

Milton, Aug. 17, 1778, Monday, but the post goes not out from Cambridge till tomorrow.

Dear Sir,

WITHOUT any kind of expectation to meet with Rowley in Bale or Pits, I have searched the indexes of both, for in quest of such a great poet or notorious imposter no doubt all the purlieus

---

3. HW refers to the tomb of Robert Walby or Waldby (d. 1398), Abp of York, in the Chapel of St Edmund in Westminster Abbey. The print (in John Dart,

of every city, borough, village and hamlet have been ransacked by those who are interested in finding him out.

I am sorry you mean not to publish your narrative. As I have a copy of it, it can make no great odds to me, but I have another reason for my concern. You told me in a former letter that you meant to do so, and at the same time you gave me a caution not to say anything about it, as you was not positively determined. I never opened my lips till Saturday evening, when Dr Glynn called here to drink coffee, when, knowing that Mr Lort had mentioned it already,[1] I made no scruple to read to him some passages in it, particularly relating to your having never seen him, of which he was persuaded that you had. He was delighted with it, and asked me to let him have it home, and it was a trifle that would have turned the scale, as I really thought it printed already and near publication. But if your narrative takes up thirty small quarto sheets of your writing, surely that lent me by Mr Lort in his own handwriting can't be the same, for it makes only eight or nine of mine in my book, viz., exactl$<$y two$>$[1a] folio leaves or four half-sheets in my book. Dr Glynn is full as earnest in his research after Rowley as ever, and speaks indifferently of Mr Lort, to whom he communicated all his knowledge on the subject, for his retentiveness to him on the subject.[2] He went to Bath and Bristol some four or five months ago, and till last Saturday [I] had not seen or heard of him, though he has been returned this month or six weeks for the same period.

What I am going to mention is not my interest to do so, as it may still interrupt Mr Baker. Dr Glynn mentioned that in the late publication of Chatterton's *Poems,* which I have not seen, that one of them was glancing at your *Castle of Otranto,* and done in resentment, as he supposed, for your neglect of him.[3] I told him that I had seen (and which I had made a memorandum of, in order to com-

---

Westmonasterium, [1742?], i. 127) represents Waldby in his mass-habit; the inscription is a line of Latin on each of the four sides of the plate. HW's error may be partly accounted for: in Dart, ibid. i. 71, Waldby is listed as 'Robert Walby, Bishop of Durham,' but this error is corrected in pp. 126–8 and 'Dalby' is probably a mere slip of the pen, influenced by 'Dart' and 'Durham.'

———

1. '(the Master of Emmanuel [Richard Farmer] told me Aug. 7 that he had mentioned the narrative to him)' (addition in Cole's copy).

1a. Figure supplied from Cole's copy.

2. For Lort's denial of the charge that he withheld information, see *ante* 14 June 1778.

3. HW figures in Chatterton's 'Memoirs of a Sad Dog,' first printed in *The Town and Country Magazine,* July and August 1770 (ii. 374–6, 431–3), and reprinted in his *Miscellanies,* 1778, pp. 184–208. HW is 'the

municate to you the first opportunity) a sort of oblique criticism on that book in an account of a late romance called *The English Baron* in *The Gentleman's Magazine* for last month, pp. 324–5.[4] He said it was not that, so I leave it with you, as I have not the book.

In the same magazine, at p. 321, is Kippis's note in relation to your charge against the old Biographers, with his impertinent hint of not being *too milky*, etc.[5] But I suspect the whole article, which is a long one, to be a puff of the new *Biography* from the editors to recommend it and to make it more publicly known.

Now I am on this subject, I am <also to in>form you of what perhaps may not have fallen in your way, except you tak<e in the> *Critical Review*, that in the last,[6] at p. 9, is a formal advertisement from Lord Hardwicke, apologizing for his printing the letter about Jane Shore. It looks extremely as if his Lordship was very familiar and in close connection with these Critics. I can give a sort of guess how it came there. The apology is ruder than the insertion.[7]

I would not repeat it, but I know by Mr Lort that you have already packed up the prints[8] you was so kind to promise me for Mr Kerrick. His impatience about them almost make[s] me impertinent.

I am, dear Sir,

Your most obliged and faithful servant,

WM COLE

redoubted Baron Otranto, who has spent his whole life in conjectures.' He reads the faint characters on a broken stone (the original inscription was, 'James Hicks lieth here, with Hester his wife') as 'Hic jacet corpus Kenelmae Legero. Requiescat, etc., etc. . . . Elated with the happy discovery, the baron had an elegant engraving of the curiosity executed, and presented it to the Society of Antiquaries' (*Miscellanies* 198–202).

4. The reviewer of Clara Reeve's *English Baron*, 1778, says that 'the author has endeavoured . . . to avoid what she deems the only fault in *Otranto*, viz., "such a degree of the marvellous as excites laughter."' Miss Reeve's preface is almost entirely devoted to *The Castle of Otranto*.

5. For this note, see *ante* 14 June 1778. It appears in a review of *Biographia Britannica²*, vol. 1, in GM July 1778, xlviii, 320–2.

6. That is, for July.

7. HW first printed the letter from Richard III to the Bp of Lincoln in *Historic Doubts*, 1768, pp. 118–9, as he notes in his copy of Hardwicke's *Miscellaneous State Papers* i. 573–4, where it is reprinted without acknowledgment to HW. Hardwicke's apology appears at the end of a review of *State Papers*: 'The editor of this collection wishes for an opportunity of acknowledging his mistake in giving the letter about Jane Shore, as printed for the first time, when it had been already communicated to the public by Mr Walpole, in his *Historical Doubts*. Should these *Papers* come to a second edition, the error shall be set right, by omitting this letter, and inserting some other' (*Critical Review*, Ser. I, vol. 46, p. 9). Cole's 'guess how it came there' is not further explained.

8. From *Anecdotes*.

To Cole, Saturday 22 August 1778

Add MS 5953, ff. 34–5.

Address: [From Cole's copy, Add MS 5824, f. 159v.] To the Rev. Mr Cole at Milton near Cambridge.

Strawberry Hill, Aug. 22, 1778.

I BEG you will feel no uneasiness, dear Sir, at having shown my narrative[1] to Dr Glynn. I can never suspect you, who are always giving me proofs of your friendship and solicitude for my reputation, of doing anything unkind. It is true, I do not think I shall publish anything about Chatterton. Is not it an affront to innocence not to be perfectly satisfied in her? My pamphlet, for such it would be, is four times as large as the narrative in your hands, and I think, would not discredit me—but in truth I am grown much fonder of peace than fame; and scribblers or their patrons shall not provoke me to sacrifice the one to the other. Lord Hardwicke, I know, has long been my enemy—latterly, to get a sight of the Conway papers,[2] he has paid great court to me, which, to show how little I regarded his enmity, I let him see, at least the most curious. But as I set as little value on his friendship, I did not grant another of his requests. Indeed I have made more than one foe by not indulging the vanity of those that have made application to me; and I am obliged to them when they augment my contempt by quarrelling with me for that refusal. It was the case of Mr Masters,[3] and is now of Lord Hardwicke. He solicited me to reprint his Boeotian volume of Sir Dudley Carleton's papers,[4] for which he had two motives. The first he inherited from his father, the desire of saving money; for though his fortune is so much larger than mine, he knew I would not let out my press for hire, but should treat him with the expense, as I have done for those I have obliged. The second inducement was, that the rarity of my editions makes them valuable, and though I cannot make men read dull books, I can make them purchase them. His Lordship therefore has bad grace in affecting to overlook one whom he had in vain courted; yet he again is grown my enemy, because I

1. That is, Cole's copy of HW's letter to Bewley 23 May 1778.

2. See HW to Montagu 20 Aug. 1758; to Conway 2 Sept. 1758; and to Zouch 5 Oct. 1758. They were edited by Marjorie Hope Nicolson in *Conway Letters, the* *Correspondence of Anne, Viscountess Conway, Henry More, and their Friends, 1642–1684,* New Haven, 1930.

3. It is not known what Masters offered to the SH Press.

4. See HW to Hardwicke 12 Jan. 1775.

would not be my own. For my writings they do not depend on him or the venal authors he patronizes (I doubt very frugally) but on their own merits or demerits. It is from men of sense they must expect their sentence, not from boobies, and hireling authors; whom I have always shunned with the whole fry of minor wits, critics and monthly censors. I have not seen the review you mention, nor ever do, but when something particular is pointed out to me. Literary squabbles I know preserve one's name, when one's works will not; but I despise the fame that depends on scolding till one is remembered—and remembered by whom? the scavengers of literature! Reviewers are like sextons, who in a charnel-house can tell you to what John Thompson or what Tom Matthews such a skull or such belonged—but who wishes to know? The fame that is only to be found in such vaults, is like the fires that burn unknown in tombs, and go out as fast as they are discovered. Lord Hardwicke is welcome to live amongst the dead if he likes it, and can contrive to exist nowhere else.

Chatterton did abuse me under the title of Baron of Otranto, but unluckily the picture is much more like Dr Milles and Chatterton's own devotees than to me, who am but a recreant antiquary, and as the poor lad found by experience, did not swallow every fragment that was offered to me as antique; though that is a feature he has bestowed on me.

I have seen too the criticism you mention on *The Castle of Otranto* in the preface to *The English Baron*. It is not at all oblique, but though mixed with high compliments, directly attacks the visionary part, which, says the author, or authoress, makes one laugh. I do assure you I have not had the smallest inclination to return that attack. It would even be ungrateful, for the work is a professed imitation of mine, only stripped of the marvellous; and so entirely stripped, except in one awkward attempt at a ghost or two, that it is the most insipid dull nothing you ever saw. It certainly does not make one laugh, for what makes one doze, seldom makes one merry.

I am very sorry to have talked for near three pages on what relates to myself, who should be of no consequence, if people did not make me so, whether I will or not. My not replying to them, I hope, is a proof I do not seek to make myself the topic of conversation—how very foolish are the squabbles of authors! They buzz and are troublesome for a day, and then repose forever on some shelf in a college library close by their antagonists, like Henry VI and Edward IV at Windsor.[5]

I shall be in town in a few days, and will send you the heads of painters, which I left there; and along with them for yourself a translation of a French play that I have just printed here.[6] It is not for your reading, but as one of the Strawberry editions, and one of the rarest, for I have printed but 75 copies. It was to oblige Lady Craven, the translatress; and will be an aggravation of my offences to *Sir Dudley Statepapers*.[7]

I hope this Elysian summer, for it is above Indian, has dispersed all your complaints. Yet it does not agree with fruit; the peaches and nectarines are shrivelled to the size of damsons, and half of them drop. Yet you remember what portly bellies the peaches had at Paris, where it is generally as hot. I suppose our fruit trees are so accustomed to rain, that they don't know how to behave without it. Adieu!

Yours ever,

H. W.

PS. I can divert you with a new adventure that has happened to me in the literary way. About a month ago I received a letter from a Mr Jonathan Scott[8] at Shrewsbury, to tell me he was possessed of a MS of Lord Herbert's account of the court of France, which he designed to publish by subscription, and which he desired me to sub-

---

5. Henry VI and Edward IV are buried in the Royal Chapel at Windsor: the former at the east end of the north aisle, and the latter near the choir door in the opposite aisle. Cf. Pope:

Let softer strains ill-fated Henry mourn,
And palms eternal flourish round his urn.
Here o'er the martyr-king the marble weeps,
And, fast beside him, once-feared Edward sleeps: . . .
The grave unites; where ev'n the great find rest,
And blended lie th' oppressor and th' oppressed!
—'Windsor Forest,' ll. 311–8.

6. *The Sleep-Walker, a Comedy: In two Acts. Translated from the French, in March. M.DCC.LXXVIII*, SH, 1778. The author of the original play (*Le Somnam-*

bule) was Antoine de Ferriol (1697–1774), Comte de Pont-de-Veyle, one of Mme du Deffand's most intimate friends (see her letters, *Paris Jour.*, and HW to Gray 25 Jan. 1766). The play was translated by Elizabeth Berkeley (1750–1828), Baroness Craven, afterwards (1791) Margravine of Anspach. According to HW's entry in *Jour. Print. Off.*, the printing of the play was not finished until 30 Aug. (see *Jour. Print. Off.* 19, 63).

7. Lord Hardwicke, the editor of Sir Dudley Carleton's *Letters*, and *State Papers*.

8. The correspondence between HW and Scott is missing. As Scott died in Aug. 1778, HW heard no more of his plan of publishing Lord Herbert's account. See DNB, *sub* John Scott [afterwards -Waring] (1747–1819). The whereabouts of the MS of Lord Herbert's account is not known.

scribe to, and to assist in the publication. I replied, that having been obliged to the late Lord Powis and his widow,[9] I could not meddle with any such thing, without knowing it had the consent of the present earl[10] and his mother. Another letter, commending my reserve, told me Mr Scott had applied for it formerly and would again now. This showed me they did not consent. I have just received a third letter, owning the approbation is not yet arrived; but to keep me employed in the meantime, the modest Mr Scott, whom I never saw, nor know more of than I did of Chatterton, proposes to me to get his fourth son[11] a place in the civil department in India, the father not choosing it should be in the military, his three elder sons being engaged in that branch already[12]—If this fourth son breaks his neck, I suppose it will be laid to my charge!

PS. 25th. I shall [send] the prints to the coach tomorrow.

From COLE, Saturday 29 August 1778

VA, Forster MS 110, ff. 197–8. COLE's copy, Add MS 5824, ff. 163v, 164v.
Address: The Honourable Horace Walpole, Strawberry Hill, Twickenham, Middlesex. Free S. Gideon. *Postmark:* 4 SE.

Milton, Aug. 29, 1778, Saturday.

Dear Sir,

LAST night I received the packet of prints and play, and am greatly obliged to you for both. The prints will make Mr Kerrich happy, and I am already, and by the enclosed[1] you will see I am going to be further obliged to him. I sat for my picture last year to

9. Henry Arthur Herbert (1703?–72), 1st E. (n.c.) of Powis, m. (1751) Barbara Antonia Herbert (1735–86?). HW was indebted to them for permission to print *The Life of Edward Lord Herbert of Cherbury* at SH in 1764.

10. George Edward Henry Arthur Herbert (1755–1801), 2d E. of Powis.

11. Scott's fourth son, Folliott, did not go to India, but his fifth son, Henry, entered the service of the East India Company, and became commissioner of police at Bombay. He later returned to Shrewsbury (see Burke, *Commoners* ii. 505).

12. The sons were: John Scott (1747–1819), afterwards Scott-Waring, the zealous but tactless agent for Warren Hastings; Richard Scott (d. before 1829), a Lieutenant-Colonel; and Jonathan Scott (1754–1829), the orientalist. They went to India together in 1767.

———

1. A letter from Tyson to Cole 21 Aug. 1778 (see below). Kerrich had promised to send Tyson a portrait of Cole.

him, and now Mr Tyson desires it. He is very happy in taking like-
nesses, but he does it in crayons, which I think has the least merit.

Lord Hardwick showed his judgment in endeavouring to connect
himself with you and your press: a person who so soon discovered
the forgeries of Chatterton was not likely to be caught by the cunning of the other. Though so humble as my station is, yet I never
could bring myself to pay the usual homage in fashion here, to go
and dine at Wimpole.[2] The natural and inherent meanness of the
whole race has ever disgus<ted> me, and though I have no reason
to think I should be worse re<ceive>d than anyone else, yet there is
something so very forbidding <in t>he manner of his Lordship that
I could never persuade myself to pay court to a person whom I could
not honour.

Thank God, this very burning summer, however disagreeable
otherwise, has chased the gout, and I have my leathern shoes on,
which I have not had for two years before, and never thought I ever
should again, yet I feel the symptoms, since the weather is altered,
in my feet, fingers and collar-bones. I never sent for fruit to Cambridge before the day before yesterday. My own garden has not a
peach, and only four nectarines, and Lord Montfort's garden is no
more,[3] where I used to have supplies. My servant brought me six
peaches, twopence each, which literally I would have thrown to the
hogs another year. Walnuts are the only fruit, if I may call them so,
and nonpareils, of which I have plenty in my poor garden. I am
sorry you are so badly off for wall-fruit, as I think you are fond of
them.

I am quite sorry for Mr Scott's assurance, for I suppose he is in
possession of the MS he mentions, and though your delicacy might
not choose to be concerned in the publication, yet I shall be heartily
glad to be a subscriber. Your specimen has given me a relish to his
(Lord Herbert's) manner, and his description of the court of France
must be curious and entertaining. I could wish your Chattertons and
Scotts would make their essays on less discerning persons, and that
the public might not suffer by such mortifying discouragements.

I send you the enclosed, which I received the same day with your

2. Lord Hardwicke's seat, in Cambridgeshire, near Royston, Herts.

3. Lord Montfort, 'having involved
himself in embarrassments,' was obliged to
advertise his estates for sale in 1776. Horse-

heath Hall had been stripped of its furniture in 1775, and the Hall itself was sold
in 1777 for the materials. The estate was
sold in 1783 to Stanlake Batson (see Ly-
sons, *Mag. Brit.* ii. 217).

last letter, not that you may see the compliments paid to me, but for the news it contains relating to Chatterton and the mention of your name in it.[4] I had desired Mr Tyso<n> (who lodges at Chigwell till he can get into his own parson<age> house at Lamborne,[5] adjoining) to take me a drawing of Archbishop Harsnet's monument.[6] You may send me the letter again if you have an opportunity. If not, please to burn it, for it is of no consequence.

I have just finished an account of a manor for Sir Sampson Gideon, the lord of it, and am sending it to him, so will send this double letter to him and beg him to frank it.

As you seem doubtful still about publishing your narrative, I am very glad, however, that I did not let Dr Glynn have it home with him, but am sorry still you do not print it.

That Mr Baker was generally supposed to have thoughts of writing an history of the Cambridge writers is evident from some quotations in my former papers on his subject. Mr Drake, in his *Eboracum*, p. 378, speaking of one Christopher Cartwright,[7] has this:

The account of this man is taken wholly from Sir Tho. Widdrington[8] for,

4. Cole kept a copy of Tyson's letter (Add MS 5824, ff. 161v, 162v) from which the following paragraphs are quoted:

'The publication of Chatterton's pieces are under the direction of Dr Percy and Stevens [George Steevens, the Shakespearean scholar], in order to renew the controversy about Rowley's poems. I hear the Dean of Exeter is going to publish a quarto edition of those poems, with notes to prove their antiquity. Heaven send him a good deliverance! Where is Mr Walpole? I long much to renew the honour of the connection and correspondence I once had with him, and wish I could do anything that might be acceptable to him.

'Mr Kerrich promised to send me a portrait of you. Pray tell him that I would rather have it than the whole *Capella Sistina*, and the Vatican into the bargain.'

Cole's copy of his reply to Tyson 29 Aug. 1778, contains the following paragraph:

'The same post which brought your obliging letter, conveyed one from Strawberry Hill. He [HW] tells me that he shall not publish his narrative about Chatterton, but if our Dean is going into the

world with a fresh edition of Rowley, with notes, etc., it may probably determine the publication of it: as some things may occasionally be thrown out, that may provoke him to it. As you mention his name with respect, with a desire of renewing your correspondence with him, without your leave I have taken the liberty to send your letter to him by this same post, and as I am writing to Sir Sampson Gideon, shall put all under a cover to him, and beg him to frank them' (Add MS 5824, f. 163v).

5. Tyson's house at Lambourne 'was occupied by his predecessor's family till Christmas, by agreement after a lawsuit' (Cole's note, Add MS 5824, f. 161v).

6. Samuel Harsnett (1561–1631), Abp of York, who founded schools at Chigwell, and was buried in the parish church, where is a fine brass, executed after his own design.

7. (1602–58), a clergyman in York.

8. Sir Thomas Widdrington (d. 1664), Kt; Speaker of the House of Commons, and author of a history of York, which was not published until 1897.

as the learned world is not yet made happy with a history of the Cambridge writers, though it is much expected from the labours of that great antiquary Mr. Baker of St. John's, I am not able to give any further intelligence concerning Mr. Cartwright's life and writings.

In a curious pedigree of Peverel and Peche, Barons of Brunne[9] in Cambridgeshire, lately put into my hands, I find John Walpole, who lived about the time of Edward II, as well as I can guess, married Elizabeth, the daughter of Gilbert de Peche, by Isolda his wife; which Elizabeth was great-great-granddaughter to Sir Hamon de Peche, who married Alicia, the daughter and heir of Pagan Peverel, temp. Henry I, and founder of Barnwell Abbey near <Cam>bridge. I see there are more Johns than one in your <pedi>gree, and about the time mentioned, but their matches are different. Perhaps this lady might have been a first or second wife.

I will tire you no longer than in repeating my thanks for your kindness to, dear Sir,

Your ever faithful and obliged servant,

WM COLE

Lord Montfort's servant was here yesterday. He tells me that his Lordship has an house at Sunbury in your neighbourhood, though I suppose you know nothing of him. I have not heard from him since he left Horseth four years ago.

To COLE, Tuesday 1 September 1778

Add MS 5953, ff. 36–7.

Address: [From COLE's copy, Add MS 5824, f. 164v.] Rev. Mr Cole at Milton near Cambridge.

[Strawberry Hill,] Sept. 1, 1778.

I HAVE now seen the *Critical Review* with Lord Hardwicke's note, in which I perceive the sensibility of your friendship for me, dear Sir, but no rudeness on his part. Contemptuous it was to reprint Jane Shore's letter without any notice of my having given it before; the apology too is not made to me—but I am not affected by

9. Cole's copy reads *Bourne.*

such incivilities, that imply more ill will than boldness. As I expected more from your representation, I believe I expressed myself with more warmth than the occasion deserved; and as I love to be just, I will, now I am perfectly cool, be so to Lord H. His dislike of me was meritorious in him, as I conclude it was founded on my animosity to *his* father, as mine had been, from attachment to *my own*, who was basely betrayed by the late Earl.[1] The present has given me formerly many peevish marks of enmity; and I suspect, I don't know if justly, that he was the mover of the cabal in the Antiquarian Society against me—but all their understandings were of a size that made me smile rather than provoked me. The Earl, as I told you, has since been rather wearisome in applications to me, which I received very civilly, but encouraged no farther. When he wanted me to be his printer, I own I was not good Christian enough, not to be pleased with refusing, and yet in as well-bred excuses as I could form, pleading, what was true at the time as you know, that I had laid down my press—but so much for this idle story. I shall think no more of it, but adhere to my pacific system. The antiquaries will be as ridiculous as they used to be; and since it is impossible to infuse taste into them, they will be as dry and dull as their predecessors. One may revive what perished, but it will perish again, if more life is not breathed into it than it enjoyed originally. Facts, dates and names will never please the multitude, unless there is some style and manner to recommend them, and unless some novelty is struck out from their appearance. The best merit of the Society lies in their prints; for their volumes,[2] no mortal will ever touch them but an antiquary. Their Saxon and Danish discoveries are not worth more than monuments of the Hottentots; and for Roman remains in Britain, they are upon a foot with what ideas we should get of Inigo Jones, if somebody was to publish views of huts and houses that our officers run up at Senegal and Goree. Bishop Lyttelton used to torment me with barrows and Roman camps, and I would as soon have attended to the turf graves in our churchyards. I have no curiosity to know how awkward and clumsy men have been in the dawn of arts or in their decay.

I exempt you entirely from my general censure on antiquaries,

1. Philip Yorke (1690–1764), 1st E. of Hardwicke. For HW's biased account of Hardwicke's character and his betrayal of Sir Robert Walpole, see *Mem. of the Reign of George II* i. 158–61.

2. *Archaeologia.*

both for your singular modesty in publishing nothing yourself, and for collecting stone and brick for others to build with. I wish your materials may ever fall into good hands—perhaps they will! Our empire is falling to pieces; we are relapsing to a little island. In that state, men are apt to inquire how great their ancestors have been; and when a kingdom is past doing anything, the few, that are studious, look into the memorials of past time; nations, like private persons, seek lustre from their progenitors, when they have none in themselves, and the farther they are from the dignity of their source. When half its colleges are tumbled down, the ancient University of Cambridge will revive from your collections, and you will be quoted as a living witness that saw it in its splendour!

Since I began this letter, I have had another curious adventure. I was in the Holbein chamber, when a chariot stopped at my door. A letter was brought up[3]—and who should be below but—Dr Kippis. The letter was to announce himself and his business; flattered me on my writings, desired my assistance, and particularly my direction and aid for his writing the life of my father. I desired he would walk up, and received him very civilly, taking not the smallest notice of what you had told me of his flirts at me in the new *Biographia*. I told him, that if I had been applied to, I could have pointed out many errors in the old edition, but as they were chiefly in the printing, I supposed they would be corrected. With regard to my father's life, I said, it might be partiality, but I had such confidence in my father's virtues, that I was satisfied the more his life was examined, the clearer they would appear. That I also thought that the life of any man written under the direction of his family, did nobody honour; and that as I was persuaded my father's would stand the test, I wished that none of his relations should interfere in it. That I did not doubt but the Doctor would speak impartially, and that was all I desired. He replied, that he did suppose I thought in that manner, and that all he asked was to be assisted in facts and dates. I said, if he would please to write the life first, and then communicate it to me, I would point out any errors in facts that I should perceive.[4] He seemed mighty well satisfied—and so we parted—but is it not odd, that people are continually attacking me, and then come to me for

---

3. The letter is missing.
4. As only five volumes and part of a sixth of the second edition of *Biographia*

Britannica were published, Kippis (presumably) never wrote the life of Sir Robert Walpole.

assistance?—but when men write for profit, they are not very delicate.

I have resumed Mr Baker's Life, and pretty well arranged my plan, but I shall have little time to make any progress till October, as I am going soon to make some visits.[5]

I hope you have received the heads of the painters.

Yours ever,

H. W.

From Cole, Thursday 3 September 1778

VA, Forster MS 110, ff. 199–200. Cole's copy, Add MS 5824, ff. 165v, 166v.
Address: For the Honourable Horace Walpole at Strawberry Hill in Twickenham, Middlesex. *Postmark:* Cambridge 4 SE.

Milton, Sept. 3, 1778, Thursday morning.

Dear Sir,

THIS moment the turnpike woman brought me your kind letter, which I ought to have had yesterday, but though I have wrote to you a week ago in answer to your former letter and to thank you for the prints, it is probable you may have not yet received it, as I sent that and another to Mr Tyson to Sir Sampson Gideon to frank for me, yours being a double one, and as I then thought him at Abington and was sending to him. Yesterday morning Sir <John> Cotton and Mr Greaves in their return from dining with <the Bishop> of Ely, called here in the morning (for they laid at Ely): Mr Greaves told me that Sir Sampson was in Sussex at Lord Gage's,[1] so whether they will send my letters after him, or keep them till his return, I don't know. Happily it is of no consequence either way.

I send this letter today, as my man passes through Cambridge to excuse my dining at Madingley, where Sir John had invited me yesterday, but a bad night without sleep, and a fresh attack of a dis-

5. In Sept. HW visited at Park Place (Conway's) and at Nuneham (Lord Harcourt's) (see HW to Harcourt 17 and 27 Sept. 1778).

1. William Hall Gage (1718–91), 2d Vct

Gage [I.], 1st Bn Gage of Firle [G.B. 1780] and of High Meadow [G.B. 1790], m. (1757) Elizabeth Gideon (1739–83), Sir Sampson's youngest sister. See Sir Herbert Croft, *Abbey of Kilkhampton,* 1780, p. 9.

order that weakens me exceedingly, and which had left me for three days after having been very troublesome for six or seven days and nights before, prevents my attempting to go out.

Lord Hardwicke's little enmities and meannesses are not unknown to this county. I heard a master of a college² say in public company last year, and before some of his particular friends who endeavoured to defend him, that when he and his brethren³ paid their annual dining visit, they were always glad to get into their coach, for if he said nothing offensive, which was sometimes the case, his behaviour was so chilling and forbidding that, was it not for the disrespect, he would never go again. I heard Mr Lort say much to the same purpose two years ago.⁴ Since that time he has paid greater court there, and perhaps may be better reconciled to his manner.

Dr Kippis's visit by no means surprises me. There are a certain set of people whose assurances are steeled to every modest feeling. He shows his judgment, however, to endeavour to conciliate your favour.

In your former letter you say the play is not for my reading. I have, however, read it, but I don't think it a translation.

Adieu, dear Sir, and with the truest esteem, I remain

Your ever faithful and obliged servant,

WM COLE

What you mention in respect to Lord Hardwicke being the mover of the cabal in the Antiquary Society against you may be very just, but of that I know nothing. But, following your good example of

2. 'Dr Farmer at Mr Tyson's before Mr and Mrs Chettoe, who would aim at defending him. Mr Masters, who agreed in the charge, was there also' (note in Cole's copy. It is enclosed in brackets, and marked by Cole, 'not sent'). Mr and Mrs John Chettoe of Chesterton, Cambs, were Cole's friends. He records that he dined with them, 3 Oct. 1778 (see Palmer, *Monumental Inscriptions* 248). Mrs Chettoe died 3 Feb. 1798, when she is referred to as the 'relict of John Chettoe, Esq.' (GM Feb. 1798, lxviii. 175b).

3. 'the heads of colleges' (Cole's note in his copy). Hardwicke was High Steward of the University and appears to have given them an official dinner.

4. Cole notes on his copy: 'What I allude to in respect to Mr Lort in the following letter is this: about two years ago, after a visit at Wimpole, where he unluckily called a spade a spade, viz., in speaking of the Grand Rebellion, he called it the Rebellion, with which Lord H. was so incensed that, although in his own house, he took a liberty of chiding Mr Lort, which was then much resented by him, as he told me himself. I remember Lord Clare [Robert Nugent (1720?–88), cr. (1766), Bn Nugent and Vct Clare, and afterwards (1776) E. Nugent] served me so at Lord Temple's [Richard Grenville-Temple (1711–79), 2d E. Temple] at Stow.'

being scrupulously just, I must acquit a person whom you have no reason to dislike, as he wrote so poorly against you, which is always an advantage, and whom I can never like for his dirtiness: I mean my neighbour Masters, who joins in the general cry about Lord Hardwicke, as I have often remarked. Indeed, I hardly ever heard one speak in his favour, so contemptible is his character, as also that of the whole *razzo*.

I have just been reading three numbers of an *History of Norfolk* under the direction of a Captain Gardiner,[5] who seems to be of a lively genius. Do you know anything of him?

I had almost forgotten to beg another favour for my friend Mr Kerrich: a ticket to see Strawberry Hill and its rarities. He goes to town about the exhibition time in the spring generally, and would be greatly delighted to see what he will not have an opportunity of seeing anywhere else.

To COLE, Thursday 10 September 1778

Add MS 5953, ff. 38–9.

Address: [From COLE's copy, Add MS 5824, f. 166v.] Rev. Mr Cole at Milton near Cambridge. Free T. Caswall.

Strawberry Hill, Sept. 10, 1778.

I WRITE a few words to satisfy you, dear Sir, that I received both your letters together. If I did not mention them, you might think the franked one had strayed.

I rejoice that the heat of the weather has been so serviceable to you, and I hope the little return of tenderness in your feet will not last, as the season continues so dry.

I have run through the new articles in the *Biographia,* and think them performed but with a heavy hand. Some persons have not trusted the characters of their ancestors, as I did my father's, to their

5. This is evidently the same work mentioned *ante* 10 May 1778. Richard Gardiner (1723–81), alias Dick Merryfellow, a captain (afterwards major) in the army, claimed to be the natural son of HW's brother, Lord Walpole (see Mann to HW 22 Sept. 1744). HW denied the relationship (HW to Mann 19 Oct. 1744), but Mr R. W. Ketton-Cremer writes that among the papers at Felbrigg Hall, Norfolk, is contemporary evidence of Lord Walpole's liaison with Gardiner's mother. See also *Memoirs of the Life and Writings . . . of R–ch––d G–rd–n–r, Esq.,* 1782, p. 34 and n. Gardiner was a second-rate satirist who 'prepared some articles for a projected county history of Norfolk,' but Cole is probably wrong in attributing to him the 'direction' of it.

own merit. On the contrary, I have met with one whose corruption
is attempted to be palliated by imputing its punishment to the revenge of *my father*—which by the way I think is confessing the guilt
of the convict. This was the late Lord Barrington,[1] who, I believe,
was a very dirty fellow, for, besides being expelled the House of
Commons on the affair of the Harburgh lottery, he was reckoned to
have twice sold the Dissenters to the Court—but in short what credit
can a *Biographia Britannica,* which ought to be a standard work, deserve, when the editor is a mercenary writer, who runs about to relations for directions, and adopts any tale they deliver to him? This
very instance is a proof that it is not a job more creditable than a
peerage. The authority is said to be a nephew of Judge Foster;[2] (consequently I suppose a friend of Judge Barrington)[3] and he pretends
to have found a scrap of paper, nobody knows on what occasion
written, that seems to be connected with nothing, and is called a
palliative, if not an excuse, of Lord B.'s crime. A man is expelled
from Parliament for a scandalous job, and it is called a sufficient excuse to say the minister was his enemy; and this near forty years
after the death of both! and without any impeachment of the justice
of the sentence! Instead of which we are told that Lord B. was *suspected* of having offended Sir R. W. who took that opportunity of
being revenged—Supposing he did, which at most you see was a
suspicion grounded on a suspicion, it would at least imply that he
had found a good opportunity—a most admirable acquittal! Sir
R. Walpole was expelled for having endorsed a note that was not for
his own benefit,[4] nor ever supposed to be, and it was the act of a
whole outrageous party; yet abandoned as Parliaments sometimes

1. John Shute Barrington (1678–1734),
1st Vct Barrington, who was expelled from
the House of Commons in 1723 for his
connection with the Harburg lottery.

2. Michael Dodson (1732-99), lawyer and
editor (see DNB), was the nephew of Sir
Michael Foster (1689–1763), judge of King's
Bench. Dodson communicated an unpublished account of the Harburg lottery affair, by Judge Foster, which, according to
Kippis, 'will greatly contribute to extenu-
ate, if not justify, the conduct of his lordship in this transaction.' In the last paragraph are these remarks by Judge Foster:
'This matter [of the Harburg lottery] was
made an occasion of bringing this severe
censure [expulsion from the House of
Commons] on Lord Barrington; who was
suspected to have formerly taken some
steps very disagreeable to the reigning
minister, Sir Robert Walpole . . . [who]
could not forget the part which Lord Barrington had acted against him' (*Biographia Britannica*[2] i. 625–6 nn).

3. Hon. Daines Barrington (1727–1800),
son of 1st Vct Barrington; antiquary and
naturalist; correspondent of Gilbert White.

4. He was expelled from the House of
Commons and imprisoned in the Tower in
1712 on a charge of venality in the Navy
Office.

are, a minister would not find them very complaisant in gratifying his private revenge against a member, without some notorious crime. Not a syllable is said of any defence the culprit made; and had my father been guilty of such violence and injustice, it is totally incredible that he, whose minutest acts and his most innocent, were so rigorously scrutinized, tortured and blackened, should never have heard that act of power complained of. The present Lord Barrington,[5] who opposed him, saw his fall, and the Secret Committee appointed to canvass his life, and when a retrospect of twenty years was denied, and only ten allowed, would certainly have pleaded for the longer term, had he had anything to say in behalf of his father's sentence. Would so warm a patriot then, though so obedient a courtier now, have suppressed the charge to this hour? This Lord B. when I was going to publish the second edition of my *Noble Authors,* begged it as a favour of me to suppress all mention of his father[6]—a strong presumption that he was ashamed of him—I am well repaid! but I am certainly at liberty now to record that good man. I shall—and shall take notice of the satisfactory manner in which his sons have whitewashed their patriarch![7]

I recollect a saying of the present peer that will divert you, when contrasted with forty years of servility, which even in this age makes him a proverb. It was in his days of virtue. He said, 'If I should ever be so unhappy as to have a place, that would make it necessary for me to have a fine coat on a birthday, I would pin a bank-bill on my sleeve.'—he had a place in less than two years, I think—and has had almost every place that every administration could bestow. Such were the patriots that opposed that excellent man my father, allowed by all parties to have been as incapable of revenge as ever minister was[8]—but whose experience of mankind drew from him

5. William Wildman Barrington (1717–93), 2d Vct Barrington; Chancellor of Exchequer, 1761; Secretary at War, 1755–61, 1765–78. See HW's character and description of him in *Mem. of the Reign of George II* ii. 141–2.

6. 'After the first edition of this work was published, I was told that I had omitted one noble author, Lord Barrington. As I intended a second edition, I applied to the son and heir of that lord for a list of his father's writings. The answer I received was, that his lordship would be obliged to

me if I would continue to omit all mention of his father—and to oblige his lordship I did, though it left my work, which I had enlarged with former omissions, still imperfect' (*Roy. & Nob. Authors, Works* i. 546).

7. See *Roy. & Nob. Authors, Works* i. 523, 543–8. HW enlarged the defense of his father, and warmly defended him against the insinuations in Foster's account.

8. 'Lord Chesterfield, one of his warmest opponents and satirists, who knew him better than Judge Foster or Mr Dobson

that memorable saying, 'That very few men ought to be Prime Ministers, for it is not fit many should know how bad men are.'—One can see a little of it without being a Prime Minister! If one shuns mankind and flies to books, one meets with their meanness and falsehood there too!—One has reason to say, There is but one good, that is God—Adieu!

Yours ever,

H. Walpole

To Cole, Wednesday 14 October 1778

Add MS 5953, ff. 40–1.

Address: [From Cole's copy, Add MS 5826, f. 166v.] Rev. Mr Cole, Milton near Cambridge. Free Beauchamp.

[Strawberry Hill,] Oct. 14, 1778.

I THINK you take in no newspapers,[1] nor I believe condescend to read any more modern than the *Paris à la Main* at the time of the Ligue[2]—consequently you have not seen a new scandal on my father, which you will not wonder offends me. You cannot be interested in his defence, but as it comprehends some very curious anecdotes, you will not grudge my indulging myself to a friend in vindicating a name so dear to me.

In the account of Lady Chesterfield's death and fortune,[3] it is said

[sic] could, has said in his character of Sir Robert Walpole, *that he was not vindictive, but on the contrary placable to those who had injured him most*' (*Roy. & Nob. Authors, Works* i. 545–6). HW's quotation (not exact) is from Lord Chesterfield's *Characters of Eminent Personages of his Own Time,* 1777. This supplementary account of Lord Barrington was first printed in 1787 (*Jour. Print. Off.* 20) and formed pp. 546–53 of *Roy. & Nob. Authors* in HW's proposed edition of *Works.* There were three copies of this edition in the sale of Kirgate's library, 1810, one the Merritt copy in Harvard College Library, and a second WSL. No other copies have apparently been recorded.

———

1. Cole received the *Cambridge Chronicle* (see following letter).

2. The *Paris à la Main* was apparently one of the *nouvelles à la main* which flourished in France in the seventeenth century —newspapers or pamphlets in manuscript or clandestinely printed and circulated, giving the news of the court or town (see *La Grande Encyclopédie, sub Nouvelle à la main*). The 'Ligue' (the Holy League) flourished 1576–94.

3. Melusina de Schulenburg (1693–1778), *suo jure* Countess of Walsingham, illegitimate dau. of George I by his favourite mistress Ermengarde Melusina de Schulenburg, *suo jure* Duchess of Kendal; m. (1733) Philip Dormer Stanhope, 4th E. of Chesterfield. She died 16 Sept. 1778. The story of her 'death and fortune' appeared in *The London Chronicle* 8–10 Oct. 1778, in *Lloyd's Evening Post* 9–12 Oct. 1778, and doubtless in other newspapers of the

that the late King, at the instigation of Sir R. W., burnt his father's will, which contained a large legacy to that his supposed daughter, and I believe his real one, for she was very like him, as her brother General Schulembourg[4] is in black, to the late King. The fact of suppressing the will is indubitably true, the instigator most false, as I can demonstrate thus.

When the news arrived of the death of George I[5] my father carried the account from Lord Townshend[6] to the then Prince of Wales. One of the first acts of royalty is for the new monarch to make a speech to the Privy Council. Sir Robert asked the King who he would please to have draw the speech, which was in fact asking, who was to be Prime Minister. His Majesty replied, Sir Spencer Compton.[7] It is a wonderful anecdote, and little known, that the new Premier, a very dull man, could not draw the speech, and the person to whom he applied, was—the deposed Premier. The Queen,[8] who favoured my father, observed how unfit a man was for successor, who was reduced to beg assistance of his predecessor. The Council met as soon as possible, the next morning at latest. There, Archbishop Wake,[9] with whom one copy of the will had been deposited (as another was, I think, with the Duke of Wolfenbuttle,[10] who had a pension for sacrificing it, which, *I know*, the late Duke of Newcastle transacted) advanced and delivered the will to the King, who put it into his pocket, and went out of council without opening it, the Archbishop not having courage or presence of mind to desire it to be read, as he ought to have done.

day, in any one of which HW may have seen it. Both the above accounts follow the version mentioned by Cole in his next letter: the will was put in the hands of the Abp of York, and the amount of the legacy and the amount recovered, £80,000. HW's version is generally accepted (see DNB, *sub* Stanhope, Philip Dormer, 4th E. of Chesterfield). HW gives a similar account in *Reminiscences* 54–6.

4. Count Adolf Friedrich von Schulenburg (1685–1741), a nephew of the Duchess of Kendal, and therefore a cousin, not a brother, of the Countess of Chesterfield (see *Allgemeine Deutsche Biographie*, vol. 32). It is possible that HW meant to write 'and' for 'as' and 'was' for 'is,' or that he was using 'in black' for 'brunette.'

5. George I died 12 June 1727, and Sir Robert Walpole went to the Prince 14 June.

6. Charles Townshend (1674–1738), 2d Vct Townshend, then (1727) secretary for the northern department. He was Sir Robert Walpole's brother-in-law, having married, in 1713, as his second wife, Dorothy Walpole, Sir Robert's sister.

7. (1673?–1743), afterwards 1st E. of Wilmington.

8. Caroline (1683–1737).

9. William Wake (1657–1737), Abp of Canterbury 1716–37.

10. Augustus Wilhelm (d. 1731), D. of Brunswick-Wolfenbüttel 1714–31.

These circumstances, which I solemnly assure you are strictly true, prove that my father neither advised, nor was consulted; nor is it credible that the King in one night's time should have passed from the intention of disgracing him, to make him his bosom confidant on so delicate an affair.

I was once talking to the late Lady Suffolk,[11] the former mistress, on that extraordinary event. She said, 'I cannot justify the deed to the legatees, but towards his father, the late King was justifiable, for George I had burnt two wills made in favour of George II.'—I suppose, they were the testaments of the Duke and Duchess of Zell,[12] parents of George I's wife,[13] whose treatment of her they always resented.

I said *I know* the transaction of the D. of N.—The late Lord Waldegrave[14] showed me a letter from that Duke to the first Earl of Waldegrave,[15] then ambassador at Paris, with directions about that transaction, or at least about payment of the pension, I forget which. I have somewhere, but cannot turn to it now, a memorandum of that affair,[16] and who the Prince was, whom I may mistake in calling Duke of Wolfenbuttle. There was a third copy of the will, I likewise forget with whom deposited. The newspaper says, which is true, that Lord Chesterfield filed a bill in Chancery against the late King to oblige him to produce the will, and was silenced, I think, by payment of £20,000. There was another legacy to his own daughter the Queen of Prussia,[17] which has at times been, and I believe, is still claimed by the King of Prussia.

11. Henrietta Hobart (1681?–1767), m. (1706) Charles Howard, afterwards 9th E. of Suffolk. In her old age she became the friend and correspondent of HW, and the source of his *Reminiscences* and *Notes of Conversations with Lady Suffolk*, ed. Paget Toynbee, Oxford, 1924.

12. George William (1624–1705), and Eléonore d'Olbreuse (fl. 1665–90), D. and Duchess of Zell, or Lüneburg-Celle. Elsewhere HW says that the wills were those of the D. of Zell and Sophia Dorothea, which is the accepted account (see *Reminiscences* 56; *Mem. of the Reign of George II* iii. 309–15; *Allgemeine Deutsche Biographie*).

13. Sophia Dorothea (1666–1726), m. (1682) George, afterwards George I of England, who divorced her in 1694, and imprisoned her for life.

14. James Waldegrave (1715–63), 2d E. Waldegrave, who m. HW's niece, Maria Walpole (afterwards Duchess of Gloucester).

15. James Waldegrave (1685–1741), 1st E. Waldegrave. He was ambassador at Paris 1730–40; his correspondence (1728–39) is in the British Museum.

16. HW doubtless refers to the account in his *Mem. of the Reign of George II* iii. 307–9, which generally agrees with that given here.

17. Sophia Dorothea (1687–1757), m. (1706) Frederick William I (1688–1740), King of Prussia.

Do not mention any part of this story, but it is worth preserving, as I am sure you are satisfied of my scrupulous veracity.[18] It may perhaps be authenticated hereafter by collateral evidence that may come out. If ever true history does come to light, my father's character will have just honor paid to it. Lord Chesterfield, one of his sharpest enemies, has not with all his prejudices left a very unfavorable account of him,[19] and it would alone be raised by comparison of their two characters. Think of one who calls Sir Robert the corruptor of youth,[20] leaving a system of education to poison them from their nursery! Chesterfield, Pulteney[21] and Bolingbroke[22] were the saints that reviled my father!

I beg your pardon, but you allow me to open my heart to you when it is full.

Yours ever,

H. W.

From Cole, Sunday 18 October 1778

VA, Forster MS 110, ff. 201–2. Cole's copy, Add MS 5826, ff. 167v, 168v.
Address: The Honourable Horace Walpole, Strawberry Hill, Twickenham, Middlesex. *Postmark:* Cambridge 19 OC.

Milton, Oct. 18, 1778.

Dear Sir,

THAT the world grows viler and viler is my settled opinion, and that it should do so is natural, from the utter loss of principle among all ranks of mankind. Some time ago religion of some sort or other had a check upon people's consciences: it might be supersti-

18. HW's object in writing this letter was doubtless to embed it in Cole's papers, where it stood as much chance of being seen by posterity as in any private place he could have chosen.

19. In *Characters of Eminent Personages of his Own Time*, 1777. Cf. HW to Mason 18 April 1777.

20. 'He [Sir Robert] would frequently ask young fellows, at their first appearance in the world, while their honest hearts were yet untainted, "Well, are you to be an old Roman? a patriot? You will soon come off that, and grow wiser." And thus he was more dangerous to the morals than to the liberties of his country, to which I am persuaded he meant no ill in his heart' (*The Letters of Philip Dormer Stanhope 4th Earl of Chesterfield*, ed. Bonamy Dobrée, 6 vols, 1932, i. 28).

21. William Pulteney (1684–1764), 1st E. of Bath.

22. Henry Saint-John (1678–1751), 1st Vct Bolingbroke.

tion, it might be enthusiasm. At present the disregard to it, even among the clergy, has let in such a torrent of infidelity and looseness of morals that the prospect of it is most alarming. But I forget myself, and am preaching a sermon instead of thanking you for your last kind letter. The circumstance you mention was in our vile Cambridge paper of yesterday:[1] a paper, with others of the same kind, calculated to circulate lies, scandal and sedition in every part of the kingdom it reaches. However, like all other violent measures, it defeats its own purpose: it is too scandalous to be credited, like a small publication at the same press within this month by the Anabaptist teacher at Cambridge,[2] whose virulence against the hierarchy is only equalled by the writing of 1643, and might have done service to his cause, had it been written [with] temper. As it is, it only shows the man's malice and to what lengths the party would go had they it in their power. Even Burnet and Hoadley are not spared.[3] The man says the poison lies in the office, not in the men.[4] But I get I know not whither. This man is the friend and agent of Kippis here.

In our paper the accusation of your father is as you mention, but it puts the will into the hands of the Lord Almoner, Archbishop of York,[5] and the sum recovered by Lord Chesterfield £80,000. But lies are much easier come at than truth, and when they are to aid scandal and defamation are readily swallowed with appetite. I hope you, who are so well able, will leave an antidote to such poisoners of true history. If I am not mistaken, Mrs Macaulay has been as guilty of abus-

---

1. Cole refers to the account of the death and fortune of the Countess of Chesterfield, which appeared in the *Cambridge Chronicle* 17 Oct. 1778. He placed the clipping in one of his MS volumes, now Add MS 5826, f. 170.

2. *A Plan of Lectures on the Principles of Nonconformity*, Cambridge, 1778, by Robert Robinson. Cole's account of his virulence is not exaggerated.

3. Benjamin Hoadly (1676–1761), Bp successively of Bangor, Hereford, Salisbury, and Winchester. Robinson says, 'Burnets and Hoadlys—and other tolerant prelates—preach rightly—but in vain—nobody is relieved by their declamations—they live down their own doctrine—find apologies—and salvos—and subtle distinctions neces-

sary—and do much damage to religion by inventing and publishing them' (*Plan of Lectures*, 5th edn, 1781, p. 53).

4. Robinson condemns prelatical hierarchy as unconstitutional, unsound at heart, etc., and distinguishes between persons and things: 'some prelates may be laudable—but all prelacy is execrable . . .' (ibid. 10, 27). Cole's copy contains the following additional sentence: 'The writer is the great friend and agent of Kippis here, and being a man of ingenuity, though bred a barber, had met with many friends in the University.'

5. Lancelot Blackburne (1658–1743), Abp of York 1724–43. The newspaper account was incorrect: Abp Wake was the custodian of the will (see preceding letter).

ing your father's memory as anyone.[6] I am entirely of your opinion
that the character of Lord Orford will appear with greater lustre
when opposed to the mock patriots who have succeeded him, and as
no one can do it so well, as no one is more interested to see justice
done him, which I am satisfied you have it in your power to do, I
make no doubt but your filial piety to so great and excellent a man
and so worthy a parent will force you to do it.

In the last *London Magazine*, p. 420, which, as I suppose, you do
not take, is this paragraph relating to Chatterton, whose life is the
subject of the paper:[7]

One of his first efforts to emerge from a situation so irksome to him, was
an application to a gentleman well known in the republic of letters,
which, unfortunately for the public and himself, met with a very cold
reception, and which the disappointed author always spoke of with a high
degree of acrimony, whenever it was mentioned to him.

You see this is civil to what has been said. Your narrative would un-
deceive the world, who are fated to be fed with falsehood.

I made a request to you in a former letter for the favour of a
ticket for Mr Kerrich to see Strawberry Hill some time in the spring,
which, if you are kind enough to let him have, he may then see it,
even if I should not be in a capacity to ask it then, for though I am
at this present better than I have been these three years, yet a winter
and spring such as the last may put it out of my power to solicit it.

Mr Lort, I hear, is at Cambridge, but I have not seen him yet.[8] I
have the Cowdray print,[9] which I don't like. I love portraits of great
men, and prints not so crowded.

It was very singular, but on Thursday morning the Master of
Benet[10] brought me the broad seal in plaster of Paris, taken from the
original matrix in brass, of Henrietta, King Charles I's Queen, four

6. If she did so in print, it has not been
located. This is a dig at HW's 'Republican' sympathies.

7. A review of Chatterton's *Miscellanies*.
The passage quoted by Cole is taken from
that work, pp. xviii–xix (cf. *ante* 24 July
1778 n. 1). It appears from MS Cat. that
HW had 16 vols of the *London Magazine*
(B.5.1–16), 1732–47. They were sold SH v. 3.
It is not clear why Cole supposed HW did
not take it unless he was referring to HW's
alleged indifference to public opinion.

8. 'but probably shall today at dinner.
He came down to Dr Ewin's trial in the
Vice-Chancellor's Court, which was last
Wednesday, and adjourned to that day
sennight, when it is supposed censure will
be passed' (addition in Cole's copy).

9. See *ante* 26 March 1776.

10. William Colman, who had been
elected 25 June of this year.

inches and an half diameter, very beautiful: on one side she is standing under a canopy; the reverse, her arms in a lozenge, viz., England
impaling France and Navarre, supported by a lion and an angel of
France. Within ten minutes, and while the Master was with me, in
comes Mr Kerrich with a printed plate of the same seal:[11] neither of
which had I ever before heard a word of.

I am, dear Sir,

Your ever devoted and affectionate servant,

WM COLE

To COLE, Monday 26 October 1778

Add MS 5953, ff. 42–3.
Address: To the Reverend Mr Cole at Milton near Cambridge.
Postmark: 26 OC.

Strawberry Hill, Oct. 26, 1778.

M R Kerrich shall have a ticket, dear Sir, to see Strawberry whenever he wishes for it next spring.

I have finished the life of Mr Baker, will have it transcribed, and
send it to you. I have omitted several little particulars that are in
your notes, for two reasons, one, because so much is said in the *Biographia,* and the other, because I have rather drawn a character of
him, than meant a circumstantial life. In the justice I have done to
him, I trust I shall have pleased you. I have much greater doubt of
that effect in what I have said on his principles and party. It is odd
perhaps to have made use of the life of a High Churchman for ex-
patiating on my own very opposite principles, but it gave me so fair
an opportunity of discussing those points, that I very naturally embraced it. I have done due honour to his immaculate conscience, but
have not spared the cause in which he fell, or rather rose, for the
ruin of his fortune was the triumph of his virtue.

As you know I do not love the press, you may be sure I have no
thoughts of printing this life at present; nay, I beg you will not only

11. The seal was engraved by James Basire as Plate XXIV in *Archaeologia,* vol. 5.
A 'Description of a third unpublished
royal Seal, in the Possession of Owen Salus-
bury Brereton, Esq.' was read before the
Society of Antiquaries, 29 Jan. 1778, and
was printed in *Archaeologia* v. 280–1. See
also *post* 2 June 1779, where HW refers to
'three pretty prints of reginal seals.'

not communicate it, but take care it never should be printed without my consent. I have written what presented itself; I should perhaps choose to soften several passages; and I trust it to you for your own satisfaction, not as a finished thing, or as I am determined it should remain.[1]

Another favour I beg of you, is to criticize it as largely and severely as you please. You have a right so to do, as it is built with your own materials; nay, you have a right to scold, if I have, nay, since I have, employed them so differently from your intention. All my excuse is, that you communicated them to one who did not deceive you, and who you was pretty sure would make nearly the use of them that he has made. Was not you? Did not you suspect a little that I could not write even a life of Mr Baker without talking Whiggism?—Well, if I have ill treated the cause, I am sure I have exalted the martyr. I have thrown new light on his virtue from his notes on the *Gazettes*,[2] and you will admire him more, though you may love me less, for my chemistry. I should be truly sorry if I did lose a scruple of your friendship. You have ever been as candid to me, as Mr Baker was to his antagonists, and our friendship is another proof that men of the most opposite principles can agree in everything else, and not quarrel about them.

As my MS contains above twenty pages of my writing on larger paper than this, you cannot receive it speedily—however I have performed my promise, and I hope you will not be totally discontent, though I am not satisfied myself. I have executed it by snatches and with long interruptions; and not having been eager about it, I find I wanted that ardour to inspire me; another proof of what I told you, that my small talent is waning, and wants provocatives. It shall be a warning to me. Adieu!

PS. I have long had a cast of one part of the Great Seal of Queen Henrietta, that you mention, as you may find in the catalogue of Strawberry in the green closet. It is her figure under a canopy.[3]

1. HW made no changes in the 'Life.' Cole received the MS 26 Jan. 1779, and, with HW's permission, copied it into one of his volumes, now Add MS 5850, ff. 205v–222v. It follows exactly the text printed in *Works* ii. 339–62.

2. For Baker's notes on the *London Gazette*, see Appendix 1, and cf. HW's 'Life of Baker,' *Works* ii. 345–50.

3. The 'impression of the great seal of Queen Henrietta Maria' was 'over the window' 'at the end of the closet towards the Thames' (*Description of SH, Works* ii. 433).

From Cole, Sunday 1 November 1778

VA, Forster MS 110, f. 203. Cole's copy, Add MS 5850, f. 223.
Address: To the Honourable Horace Walpole, Strawberry Hill in Twickenham, Middlesex. *Postmark:* Cambridge 2 NO.

Milton, Sunday, Nov. 1, 1778.

Dear Sir,

AM I to thank you for the trouble you have taken to oblige me,[1] or am I not? In good truth I am at loss to decide which. Your letter threatens so severely that I almost wish you had not undertaken it. I dread to receive it, yet am impatient to see it. At all events I am sure to be a gainer, for however I may dislike the politics, the way of treating them will be sure to please me. I own I always suspected that more Whiggism would be mixed with it than was likely to be relished by my old-fashioned principles, but I could never conceive that you would lay hold of an opportunity to discuss a point so diametrically opposite to the sentiments of the hero whose life you wrote, and decide against him. I could now maliciously wish, what I do not suspect, that your talents are upon the wane, and as I am pretty sure not to find them so, it makes it necessary for me to beg that you will return with the life all the rubbish I sent you, even to the smallest article, that, if I don't like your performance, I may compile one from them in the true style of honest Anthony Wood. I will observe your caution about not communicating it or printing it without your approbation. However, I must be thus ingenuous, before you part with it out of your power, to inform you that I ever held all papers of your composition in that esteem as not to throw them away, and such an one as you promise to send me, though I shall not show it without your leave, yet being committed to my book, some twenty years after my death it will be in the power of anyone to see it that pleases. Neither can I conceive that you mean that so much trouble, and on a curious subject, should be confined to my perusal only. It is pity it should. It never was my method, and I shall hardly begin it now, to press what may be disagreeable, but I wish, without violent struggle, you would alter your mind and print yourself what I am satisfied will give general pleasure. But I am

1. In writing the 'Life of Baker.'

afraid to say more till I see in what manner you have handled worthy
Mr Baker, and his sincere admirer as well as yours,

WM COLE

A note from Mr Lort yesterday informs me that he sat[2] out for
town in the morning, and returns to Cambridge within a week. I
write to him upon another commission, and will beg him to call in
Arlington Street, when possibly the MS may be transcribed, though
I shall not tell him the subject of it.

Apropos, Mr Knight of this parish calling here this week, told me
that he had been in Norfolk and that he had seen a MS of your narrative about Chatterton[3] (or that he had said he had one) with Mr
Nicols,[4] the correspondent of Mr Gray.

To COLE, Wednesday 4 November 1778

Add MS 5953, ff. 44–5.

The letter and the address are in Kirgate's hand.

Address: To the Reverend Mr Cole at Milton near Cambridge.

Postmark: EK 4 NO.

Arlington Street, Nov. 4, 1778.

YOU will see by my secretary's hand that I am not able to write
myself, indeed I am in bed with the gout in six places; like
Daniel in the den, but as the lions are slumbering round me, and
leave me a moment of respite, I employ it to give you one. You have
misunderstood me, dear Sir. I have not said a word that will lower
Mr Baker's character; on the contrary, I think he will come out
brighter from my ordeal. In truth, as I have drawn out his life from
your papers, it is a kind of political epic in which his conscience is
the hero that always triumphs over his interest upon the most opposite occasions. Shall you dislike your saint in this light?

I had transcribed about half when I fell ill last week. If the gout
does not seize my right hand, I shall probably have full leisure to

2. 'Frequent [for *set*] in inferior writers
of the second half of the 18th c' (OED).

3. This was HW's letter to Bewley (see
following letter).

4. Norton Nicholls (1742?–1809), who
became acquainted with Gray in 1761,
Nicholls then being an undergraduate at
Cambridge (see *Gray's Corr., passim*). He
became rector of Lound and Bradwell in
Suffolk, 1767, and accompanied Gray on a
tour through the midland counties, 1770.
On first acquaintance with Nicholls, HW
thought highly of him, but gradually tired
of his gossip.

finish it during my recovery, but shall certainly not be able to send it to you by Mr Lort.

Your promise fully satisfies me. My life can never extend to twenty years: anyone that saw me this moment would not take me for a Methusalem. I have not strength to dictate more now, except to add, that if Mr Nickolls has seen my narrative about Chatterton, it can only be my letter to Mr Bewley, of which you have a copy; the larger one has not yet been out of my own house.

I am, dear Sir, Yours most sincerely,

H. W.

PS. I forgot to say that you shall certainly have every scrap of your MSS carefully returned to you; and you will find that I have barely sipped here and there, and exhausted nothing.

From COLE, Sunday 8 November 1778

VA, Forster MS 110, f. 204. Cole kept no copy.
Address: To the Honourable Horace Walpole in Arlington Street, Piccadilly, London. *Postmark:* Cambridge 9 NO.

Milton, Sunday, Nov. 8, 1778.

Dear Sir,

I AM much more concerned to find you in the gout than about the manner you have treated Mr Baker and my politics. Indeed all I said was irony, and if I have expressed myself in another mode, it was for want of knowing how to do it better.

May the lions keep dozing and slumbering till you get out of their den, which I heartily wish may be soon. It is too early to begin a gouty winter, and the six months betwixt this and May is enough to make the stoutest of us to tremble. I received your letter only yesterday. I ought to have had it on Friday, and passed by the turnpike where it laid for me. The day I received it, viz., yesterday, I had an attack in one foot, after a respite of many months. Thank God it is much better this morning. May yours be a short visit too. I am obliged to be in an hurry, as a boy waits to carry this to Cambridge.

Never trouble yourself a moment about sending the packet. My curiosity and impatience are too humane to desire you to give yourself a minute's uneasiness either in body or mind to gratify them.

The Critical Reviewers and Dr or Mr Henry, the Scotch historian, are quarrelling about a quotation from your *Royal Authors*.[1] One alludes to the first and the other to the second edition, which has obliged brothers to fall out with one another.

I am, dear Sir,

Your ever faithful and affectionate servant,

WM COLE

To COLE, Sunday 3 January 1779

Add MS 5953, ff. 46–7.

Cole notes on the cover: 'Print of Captain Robert Knox. *V.* my vol. 3 of A.C.M., p. 517, No. 560, and p. 551, no. 673.' Robert Knox (1640?–1720) was the author of *An Historical Relation of the Island of Ceylon* . . ., 1681, and the captain of a ship in the service of the East India Company. His portrait was engraved in 1695 by Robert White. A.C.M. stands for *Athenae Cantabrigiae MSS*, in which he had copied some of Knox's letters to his cousin John Strype (see *Index to the Additional Manuscripts . . . in the British Museum . . . 1783–1835*, 1849, *sub* Knox).

Address: To the Reverend Mr Cole at Milton near Cambridge.
Postmark: Isleworth 4 IA.

Strawberry Hill, Jan. 3, 1779.

AT last after ten weeks I have been able to remove hither, in hopes change of air and the frost will assist my recovery; though I am not one of those ancients that forget the register, and think they are to be as well as ever after every fit of illness. As yet I can merely creep about the room in the middle of the day.

I have made my printer, now my secretary, copy out the rest of Mr Baker's Life, for my own hand will barely serve to write neces-

1. A writer in the *Critical Review* (Jan. 1778, Ser. I, vol. 45, p. 38), in a review of the third volume of *The History of Great Britain*, by Robert Henry (1718–90), HW's correspondent, condemns Henry for making false statements concerning the account of Richard I in *Roy. & Nob. Authors*. Henry's letter of explanation, dated 24 March 1778, was printed in the *Critical Review*, Oct. 1778 (Ser. I, vol. 46, p. 320). The reviewer consulted the first edition of *Roy. & Nob. Authors*, while Henry, without mentioning the edition, quoted from the second, 'because I did not imagine that anybody read the first edition, when a second one, corrected and enlarged, had been published above eighteen years, with which all men of learning are well acquainted.'

sary letters, and complains even of them. If you knew of any very trusty person passing between London and Cambridge, I would lend it to you; but should not care to trust it by the coach, nor to any giddy undergraduate that comes to town to see a play: and besides I mean to return you my own notes.¹ I will say no more than I have said in apology to you for the manner in which I have written this life. With regard to Mr Baker himself, I am confident you will find that I have done full justice to his worth and character—I do not expect you to approve the inferences I draw against some other persons—and yet if his conduct was meritorious, it would not be easy to excuse those who were *active* after doing what he would not do.² You will not understand this sentence, till you have seen the life.

I hope you have not been untiled nor unpaled by the tempest on New Year's morning. I have lost two beautiful elms in a row before my windows here, and had the skylight demolished in town. Lady Pomfret's³ Gothic house in my street lost one of the stone towers like those at King's Chapel, and it was beaten through the roof. The top of our cross too at Ampthill was thrown down, as I hear from Lady Ossory this morning.⁴ I remember to have been told that Bishop Kidder and his wife were killed in their bed in the palace at Gloucester in 1709, and yet his heirs were sued for dilapidations.⁵

Lord de Ferrers,⁶ who deserves his ancient honours, is going to repair the Castle of Tamworth,⁷ and has flattered me that he will consult me. He has a violent passion for ancestry—and consequently I trust will not stake the patrimony of the Ferrarii, Townshends and

1. This passage probably should read *your own notes,* which Cole had asked to be returned.

2. HW refers to his remarks on 'those Jacobites, who did take the oaths to King William and the succeeding princes down to the present reign, and yet constantly promoted the interests of a family they had so solemnly abjured!' ('Life of Baker,' *Works* ii. 347.)

3. Anna Maria Draycott, formerly Delagard (1736–87), a great heiress, m. (1764) George Fermor (1722–85), 2d E. of Pomfret. In his letter to Lady Ossory 3 Jan. 1779, HW wrote: 'One of the stone Gothic towers at Lady Pomfret's house (now Single-Speech Hamilton's) in my street fell through the roof, and not a thought of it remains. There were only two maids in the house, who luckily lay backwards.' The house, which was last owned by Lord Farringdon, was demolished in 1934.

4. This letter is missing.

5. Richard Kidder (1633–1703), Bp of Bath and Wells, and his wife were 'killed in their bed in the palace at Wells by the falling of a stack of chimneys through the roof in the great storm of 26 Nov. 1703' (DNB: Canon Overton). Cole corrected HW's mistake to '[Wells] in [1703]' in his copy.

6. George Townshend (1753–1811), Lord Ferrers and Lord Compton, cr. E. of Leicester in 1784, suc. his father as 2d M. Townshend in 1807. He was elected President of the Society of Antiquaries in 1784, and a Trustee of the British Museum in 1787.

7. In Staffordshire.

Comptons, at the hazard table. A little pride would not hurt our nobility, cock or hen.[8] Adieu! dear Sir, send me a good account of yourself.

Yours ever,

H. W.

From Cole, Sunday 3 January 1779

VA, Forster MS 110, f. 205. Cole kept no copy.

Address: The Honourable Horace Walpole, Arlington Street, Piccadilly, London. *Postmark:* Cambridge 5 IA.

Sunday, Jan. 3, 1779, Milton.

Dear Sir,

MY patience is quite worn out in respect to your health and welfare: I am afraid to write, and yet I can't help it. While Mr Lort was in London I had an opportunity of inquiring by him after you. He has been in Cambridge these three weeks, and once or twice sent to inquire of me what I wish to give him a good account of.[1]

I hope the hurricane on Thursday night or Friday morning did not alarm you.[2] I assure you I often thought of you in the storm. My old timber house shook like a cradle without intermission till three in the morning. I dared not get up, as I knew no place more secure than where I was. My servants dared not go to bed. However, we had no mischief done in the parish, except unroofing the church, and a few old barns and hovels and some trees close to my garden blown down. Neither has there been much damage at Cambridge, except among the fine elms at St John's, Trinity, our college, and some chimneys and barns blown down. I dread to hear the account from sea, where it must have been terrible.

Pray God send me a good account of yourself. I have been free from gout ever since that hot weather in the summer, and I hope and pray God you may be well, or getting so. My pen will hardly stick between my fingers that I can hardly say I am, dear Sir,

Your ever faithful and obliged servant,

Wm Cole

8. 'The last sentence alludes to the number of divorces between people of quality at this time' (Cole's note, Add MS 5850, f. 224).

1. That is, HW's health.

2. Cole had not yet received the preceding letter, which HW wrote on the same day—3 January.

From COLE, Monday 11 January 1779

VA, Forster MS 110, f. 206. Cole kept no copy.
Address: Honourable Horace Walpole, Strawberry Hill in Twickenham, Middlesex. *Postmark:* Cambridge 13 IA.

Dear Sir,   Milton, Jan. 11, 1779, Plough Monday.

A GENTLEMAN from Ely calling here in his way to Cambridge is so obliging to stay till I write this letter. I should have wrote yesterday, but this east wind always gives me a sore throat, though I get no farther than the fireside.

Thank God you are well and on your legs again. It was that that occasioned my former letter, which passed yours on the road. I was very uneasy to know what state you was in, and fearful at the same time. Pray take care of this extreme cold, and be not too venturesome at Strawberry Hill. Thank God none of your chimneys crushed you. I find some in your street that fell down besides Lady Pomfret's. I think tin or copper chimneys for those that can afford it, would be no bad practice.

Dr Glynn called here on Saturday. A friend of his of the Temple, son to a Dr Jacob,[1] a physician at Salisbury, comes to College this week to take his degree, and he promised me to write to him to call at Arlington Street for the papers, which, though I long to see, yet my real concern was about your health. As to Mr Baker's politics, I make no doubt but you have represented them fairly. I have met with an original letter of his very lately, that fully convinces me of his moderate principles. I will send it to you if you desire it.

Once more I bid you adieu, and pray take care of yourself. I am sadly afraid to be deserted in this desert of a wide world which every day gets new inhabitants and deprives one of one's old friends. I lost four very particular ones last year[2]—no small havoc at my age. Old friends are like old gold.

Adieu, dear Sir, and God bless you!

WM COLE

1. The son was John Henry Jacob (1755–1828), Eton and King's (B.A. 1779, Fellow 1778–89); admitted student of Lincoln's Inn 12 Nov. 1778; prebendary of Salisbury 1805–28, and rector of Mamhead, Devon, 1806. He inherited property from Dr Glynn, his father's intimate friend. His father, John Jacob (1722?–89), was also Eton and King's (B.A. 1744–5, M.D. 1758, Fellow 1744–54). He m. Mary, dau. of John Clarke, Dean of Salisbury (see *Eton Coll. Reg. 1698–1752* and *1753–90;* Brydges, *Restituta* iii. 228–9).

2. They were John Allen, John Barnard-

To Cole, Friday 15 January 1779

Add MS 5953, f. 48.

Address: [From Cole's copy, Add MS 5850, f. 224.] To the Rev. Mr Cole at Milton near Cambridge.

Postmark: None. [HW enclosed the letter in the packet with his 'Life of Baker'; see below.]

[Arlington Street,] Jan. 15, 1779.

I SEND you by Dr Jacob,[1] as you desired, my Life of Mr Baker, and with it, your own materials. I beg you will communicate my MS to nobody—but if you think it worth your trouble, I will consent to your transcribing it—but on one condition, and a silly one for me to exact, who am as old as you, and broken to pieces, and very unlikely to survive you; but should so improbable a thing happen, I must exact that you will keep your transcript sealed up, with orders written on the cover to be restored to me in case of an accident, for I should certainly dislike very much to see it printed without my consent. I should not think of your copying it, if you did not love so much *to transcribe,* and sometimes things of as little value as my MS. I shall beg to have it returned to me by a safe hand, as soon as you can, for I have nothing but the foul copy, which nobody can read, I believe, but I and my secretary.

I am actually printing my justification about Chatterton, but only 200 copies to give away,[2] for I hate calling in the whole town to a fray, of which otherwise probably not one thousand persons would ever hear. You shall have a copy as soon as ever it is finished, which my printer says will be in three weeks. You know my printer is my secretary too: do not imagine I am giving myself airs of a numerous household of officers.

I shall[3] be glad to see the letter of Mr Baker you mention. You will perceive two or three notes in my MS in a different hand from mine or that of my *amanuensis* (still the same *officer*) they were added by a person[4] I lent it to, and I have effaced part of the last.

iston, Joseph Bentham, and Pulter Forester. The last-named was Chancellor of the diocese of Lincoln 1766–78, and Archdeacon of Buckingham 1769–78. He died 20 July 1778 (see *Blecheley Diary, passim;* Brydges, *Restituta* iv. 241).

———

1. HW misunderstood Cole, who said that Dr Jacob's son would call for the MS (see preceding letter).

2. HW could not have given many away, for the majority of copies that appear today are in mint state.

3. MS reads *I am shall.*

4. Not identified.

I must finish, lest Dr Jacob should call and my parcel not be ready. I hope your sore throat is gone; my gout has returned again a little with taking the air only, but did not stay—however I am still confined, and almost ready to remain so, to prevent disappointment.

Yours most sincerely,

HOR. WALPOLE

From COLE, Tuesday 26 January 1779

VA, Forster MS 110, ff. 207–8. Cole kept no copy.

Address: The Honourable Horace Walpole, Arlington Street, Piccadilly, London. *Postmark:* Cambridge 26 IA.

Tuesday night, Jan. 26, 1779, Milton.

Dear Sir,

I JUST now safely received your packet from Mr Lort, though your letter is dated eleven days before, yet I thought you would be glad to hear of its safe arrival. Mr Lort writes me word that he shall return to town in a few days. If it is possible, he shall convey your MS to you again, but unfortunately, and what does not happen once in a twelvemonth, I had this day a note to let me know that a godson and his lady[1] would be with me tomorrow by dinner, and I a little expect the ⟨y plan⟩ to stay a day or two, which will probably interrupt me in m⟨y having⟩ it done time enough for Mr Lort's conveyance, which I shall ⟨certain⟩ly endeavour. Otherwise, I will take all possible care that the bearer will be a secure one and steady one, and that you receive the MS safely. Indeed it deserves the greatest precautions, and am noways surprised at your fears about it. I read it over with rapture, and in general am delighted with it:[2] to say

1. Doubtless John Ward (b. ca 1742), 2d son of Thomas Watson Ward of Great Wilbraham, Cambs, and Cole's godson; m. (1766) Dorothea Plumptre (d. before 1815), only dau. of Russell Plumptre, Regius Professor of Physic at Cambridge (Henry P. Stokes, *A History of the Wilbraham Parishes,* in *Cambridge Antiquarian Society, Octavo Publications,* No. L, Cambridge, 1926, p. 70; LA ix. 556; Burke, *Landed Gentry,* 1838, iii. 76). On 30 Sept. 1766 Cole learned 'that Miss Plumptre married my godson Ward without the knowledge or consent of her parents; that her aunt had just left her £10,000 independent of her father, which enables her to marry Mr Ward, who has no profession, no fortune and no economy; and that she made the offer herself' (*Blecheley Diary* 129). The Wards lived at Quy Hall, about five miles east of Cambridge (Palmer, *Monumental Inscriptions* 279).

wholly would not be telling truth and acting candidly. You did not expect I should be pleased with all, and indeed I cannot, yet I readily agree that that makes no abatement in your performance. To be particular is not necessary. At my age, going out of the world, it is very immaterial what my political or religious principles are: all I can say about them is, I have never seen occasion to alter them, and shall hardly think of doing so now. I took the world as I found it, but never made any exceptions to what I may have disliked, but have endeavoured to jog on quietly without giving offense by my mumpsimus[3] to anyone. The charge you lay on me I shall religiously observe, and I shall take every precaution in my power to prevent its either being seen or published, but must add what I said in a former letter that I wish you would put it out of my power to give you any disquiet on that head by publishing it yourself. I am satisfied that the world would be highly obliged and as much entertained as by any publication they have been presented with.

I was determined to write thus much to advertise you of its arrival, and to thank you for the favour of communicating it to me. Assure yourself no one shall see it, though it is shameful to hide such a jewel from the eyes of the public. But for these reasons, I should have excused myself from writing, for within these ten days or a fortnight the gout has laid siege to me, has seized the calf of one leg and the muscles and sinews under one of the joints of my knee, with feverishness and queerness which you are a better judge of, than I know how to describe.

I will send you the letter I mentioned, or a copy, with two or three other things of the same sort, which lower Mr Baker, perhaps, in my esteem, and will exalt him in yours.

Pray, in your collection of heads, have you one of Captain Robert Knox[4] in Charles II's time? He is not mentioned in Mr Granger's book, nor did I ever see one of him, yet by two letters at various periods to Mr Strype I know he had a print of himself.

Dear Sir, adieu! Take care of yourself this cold weather which won't do for us gouty folk to air in. I am,

Yours most cordially,

WM COLE

2. Deliberation changed Cole's opinion. See his next letter to HW 30 Jan. 1779, and Appendix 2.

3. *Stubbornness;* see OED.

4. See *ante* 3 Jan. 1779, introductory n.

Mr Lort says he saw you but in company. I have not seen him since his return, but did you observe not how ill he looked? if he was not much recovered when he called upon you. I do not know I ever saw a man so changed as he was in so small a time.

I am glad to hear Chatterton is gone to the press, and shall be much obliged to you for a copy: I hoard them as relics, and shall be glad to increase my number. Mr Lort, in a letter about three weeks ago, before I wrote to you, told me that in your confinement to your bed you dictated some tales in the style of *The Castle of Otranto*.[5] Is it true? I suppose they are not printed or probably you would have mentioned it.

To COLE, Thursday 28 January 1779

Add MS 5953, ff. 49–50.

Address: To the Reverend Mr Cole at Milton near Cambridge.
Postmark: DW 29 IA.

Arlington Street, Jan. 28, 1779.

I WRITE in as much hurry as you did, dear Sir, and thank you for the motive of yours: mine is to prevent your fatiguing yourself in copying my MS[1] for which I am not in the least haste; pray keep it till another safe conveyance presents itself. You may bring the gout, that is I am sorry to hear flying about you, into your hand by wearying it.

How can you tell me I may well be cautious about my MS and yet advise me to print it?—No, I shall not provoke nests of hornets, till I am dust, as they will be too.

If I dictated tales when ill in my bed, I must have been worse than I thought, for, as I know nothing of it, I must have been light-headed. Mr Lort was certainly misinformed, though he seems to have told you the story kindly to the honour of my philosophy or spirits—but I had rather have no fame, than what I do not deserve. I am fretful or low-spirited at times in the gout, like other weak old men, and have less to boast than most men. I have some strange things in my drawer, even wilder than the *Castle of Otranto,* and

5. Cole refers to *Hieroglyphic Tales,* of which 'six copies, besides the revised copy' were printed at SH in 1785. The tales were reprinted in *Works* iv. 319–52. In 'Short Notes' for 1772, HW says: 'This year, the last, and some time before, wrote some *Hieroglyphic Tales.* There are only five' (see *Jour. Print. Off.* 20, 69–71).

1. 'Life of Baker.'

called *Hieroglyphic Tales*—but they were not written lately, nor in the gout, nor, whatever they may seem, written when I was out of my senses. I showed one or two of them to a person[2] since my recovery, who may have mentioned them, and occasioned Mr Lort's misintelligence. I did not at all perceive that the latter looked ill; and hope he is quite recovered. You shall see Chatterton soon. Adieu!

From Cole, Saturday 30 January 1779

VA, Forster MS 110, f. 209. Cole's copy, Add MS 5850, ff. 225v, 226.

At the end of his copy of the letter, Cole has the following note: 'Mr Knight of Milton going to town on Tuesday [2 Feb.], I entrusted the MS to his care, who promised to deliver it with his own hand. I had the following letter [that is, HW's letter of 4 Feb. 1779] on Friday, Feb. 5.' As no postmark appears on this letter, Cole must have enclosed it in the packet with the MS.

Address: For the Honourable Horace Walpole, in Arlington Street, Piccadilly, London.

Milton, Jan. 30, 1779. Saturday morning.
Dear Sir,

I HAD packed up your MS and sent it with a long letter[1] to Mr Lort last night, in order that you might receive them this evening, but having said more than I thought became me, I wrote a letter to Mr Lort before I went to bed, which my servant carried to College time enough to prevent Mr Lort's going off with it; as by your very obliging letter of last night I had your leave to keep the MS for some time longer. In that letter you say I used the word *cautious:* if I did, as I make no doubt of it, it must be in a sense different from what you seem to put it to. To be ingenuous, my long letter was to beg that the preceding one, giving you an account of my safe receipt of the MS, might be looked upon as unwritten and unsaid, being wrote in a great hurry; and smitten with the beauties of the chief part of the work, I was afraid that I had said more than I could safely and honestly say, when I had read other parts of it, with more attention. Yet, though I recall my approbation of the whole, I should be extremely injurious not to acknowledge the merit of the greater part, and not to return my thanks for the pains you

2. Doubtless the person referred to *ante* 15 Jan. n. 4.

1. This letter, which Cole never sent to HW, is printed in Appendix 2.

have so courteously bestowed on a subject which I threw in your way, and which you had a right to execute in the way you liked best. I will send the MS by the first safe conveyance I can meet with, and in the meanwhile have carefully sealed it up, that it is obvious to no one. You, who declared your love for truth, cannot, I hope, be offended at my sincerity. I shall be extremely unhappy if you are, because I find it impossible to contradict what I have said; and shall <este>em it as a great favour if I never more hear a word about it, as altercation and <deb>ate will do neither of us any good.

My gout has now fixed itself in the muscles under my knee and calf of my leg. I hope you are free from it in every part.

I am, Sir, with great esteem and sincerity,

Your ever obliged and faithful servant,

WM COLE

To COLE, Thursday 4 February 1779

Add MS 5953, ff. 51–2.
Address: To the Reverend Mr Cole at Milton near Cambridge.
Postmark: 4 FE.

[Arlington Street,] Feb. 4, 1779.

I HAVE received the MS and though you forbid my naming the subject more, I love truth and truth in a friend so much, that I must tell you, that so far from taking your sincerity ill, I had much rather you should act with your native honest sincerity than say you was pleased with my MS. I have always tried as much as is in human nature to divest myself of the self-love of an author; in the present case I had less difficulty than ever, for I never thought my life of Mr Baker one of my least indifferent works. You might, believe me, have sent me your long letter,[1] whatever it contained: it would not have made a momentary cloud between us. I have not only friendship but great gratitude for you for a thousand instances of kindness—and should detest any writing of mine that made a breach with a friend, and still more if it could make me forget obligations. I am,

Yours most cordially,

HOR. WALPOLE

1. Appendix 2.

From COLE, Sunday 7 February 1779

VA, Forster MS 110, ff. 210–11. Cole's copy, Add MS 5850, f. 226.

Address: For the Honourable Horace Walpole, Arlington Street, Piccadilly, London. *Postmark:* Cambridge 8 FE.

Sunday, Milton, Feb. 7, 1779.

Dear Sir,

I THANK you for your very kind and polite letter, which I received on Friday, and am glad Mr Knight was so punctual in the delivery of the packet so early. However, after such a disappointment, you must allow me to pout a little, till Time brings matters to rights again. In the meantime, though I delight not to talk on a subject that can give me no pleasure, yet as I led you into an error, it is but just that I should prevent your l<eading> others into the same mistake. I will therefore transcrib<e one> paragraph of my letter I had sent as far as Cambri<dge and re>called afterwards. It is this:

It is probable I led you into an error (if it is one), 'That he was always a welcome guest at Wimpole. p. 21.'[1] It might be so, but I have no authority for saying so. I am rather inclined to believe that he never went out anywhere. Had he been a guest at Wimpole, Lord Oxford would hardly have sent Mr Vertue to Cambridge to catch his likeness, as you have mentioned (Mr Vertue's Life, p. 8),[1a] but rather have given the painter a better opportunity to have studied his visage at Wimpole. But I remember in a letter of his, about Queen Anne's time, he mentions that he had not been at Ely for between twenty and thirty years.

What I had then only surmised, within these two or three days I have found full proof of, for in a letter to Mr Strype, dated March 8, 1717, he writes thus. I have met with near 150 of his original letters, all which I transcribed. He is speaking of the Harleian MSS at Wimpole:

1. HW did not change this passage, which reads: 'Mr Baker ever gratefully acknowledged the patronage of the noble Maecenas, to whose house at Wimpole he was always a welcome guest' (*Works* ii. 353). 'The noble Maecenas' was Edward Harley (1689–1741), 2d E. of Oxford, the friend and correspondent of Pope and Swift. Wimpole, the seat of the Earls of Oxford in Cambridgeshire until 1740, when Edward Harley, 2d E. of Oxford, sold it to Philip Yorke, 1st E. of Hardwicke, to pay a debt of £100,000. See W. S. Lewis, *Horace Walpole's Fugitive Verses*, pp. 44–5 n, for HW's allusion to this transaction in a MS copy of 'The Entail.'

1a. *Engravers*[1]; Vertue's 'Life' is appended with separate pagination.

When I see Mr W. [Wanley, Lord Oxford's librarian][2] I will discourse him about the MSS, which cannot be so well done by letter. A general catalogue I have seen, as far as they have gone, and can borrow upon occasion. The library I never saw, though I have been invited oftener than once, and have otherwise great obligations, but I go nowhere. I have seen the owner. I am, Sir, etc.

In the two last letters of the collection, which I transcribed but yesterday, there is this further proof, if it wanted any, of my assertion. They are both to Mr Strype, who possibly might have teased him overmuch to solicit subscriptions in the University for his edition of Stow.[3] The first is dated Jan. 13, 1719, the other May 22, 1720.

Stowe's *Survey* is a great work, but out of my way. Whenever you proceed in your *Annals*,[4] I think I may undertake for the College and myself. How much further I cannot yet say; for I live very retired, and hardly see anyone beyond my chamber, unless it be at chapel in the morning, where I make my bows (like a Carthusian) and see the company no more till night. From one in such retirement you will not expect much news, etc.

Worthy Sir, I am glad to hear of your health, and of your good designs for the public, which, I hope, will meet with due encouragement: I mean from such as are capable of encouraging them. For myself, I am out of the world, and live in the utmost retirement, and see nobody beyond my own chamber, nor willingly there, unless upon business, and am the most unfit man living to solicit subscriptions, etc.

If this has not tired you, I wish my next quotation in crotchets[5] does not vex you. I am sure it does me. Though one never sees them, or has a chance for it, yet it was a consolation that it was not out of one's power to do so; besides the self-satisfaction and pride one had that so noble a collection was in the kingdom. In our yesterday's *Cambridge Chronicle* was this paragraph:

We are informed that, much to the dishonour of this country, the celebrated Houghton Collection of pictures, the property of Lord Orford, and

2. The brackets and the words within them are Cole's. Humfrey Wanley (1672–1726), antiquary, was librarian to the first and second Earls of Oxford. He catalogued the Harleian MSS.

3. Strype's edition of Stow's *Survey . . . brought down . . . to the present time* was published in two parts, 1720.

4. Strype's *Annals of the Reformation in England* was published in two parts, 1708–9. Baker refers to the second edition, with continuation, 4 vols, 1725–31.

5. Cole encloses the quotation in double quotes. *Crotchet,* in the sense in which Cole uses it, does not appear in OED.

collected at a vast expense by the late Sir Robert Walpole, is actually purchased by the Empress of Russia[6] for £40,000.

I hope this, like most other things in these sort of publications, is a
lie of their own fabrication.

I am, dear Sir,

Your ever faithful and obliged servant,

WM COLE

To COLE, Thursday 18 February 1779

Add MS 5953, ff. 53–4.

Address: To the Reverend Mr Cole at Milton near Cambridge.
Postmark: 18 FE.

[Arlington Street,] Feb. 18. 1779.

I SENT you my Chattertoniad last week, in hopes it would sweeten
your pouting, but I find it has not, or has miscarried, for you have
not acknowledged the receipt with your usual punctuality.

Have you seen Hasted's new *History of Kent?*[1] I am sailing
through it, but am stopped every minute by careless mistakes. They
tell me the author had good materials, but is very negligent: and so
I perceive. He has not even given a list of monuments in the
churches, which I do not remember omitted in any history of a
county—but he is rich in pedigrees; though I suppose they have
many errors too, as I have found some in those I am acquainted with.
It is unpardonable to be inaccurate in a work, in which one nor ex-
pects nor demands anything but fidelity.

We have a great herald arising in a very noble race, Lord de Ferrars. I hope to make him a Gothic architect too, for he is going to
repair Tamworth Castle, and flatters me that I shall give him sweet
council. I enjoin him to *kernellare.*[2] Adieu!

Yours ever,

H. W.

6. Catherine II (1729–96), Empress of
Russia 1762–96.

1. *The History and Topographical Survey of the County of Kent,* 4 vols, Canterbury, 1778–99, by Edward Hasted. HW's

copy, the first three volumes only (A.1.),
was sold SH i. 69.

2. That is, to furnish with battlements,
in the manner HW instituted at SH (see
OED, *sub* kernel, kernellate, crenellate).

From Cole, Thursday 18 February 1779

VA, Forster MS 110, f. 212. Cole's copy, Add MS 5826, f. 168v.
Address: The Honourable Horace Walpole in Arlington Street, Piccadilly,
London. *Postmark:* Cambridge [19?] FE.

Dear Sir,   Milton, Feb. 18, 1779. Thursday.

I LAST night received by the Cambridge fly your most ingenious
and acceptable present.[1] I devoured it with impatience, and may
truly pronounce what Bishop Warburton on another, similar, occasion said, 'The question is now decided forever.' The editor of the
Miscellanies must be thunderstruck on reading your masterly preface to the narrative, and the irony upon his 'honest simplicity'[2] is
beyond praise: we shall have no other edition of Rowley. Mr Lort
and Dr Glynn, both violent Rowleyists, but somehow divided about
their collections[3] concerning him, must be struck dumb, though the
most noisy and clamorous about him. To Dr Glynn I shall send your
book, and if he is not convinced of the nonentity of Rowley, God
help him. I shall then rank him among the incurables: hitherto I
have only considered him as a patient of the first ward. I am glad
the man abused you, for the pleasure you have given me in his con-
futation.
I am, Sir,
Your most faithful and obliged servant,
WM COLE

From Cole, Tuesday 2 March 1779

VA, Forster MS 110, f. 213. Cole's copy, Add MS 5826, ff. 166, 170v.
Address: The Honourable Horace Walpole, Arlington Street, Piccadilly,
London. [Essex conveyed the letter to HW; see below.]

Dear Sir,   Milton, March 2, 1779.

YESTERDAY Mr Essex came and drank tea here, and informed
me of his going to town tomorrow, and intention of calling
upon you. I seized the opportunity it gave me of thanking you for

1. HW's *Letter to the Editor of the Mis-*
cellanies of Thomas Chatterton. Cole's
copy is now WSL. He wrote on the verso

of the title-page: 'Sent to me by Mr Walpole, February 14, 1779. Wm Cole.'
2. '. . . there is such honest simplicity

your last of February 18, the very date of my last to you, to thank you for your Chattertoniad, and with my sentiments of it. I assure you I have no reserves or wishes to recall that letter, which I hope you received after it passed yours on the road to me. The reason I wrote no sooner was (as I mentioned in the letter) that I received your excellent book only the evening before, and then by mere accident, for had I not expected a <parcel of> tea by the fly, which I sent for and received, it m<ight possi>bly have laid there till this time, having not been at Cambridge since the day after the high wind.

I have not seen Hasted's *History:* new books of price do not agree with my pocket, and since the loss of Mr Tyson,[1] who was very friendly in sending me all new publications, I rarely see any. Your account of it lessens my curiosity about it.

I want to know whether Captain Grose has published his additional volume.[2] Above a year ago I drew up an account of Pythagoras's school at Cambridge for him, but whether it is printed,[3] I know not.

I am glad to hear Lord de Ferrers is so good an herald, the foundation of an antiquary, a *sine qua non* to make one; and for his improvement in Gothic architecture I am sure he needs no better tutor than he has judiciously pitched upon. For ancient and modern heraldry, viz., names of persons with their arms, I have a large folio which I think would suit his Lordship: it is of my own writing, but I can't be without it a week. A castle without crenellation would be no castle: it is as necessary as port-holes and portcullis.

in condemning a man first, and then desiring him to tell you his story, that it would be unpardonable to be angry with or to deceive you, and I give you my word I will be guilty of neither' (*Works* iv. 210).

3. Part of Glynn's Rowleian Collection is now WSL.

———

1. That is, since Tyson moved to his living at Lambourne, Essex.

2. Francis Grose (1731?–91), antiquary, and captain and adjutant in the Surrey militia from about 1778 to his death, published *The Antiquities of England and Wales,* by subscription in numbers, the whole being reissued in 6 vols, 1773–87. The last two volumes have the title, *Supplement to the Antiquities.* By 'additional

volume' Cole means vol. 5, or the first volume of the *Supplement,* in which his account of Pythagoras's school appeared under Cambridgeshire. It is illustrated by an engraving by Sparrow, which was 'published 13th Augt. 1783 by S. Hooper.' The title-page of this volume reads 1777, but some of the plates are dated as late as 1787. (Professor R. S. Crane writes that publishing in parts by subscription was fairly common at this time.) Cole's account was reprinted in the second edition of Grose's work, 8 vols, [1783–97], i. 23–6, and in *The Account of Pythagoras's School in Cambridge; as in Mr Grose's Antiquities . . . and other Notices,* [Cambridge? 1790?] pp. 5–15.

3. Cole's copy reads: 'whether it is pub-

I have sent Chatterton to the Vice-Chancellor,[4] Dr Farmer, Master of Emanuel, and Dr Glynn. It has been with them a week, but I have heard nothing from them since.

I am, dear Sir, wishing you a perfect enjoyment of health,

Your most obliged and faithful servant,

Wm Cole

To Cole, Sunday 28 March 1779

Add MS 5953, ff. 55–6.

Address: To the Reverend Mr Cole at Milton near Cambridge.
Postmark: 29 MR.

Strawberry Hill, March 28, 1779.

YOUR last called for no answer; and I have so little to tell you, that I only write today to avoid the air of remissness. I came hither on Friday, for this last week has been too hot to stay in London; but March is arrived this morning with his north-easterly malice, and I suppose will assert his old-style claim to a third of April. The poor infant apricots will be the victims of that Herod of the almanac.

I have been much amused with new *Travels through Spain* by a Mr Swinburne[1]—at least with the account of the Alhambra, of the inner parts of which there are two beautiful prints.[2] The Moors were the most polished and had most taste of any people in the Gothic ages; and I hate the knave Ferdinand and his bigoted Queen for destroying them. These new *Travels* are simple, and do tell one a little more than late voyagers, by whose accounts one would think there was nothing in Spain but muleteers and fandangos—In truth, there does not seem to be much worth seeing but prospects—and those, unless I were a bird, I would never visit, when the accommodations are so wretched.

lished I know not: it was printed and sent to me a year ago.' LA iii. 656 states that the first number of the *Antiquities of England and Wales* was 'published' in 1773, and that the whole was completed in 1776.

4. William Colman.

1. *Travels through Spain, in the Years* 1775 and 1776. In which several Monuments of Roman and Moorish Architecture are illustrated by accurate Drawings taken on the Spot, 1779, by Henry Swinburne (1743–1803). HW's copy was sold SH v. 134.

2. For the account of the Alhambra, see Swinburne, ibid., letter 23, pp. 171–88. HW refers to the two folding plates, 'Court of

Mr Cumberland has given the town a masque called *Calypso*,[3] which is a prodigy of dullness. Would you believe that such a sentimental writer would be so gross as to make cantharides one of the ingredients of the love-potion for enamouring Telemachus? If you think I exaggerate, here are the lines,

> To these, the hot Hispanian fly,
> Shall bid his languid pulse beat high.

Proteus and Antiope are Minerva's missioners for securing the Prince's virtue, and in recompense they are married and crowned King and Queen![4]

I have bought at Hudson's sale[5] a fine design of a chimney-piece by Holbein for Henry VIII—if I had a room left, I would erect it. It is certainly not so Gothic as that in my Holbein room; but there is a great deal of taste for that bastard style. Perhaps it was executed at Nonsuch.[6] I do intend under Mr Essex's inspection to begin my offices next spring—It is late in my day, I confess, to return to brick and mortar, but I shall be glad to perfect my plan, or the next possessor will marry my castle to a Doric stable. There is a perspective through two or three rooms in the Alhambra, that might easily be improved into Gothic, though there seems but small affinity between them; and they might be finished within with Dutch smiles[7] and painting, or bits of ordinary marble, as there must be gilding. Mosaic seems to have been their chief ornament, for walls, ceilings and floors. Fancy must sport in the furniture, and mottoes might be

the Lions' and the 'Entrance of the Torre de las dos Hermanas,' by F. Giomignani, after drawings by Swinburne.

3. Richard Cumberland (1732–1811), dramatist and miscellaneous writer. His *Calypso* was first performed at Covent Garden Theatre, 20 March 1779, where it lasted for only three performances (see Stanley Thomas Williams, *Richard Cumberland*, New Haven, 1917, p. 151). It was published in the same year: *Calypso; A Masque, in three Acts. As it is performed at the Theatre Royal.* HW's copy, which formed part of his 'Theatre of Geo. 3,' is now WSL. HW has noted on the title, 'acted for the first time March 20th.'

4. HW misquotes:

'I've gleanings of Hesperian fruit,
With rank Satyrion's guilty root;

These, with the hot Hispanian fly,
Shall make his languid pulse beat high.'
(*Calypso*, Act iii, p. 43.)

HW, who disliked Cumberland personally, also distorts the plot.

5. Thomas Hudson (1701–79), portrait-painter, died at Twickenham 26 Jan. 1779, and in the following March his collection, including drawings, prints and other works of art, was sold by auction.

6. Nonsuch Palace in Surrey, begun by Henry VIII as a royal residence, was placed by Charles II (in 1670) in trust for Barbara Villiers, Duchess of Cleveland. It was dismantled and its contents sold in order to settle her financial difficulties.

7. MS is clear, but possibly HW meant 'tiles.'

galant, and would be very arabesque. I would have a mixture of colours, but with strict attention to harmony and taste; and some one should predominate, as supposing it the favourite colour of the lady who was sovereign of the knight's affections who built the house. Carpets are classically Mahometan, and fountains—but alas! our climate till last summer was never romantic! Were I not so old, I would at least build—a Moorish novel—for you see my head runs on Granada—and by taking the most picturesque parts of the Mahometan and Catholic religions, and with the mixture of African and Spanish names, one might make something very agreeable—at least I will not give the hint to Mr Cumberland. Adieu!

Yours ever,

H. W.

From Cole, Wednesday 7 April 1779

VA, Forster MS 110, ff. 214–5. Cole's copy, Add MS 5826, ff. 171v, 172v.
Address: The Honourable Horace Walpole, Arlington Street, Piccadilly, London. *Postmark:* 8 [AP.]

Milton, April 7, 1779.

Dear Sir,

YOUR kind letter found me just packed up with a fresh fit of the gout in one foot. It happily made me but a short visit, and is already gone except a little puffing and swelling in the ankle. I had not been out since Nov. 5, but the fine weather tempted me March 26 and 27 to pay two visits,[1] and I was called to account the next day for my excursions, so that I may truly accuse the northeasterly wind of malice, as well as my few poor fruit trees, where Herod has been gratifying his cruelty on the poor infant buds, which, from the finest blow, are now all slain and prostrate. What grieves me most is that you gave me some six years ago a dozen fine roots of jonquils, which blowed finely the year after, and have ceased ever since, though they thrive and multiply exceedingly. I will transplant them.

I have not seen Mr Swinburne's *Travels.* About five years ago I gave Mr Essex a curious book of prints of old castles in France and

1. 'one at Cambridge and the other at Quy Hall' (addition in Cole's copy). See *ante* 26 Jan. 1779 n. 1.

Spain, in quarto, among which was one or two of the Alhambra.[2]
You can, if you set about it, build either a Moorish castle or novel
with equal taste and expedition. A Moorish apartment in a Gothic
castle, fitted up for the reception of a captive lady or knight of
Granada would not be incongruous, and an history of that lady or
knight in your hands would be no bad companion of Matilda and
Otranto. At present we bid as fair for the introduction of Mahomet-
ism or any other *ism* as possible, when the old religion seems to be
worn to the stumps, and scouted by everyone, not omitting the
clergy, yet whether their luscious doctrines will be an equivalent for
their circumcision, fastings, regular prayers, disuse of wine and pork,
etc., is more than I can say. No doubt the giving up the Trinity, both
by the Church and Dissenters, is no small compliment to them, as
well as all mysteries. Yet I believe the mysteries among them are of
as hard digestion. Lady Mary W. Montagu speaks of them with great
partiality,[3] yet possibly her Ladyship might not have found her account in a religion where one man may have as many women as he
pleases. Her son[4] had more advantages in his profession of it.

Last week but one, when I was at Cambridge, I called at an alderman's[5] who has purchased an old gold ring found[6] in a field about
three miles off. He had many things of curiosity, particularly a picture of St Peter formed by writing in a very small compass, containing the creeds,[7] Lord's Prayer, all St Peter's Epistle, etc., and all
within the compass of a crown piece or somewhat larger. He asks immoderately for it—seven guineas.[8] It is set in silver gilt. I imagine it
to have been a picture hanging from a ribbon belonging to the Order of St Peter, for such an order was instituted by Pope Leo X[9] to
fight against our friends the Mahometans. But the things that struck
me most were half a dozen dessert plates of copper, painted admirably in gray, by Rubens,[10] both within and without, the stories out

2. 'I thought myself under obligations
to him for designing my cottage, for which
he would take nothing' (addition in Cole's
copy).

3. *Letters . . . written during her Travels in Europe, Asia and Africa*, by Lady
Mary Wortley Montagu (1689–1762), were
published posthumously, 3 vols, 1763 (vol.
4, 1767).

4. Edward Wortley Montagu (1713–76),
author and traveller, who became a convert
to Mohammedanism.

5. Not identified.

6. 'in Shelford Field' (addition in Cole's
copy).

7. 'Ave Mary' (addition in Cole's copy).

8. 'though the silver gilt frame and back
to it can't be worth above 20s.' (addition in
Cole's copy).

9. Leo X (Giovanni de' Medici) (1475–
1521), Pope 1513–21.

10. But see *post* 20 April 1779.

of Ovid's *Metamorphosis:*[10a] all in the most perfect preservation. He asks twelve guineas for them.

As I don't know whether you ever read the *Life of John Stow*[11] by Mr Strype, I will transcribe a paragraph at p. xviii:

One observation more made by Stow may here be mentioned, which I have from George Buck Esq.,[12] who saith of him [viz., of Stow][13] that *he was a man indifferently inquisitive after the verbal relations of the persons of princes, and curious in the descriptions of their features and lineaments.* And that in all his inquiries, he could find no such note of deformity in King Richard III as historians commonly relate: and that he acknowledged *viva voce* that he had spoken with some ancient men, who, from their own sight and knowledge affirmed, that he was of bodily shape comely enough; only of low stature.

This is very particular. Perhaps Buck may have the same, but as I have not Buck, I choose to send it you as I find it.

As in two or three of your late letters you have mentioned Lord De Ferrers's turn and taste for antiquity, heraldry and ped<igree, it> may not be amiss to mention that I have been just transcribing a very fi<ne pedigree> of Lord Chancellor Bromley, in which, as a collateral branch, is a long pedigree of De Ferrers Earls of Derby, etc., finely illuminated. Lord Montfort gave me the pedigree[14] five years ago, not caring a groat for it, and I was glad to have it, to secure it to the family (if there should be one),[15] and prevent its falling into worse hands. As it was my own (though in my will I have ordered it to be delivered to the heir of the family)[16] I neglected look-

---

10a. Cole's habitual spelling.

11. Prefixed to the first volume of Strype's edition of Stow's *Survey of the Cities of London and Westminster,* 2 vols, 1720. HW's copy of Stow's work (E.2.24) was another edition, 1633, and was sold SH ii. 91 to Thos. Baylis, Esq.

12. Sir George Buc or Buck (d. 1623), Kt, poet, historian and Master of the Revels, was the author of *The History of the Life and Reigne of Richard the Third,* which was first published in 1646 as the work of 'George Buck, Esq.' As HW used some of Buck's arguments in *Historic Doubts,* he doubtless was once familiar with this passage, which Strype closely paraphrases from Buck, op. cit. 79. It appears from the following letter, however, that HW had

forgotten it. HW's copy (C.6.28), dated 1647, was sold SH i. 150.

13. The brackets and interpolation are Cole's.

14. 'five yards in length' (addition in Cole's copy).

15. 'and as I am a small appendage of it myself' (addition in Cole's copy). Cole's stepmother, his father's fourth wife, was related to the first Lord Montfort (see LA viii. 382).

16. Cole's final will was signed 12 Dec. 1782, only four days before his death. It contains the following provision: 'Whereas my Lord Montford gave me some six or seven years ago a noble pedigree of his family on vellum down to Lord Chancellor Bromley, with additions since, which pedi-

ing at it till about three weeks ago, when I received a letter signed *Robert Bromley*[17] dated from *Tenterden Street, Hanover Square,* to inform me that he had just before called on Lord Montfort to have a sight of the pedigree, who had directed him to me, and given his consent that he might see it and return it to me. He wanted it to correct the pedigree, as a friend of his was preparing an *History of Worcestershire,* and he was desirous his pedigree should be as perfect as it might be.[18] Accordingly I sent it to him last week by one of the Master of Queens's sons,[19] who was going[20] to stay a little with his uncle in Jermin Street, Mr Plumptre,[21] where it is now, and I write to Mr Bromley by this post to inform him of it, that he may send for it there, and if Lord De Ferrers is curious to see it, his Lordship may make use of my name at either place (but probably Mr Bromley will send for it immediately) and have it to his house and return it to Mr Bromley again: except you should be curious to see it, and in that case I will write to Mr Bromley and desire him to send it to you as soon as he has done with it, from whom I may receive it when you and Lord Ferrers have satisfied your curiosity.

Yours most sincerely,

Wm Cole

gree, in length 4 yards and a half, I lent two years ago to Mr Robert Bromley, of Worcester, and is not returned, and as I meant only to save it for his lordship's family when he gave it me, I think it proper that Lord Montford may be acquainted where it is lodged now' (quoted in Palmer, *William Cole* 29).

17. (1732–1803), of Abberley Lodge, Worcs. He died in Albemarle Street, London, 11 March 1803 (see GM March 1803, lxxiii. 292a).

18. Treadway Russell Nash (1725–1811) published *Collections for the History of Worcestershire,* 2 vols, 1781–2. The Bromley pedigree there printed (i. 595) begins with the parents of Sir Thomas ('Lord Chancellor') Bromley.

19. Robert Plumptre (1723–88), President of Queens' College 1760–88; m. (1756) Anne Newcome, 2d dau. of Dr Henry New-

come of Hackney, by whom he had ten children (see DNB). It appears from an entry in one of Cole's MS volumes (Add MS 5825, f. 167v) that Plumptre's eldest son, Joseph (1759–1810), carried the pedigree to London. The latter was of Queens' College (B.A. 1779, and Fellow), and afterwards rector of Newton in the Isle of Ely and of Stretton, Rutland. He d. 16 Oct. 1810 at St Martin's, Stamford Baron, Lincs (see GM Oct. 1810, lxxx. 397b).

20. 'for a few days to see my niece Newcome (and his aunt) at Hackney, and from thence to stay a week or two with his uncle Plumptre' (addition in Cole's copy).

21. John Plumptre or Plumtre (1710–91), of Fredville in Kent; M.P. for Penryn 1758–61; for Nottingham 1761–74. He died 23 Feb. 1791 at his house in Jermyn Street (see *Alumni Cantab.*; GM March 1791, lxi. 280b).

To Cole, Monday 12 April 1779

Add MS 5953, ff. 57–8.

Cole wrote the following notes on the cover: 'Hasted. Lord Hardwicke. Chatterton. V. Ch.' They appear to be an echo of *ante* 2 March, but Cole did not use them.

Address: To the Reverend Mr Cole at Milton near Cambridge.
Postmark: 12 AP.

Arlington Street, April 12, 1779.

AS your gout was so concise, I will not condole on it, but I am sorry you are liable to it, if you do but take the air.

Thank you for telling me of the vendible curiosities at the alderman's. For St Peter's portrait to hang to a fairy's watch, I shall not think of it, both as I do not believe it very like, and as it is composed of invisible writing, for which my eyes are not young enough. In truth I have almost left off making purchases; I have neither room for anything more, nor inclination for them, as I reckon everything very dear, when one has so little time to enjoy it. However, I cannot say but the plates by Rubens do tempt me a little—yet, as I do not care to buy even Rubens in a poke, I should wish to know if the alderman would let me see if it were but one. Would he be persuaded? I would pay for the carriage, though I should not buy them.

Lord De Ferrers will be infinitely happy with the sight of the pedigree, and I will certainly tell him of it, and how kind you are.

Strype's account, or rather Stow's, of Richard's person is very remarkable—but I have done with endeavouring at truth. Weeds grow more naturally than what one plants. I hear your Cantabrigians are still unshaken Chattertonians. Many men are about falsehood, like girls about the first man that makes love to them; a handsomer, a richer, or even a sincerer lover cannot eradicate the first impression—but a sillier swain or a sillier legend sometimes gets into the head of the miss or the learned man and displaces the antecedent folly. Truth's kingdom is not of this world.

I do not know whether our clergy are growing Mahometans or not: they certainly are not what they profess themselves—but as you and I should not agree perhaps in assigning the same defects to them, I will not enter on a subject which I have promised you to drop. All I allude to now is the shocking murder of Miss Ray by a divine.[1] In

1. Martha Ray, the mistress of Lord Sandwich, was shot dead by James Hack- man (1752–79), a clergyman, as she was leaving Covent Garden Theatre 7 April

my own opinion we are growing more fit for Bedlam than for Mahomet's paradise. The poor criminal in question I am persuaded is mad—and the misfortune is, that the law does not know how to define the shades of madness; and thus there are twenty out-pensioners of Bedlam for one that is confined. You, dear Sir, have chosen a wiser path to happiness by depending on yourself for amusement. Books and past ages draw one into no scrapes;[2] and perhaps it is best not to know much of men till they are dead. I wish you health; you want nothing else.

Yours most truly,

H. W.

To Cole, Tuesday 20 April 1779

Add MS 5953, ff. 59–60.
Address: To the Reverend Mr Cole at Milton near Cambridge.
Postmark: EK 20 AP.

Arlington Street, April 20, 1779.

Dear Sir,

I HAVE received the plates very safely,[1] but hope you nor the alderman will take it ill that I return them. They are extremely pretty and uncommonly well preserved—but I am sure they are not by Rubens, nor I believe after his designs, for I am persuaded they are older than his time. In truth I have a great many of the same sort, and do not wish for more. I shall send them back on Thursday by the fly, and will beg you to inquire after them, and I trust they will arrive as safely as they did to

Yours ever,

H. W.

1779, after the performance of Bickerstaffe's *Love in a Village*. Hackman was hanged at Tyburn 19 April 1779. Cole has the following note at the end of his copy of HW's letter (Add MS 5826, f. 173v): 'For an account of this horrid murder, see what I have said in my volume *Initials*, p. 75. Sir John Hynde Cotton calling on me this morning, Wednesday, April 14, told me that he received a letter yesterday from Lord Sandwich, who was to be baited on Monday by Mr Walpole's friends, the Patriots, desiring him to come up to town to serve him in the House of Commons, concluded his letter thus: "I suppose you have heard of the late accident: pray God keep you and yours from such severe trials." I was told last week by Mr Lort that Mr Walpole, on account of Bishop Hinchliffe's patriotism, was grown very fond of him, sent him his Chatterton, and invited him to dine at Strawberry Hill.' Bishop Hinchliffe was an eloquent supporter of liberalism in the House of Lords: he favoured conciliation with the American colonies and toleration toward Roman Catholics.

2. HW has, for the moment, forgotten *Historic Doubts* and Milles and Masters.

1. See *ante* 7 April 1779.

From COLE, Tuesday 20 April 1779

VA, Forster MS 110, f. 216. Cole kept no copy.
Address: The Honourable Horace Walpole, Arlington Street, Piccadilly, London. *Postmark:* Cambridge 22 AP.

Tuesday, April 20, 1779.

Dear Sir,

I SHOULD have wrote before, but Mr Lombe,[1] a gentleman at Cambridge, who has a large collection of pictures, calling on me on Friday with a prized *Catalogue of the Houghton Collection*,[2] I sent a note by him to the alderman signifying your desire to see a specimen before you purchased the plates, at the same time telling him that if he agreed to send one up, I desired he would let me know the day, and I would advertise you of it. I desired Mr Lombe to give me his opinion about them, and let me know it. To my surprise, when I sent my servant this morning for the apothecary to come to me, he brought me a note from the alderman, telling me he had sent them, agreeable to my address, on Monday. So I suppose you have them already, being sent by the fly in Gray's Inn Lane. I am sorry I had not notice of them earlier and to have prevented their coming, for Mr Lombe has no opinion of them.

I am so ill I can write no more. I believe it is something of a St Anthony's fire all about my neck, shoulders and breast. I wish you your health, and am, dear Sir,

Unvariably your most faithful servant,

WM COLE

1. Thomas Lombe (1719–1800), 'an attorney of eminence in Free School Lane,' Cambridge, and also a collector. He was one of the executors of Cole's will, and received a legacy of £50 and a mourning ring for his 'trouble in the execution of this my will' (Cole, quoted in Palmer, *William Cole* 67, 29; see also Cooper, *Memorials* iii. 278).

2. Cole meant to write *priced:* that is, a copy of *Aedes Walpolianae* showing the prices paid by the Empress of Russia for the pictures at Houghton (see *post* 27 April 1779).

To Cole, Friday 23 April 1779

Add MS 5953, ff. 61–2.
Address: To the Reverend Mr Cole at Milton near Cambridge.
Postmark: 23 AP.

[Arlington Street,] April 23, 1779.

I OUGHT not trouble you so often when you are not well; but that is the very cause of my writing now. You left off abruptly from disorder, and therefore I wish to know it is gone.

The plates I hope got home safe. They are pretty, especially the reverses; but the drawing in general is bad.

Pray tell me what you mean by a *prized* catalogue of the pictures at Houghton. Is it a printed one? If it is, where is it to be had?—Odd questions from *me;* and which I should not wish to have mentioned as coming from me. I have been told today that they are actually sold to the Czarina—*sic transit!*—mortifying enough, were not everything transitory! We must recollect that our griefs and pains are so, as well as our joys and glories; and by balancing the account, a degree of comfort is to be extracted—Adieu! I shall be heartily glad to receive a better account of you.

From Cole, Tuesday 27 April 1779

VA, Forster MS 110, f. 217. Cole kept no copy.
Address: The Honourable Horace Walpole, Arlington Street, Piccadilly, London. *Postmark:* Cambridge 28 AP.

Milton, April 27, Tuesday, 1779.

Dear Sir,

I HAVE two or three reasons to write, otherwise have no disposition to it. You want kindly to know how I do: I never was worse in my life: a St Anthony's fire all over my breast, neck and shoulders has so tormented me that I am worn out. God knows whether I shall get the better of it! His will be done, and so I have no great struggles, am resigned.

My servant went on purpose to the fly, met the plates, and delivered them into the alderman's hands, with a civil letter from me, and I believe all is well, for I heard no further about it.

The priced catalogue was brought to me[1] last week by Mr Lombe of Cambridge, a collector. It is a MS, and numbered according to the pages of another edition of the *Aedes Walpolianae* than that you was so kind to give me in 1749. I took a copy[2] of it and sent it back, but Mr Lombe told me that he had with it a letter from a dilettante in town, giving some account of the affair. I asked him to favour me with the sight of it, which he promised to send to me, but has forgot it. If you are curious to have it, I will privately get it, or send you a copy of the prices, which totally are £40,555.

I can write no longer. Adieu, dear Sir,

WM COLE

To COLE, Friday 21 May 1779

Add MS 5953, ff. 67–8.

Cole notes on the cover: 'Mélanges d'Histoire et de Literature par Dom Bonaventure d'Argogne Chartreux, vol. 1, p. 252, where a curious account of Lady Venetia Digby and her miniature picture in your possession.' For his use of the note, see *post* 14 Nov. 1779.

Address: To the Reverend Mr Cole at Milton near Cambridge.
Postmark: RD 21 MA.

Arlington Street, May 21, 1779.

AS Mr Essex has told me that you still continue out of order, I am impatient to hear from yourself how you are. Do, send me a line; I hope it will be a satisfactory one.

Do you know that Dr Ducarel has published a translation of a history of the Abbey of Bec?[1] There is a pretty print[2] to it; and one very curious circumstance, at least valuable to us disciples of *Alma Mater Etonensis*. The ram-hunting was derived from the manor of Wrotham in Norfolk, which formerly belonged to Bec, and being

---

1. MS reads *me to*. The effect of Cole's illness appears in his handwriting, which is not as clear as usual.

2. As it does not appear in Cole's MSS, it is possible that he made the copy in the 1747 *Aedes* which HW sent him.

---

1. *The History of the Royal Abbey of Bec, near Rouen in Normandy.* By Dom. John Bourget [(1724–76)], Benedictine Monk of the Congregation of St Maur in

the said House, and F.S.A. Translated from the French. Printed for J. Nichols, 1779. 'This tract (which he presented to Dr Ducarel in 1764) is only an abstract' of a larger work on the same subject (John Nichols, Advertisement, pp. vii–viii). It was translated from the French by Nichols (see *BM Catalogue*).

2. A print engraved by Pouncy, 'The Church of the Benedictine Abbey of Becc in Normandy,' faces the title-page.

forfeited with other alien priories, was bestowed by Henry VI on our college.[3] I do not repine at reading any book from which I can learn a single fact that I like to know. For the lives of the abbots, they were, according to the author, all pinks of piety and holiness—but there [are] a few other facts amusing, especially with regard to the customs of those savage times—especially, that the Empress Matilda was buried in a bull's hide, and afterwards had a tomb covered with silver.[4]

There is another new book called *Sketches from Nature* in two volumes by Mr G. Keate,[5] in which I found one fact too that, if authentic, is worth knowing. The work is an imitation of Sterne, and has a sort of merit, though nothing that arrives at originality. For the foundation of the church of Reculver, he quotes a MS[6] said to be

3. 'When the harvest work was finished by the tenants [of the manor of East or Great Wrotham], they were to have half an acre of barley, and a ram let loose in the midst of them; and if they catched him, he was their own to make merry with; but if he escaped from them, he was the lord's: which custom is still kept at Eton College, there being a ram every year let loose among the scholars, on a certain day, to be run down by them, the original of which might come from the custom of this manor' (Bourget, op. cit. 130–1). Henry VI settled the manor 'on his college of Eton, at the time of its foundation, and confirmed it afterwards by his charter in 1444; and in 1460 it was re-confirmed by King Edward IV' (ibid. 134). HW's copy of *Topographical Survey of the Great Road from London to Bath and Bristol*, by Archibald Robertson, 2 parts, 1792, is in the British Museum (C.61.c.13), and contains the following note in HW's hand: 'I remember another ancient custom or tenure at Eton College, which was hunting the ram. On a certain day in August, a ram was turned loose in the playing-fields and the boys hunted it with knotted clubs till they killed him. Latterly he was hamstringed before turned out and immediately dispatched. Now I believe the practice is totally dropped.' See also Henry C. Maxwell Lyte, *History of Eton College, 1440–1910*, 1911, pp. 297–8, where he states that shortly after the innovation of hamstringing the ram and beating it to death, the custom was abolished in 1747.

4. Matilda (1102–67), dau. of Henry I of England, m. the Emperor Henry V. Before the high altar of the Abbey of Bec, 'in the middle of the sanctuary, rests the body of Matilda. . . . She was buried in 1167, before our Lady's altar; and in 1282, as they were lengthening the church, they found her corpse, before the place of the high altar, buried in an ox's hide' (Bourget, op. cit. 98–9; cf. 38–9). In the fifteenth century, the English 'plundered the treasury . . . and pulled off the silver plates that covered the tomb of the Empress Matilda' (ibid. 62).

5. *Sketches from Nature; taken, and coloured, in a Journey to Margate. Published from the Original Designs*, 2 vols, 1779, by George Keate (1729–97), author, painter and friend of Voltaire. The work passed through several editions (5th edn, 1802), and was translated into French.

6. Keate apparently embellished a current popular legend, and made it a plausible story (see his *Sketches from Nature*,' 1779, ii. 111–53). In John Nichols's *Bibliotheca Topographica Britannica*, No. 6, pt 2, 1793, p. 79, it is said: 'The beautiful spires of Reculver have furnished Mr Keate with an ingenious legendary tale in his *Sketches from Nature*.' George Dowker, in an article on 'Reculver Church' in *Archaeologia Cantiana*, xii. 248–68, refers to the legend, but assigns it to the twelfth century, not the sixteenth, as Keate does.

written by a Dominican friar of Canterbury and preserved at Louvain. The story is evidently metamorphosed into a novel, and has very little of an antique air; but it affirms that the monkish author attests the beauty of Richard III.[7] This is very absurd if invention and has nothing to do with the story; and therefore one should suppose it genuine. I have desired Dodsley to ask Mr Keate, if there truly exists such a MS—if there does—I own I wish he had printed it rather than his own production; for I agree with Mr Gray, 'That any man living may make a book worth reading, if he will but set down with truth what he has seen or heard, no matter whether the book is well written or not'[8]—Let those, who can[9] write, glean.

From Cole, Tuesday 25 May 1779

VA, Forster MS 110, f. 218. Cole kept no copy.
Address: Honourable Horace Walpole, Arlington Street, Piccadilly, London.
Postmark: Cambridge 26 MA.

Milton, Tuesday, May 25, 1779.

Dear Sir,

YOUR letter was a cordial to me both in its kindness and as I wanted one in my present situation. I wanted to write to you, but could not; and by this scrawl you will perceive how ill qualified for it. I have wrote none since my last to you. Thank God, I think I am better, but my arm, collar-bone and shoulder still continue so uneasy and troublesome with pain and smart, that I am now uneasier for its long continuance. For the last three evenings I have been out for airing.

I did not know Dr Ducarel was the translator: I shall send for the book. I am much afraid the Dominican friar's MS will turn out a fiction. I am told the ram-hunting is lately left off at Eton: as I love old customs, even wh<en> absurd, I am grieved at it.

7. According to Keate, 'it is worthy of being remembered, that there are encomiums bestowed on the character, and person of Richard; upon both of which, historians have thrown so much deformity' (*Sketches from Nature*[2] ii. 129).

8. Gray made the remark apropos of Boswell's *Account of Corsica*: 'The pamphlet proves what I have always maintained, that any fool may write a most valuable book by chance, if he will only tell us what he heard and saw with veracity' (Gray to HW 25 Feb. 1768). See also HW to Mme du Deffand 6 March 1772.

9. Cole's copy reads *can't*.

Have you seen the new *Archaeologia?*[1] I find I am e<mbalmed>
in it.[2] Mr Gough wrote me word[3] that he would send me a parcel of
my performance in a detached state. When they come, I will send
one to you, in full payment for those numerous bounties I have received at your hands. This serves, however, to correct an error I may
have made, when formerly I told you[4] that he had sent down twenty
or more of Mr Masters's essay against you, as it seems to be official
and not particular, which I did not know before.

The first article in the new volume[5] is absurd to the last degree.
Mr Pegge has thought proper in a very long, solemn and elaborate
performance to vindicate St George against a pleasant ballad by Dr
Byrom of Manchester or Lancaster,[6] who, in a bantering, jocose manner, as was his turn, [?pretended] to suppose that St George was a
mistake for St Gregory, who sent over St Augustine the monk to convert us, and so properly the patron of England.

I can write no longer, and think you'll hardly be able to read this
from, dear Sir,

Your most affectionate faithful servant,

WM COLE

You say nothing of the Houghton Collection, therefore I suppose
you have the priced catalogue.

1. Vol. 5.
2. Cole's contribution is entitled, 'Some
Observations on the Horns given by Henry
I to the Cathedral of Carlisle,' *Archaeologia* v. 340–5.
3. MS reads 'me word he word that he
would . . .', obviously a slip of Cole's
pen. The writing in this letter is affected
by Cole's illness.
4. See Cole to HW 6 Jan. 1773 (i. 290),
i. 294, n. 12, and i. 309, n. 3.
5. 'Observations on the History of St
George, the Patron Saint of England,' pp.
1–32, by Samuel Pegge (1704–96) the elder,
antiquary and prebendary of Lichfield
(1757–96) and of Lincoln (1772–96).
6. John Byrom (1692–1763), teacher of
shorthand, poet and diarist, of Manchester,
was the author of a poem, 'On the Patron
of England, In a Letter to Lord Wil-

loughby, President of the Antiquarian Society,' which was printed in his *Miscellaneous Poems*, 2 vols, Manchester, 1773, i.
100–4. The last stanza contains the following lines:

'One may be mistaken—and therefore
    would beg
That a *Willis*, a *Stukeley*, an *Ames*, or a
    Pegge . . .
To search this one question, and settle, I
    hope,
Was Old England's old patron, a Knight
    or a Pope?'

As Willis, Stukeley and Ames were dead
in 1773, when the poem appeared, Pegge
took it upon himself to reply to Byrom,
and his paper, though dated 20 July 1773,
was not read before the Society of Antiquaries until 10 April 1777.

To Cole, Wednesday 2 June 1779

Add MS 5953, ff. 63-4.

Cole notes on the cover: 'In a late letter [i.e., in this letter] you desired to know how Hobart came to impale Boleyn. That I can't resolve, but by a book I just now received from the editor, Mr Gough, who has published Tom Martin's *History of Thetford,* at p. 290 it is evident that Sir Robert Clere, who is buried in Blickling Church, married Alice, daughter of Sir William Boleyn, to whom Blickling Manor belonged. Sir Edward Clere, Knight of the Order of St Michael, sold the chief seat of his family, Blickling, to Sir Henry Hobart, Lord Chief Justice of the Common Pleas.' This note, with a few minor changes, is written to HW 14 Nov. 1779.

Address: To the Reverend Mr Cole at Milton near Cambridge.
Postmark: Isleworth 3 IV.

Strawberry Hill, June 2, 1779.

I AM most sincerely rejoiced, dear Sir, that you find yourself at all better, and trust it is an omen of farther amendment. Mr Essex surprised me by telling me that you, who keep yourself so warm and so numerously clothed, do yet sometimes, if the sun shines, sit and write in your garden for hours at a time. It is more than I should readily do, whose habitudes are so very different from yours. Your complaints seem to demand perspiration—but I do not venture to advise. I understand no constitution but my own, and should kill Milo,[1] if I managed him as I treat myself. I sat in a window on Saturday with the east wind blowing on my neck till near two in the morning—and it seems to have done me good, for I am better within these two days than I have been these six months. My spirits have been depressed, and my nerves so aspen, that the smallest noise disturbed me. Today I do not feel a complaint, which is something at near sixty-two.

I don't know whether I have not misinformed you, nor am sure it was Dr Ducarel who translated the account of the Abbey of Beck—he gave it to Mr Lort, but I am not certain he even published it.[2] You was the first that notified to me the fifth volume of the *Archaeologia.* I am not much more edified than usual; but there are three pretty prints of reginal seals.[3] Mr Pegge's tedious dissertation, which he

1. The celebrated strong-man of antiquity.
2. See *ante* 21 May 1779 n. 1.
3. Prints of the great seals of Queen

Catherine Parr, Queen Mary d'Este (Modena) and Queen Henrietta Maria (see *Archaeologia* v, Plates XIX, XXIV). The third seal is identical with that mentioned

calls a brief one,[4] about the foolish legend of St George, is despicable. All his arguments are equally good for proving the existence of the dragon.

What diversion might laughers make of the Society! Dolly Pentraeth, the old woman of Mouse-hole, and Mr Penneck's nurse, *v.* p. 81, would have furnished Foote with two personages for a farce.[5] The same grave judge's dissertation on patriarchal customs[6] seems to have as much to do with British antiquities, as the Lapland witches that sell wind—and pray what business has the Society with Roman inscriptions in Dalmatia?[7] I am most pleased with the account of Nonsuch,[8] imperfect as it is. It appears to have been but a villa, and not considerable for a royal one. You see lilacs were then a novelty[9]— Well, I am glad they publish away. The vanity of figuring in these repositories will make many persons contribute their MSS, and every

by Cole and HW in their letters of 18 and 26 Oct. 1778. The plates were engraved by Basire.

4. 'On the History of St George' (see preceding letter). Pegge's words are: 'though the matter be treated with all possible brevity, yet sufficient, I trust, will be said, to convince all impartial and competent judges' (*Archaeologia* v. 2).

5. Daines Barrington contributed a paper, 'Mr Barrington on some additional Information relative to the Continuance of the Cornish Language. In a Letter to John Lloyd, Esq.' It was read before the Society 21 March 1777, and it appeared in *Archaeologia* v. 81–2. The passage which HW ridicules is as follows: 'Dolly Pentraeth [1685–1778] (the old woman of Mousehole . . .) is still alive, being supposed to be ninety years of age, and is now grown excessively deaf. She is conceived by some, to be the only person now existing who can speak Cornish; but Mr Penneck's nurse, who died about twenty years ago, could likewise converse in the same language' (p. 81). For further particulars concerning Dolly Pentraeth, whose married name was Jeffers or Jeffery, see 'On the Expiration of the Cornish Language. In a Letter from the Hon. Daines Barrington . . . to John Lloyd, Esq.,' *Archaeologia* iii. 278–84. 'Peter Pindar' ridiculed Barrington for his part in this affair in *Lyric Odes for the Year 1785*, Ode xxi:

'Hail Mousehole! birth place of old Doll Pentreath,
The *last* who jabber'd Cornish—so says Daines,
Who, bat-like, haunted ruins, lane and heath,
With Will o' Wisp, to brighten up his brains.'

See also an account, with a print of her, in *The Universal Magazine*, Jan. 1781, lxviii. 21–4; Musgrave, *Obituary*.

6. 'Observations on Patriarchal Customs and Manners. By the Hon. Daines Barrington,' *Archaeologia* v. 119–36.

7. HW refers to 'A further Account of some ancient Roman Inscriptions, lately observed in the Provinces of Istria and Dalmatia, and also in Italy, with Remarks. In a Letter to the Rev. Dr Milles . . . from John Strange, Esq., F.R.S., his Majesty's Resident at Venice,' ibid. 169–81.

8. 'A Survey of Nonsuch House and Park, *cum pertinentiis, Anno Domini* 1650,' ibid. 429–39. The account was taken 'from the original in the Augmentation Office.'

9. A fountain of white marble 'is set round with six trees called lelack trees, which trees beare no fruite but only a very pleasant flower' (ibid. v. 434). The first reference to lilacs in OED is 1625.

now and then something valuable will come to light, which its own intrinsic merit might not have saved.

I know nothing more of Houghton.[10] I should certainly be glad to have the priced catalogue; and if you will lend me yours, my printer shall transcribe it—but I am in no hurry. I conceive faint hopes, as the sale is not concluded—however I take care not to flatter myself.

I think I told you[11] I had purchased at Mr Ives's sale a handsome coat in painted glass of Hobart impaling Boleyn—but I can find no such match in the pedigree—yet I have heard that Blickling belonged to Anne Boleyn's father.[12] Pray reconcile all this to me.

Lord De Ferrers is to dine here on Saturday; and I have got to treat him an account of ancient paintings formerly in the hall of Tamworth Castle; they are mentioned in Warton's *Observations on the Fairy Queen*, vol. 1, p. 43.[13]

Do not put yourself to pain to answer this. Only be assured that I shall be happy to know when you are able to write with ease. You must leave your cloister, if your transcribility leaves you.

From Cole, Wednesday 9 June 1779

VA, Forster MS 110, ff. 219–20. Cole's copy, Add MS 5826, ff. 174v, 175v.
Address: Honourable Horace Walpole, in Arlington Street, Piccadilly, London.
Postmark: Cambridge.

Milton, June 9, Wednesday, 1779.

Dear Sir,

THANK God I am much better of my complaint[1] than I have been, and can use my pen with tolerable ease, so that I hope to continue in my cloister[2] for this bout at least. I am concerned that your spirits have been less vigorous, and should be sorry you would continue the receipt of the window to mend them: an east wind even

10. That is, concerning the sale of the Houghton collection of pictures to the Empress of Russia.

11. See *ante* 20 Feb. 1777.

12. Sir Thomas Boleyn (1477–1539), afterwards E. of Wiltshire.

13. HW refers to Thomas Warton's *Observations on the Fairy Queen of Spenser*, 2d edn, corrected and enlarged, 2 vols, 1762. HW's copy (K.4.8–9) was sold SH iii. 163.

———

1. Erysipelas, or 'St Anthony's Fire.'

2. 'and not be a *moine defroqué*' (addition in Cole's copy).

by my fireside kills me. I even suffered by that which you fancy did you service on Saturday. Sore throats and fevers are sure to visit me with that diabolical blast, and the only good I ever heard of it was from you: may you never feel its bad influence. It must be an ill wind indeed that blows no good.

Mr Essex's information might well surprise you. Half of it was literally true. I suppose no one, much against inclination, goes so wrapped up as myself. As to sitting and writing in the garden, about nine years ago, for half an hour at most each time, I twice made the experiment, once in a little building in it,[3] which was too hot, the other under some filbert trees, and was too exposed, and never more after in my life. Nay, for these five years I have not even ventured to sit on a bench in the garden for three minutes together.[4] So far for Mr Essex, who was here a fortnight ago, and is going with his family to Margate.

You are so far in the right in respect to my constitution, in wanting perspiration, that I even envy the offensiveness of my servants' sweaty feet. I don't know hardly what it is to perspire, and have a mind to try the bootikins you was so kind to send me three or four years ago, which are still new.

Dr Ducarel, I am informed, with Mr Nicols[5] the printer, and Mr Gough, published the Bec *History*. I suppose Dr Ducarel might lend the book and partly translate it. I am told he is now, with Mr Nicols, on the eve of publishing an account of our alien priories, with some neat prints.[6] I know he had such a design many years ago.

As it will be less trouble to me, who do not write with great ease, to send you my priced catalogue,[7] although copied into your kind present many years ago, I will convey it to you, I hope, by Mr Lort, tomorrow or next day, in hopes that you will return it to me again.

Tomorrow is the election at Cambridge for the University.[8] The

3. Cole's copy reads 'once in the hermitage.'

4. 'Mr Essex must have dreamt what he mentioned' (addition in Cole's copy).

5. John Nichols (1745–1826), of LA and LI, correspondent of HW and Cole.

6. 'which Mr Essex saw when lately in town' (addition in Cole's copy). Essex presumably was Cole's informant concerning the *History of the Abbey of Bec*. Nichols published *Some Account of the Alien Priories, and of such Lands as they are* known to have possessed in England and Wales, 2 vols, 1779, collected from the MSS of John Warburton and Ducarel.

7. Cole afterwards copied the prices from his copy and sent them to HW (see *post* 12 July 1779). He possibly had other MS notes in it which he was not willing for HW to see.

8. Charles Manners, M. of Granby, and M.P. for the University, had succeeded to the Dukedom of Rutland 29 May 1779.

Vice-Chancellor called here yesterday, and told me that Mr Townshend,[9] had the election been after the Commencement, three weeks
hence, would certainly have carried it,[10] and may have a good chance
now. Lord Hyde[11] is of the same college, St John's, which is consequently divided.[12] King's no doubt will be for Mr Mansfield,[13] the
counsellor. As far as I can hear, it will be a hard-run affair. It is reported that Lord Townshend[14] gives his interest to Lord Hyde, because he is his relation, as he expressed it. Is not Mr Townshend[15] a
nearer? The ministry are for Lord Hyde, yet the Archbishop[16] <and
Bishop> of Ely are for Mr Townshend. How are these things to be
reconciled? <I sup>pose Mr Lort will come down.

Mr Pennant lately sent me two prints,[17] which I send in the *Aedes
Walpolianae* for you to keep or return, as you judge proper.

Here is a self-taught genius at Cambridge[18] who paints exceedingly
well upon glass. I have two of his heads exceedingly like. It has the
appearance of standing the weather.[19]

Mr Lort did not come,[20] so am disappointed in sending the book,

9. '(notwithstanding his affair of being
turned out of the coach by Lady Granby
last year)' (addition in Cole's copy). Hon.
John (afterwards Lord John) Townshend
(1757–1833), 2d son of George Townshend,
4th Vct and 1st M. Townshend; M.P. for
Cambridge University 1780–4 (see *Eton
Coll. Reg. 1753–90*). Mary Isabella Somerset, Lady Granby (1756–1831), 5th dau. of
Charles Noel Somerset, 4th D. of Beaufort,
m. (1776) Charles Manners (1754–87), afterwards 4th D. of Rutland. In 1786 Townshend stood trial for criminal conversation.

10. 'by means of the younger Masters of
Arts' (addition in Cole's copy).

11. Thomas Villiers (1753–1824) suc. his
father (11 Dec. 1786) as 2d E. of Clarendon;
Eton and St John's, Cambridge (M.A.
1773); M.P. for Christchurch 1774–80; for
Helston 1780–6.

12. 'Trinity is also about equally divided
between them' (addition in Cole's copy).

13. James Mansfield (originally Man-
field) (1733–1821), M.P. for Cambridge University 1779–84; solicitor-general 1780–2;
Lord Chief Justice of the Common Pleas,
and knighted, 1804.

14. George Townshend (1724–1807), 4th
Vct Townshend, afterwards (1787) 1st M.
Townshend.

15. Cole's copy reads 'his son.'

16. Hon. Frederick Cornwallis (1713–83),
Abp of Canterbury 1768–83, noted for his
hospitality at Lambeth Palace.

17. 'of Mr Lloyd and Sir John Gwynn'
(addition in Cole's copy). John Lloyd
(1733–93), rector of Caerwis, was Pennant's
companion on his tour in Wales. EBP states
that this print was engraved by P. Mazell
after Moses Griffith, and that it was a plate
to Pennant's *Tour in Wales*, 1778, but it
has not been found in any copy seen and it
is not mentioned in the List of Plates. 'Sir
John Gwynn' is Cole's mistake for Sir John
Wynn or Wynne (1553–1626), of Gwydir,
Bt and antiquary, whose print, engraved by
W. Sharp, was Plate III (opp. p. 140) of
Pennant's *Journey to Snowdon*, 1781, the
second part of his *Tour in Wales*. Pennant
allowed Daines Barrington to use the print
in his *Miscellanies*, 1781, as a frontispiece
to 'The History of the Gwedir Family' (see
EBP).

18. 'Charles Freeman' (addition in Cole's
copy). He is listed as a 'painter' in *Universal British Directory*, 5 vols, 1791–8?, ii.
491.

19. 'being burnt in' (addition in Cole's
copy).

20. This paragraph was evidently writ-

which I will send by some early conveyance. Mr Mansfield had 157 votes, Mr Townshend 145, Lord Hyde 138. The two mitres interested themselves for Mr Mansfield, as I am since informed.

To COLE, Monday 12 July 1779

Add MS 5953, ff. 65–6.

A letter from Cole, which he presumably sent with the list of prices, mentioned below, is missing.

Address: To the Reverend Mr Cole at Milton near Cambridge.

Postmark: EK 13 IY.

Strawberry Hill, July 12, 1779.

I AM concerned, dear Sir, that you gave yourself the trouble of transcribing the catalogue and prices,[1] which I received last night, and for which I am exceedingly obliged to you. Partial as I am to the pictures at Houghton, I confess I think them much overvalued. My father's whole collection of which alone he had preserved the prices, cost but forty thousand pounds; and after his death there were three sales of pictures,[2] among which were all the whole lengths of Vandyck but three, which had been sent to Houghton, but not fitting any of the spaces left, came back to town. Few of the rest sold were very fine, but no doubt Sir Robert had paid as dear for many of them; as purchasers are not perfect connoisseurs at first.

Many of the valuations are not only exorbitant, but injudicious. They who made the estimate[3] seem to have considered the rarity of the hands more than the excellence. Three, 'The Magi Offering' by Carlo Maratti,[4] as it is called, and two supposed Paul Veroneses[5] are

ten on or after 10 June, as the election was held on that day. It does not appear in Cole's copy.

———

1. A list of the prices at which the pictures in the Houghton Collection were valued. A priced list of the Houghton Collection was printed in *The European Magazine*, Feb. 1782 (i. 96–9).

2. Not identified.

3. It appears from two letters, formerly in the Morrison Collection, from Lord Orford to Christie, the auctioneer, dated 30 Oct. and 2 Dec. 1778, that the valuation of the pictures in the collection was entrusted to Christie, and that 'the most profound secrecy' was to be observed (see

Catalogue of the Collection of Autograph Letters . . . formed . . . by Alfred Morrison, vol. 5, Privately Printed, 1891, pp. 48–9).

4. 'The Adoration of the Magi, by Carlo Maratti. He has painted another of them in the Church of the Venetian St Mark at Rome. Six feet eleven inches high, by four feet wide' (*Aedes, Works* ii. 276). It was in the gallery at Houghton, and was valued at £300, according to a contemporary MS list now WSL (see also *European Magazine* i. 98b).

5. Probably two pictures in the Marble Parlour at Houghton, 'The Ascension,' and 'The Apostles after the Ascension,' assigned to Paul Veronese (see *Aedes, Works*

very indifferent copies, yet all are roundly valued, and the first ridiculously. I do not doubt of another picture in the collection but 'The Last Supper' by Raphael,[6] and yet that is set down at 500*l*. I miss three pictures at least that are not set down, the Sir Thomas Wharton,[7] the Laud[8] and Gibbons.[9] The first is most capital. Yes, I recollect, I have had some doubts on the Laud, though the University of Oxford once offered 400*l*. for it—and if Queen Henrietta is by Vandyck,[10] it is a very indifferent one. The affixing a higher value to the Pietro Cortona[11] than to the octagon Guido[12] is most absurd—I have often gazed on the latter and preferred it even to the 'Doctors.'[13]

ii. 263). 'The Ascension' is valued at £200 in the MS referred to in the preceding note; 'The Apostles after the Ascension' is not valued at all, but in *The European Magazine* i. 98a, it is valued at £200, and 'The Ascension' is omitted. A third Veronese, valued at £100, hung in the gallery, but HW's eulogistic description of it in *Aedes* is inconsistent with a picture of doubtful authenticity (see *Works* ii. 272).

6. 'It was in the Arundel collection, and is mentioned in the catalogue of those pictures; from thence it came into the possession of the Earl of Yarmouth, and from him to Sir John Holland, of whom Lord Orford bought it. It is in fine preservation. One foot eight inches high, by two feet eight and a half wide. There are various prints from it' (*Aedes, Works* ii. 277). It was in the Gallery at Houghton.

7. (1610–84), 'brother to Philip Lord Wharton, and Knight of the Bath; whole length, by Van Dyck. From the Wharton Collection' (*Aedes, Works* ii. 263). It was in the Marble Parlour at Houghton, and was bought by the Empress of Russia (see Gustav Glück, *Van Dyck*, Stuttgart and Berlin, [1931], pp. 468, 572).

8. 'Archbishop Laud, the original portrait of him; three quarters, by Van Dyck. The University of Oxford once offered the Wharton family four hundred pounds for this picture' (*Aedes, Works* ii. 247). It was in the Drawing Room at Houghton, and it also was bought by the Empress of Russia (see Glück, op. cit. 443, 569). It was engraved for John Boydell, *Collection of Prints, engraved after the most capital Paintings in England*, 9 vols, ii. No. 11.

9. A portrait of Grinling Gibbons by Sir Godfrey Kneller. 'It is a masterpiece, and

equal to any of Van Dyck's' (*Aedes, Works* ii. 242). It was in the Common Parlour at Houghton. The portraits of Wharton, Laud and Gibbons are not mentioned in the MS list now wsl, or in *The European Magazine*.

10. The portrait of Henrietta, in the Drawing Room at Houghton, was valued, together with Van Dyck's portrait of Charles I, at £400 (see *European Magazine* i. 97a; the MS list does not include this valuation). See also Glück, op. cit. 391, 562. The portrait was engraved for Boydell, op. cit. ii. No. lxviii.

11. 'Abraham, Sarah, and Hagar, by Pietro Cortona. . . . Six feet ten inches high, by six feet one wide' (*Aedes, Works* ii. 273). It was in the Gallery at Houghton, and was engraved for Boydell, op. cit. i. No. xxvii. It was valued at £1,000.

12. 'The Adoration of the Shepherds, octagon, a most perfect and capital picture of Guido [Guido Reni, 1575–1642], not inferior to The Doctors: the beauty of the Virgin, the delicacy of her and the Child . . . the awe of the shepherds, and the chiaroscuro of the whole picture, which is in the finest preservation, are all incomparable. . . . Three feet three inches and a half every way' (*Aedes, Works* ii. 274). It was in the Gallery at Houghton and was valued at £400.

13. 'Over the farthest chimney [in the Gallery at Houghton] is that capital picture, and the first in this collection, The Doctors of the Church: they are consulting on the immaculateness of the Virgin, who is above in the clouds. . . . In this picture, which is by Guido in his brightest manner, and perfectly preserved, there are six old men as large as life. The expression, draw-

In short the appraisers were determined to consider what the Czarina *could* give, rather than what the pictures were really worth—I am glad she seems to think so, for I hear no more of the sale—It is not very wise in me still to concern myself and at my age, about what I have so little interest in—It is still less wise to be anxious on trifles when one's country is sinking. I do not know which is most mad, my nephew or our ministers—both the one and the others increase my veneration for the founder of Houghton!

I will not rob you of the prints you mention, dear Sir. One of them at least I know Mr Pennant gave me.[14] I do not admire him for his punctiliousness with you.[15] Pray tell me the name of your glass-painter:[16] I do not think I shall want him, but it is not impossible. Mr Essex agreed with me that Jarvis's windows[17] for Oxford after Sir Joshua Reynolds, will not succeed. Most of his colours are opaque, and their great beauty depending on a spot of light for sun or moon, is an imposition. When his paintings are exhibited at Charing Cross,[18] all the rest of the room is darkened to relieve them. That cannot be done at New College; or if done, the chapel would be too dark. If there is other light, the effect will be lost.

This sultry weather I hope will quite restore you. People need not go to Lisbon and Naples, if we continue to have such summers.

Yours most sincerely,

H. Walpole

ing, design, and colouring, wonderfully fine. . . . After Sir Robert had bought this picture, and it was gone to Civita Vecchia to be shipped for England, Innocent XIII, then Pope, remanded it back, as being too fine to be let go out of Rome; but on hearing who had bought it, he gave permission for its being sent away again' (*Aedes, Works* ii. 266–8). It was engraved for Boydell, op. cit. ii. No. lviii, and was valued at £3,500. According to HW, Sir Robert paid 'but a little above six hundred pounds' (HW to Mann 1 May 1774). Lord Orford wrote to Christie 30 Oct. 1778: 'Sir Joshua Reynolds formerly offered me two thousand guineas for one picture only (The Doctors), and assured me that if I would part with it to him he meant to keep it' (see Alfred Morrison, *Catalogue*, loc. cit.).

14. Which one is not known. The London Sale Catalogue mentions neither, but the print of Lloyd may have been in one of the lots, v. 626–31, 'Dignified and Other Clergy' of the reign of George III, who are not all mentioned by name. The rare print of Sir John Wynn by Vaughan (see EBP) was i. 130.

15. What this was is not known.

16. Charles Freeman (see following letter).

17. Thomas Jervais or Jarvis (d. 1799) began in 1777 to paint the glass for the great west window of New College Chapel, and completed it in 1787.

18. Jervais 'held an exhibition at Charing Cross of specimens from his works, including effects of moonlight, firelight, and winter scenes' (DNB: Lionel Cust). This was

From Cole, Saturday 24 July 1779

VA, Forster MS 110, ff. 221–2. Cole's copy, Add MS 5826, ff. 176v, 177v.
Address: Honourable Horace Walpole, Strawberry Hill, in Twickenham, Middlesex. *Postmark:* 27 IY.

Milton, July 24, 1779.

Dear Sir,

I HOPE the pictures will keep their station, on many accounts: it is a fine repository for them, and though a most capital palace, yet when the pictures have unfurnished it, it will be disregarded, at least for a time, and till they are forgotten. I am told by a Norfolk gentleman,[1] who has it from Lord Orford, that the reason he gives for parting with them is the burden upon him of paying the interest of £40,000, which this would ease him from. Yet, methinks the honour of his family, the way he lives in, no children to provide for, and the great fortune that must come in on the death of his mother,[2] might be supposed to balance the weight of the interest, except he is more pressed than I apprehend he is. I am rather partial to him, having met him two or three times at Horsheth, when his agreeable and polite behaviour much pleased me.

The glass-painter at Cambridge is one Charles Freeman, a common coach- and house-painter. He has an elder brother[3] at Cambridge, self-taught also, and from his appearance the least likely to prove a genius that you can meet with. They are both originals, well behaved and ingenious. The elder brother is a most admirable copier, and did a great deal in that way, but he got his prices to be high.[4] He now is so employed in surveying estates that he has in a manner dropped his pencil. I wish you could see a coat of arms that he did lately for Tyson and his wife.[5] He brought it over to me, by

in 'the Great Room, in Spring-Gardens, Charing Cross,' where the Incorporated Society of Artists of Great Britain held their exhibitions until 1772.

---

1. Probably Thomas Kerrich.
2. Margaret Rolle, wife of Robert Walpole, 2d E. of Orford. At this time she was living in Italy with the Cavaliere Mozzi. She died 13 Jan. 1781 (cf. *post* 7 Feb. 1781).
3. Joseph Freeman, land-surveyor and

painter. He died 'suddenly, at his house near St Peter's College, Cambridge,' 10 March 1799 (GM March 1799, lxix. 260a).
4. 'I would have had a picture of Bishop Gardiner from the original in Trinity Hall Lodge, not bigger than that of Mr Gray you gave to Pembroke Hall, but he asked three guineas for it: that deterred me' (addition in Cole's copy).
5. 'the colouring, drawing and disposition of which, with diapering, is beyond

great persuasion, for he is shy, diffident and reserved to a great degree.[6] Mr Tyson might easily convey it to you, and will do so, if you choose to let me know whether it would be agreeable to you, and I would write to him. He is doing something for me,[7] but when it will be finished is more than I can say, for I have no opportunity of seeing him, not being well enough to go to Cambridge.

I hope the Lisbon and Neapolitan weather will be of service, for I never was in such a perspiration. It was the hope of its service that made it tolerable: otherwise it was the most fatiguing and disagreeable weather I ever experienced. I hope it agreed with you, and that you find the benefit of it.

Mr Bryant was at Cambridge for five days in the Commencement Week, where he has not been for years. He was so caressed that dining here was impracticable when heads and professors vied with each other to engage him, and I thought he much distinguished me by coming to see me two mornings together. Dr Glynn came with him both times, and though he said not a word to me, yet I find by others that he can't digest or relish your Chatterton book. He is indeed Rowley-mad. Mr Bryant seemed much pleased with a kind letter he had received from you.[8] He told me that the mastership of the Charterhouse, without any application from him, had been[9] offered to him, but that he had declined it. I was much surprised at it, as it was a most honourable retreat and retirement in the decline of life and in the literary way. I told him so.[10] I can only add my name, and that I am,

Yours,

WM COLE

I send this by Mr Essex, who, with his family, set off for Margate tomorrow.

any I ever saw, ancient or modern. Mr Essex says the colours will stand' (addition in Cole's copy).

6. 'which is not commonly the case of genii, who generally are pretty confident of their own merit' (addition in Cole's copy).

7. Freeman was making a painted-glass portrait of Cole from a drawing by Kerrich (see *post* 30 Dec. 1779).

8. This letter is missing. Apparently none of the HW-Bryant correspondence has survived.

9. Cole's copy reads 'had been twice offered. . . .' Cf. DNB.

10. 'especially as he seemed to wish for a town house, and mentioned my cousin Dr Cock's house in Abington Buildings as what would suit him' (addition in Cole's copy).

To Cole, Thursday 12 August 1779

Add MS 5953, ff. 69–70.

Address: To the Reverend Mr Cole at Milton near Cambridge.
Postmark: Isleworth [1]3 [A]V.

Strawberry Hill, Aug. 12, 1779.

I WRITE from decency, dear Sir, not from having anything particular to say, but to thank you for your offer of letting me see
the arms of painted glass, which however I will decline, lest it should
be broken; and as at present I have no occasion to employ the
painter.[1] If I build my offices, perhaps I may have; but I have
dropped that thought for this year. The disastrous times do not inspire expense. Our alarms,[2] I conclude, do not ruffle your hermitage.
We are returning to our state of islandhood, and shall have little, I
believe, to boast, but of what we have been!

I see a *History of Alien Priories*[3] announced; do you know anything of it, or of the author?

I am, ever yours most sincerely,

H. Walpole

From Cole, Sunday 14 November 1779

VA, Forster MS 110, ff. 223–4. Cole's copy, Add MS 5826, ff. 177v, 178v.

Address: The Honourable Horace Walpole, Arlington Street, London.
Postmark: Cambridge 16 NO.

Milton, Sunday, Nov. 14, 1779.

Dear Sir,

YOUR instructive good manners is thrown away on a clown, or
the beginning of your last (on the frightful 12 August) would
have taught me better behaviour. It begins thus: 'I write from decency, not from having anything particular to say,' etc. What a re-
buke is this to my negligence! Indeed it is shameful, and I assure you
I am thoroughly sensible of it, but an unaccountable indolence has

1. Charles Freeman.   3. See *ante* 9 June 1779.
2. See HW to Mason 9 and 18 Aug. 1779.
An invasion by the French and Spanish
was feared.

seized me in respect to epistolizing, for in nothing else do I feel its influence, and am never idle—if my greatest labours may not be termed idlenesses. My greatest excuse must be what is reality: that if I have not wrote to you, my oldest, worthiest friend, I have been as silent everywhere else. I have a letter by me from Mr Gough with queries for a book, which I have at last procured answers to from St John's, but I believe the book is printing before my answer gets to him.

I suppose you have seen Dr Lort since his doctorate.[1] He told me that he meant to call on you very soon. He dined with me this day fortnight, the day before he left college for his new lodgings in the Lollards' Tower at Lambeth.[2] He made me very happy on leaving me, by giving me his picture, well painted and like. Indeed I have a great loss in him. Friends at this place fly off unaccountably fast of late. Mr Tyson's loss, in communicating books and new publications, I can never retrieve. I received a letter from him on Friday,[3] which, had I a frank, I would send you entire. As I have none, I will transcribe part of it.

I shall give you some account of our late ramble, as I was very busy the whole time as an antiquary. Our first stage was to Hatfield Priory, the noble house of Mr Wright,[4] indeed so elegant and so comfortable that one almost forgives his pulling down the old Priory with its fine bay window. In the hall of his house are three busts in terra cotta of Henry VII, Bishop Fisher and Henry VIII, *aet.* 19.[4a] They are said to be the work of Pietro Torregiano, who executed the magnificent tomb of Henry VII, and were taken out of the room over the Holbein gate at Whitehall.[5] Perhaps Mr

1. The degree of D.D. was not conferred until 1780 (cf. *post* 2 July 1780).

2. Lort was domestic chaplain to Archbishop Cornwallis from 1779 to 1782, and in 1785 he became librarian at Lambeth. Cf. *post* 30 Oct. 1782.

3. The letter is dated 10 Nov. 1779. Cole's copy is in Add MS 5825, ff. 53v, 54v.

4. John Wright, a coachmaker of Long Acre, bought, about 1764, Hatfield Peverell (or Priory), near Witham in Essex. He demolished the remains of the Priory, which adjoined the church, 'and built a handsome house on a little knoll about 100 yards more south, commanding some pleasant views' ('S.H.,' in a letter in GM Aug. 1786, lvi. 664–5; see also Gough, *Sepulchral Monuments*, vol. 1, pt 1, p. 16).

4a. During 1935 the bust of Henry VII was acquired by the Victoria and Albert Museum; that of Henry VIII by Mr William Randolph Hearst; that of Bishop Fisher by the Metropolitan Museum of Art, New York. Tyson's reference to the busts is the first of many which are summarized by Charles R. Beard, *The Connoisseur* lxxxiv. 77 ff. (Aug. 1929) and by Preston Remington, *Bulletin of the Metropolitan Museum of Art*, xxxi (Nov. 1936). 223–9. The three busts are reproduced in both articles. The identity of the bust of Henry VII is alone unquestioned.

5. See following letter.

Walpole would like to know the fate of these very singular busts. In the
Priory Church is the oldest specimen of monumental sculpture in England, the effigies in stone of Lady Peverel,[6] the foundress, concubine to
William the Conqueror. Of this I made an accurate and measured drawing. From Hatfield I paid my respects to the old cross-legged knights at
Danbury, which Mr Strut points out to show how early we were advanced
in sculpture.[7] These are in wood, and the workmanship better than one
commonly meets with. There are three of them, called St Clair's.[8] At Little
Baddow are two very ancient wooden figures of ladies under an arch in
the wall, but resting on altar tombs. Mr Strut tells us[9] that the wood being
decayed, the bones, and even the dress, of the corpse may be seen: however, I could find only a heap of stones and earth, nor can I think that a
body could be buried in a church without its being enclosed in lead, besides the box of stone. At Earls Colne we met with the most cordial reception from Mrs Tyson's relation, Mrs Holgate,[10] the present Prioress, who
in respect to hospitality equals any of the former. Here I had much employment among the Veres,[11] and she gave me several old deeds to copy
the seals from. I brought home with me the only remaining MS belonging
to this Priory, a chartulary. My munificent friend Mr Gough intends to
have all my drawings of the monuments engraved, at the vast expense of
ten guineas each plate, and also intends to write a history of the <Priory
of> Earls Colne. If you should like to have the MS chartulary to transcribe,[12] I will take some opportunity of sending it to you, for I may keep
it as long as I think proper. From Sir John Cullum's, Hardwick House,[13]
formerly a seat belonging to the Abbot of Bury, I visited the de la Pole's
at Wingfield,[14] etc.

I thought this might entertain you.

I see Mr Nichols has published his two small volumes of *Alien
Priories,* which I may buy, if you have seen them and approve them.
As yet I have not seen them or heard anything of them.

6. 'Ingelrica, wife of Ranulph de Peverell. . . . Her figure cut in stone, with a
lion at her feet' (Gough, op. cit. vol. i, pt
1, p. 16). An engraving by Basire after Tyson's drawing appears opp. p. 16.

7. See Joseph Strutt, *A Compleat View
of the Manners, Customs . . . etc. . . . of
England,* 2 vols, 1775–6, ii. 25.

8. That is, supposed to be members of
the St Clere family. Two of the figures are
engraved in Gough, *Sepulchral Monuments,* vol. 1, pt 1, opp. p. 30; see also p. 32.

9. Strutt, op. cit., ii. 105.

10. Not identified.

11. Tyson's drawings of members of the
Vere family were afterwards engraved in
Gough's *Sepulchral Monuments.*

12. Cole's copy of the chartulary is in
Add MS 5860, ff. 215 ff.

13. In Suffolk, about two miles from
Bury St Edmunds.

14. Wingfield Castle, fortified manor-
house of the De la Pole family.

Probably you may have seen it: if not, in vol. 1, p. 252 of Dom Bonaventure D'Argogne's *Mélanges d'Histoire et de Literature,* is a curious account of Lady Venetia Digby and her miniature picture now in your possession.[15]

In a former letter[16] you desired to know how Hobart came to impale Boleyn. That I cannot resolve, but by a book I lately received from the editor, Mr Gough, who has published Tom Martin's *History of Thetford,*[17] at p. 290 it appears that Sir Robert Clere, who is buried in Blickling Church, married Alice, daughter of Sir William Boleyn,[18] to whom Blickling Manor belonged. Sir Edward Clere,[19] Knight of the Order of St Michael, sold the chief seat of his family, Blickling, to Sir Henry Hobart,[20] Lord Chief Justice of the Common Pleas.

I hope you continue well. Thank God, I have not had such a respite these five years as this autumn. May it continue, but I feel warnings not to be too much flushed on the occasion. Adieu! dear Sir, and that nothing may disturb your health or quiet is the constant wish of

Your affectionate and obliged servant,

WM COLE

To COLE, Tuesday 16 November 1779

Add MS 5953, ff. 71–2.

Address: To the Reverend Mr Cole at Milton near Cambridge.
Postmark: GC 16 NO.

Berkeley Square,[1] Nov. 16, 1779.

YOU ought not to accuse yourself only, when I have been as silent as you. Surely we have been friends too long to admit cere-

15. Cf. *ante* 16 May 1762 nn. 55, 57.

16. That of 2 June 1779.

17. *The History of the Town of Thetford, in the Counties of Norfolk and Suffolk, from the earliest Accounts to the present Time,* by the late Mr Thomas Martin of Palgrave, Suffolk, F.A.S., 1779. Cole was a subscriber to the work. The account to which Cole refers appears at pp. 290–1.

18. Sir Robert Clere (d. 1529), Kt, m., as his 2d wife, Alice Boleyn (d. 1538), 4th dau. of Sir William Boleyn (d. 1505), K.B., of

Blickling (see Blomefield, *Norfolk*[2] vi. 387–8, 392–3).

19. (d. 1606), great-grandson of Sir Robert Clere, was knighted by Queen Elizabeth. 'He travelled into foreign parts, was in such esteem at the French Court, that he was elected one of the Knights of the Gallic Order of St Michael; but affecting much grandeur, and keeping a vast retinue, he contracted a large debt, and was forced to sell a great part of his estate,' including Blickling (ibid. vi. 395).

20. (d. 1625), 1st Bt.

mony as a go-between. I have thought of writing to you several times, but found I had nothing worth telling you. I am rejoiced to hear your health has been better. Mine has been worse the whole summer and autumn than ever it was without any positive distemper, and thence I conclude it is a failure in my constitution—of which, being a thing of course, we will say no more. Nobody but a physician is bound to hear what he cannot cure—and if we will pay for what we cannot expect, it is our own fault.

I have seen Dr Lort who seems pleased with becoming a limb of Canterbury. I heartily wish the mitre may not devolve before it has beamed substantially on him. In the meantime he will be delighted with ransacking the library at Lambeth; and to do him justice, his ardour is literary, not interested.

I am much obliged to you, dear Sir, for taking the trouble of transcribing Mr Tyson's journal, which is entertaining. But I am so ignorant as not to know where Hatfield Priory is. The three heads I remember on the gate of Whitehall;[2] there were five more.[3] The whole demolished structure was transported to the Great Park at Windsor by the late Duke of Cumberland,[4] who intended to re-edify it, but never did; and now I suppose

Its ruins ruined, as its place no more.[5]

I did not know what was become of the heads, and am glad any are preserved. I should doubt their being the works of Torreggiano.[6]

Pray who is Mr Nichols, who has published the *Alien Priories?* There are half a dozen or more, very pretty views of French Cathedrals. I cannot say that I found anything else in the book that

1. HW acquired his house in Berkeley Square early in August, and took possession of it 14 Oct. 1779 (see HW to Lady Ossory 7 Aug., 14 Oct. 1779).

2. This statement of HW's has not been discussed by the historians of these busts, who treat as 'traditional' Pennant's statement in *London,* 1790, p. 93, that the busts formed part of the 'Holbein Gate' in Whitehall.

3. Two of these were later taken to Hampton Court, where they were made to do duty as two Roman emperors (see Henry B. Wheatley, *London Past and Present,* 3 vols, 1891, iii. 513).

4. William Augustus (1721–65), D. of

Cumberland, after the gate was demolished in Aug. 1759 'to make way for the present Parliament Street,' 'had every brick removed to Windsor Great Park, and talked of re-erecting it at the end of the Long Walk, with additions at the sides, from designs by Thomas Sandby. Nothing, however, was done' (loc. cit.).

5. 'Their ruins perish'd, and their place no more.'—Pope, *Moral Essays* v. 22. Cole's copy reads 'and.'

6. Wheatley and Mr Beard suggest that they are the work of Giovanni da Maiano; Mr Remington is inclined to accept Torrigiano.

amused me—but as you deal in ancienter lore than I do, perhaps you might be better pleased.

I am told there is a *New History of Gloucestershire,* very large, but ill executed, by one Rudhall.[7] Still I have sent for it, for Gloucestershire is a very historic county.

It was a wrong scent on which I employed you. The arms I have impaled with Hobart are certainly not Boleyn's.

You lament removal of friends—alas! dear Sir, when one lives to our age, one feels that in a higher degree than from their change of place!—but one must not dilate those common moralities. You see by my date that I have changed place myself. I am got into an excellent comfortable cheerful house; and as from necessity and inclination I live much more at home than I used to do, it is very agreeable to be so pleasantly lodged, and to be in a warm inn as one passes through the last vale. Adieu!

Yours ever,

H. W.

To Cole, Monday 27 December 1779

Add MS 5953, ff. 73–4.

Address: To the Reverend Mr Cole at Milton near Cambridge.
Postmark: GC 27 DE.

Berkeley Square, Dec. 27, 1779.

I HAVE two good reasons against writing, nothing to say, and a lame muffled hand; and *therefore* I choose to write to you, for it shows remembrance. For these six weeks almost I have been a prisoner with the gout, but begin to creep about my room. How have you borne the late deluge and the present frost? How do you like an Earl-Bishop?[1] Had not we one before in ancient days? I have not a book in town, but was not there an Anthony Beck,[2] or a Hubert de

---

7. *A New History of Gloucestershire,* Cirencester. Printed for Samuel Rudder, 1779. The author, Samuel Rudder (d. 1801), was a printer at Cirencester. HW's copy (D.1) was sold SH iv. 17.

---

1. Frederick Augustus Hervey (1730–

1803), Bp of Derry, became 4th E. of Bristol on the death of his brother, Augustus John Hervey, 3d E. of Bristol, 23 Dec. 1779.

2. Antony Bek I (d. 1310) became Bp of Durham in 1283, but he was not E. of Kent (see following letter).

Burgh[3] that was Bishop of Durham and Earl of Kent, or have I confounded them?

Have you seen Rudder's *New History of Gloucestershire?* His additions to Sir Robert Atkyns[4] make it the most sensible history of a county that we have had yet, for his descriptions of the site, soil, products and prospects of each parish are extremely good and picturesque; and he treats fanciful prejudices and Saxon etymologies, when unfounded, and vulgar traditions, with due contempt.

I will not spin this note any farther, but shall be glad of a line to tell me you are well. I have not seen Mr Lort since he roosted under the metropolitan wings of his Grace of Lambeth.

Yours ever,

H. W.

From Cole, Thursday 30 December 1779

VA, Forster MS 110, ff. 225–7. Cole's copy, Add MS 5826, ff. 179v–181v.

The name 'Thrale' in an unknown hand appears on the cover.

Address: For the Honourable Horace Walpole, Berkeley Square, London.

Postmark: [Penny Post Paid ?] O'clock.

Milton, Dec. 30, St Tho. Cant., 1779.

Dear Sir,

YOUR letter was doubly grateful to me, as it assured me of your getting better from the gout, and of your kind remembrance. The hot summer, though disagreeable, I believe did me service, but, thank God, neither the incessant late rains, no more than the severe frost, nor the breaking it, have at all affected me. I had nearer been demolished on Monday, the day you wrote your letter, than by any of the clashing of the elements, through the indiscretion of my servant. It is a long story, but as I have began it, and the impression on my spirits being so strong and recent, I hope you'll excuse me and pity me. The case was this: the Master of Emmanuel, my very good

3. Hubert de Burgh (d. 1243) was E. of Kent, but not Bp of Durham (see following letter).

4. Sir Robert Atkyns (1647–1711), Kt, was the author of *The Ancient and Present State of Glocestershire* [sic], 1712; 2d edn, 1768.

friend, just recovered himself from death's door,[1] as said commonly, invited me to dine with him on Monday. As I was very well, I went with pleasure to see him, meaning to come away when the moon was risen, but he much pressing me to stay and play a game at whist, and eat a piece of brawn only for supper, I was tempted to do so, though utterly against my practice, never tasting anything after tea for these twenty years, and staying supper at Cambridge but once, and that at Dr Lort's chambers seven years ago, for these twelve years. I stayed till eleven, and Mr Masters, my neighbour, being there also, we got into our separate carriages at the College Gate. It seems his driver was drunk, for about a mile on this side my house, I observed my driver turn about twice or three times to look behind him, and then jump down and run to the assistance of Mr Masters, who was making an horrible outcry, as his servant was under his horses' feet, and the horses trampling upon him. The instant my horses found themselves at liberty, with the reins on their backs, they set out a full gallop, and so continued till they passed through the turnpike in my village, which the gate-keeper had unluckily set wide open, not to interrupt me, on hearing the rattle of the wheels on the frost, though it then began to thaw, and was dripping rain. All this while I was seated at the bottom of the chaise, with my legs out of it, and resting on the footboard, with an intention to have jumped out, as occasion might offer, but observing the swiftness of the hinder wheels, was afraid of my gown's being entangled in it, and so might be dragged along after the carriage.[2] I had let down all the glasses at first, and in doing so, some way or other, had dropped my hat. This added to my fright, for always keeping myself so immoderately warm and hardly ever stirring out, I concluded if I escaped being dashed to pieces, I should certainly catch[3] a bad cold and fever, being exposed so late to the wind and weather and rain and without any hat. Providence, however, was more propitious to me than are my deserts, for the horses, being used to a good smooth road, galloped on without any ill accident the whole mile and cleared the turnpike, where the keeper standing and seeing no driver,[4] he ran at full stretch and stopped the horses and saved my life, for had they gone a furlong farther, to the

---

1. 'by the influenza' (addition in Cole's copy).

2. 'if I escaped without breaking my limbs' (addition in Cole's copy).

3. 'a violent cold, fever attending it, and gout in the rear' (addition in Cole's copy).

4. 'and hearing me call aloud to him' (addition in Cole's copy).

short turn out of the road, to the lane leading to my house, where were two small road bridges and ugly ditches on each side, all had been over. Thank God, I got to bed in five minutes, and my servant, frightened to death,[5] soon after came in also. Mr Masters was forced to walk home three miles,[6] discharged my servant at the turnpike, his harness broke to pieces, and his sharps to his chaise left on the road. That he was horribly frightened is evident from a civil letter, very uncommon with him, next morning, and yesterday he came to see me, and gave my servant five shillings and many kind expressions. I could get no rest that night, as you may well imagine, my spirits being too much in an hurry to allow it, and though I was a little feverish next day, probably from want of rest, I had so good a sleep for the whole night on Tuesday, that on Wednesday, yesterday, I was as well as ever. Pray excuse the overflowings of my heart in gratitude for this deliverance and escape. The week before Masters had alarmed me in another way, leaving a scrap of a dirty old cover at the turnpike to be brought to me by anyone to be picked up, with only these words on it (he is deputy to the Chancellor of the diocese):[7] 'The Bishop informs Mr Masters that Dr Apthorp of Eton is dead.' It came in a little before some company came in to dine with me,[8] and damped my spirits extremely. I went to Cambridge next day, and could find no reason for the intelligence, which was premature, for it came on 16 December, and I have heard nothing to confirm it.

The Count-Bishop formerly was my intimate acquaintance. It was when he had a mind to marry the present Lady Irwin,[9] and was often backwards and forwards with me at Horseth. I have never seen him since. He'll hardly stay in Ireland, with an estate of £12,000 per

5. 'at his own imprudence and my danger' (addition in Cole's copy).

6. 'the turnpike man leading the horses with broken traces and without sharps, for these were left at Milton, utterly broken to pieces, and his harness in shatters' (addition in Cole's copy). A sharp is 'a shaft of a cart' (OED).

7. William Compton (see *ante* 15 June 1777).

8. 'the family from Baberham Place, etc.' (addition in Cole's copy).

9. 'with whom I used to spend a great part of my time at Horseth Hall, and was often backwards and forwards with him there. Her great fortune would have at that time much accommodated him. How he has carried himself since, I don't so well know, but he was then much of a gentleman, and I was greatly prejudiced in his favour' (addition in Cole's copy). Frances Gibson, commonly called Shepherd (1734–1807), was the illegitimate dau. of Samuel Shepherd, a rich merchant, sometime M.P. for Cambridge. She m. (1758) Hon. Charles Ingram (1727–78), afterwards 9th Vct Irvine.

annum in England. Hubert de Burgh was Lord Chief Justice of England, and Earl of Kent, but no bishop. Probably you confound him with Odo, Bishop of Bayeux and Earl of Kent, half-brother to the Conqueror. Anthony de Bec, Bishop of Durham, was Patriarch of Jerusalem and Lord of the Isle of Man, but never Earl of Kent. Walcher Bishop of Durham, in the Conqueror's time, was Earl of Northumberland,[10] and his successor, Hugh de Pusey, nephew to King Stephen, was Earl of Northumberland also.[11] If Archbishop Drummond[12] had survived his brother,[13] he would have been Earl of Kinnoul.

I have not seen the *New History of Gloucestershire,* but your character of it will make me contrive to get it somewhere, but as for old women's stories and vulgar traditions, commend me to Mr Grose's *Antiquities of England and Wales,* which I had never seen to any purpose till within this month. It is a mere picture-book.

I have not yet seen the *Alien Priories.* Mr Nichols, the ostensible author of it, is the printer,[14] partner to the late Mr Bowyer,[15] and who has had many articles lately in the *Gentleman's Magazine,* particularly respecting St John's College and its fellows.

I wonder you have not seen Dr Lort. He told me when he left college about six weeks ago, that he meant to call on you very soon, nay, so soon that he offered to carry what I told him I designed for you, but as he was on horseback here, and I had no proper box to enclose it, I did not care to trust it: I mean a small picture of myself on glass,[16] which they say is like me. This is the second time I am forcing my picture upon you, and if I am not to be excused in thus being desirous to be near you, I will say that the former[17] was sent with several inedited heads of no very considerable personages,[18] to be put into your volume of *minorum gentium,* and this as an essay

---

10. Walcher (d. 1080), Bp of Durham 1071, acted as E. of Northumberland, 1074.

11. Hugh de Puiset or Pudsey (1125?–95), Bp of Durham 1153–95. He purchased the earldom of Northumberland on the accession of Richard I.

12. Robert Hay (1711–76), took the additional surname of Drummond, 1739; Abp of York 1761–76.

13. Thomas Hay (1710–87), 8th E. of Kinnoul.

14. 'to the Royal Society' (addition in Cole's copy).

15. William Bowyer (1699–1777), the younger, 'the learned printer.' Nichols afterwards published a life of him (see *post* 23, 25 July 1782).

16. 'from one by Mr Kerrich of Magdalen College' (addition in Cole's copy). The whereabouts of these painted-glass portraits of Cole is not known.

17. 'by Mr Gooch of Christ Church' (addition in Cole's copy).

18. For a list of these prints, see *ante* 18 [20] April 1775.

of a Cambridge artist[19] in a peculiar style of painting. I saw at the Master of Emmanuel's a picture done by him from a design by Mr Tyson, and for him, of a Saxon king,[20] found painted against the wall behind the altar of Westminster Abbey, when they placed a new one in its room two years ago, that would please you. Indeed I had no idea of his excellence being such: the colouring is so vivid and his drawing so exact. If you will give this picture of mine a place in some back window, you will honour me much. I wish I had one of yours done in the same way. The man did three for me, though I spoke for only one, and I was told yesterday that he has another still in his keeping. I gave <one> to Dr Lort, but he has not got it yet: it is <in> a surplice, and very popish.[21] But surely I forget myself in filling up two sheets of paper on so inconsiderable a subject. I am afraid I have tired you, and that I shall not hear from you soon.

I hope and wish that the news we had in all our papers, that the Houghton Collection of pictures are at the bottom of the sea,[22] is false. Good God! what a destruction! I am shocked when I think of it.

Adieu, dear Sir, and wishing you many and happy returns of this season, I am

Your most faithful and affectionate servant,

WM COLE

To COLE, Wednesday 5 January 1780

Add MS 5953, ff. 75–6.

Cole notes on the cover: 'Gent. Mag. for Jan. 1780. Mr Gough's Top[ography] going to be new-edited, as Mr Ty[son] has sent me a vignette for the title, of his desig[ning]. Houghton Pictures. My portr[ait].' For Cole's use of the notes, see post 12 Feb. 1780.

Address: To the Reverend Mr Cole at Milton near Cambridge.

Postmark: GC 6 IA.

Berkeley Square, Jan. 5, 1780.

WHEN you said that you feared that your particular account of your very providential escape would deter me from writing to

19. Charles Freeman (see ante 24 July 1779).

20. Sebert (d. 616?), first Christian King of the East Saxons (see DNB). See also following letter. Cole probably refers to the figure shown in Plate V of Sir Joseph

Ayloffe's An Account of Some Ancient Monuments in Westminster Abbey, 1780. The discovery was made in the summer of 1775, and not, as Cole says, 'two years ago.'

21. 'That designed for you is more laical' (addition in Cole's copy).

you again, I am sure, dear Sir, that you spoke only from modesty, and not from thinking me capable of being so criminally indifferent to anything, much under such danger as you have run, that regards so old a friend, and one to whom I owe so many obligations. I am but too apt to write letters on trifling or no occasions; and should certainly have told you the interest I take in your accident, and how happy I am that it had no consequences of any sort. It is hard that temperance itself, which you are, should be punished for a good-natured transgression of your own rules, and where the excess was only staying out beyond your usual hour. I am heartily glad you did not jump out of your chaise; it has often been a much worse precaution than any consequences from risking to remain in it—and as you are lame[1] too, might have been very fatal. Thank God! all ended so well. Mr Masters seems to have been more frightened, with not greater reason. What an absurd man to be impatient to notify so[2] disagreeable an event to you, and in so boisterous a manner, and which he could not know was true, since it was not!

I shall take extremely kind your sending me your picture in glass. I have carefully preserved the slight outline of yourself in a gown and night-cap, which you once was so good as to give me, because there was some likeness to your features, though it is too old even now. For a portrait of me in return, you might have it by sending the painter to the anatomical school, and bidding him draw the first skeleton he sees. I should expect that any limner would laugh in my face, if I offered it to him to be copied.

I thought I had confounded the ancient Count-Bishops, as I had, and you have set me right. The new temporal-ecclesiastic peer's[3] estate is more than twelve thousand a year, though I can scarce believe it is eighteen, as the last Lord said.[4]

The picture found near the altar in Westminster Abbey about three years ago was of King Sebert; I saw it, and it was well pre-

---

22. 'The celebrated Houghton collection of pictures, late the property of Lord Orford, . . . are totally lost at sea; the *Natalia*, the ship in which they were carrying to Russia, having foundered' (*Whitehall Evening Post*, 14–16 Dec. 1779). The rumour was denied in the issue of 25–8 Dec., where it was stated that 'the master of the ship . . . saw them safely unpacked in the Empress's palace.' Cf. Mann to HW 3 Jan. 1780.

1. See *ante* 19 May 1763 n. 2.
2. MS reads *notify a*. Masters had not been 'impatient' to report Dr Apthorpe's death, but insensitive in the way he did it. The last example in OED of 'boisterous' in the sense in which HW uses it is from *King John*, 1595.
3. Lord Bristol, Bp of Derry.
4. Augustus Hervey, 3d E. of Bristol.

served, with some others worse—but they have foolishly buried it again behind their new altar-piece; and so they have a very fair tomb of Anne of Cleve,[5] close to the altar, which they did not know, till I told them whose it was, though her arms are upon it, and though there is an exact plate of it in Sandford.[6] They might at least have cut out the portraits and removed the tomb to conspicuous situations—but though this age is grown so antiquarian, it has not gained a grain more of sense in that walk—witness as you instance in Mr Grose's legends; and in the Dean and Chapter reburying the crown, robes and ornaments of Edward I[7]—there would surely have been as much piety in preserving them in their treasury, as in consigning them again to decay. I did not know that the salvation of robes and crowns depended on receiving Christian burial. At the same time the Chapter transgress that Prince's will, like all their ancestors, for he ordered his tomb to be opened every year or two years, and receive a new cerecloth or pall—but they boast now of having enclosed him so substantially, that his ashes cannot be violated again.

It was the present Bishop-Dean[8] who showed me the pictures and Anne's tomb, and consulted me on the new altar-piece. I advised him to have a light octangular canopy, like the cross at Chichester,[9] placed over the table or altar itself, which would have given dignity to it, especially if elevated by a flight of steps; and from the side arches of the octagon, I would have had a semicircle of open arches that should have advanced quite to the seats of the prebends, which would have discovered the pictures; and through the octagon itself you would have perceived the shrine of Edward the Confessor, which is much higher than the level of the choir—but men, who ask advice, seldom follow it, if you do not happen to light on the same idea with themselves.

Yours most sincerely,

H. WALPOLE

PS. The Houghton pictures are not lost—but to Houghton and England![10]

5. Cf. *ante* 10 May 1778.

6. Francis Sandford, *Genealogical History of the Kings of England . . . from the Conquest . . . to . . . 1677*, 1677. HW's copy (E.1.25) was sold SH ii. 107.

7. See *ante* 14 Dec. 1775.

8. John Thomas (1712–93), Bp of Roch-ester and Dean of Westminster. For a detailed account of HW's advice to him, see HW to Mason 10–12 July 1775.

9. That is, the Market Cross, which is in HW's favourite ornate style.

10. Cole wrote the following note at the end of his copy of HW's letter (Add MS

To Cole, Saturday 5 February 1780

Add MS 5953, ff. 79–80.

Cole notes on the cover: 'V. Gen[tleman's] M[agazine], 1780, [pp.] 26, 27. Gough, v. vol. 57, p. 283. Budg[ell], Far[mer] and Col[man].' Cole used the notes in his letters of 12 Feb. and 10 March 1780.

Address: To the Reverend Mr Cole at Milton near Cambridge.
Postmark: GC 5 FE.

Berkeley Square, Feb. 5, 1780.

I HAVE been turning over the new second volume of the *Bio-graphia,*[1] and find the additions very poor and lean performances. The lives entirely new are partial and flattering, being contributions of the friends of those whose lives are recorded. This publication, made at a time when I have lived to see several of my contemporaries deposited in this national Temple of Fame, has made me smile, and reflect that many preceding authors who have been installed there with much respect, may have been as trifling personages as those we have known and now behold consecrated to memory. Three or four have struck me particularly, as Dr Birch, who was a worthy good-natured soul, full of industry and activity, and running about like a young setting dog in quest of anything, new or old, and with no parts, taste or judgment. Then there is Dr Blackwell,[2] the most impertinent literary coxcomb upon earth—but the editor has been so just as to insert a very merited satire on his *Court of Augustus.*[3] The

5826, f. 182v): 'The constant chagrin of Mr Walpole upon the Antiquaries shows that he does not forget the President [Milles] and some of their members who improperly animadverted upon his *Richard III,* though with much reason in many respects: yet not to have galled so respectable a member would have been more politic. His project for the altar-piece was certainly noble, and it is to be lamented that it could be excepted to. Had it been so executed, what an uproar should we have had from the Dissenters and Patriots, that the Church of England was setting up idolatry and offered their prayers at the shrine of St Edward the Confessor! To avoid such imputations from that quarter has been the too-studied affectation of the Church ever since Bishop Laud's time: yet the cry has not ceased, though no occasion given for it: even the late Bishop-Dean

Pearce [Zachary Pearce (1690–1774), successively Bishop of Bangor and Rochester, and Dean of Winchester] made a sufficient outcry on the putting up the painted window of St Margaret's Church, Westminster. Mr Walpole's "Life of Mr Baker" does not show a spirit that would silently have acquiesced in the erection had it been carried into execution from any other person's design.'

———

1. *Biographia Britannica*[2], ed. Kippis, vol. 2. It was published 18 Jan. 1780 (see *London Chronicle* 16–18, 21–3 Dec. 1779, 20–2 Jan. 1780).
2. Thomas Blackwell (1701–57), the younger; classical scholar; author of *An Enquiry into the Life and Writings of Homer,* 1735, and *Memoirs of the Court of Augustus,* 3 vols, 1753–64.
3. Kippis quoted from Thomas Davies'

third is Dr Browne,[4] that mountebank, who for a little time made as much noise by his *Estimate,* as ever quack did by a nostrum. I do not know whether I ever told you how much I was struck the only time I ever saw him. You know one object of the anathemas of his *Estimate* was the Italian opera[5]—yet did I find him one evening in Passion Week accompanying some of the Italian singers at a concert at Lady Carlisle's.[6] A clergyman no doubt is not obliged to be on his knees the whole week before Easter, and music and a concert are harmless amusements;[7] but when Cato or Calvin are out of character, reformation becomes ridiculous—but poor Dr Browne was mad,[8] and therefore might be in earnest, whether he played the fool or the reformer.

You recollect perhaps the threat of Dr Kippis to me, which is to be executed on my father, for my calling the first edition of the *Biographia* the Vindicatio Britannica[9]—but observe how truth emerges at last! In this new volume he confesses that the article of Lord Arlington[10] which I had specified as one of the most censur-

Miscellaneous and Fugitive Pieces, 3 vols, 1773–4, iii. 1–9, a review of Blackwell's work, 'supposed to have been drawn up by one of our most eminent living authors' (*Biographia Britannica*[2] ii. 341), which is the 'satire' HW refers to. The author of the 'satire' was Dr Johnson (see Wm P. Courtney and David N. Smith, *A Bibliography of Samuel Johnson,* Oxford, 1925, pp. 76, 116–7).

4. John Brown (1715–66), author of *Estimate of the Manners and Principles of the Times,* 2 vols, 1757–8.

5. Brown deplores the 'low and unmanly taste' shown by his contemporaries in music. 'That divine art . . . is at length dwindled into a woman's or an eunuch's effeminate trill. . . . Our concerts and operas are disgraced with the lowest insipidity of composition, and unmeaning sing-song. . . . We go not to admire the composition, but the tricks of the performer; who is then surest of our ignorant applause, when he runs through the compass of the throat, or traverses the fingerboard with the swiftest dexterity' (*Estimate*[2] i. 45–7).

6. HW mentioned this incident in his letter to Montagu 4 May 1758. Lady Carlisle was Hon. Isabella Byron (1721–95),

dau. of William Byron, 4th Bn Byron of Rochdale; she m. (1) in 1743, as his 2d wife, Henry Howard (1694–1758), 4th E. of Carlisle, and (2) in 1759, Sir William Musgrave, 6th Bt, of Hayton Castle, Cumberland.

7. HW possibly has in mind Brown's defence of himself for mixing 'with the fashionable world, as frequently as most of his profession' (ibid. ii. 122–5).

8. He committed suicide (see *Biographia Britannica*[2] ii. 673).

9. See *ante* 14 June 1778.

10. Henry Bennet (1618–85), 1st E. of Arlington, member of the Cabal ministry (see DNB). Kippis says, 'This is one of the articles censured by Mr Walpole, and on account of which he hath said, that he could not help calling our work *Vindicatio Britannica.* There is no instance, we believe, wherein the title may so justly be applied. It must be acknowledged, that the conduct of Lord Arlington is palliated beyond all truth and reason' (*Biographia Britannica*[2] ii. 188). He attributes the palliation to the 'amiableness and philanthropy of temper' of Dr Campbell (the author of the article), and not to political interest.

able, is the one most deserving that censure, and that the character of Lord Arlington *is palliated beyond all truth and reason*—words stronger than mine—yet mine deserved to draw vengeance on my father!—so a Presbyterian divine inverts divine judgment and visits the sins of the children on the parents!

Cardinal Beaton's character, softened in the first edition, gentle Dr Kippis pronounces *extremely detestable*[11]—yet was I to blame for hinting at such defects in that work!—and yet my words are quoted to show that Lord Orrery's poetry was ridiculously bad.[12] In like manner Mr Dr Cumberland who assumes the whole honour of publishing his grandfather's Lucan, and does not deign to mention its being published at Strawberry Hill,[13] (though by the way I believe it will be oftener purchased for having been printed there, than for wearing Mr Cumberland's name to the dedication)[14] and yet he quotes me for having praised his ancestor in one of my publications.[15] These little instances of pride and spleen divert me—and then make me reflect sadly on human weaknesses. I am very apt myself to like what flatters my opinions or passions, and to reject scornfully what thwarts them, even in the same persons. The longer one lives, the more one discovers one's[16] own ugliness in the features of others!

Adieu! dear Sir—I hope you do not suffer by this severe season.

Yours ever,

H. Walpole

11. While allowing 'great merit' to the former article on Beaton, Kippis admits that it is too favourable, and that Beaton's character 'on the whole, was extremely detestable' (*Biographia Britannica*² ii. 56).

12. Kippis says of the poetry of Roger Boyle (1621–79), 1st E. of Orrery: 'Mr Walpole is very severe (we wish it could not be said, too justly severe) on his Lordship's poetry' (*Biographia Britannica*² ii. 492). He then quotes the first and second paragraphs, the remarks on *Parthenissa,* and on *Poems on the Fasts and Festivals of the Church,* from HW's account of Lord Orrery in *Roy. & Nob. Authors* (*Works* i. 514–16).

13. From the marginal notes in the 'classic books' of Richard Bentley (1662–1742), 'Mr Cumberland hath published an

edition of *Lucan,* which, though not perfect throughout, is full and complete with regard to the four first books' (*Biographia Britannica*² ii. 244). According to Kippis's note, this information came 'from Mr Cumberland.'

14. This has proved to be so.

15. 'Mr Walpole, speaking of Mr Boyle's translation of the *Epistles of Phalaris,* says, "This work occasioned the famous controversy with Dr Bentley;—who alone, and unworsted, sustained the attacks of the brightest geniuses in the learned world, and whose fame has not suffered by the wit to which it gave occasion" ' (*Biographia Britannica*² ii. 243). HW's quotation is from *Roy. & Nob. Authors* ii. 129–30 (*Works* i. 442–3).

16. MS reads *one.*

PS. I remember two other instances where my impartiality or at least my sincerity have exposed me to double censure. Many, you perhaps, condemned my severity on Charles I.[16a] Yet the late Mr Hollis wrote against me in the newspapers for condemning the republicans for their destruction of ancient monuments.[17]

Some blamed me for undervaluing the Flemish and Dutch painters in my preface to the *Aedes Walpolianae*.[18] Barry the painter,[19] because I laughed at his extravagances,[20] says, in his rejection of that school, 'But I leave them to be admired by the Honourable H. W. and such judges!'[21]—Would not one think I had been their champion?[22]

16a. In *Roy. & Nob. Authors,* where HW says of him: 'His style . . . was formed between a certain portion of sense, adversity, dignity, and perhaps a little insincerity. . . . A man who studies cases of conscience so intimately, is probably an honest man; but at least he studies them in hopes of finding that he need not be so very honest, as he thought. Oliver Cromwell, who was not quite so scrupulous, knew, that casuistry is never wanted for the observance of an oath; it may to the breach of it' (*Works* i. 275–6).

17. Not located.

18. 'And as for the Dutch painters, those drudging mimics of nature's most uncomely coarsenesses, do not their earthen pots and brass kettles carry away prices only due to the sweet neatness of Albano, and to the attractive delicacy of Carlo Maratti? . . . It was not so much want of genius in the Flemish masters, as want of having searched for something better. Their only idleness seems to have been in the choice of their subjects' (*Aedes, Works* ii. 226–7).

19. James Barry (1741–1806), R.A.

20. HW did so at the Royal Academy Exhibition of 1772, as he records in one of his catalogues of the Exhibition (quoted by Cunningham, vi. 187 n). HW described Barry's 'Medea making her Incantation after the Murder of her Children' as 'wild and ill-drawn. . . . Mr H. W. happened to laugh at this picture at the Exhibition, when Barry, whom he did not know, was present. Barry resented this so much, that not long [after], in a treatise he wrote on painting, he satirised Mr W. as an admirer of the Flemish Painters. Yet Mr W. had

been censured by others for under-valuing them too much in his preface to the *Aedes Walpolianae*. Barry was of a quarrelsome temper, broke with his patron Mr [Edmund] Burke, and with the Royal Academy, and after some time ceased exhibiting. It is true, however, that he had genius and learning.' A similar account of the affair is given in *Walpoliana* ii. 91–2; and in HW to Lady Ossory 1 Feb. 1775, and to Mason 7 May 1783.

21. Barry's *Enquiry into the Real and Imaginary Obstructions to the Acquisition of the Arts in England,* first published in 1775: 'As to the Dutch taste, I shall leave it to the deep researches of the Hon. Horace Walpole, or to any other learned gentleman (if such another can be found) who may happen to have a gusto for this kind of art. It is indeed out of my way (which he will readily admit) and therefore I shall turn to the Flemings' (*Works of James Barry,* 1809, ii. 205).

22. Cole notes after his copy of HW's letter (Add MS 5826, ff. 183v, 184v): 'Mr Walpole's instancing Mr Hollis's censure of him is by no means in character. Had Mr Hollis wrote against Mr W for abusing King Charles I or II, the parallel might have been just, but the Republican Mr W. and the Republican Mr Hollis were too well agreed in their opinions relating to these monarchs. The only difference I know, Mr W. was a well-bred, and Mr Hollis a mad and brutal, Republican: and though both of them Antiquaries (for I have frequently met Mr Hollis at the Antiquarian Society with Mr Pond) [Arthur Pond (1705?–58), painter and engraver, F.S.A., 1752; see DNB; *A List of the Mem-*

From COLE, Saturday 12 February 1780

VA, Forster MS 110, f. 228. Cole kept no copy.
Address: Honourable Horace Walpole, Berkeley Square, London.
Postmark: Cambridge [13?] FE.

Milton, Saturday, February 12, 1780.

<De>ar Sir,

YOUR most agreeable, cheerful and entertaining letters of January 5 and February 5 call for my earliest thanks and acknowledgments, and though I can't have the excuse of indolence, writing as I do, yet even that would be a fair one to anyone else but yourself, who are ten times more industrious, and an hundred times more to the purpose.

I will say little of infirmities. The gout has been favourable to me in excess for this last half-year: I wish the gravel, or somewhat worse, may not be breeding and lurking in my reins, which for these few weeks past have been rather disordered. God keep you from such fears and complaints!

The *Biographia* has not yet reached me. I am promised it next Friday,[1] when, probably, I shall find occasion enough to exercise my

bers of the Society of Antiquaries, 1798, p. 11] yet the love of ancient lore was too weak to get the better of settled principles. Dr Kippis and Mr Gough are living instances of Independents by profession and principle of their party, making good antiquaries, and nothing but the aforementioned threat could have exposed the Independent teacher to the scorn of Mr Walpole, whose principles square nicely to those of the biographer. If I live long enough, I shall not be surprised to see them more intimately connected.' In another place (Add MS 5874, f. 72v) Cole has noted: 'Feb. 24, 1780. Mr Lombe sent me the second volume of the *Biographia,* which I read over cursorily, especially the new articles and additions to the old ones, before breakfast, Friday, Feb. 25, 1780, and made the following observations on them on loose pieces of paper which might be properly introduced by a letter from the Honourable Mr Horace Walpole, a gentleman too much in the same way of thinking as the editors of the work, dated Feb. 5, and which occasioned my sending for the volume to Mr Lombe, who takes it in.

It is thus, though I think he bears too hard upon Dr Browne, whose books deserve the highest encomia, whatever his self-sufficiency and arrogance may take away from their merit. He apologizes for his mixing with company in his books, and was a great admirer of music.' Then follows another copy of HW's letter, and these additional remarks: 'Mr Walpole is manifestly hurt by the threats on his father and the slights on himself. He sees not with the same eyes that I do the vile design of the work throughout; nor indeed cares for it: I mean the steady purpose of the editors to defame the Church of England and to propagate the doctrine of independency and Socinianism: a plan never out of sight: and the additions to the old articles of any orthodox clergyman of the Church of England are all on this principle' (Add MS 5874, f. 77v). Cole's notes on some of the 'Lives' then follow.

_____

1. He did not receive it, however, until Thursday, 24 Feb. (see note 22 on preceding letter).

patience. Your remarks are equally just and ingenious, and my refusal to have any connections with such a partial writer[2] does not
displease me.

If you have not seen the *Gentleman's Magazine* for last month,[3]
possibly you may be pleased with a letter in which your name is mentioned, relating to a picture painted in oil at Cheltenham, even before the time you suppose.

Mr Tyson lately sent me a neat vignette, designed by him, for the
new edition of Mr Gough's *Topography*,[4] so I guess our old one will
be of little value when the new one appears, as there are so many
additions. I guess it may be two volumes, and consequently two
guineas.[5] If it is, I shall hardly purchase it. His last guinea book of
Tom Martin's *Thetford*[5a] is, I think, the dearest purchase in the paper way I ever made.

I had a letter last post from Mr Pennant, from whom I had not
heard <for a> great while. He sends me a proof-print of his own
portrait, which he says is to be sold,[6] with some etchings by his servant
Moses Griffith,[7] well executed. His *Journey to London* is going also
to be published,[8] with a new edition of his *Quadrupeds* in quarto,
next month, greatly enlarged by the discoveries and additions from
Russia.[9]

2. That is, Kippis, the editor of the
Biographia.

3. A correspondent who signs himself
'J.M.' upholds HW's theory that oil painting was known in England before 1410 (see
Anecdotes, Works iii. 30–3). In support of
this theory, he describes an ancient portrait at Cheltenham, which he believes is
an original picture of Sir Richard Dela-
bene, who was 'created a banneret after
the glorious victory of Cressy' (GM Jan.
1780, l. 26–7).

4. Gough's *British Topography, or, An
Historical Account of what has been done
for illustrating the Topographical Antiquities of Great Britain and Ireland*, 2 vols,
1780. The vignette, designed by Tyson and
engraved by Basire, appears on the title-
page of both volumes.

5. The work was even more expensive
than Cole thought: £2.12.6 in boards (see
GM Aug. 1780, l. 377).

5a. HW's copy was sold SH v. 157.

6. The print by John Keyse Sherwin
after Gainsborough. Cole had not re-

ceived the print at this time (see *post* 10
March 1780).

7. Moses Griffith (1749–living in 1809).
He acted as draughtsman and engraver for
Pennant and Grose (see DNB). The etchings Cole mentions probably included the
ten 'Supplemental Plates to the Tours in
Wales,' with preface and explanatory notes
by Pennant, 1781. Pennant explains in the
Advertisement to his *Tour in Wales*, p. iv,
'The drawings marked Moses Griffith, are
the performances of a worthy servant,
whom I keep for that purpose. The candid
will excuse any little imperfections they
may find in them; as they are the works of
an untaught genius, drawn from the most
remote and obscure parts of North Wales.'

8. *The Journey from Chester to London*
was not published until 1782.

9. Pennant enlarged his *Synopsis of
Quadrupeds*, Chester, 1771, and published
it under the title of *History of Quadrupeds*, 2 vols, 1781. Peter Simon Pallas
(1741–1811), German traveller and ex-
plorer whom Pennant met at The Hague

This puts me in mind (and what I ought not to remind you of) [of] the Houghton Collection. By Mr Kerrich, a Norfolk man and of the neighbourhood, who was here a few days ago, he says that Lord Orford has received the Czarina's portrait,[10] and under it he has caused an inscription to be written, importing that your father, Prime Minister to two kings, and for so many years, had so little enriched himself, that his grandson was forced to sell his collection of pictures to pay his debts.[10a] Perhaps you may have heard this before.

The glass picture[11] I mentioned some time ago will go to town about 6 March by a gentleman[12] who has promised to leave it at your door.

I am now deeply engaged in transcribing an old chartulary of an abbey in Derbyshire,[13] which lately fell into my hands, and from the same person[14] I received a MS fairly written, called *The Negotiations of Cardinal Wolsey*.[15] Some of the letters may have been printed,[16] but not all, so I am tempted to begin it, though it will be a long work, but patience is the best virtue of, dear Sir,

> Your most obliged servant,
>
> WM COLE

A gentleman has called on me since I wrote this, and tells me that Mr Walpole at Lisbon[17] writes word that Admiral Rodney[18] has

in 1766, contributed largely to the *History*, especially the results of his travels and explorations in Russia (see Pennant, *History of Quadrupeds*, vol. 1, Preface).

10. It is still at Houghton and bears the inscription in Russian: 'Her Majesty Catherine II, Empress and Monarch of Russia' (transcribed by Lady Cholmondeley, June, 1936).

10a. This inscription is no longer under the picture.

11. Of Cole, by Charles Freeman after a drawing by Kerrich (see *ante* 30 Dec. 1779).

12. Not identified.

13. This was a chartulary of Derley Priory, which Cole copied into what is now Add MS 5822, p. 151 ff. Richard Farmer was the owner of the original (on vellum), and at his death it was bought by Gough for ten shillings (see *Bibliotheca Farmeriana* 7 May 1798, 35th day, lot 8087, where it is erroneously described as 'The Register and Deeds of the Abbey of Derby'). It is

now Bodley MS Gough, Derbyshire 1. See Falconer Madan, *Summary Catalogue of Western Manuscripts in the Bodleian Library*, Oxford, 1898, iv. 212.

14. That is, Richard Farmer.

15. Cole's transcript of this MS (itself a copy of the original) is now in Add MS 5860. Farmer's copy was sold in his sale (35th day, lot 8102) to James Bindley for £1.3.0.

16. See *Gray's Corr.* iii. 1119.

17. Hon. Robert Walpole (1736–1810), 4th son of Horatio Walpole, Bn Walpole of Wolterton; a clerk of the Privy Council and envoy to Lisbon (see *Eton Coll. Reg., 1698–1752*). His letter, dated 25 Jan. 1780, containing news of the victory, apparently reached London on the evening of Feb. 9 or 10, and the account first appeared in the daily papers of Friday, 11 Feb. (see *The Public Advertiser* 11 Feb. 1780; *Whitehall Evening Post*, 10–12 Feb. 1780).

18. Sir George Brydges Rodney (1719–92), afterwards 1st Bn Rodney.

taken six of the Spanish ships out of eight, and one blown up. I wish you would confirm it.[19]

To COLE, Sunday 27 February 1780

Add MS 5953, ff. 77–8.

Cole prefaced his copy with the following note: 'Dining at Cambridge March 1, my servant brought me my letters before the Ely postman had taken them. One was from Mr Walpole, and I was sorry to find the common observation that the patriots always discovered a great damp and dejection upon every piece of news that was favourable to the King and country, and exulted as much upon any misfortune that happened to them, confirmed by my friend's letter. It was in answer to one I had wrote, in which I told him that it was reported that his relation Mr Walpole, our minister at Lisbon, had sent over some good news in relation to Sir George Rodney, and I wanted to have it confirmed. They were going to illuminate at Cambridge as I came away' (Add MS 5826, f. 185v).

Address: To the Reverend Mr Cole at Milton near Cambridge.
Postmark: GC 28 FE.

Berkeley Square, Feb. 27, 1780.

UNAPT as you are to inquire after news, dear Sir, you wish to have Admiral Rodney's victory confirmed. I can now assure you that he has had a considerable advantage, and took at least four Spanish men-of-war, and an admiral, who, they say, is since dead of his wounds.[1] We must be glad of these deplorable successes—but I heartily wish we had no longer occasion to hope for the destruction of our species!—but alas! it looks as if devastation would still open new fields of blood! The prospect darkens even at home—but however you and I may differ in our political principles, it would be happy if everybody would pursue theirs with as little rancour. How very seldom does it happen in political contests, that any side can

19. On 16 Jan. 1780, Admiral Rodney, with twenty-one ships and two frigates, encountered (south of Cape St Vincent) the Spanish squadron, consisting of eleven ships and two frigates, under the command of Don Juan de Lángara y Huarte (1736–1806). One Spanish ship was blown up in action, six (four ships and the two frigates) escaped, and six (including Lángara's flagship) were captured. Of the six captured, however, only four were brought into Gibraltar, one being driven on shore dur-ing the night, and lost, and one being re-captured by the Spanish prisoners on board, who brought it to Cadiz (see David Hannay, *Rodney*, 1891, pp. 98–102; Godfrey Basil Mundy, *Life and Correspond-ence of the Late Admiral Rodney*, 2 vols, 1830, i. 220–5; *Enciclopedia Universal Ilus-trada*, vol. 29, *sub* Lángara).

1. Don Juan de Lángara was captured, seriously wounded, but he lived until 1806 (see last note to preceding letter).

count anything but its wounds! Your habitudes seclude you from meddling in our divisions; so do my age and illnesses me. Sixty-two is not a season for bustling among young partisans. Indeed if the times grow perfectly serious, I shall not wish to reach sixty-three. Even a superannuated spectator is then a miserable being; for though insensibility is one of the softenings of old age, neither one's feelings nor enjoyments can be accompanied by tranquillity. We veterans must hide ourselves in inglorious insecurity, and lament what we cannot prevent: nor shall be listened to, till misfortunes have brought the actors to their senses; and then it will be too late, or they will calm themselves faster than we could preach—but I hope the experience of the last century will have some operation, and check our animosities. Surely too we shall recollect the ruin a civil war would bring on, when accompanied by such collaterals as French and Spanish wars. Providence alone can steer us amidst all these rocks. I shall watch the interposition of its aegis with anxiety and humility—It saved us this last summer,[2] and nothing else I am sure did—but often the mutual follies of enemies are the instruments of heaven—if it pleases not to inspire wisdom, I shall be content if it extricates us by the reciprocal blunders and oversights of all parties— of which at least we ought never to despair. It is almost my systematic belief, that as cunning and penetration are seldom exerted for good ends, it is the absurdity of mankind that acts as a succedaneum, and carries on and maintains the equilibrium that heaven designed should subsist. Adieu! dear Sir, shall we live to lay down our heads in peace?

Yours ever,

H. W.

28th. A second volume of Sir George Rodney's exploits is arrived today.[3] I do not know the authentic circumstances, for I have not been abroad yet, but they [say] he has taken four men[-of-war], Spanish ships of the line and five frigates; of the former, one of 90 guns.

2. From the threatened invasion of England by the French (cf. 12 Aug. 1779).

3. Under date of 28 Feb. is this account in the GM Feb. 1780, l. 99: 'This morning an express arrived from Sir George Bridges Rodney, with a confirmation of the success of his Majesty's fleet under his command, in falling in with, and taking or destroying the Spanish fleet on the 16th of January, under the command of Admiral Langara.' The ship of 90 guns, which HW mentions, was Lángara's flagship. The information concerning the five frigates was not true.

Spain was sick of the war before—how fortunate if she would renounce it!

I have just got a new history of Leicester in 6 small volumes.[4] It
seems to be superficial—but the author is young and talks modestly,
which, if it will not serve instead of merit, makes one at least hope
he will improve, and not grow insolent on age and more knowledge.
I have also received from Paris a copy of an illumination from *La
Cité des Dames* of Christina of Pisa in the French King's library.
There is her own portrait with three allegoric figures.[5] I have learnt
much more about her and of her amour with an English peer,[6] but
I have not time to say more at present.[7]

From COLE, Wednesday 1 March 1780

VA, Forster MS 110, ff. 229–30. COLE's copy, Add MS 5826, ff. 184v, 185v.

Address: The Honourable Horace Walpole, Berkeley Square, London.
Postmark: Cambridge 2 [MR].

March 1, 1780, Milton.

\<D\>ear Sir,

SINCE I received your last kind letter of February 5,[1] I have seen
the second volume of the new *Biographia,* and am extremely glad

4. *The Memoirs of the Town and
County of Leicester,* 6 vols (12mo), Leicester, 1777, by John Throsby (1740–1803), the
parish clerk of St Martin's, Leicester. HW's
copy (B.7) was sold SH i. 82.

5. Christine de Pisan (ca 1363–ca 1431),
dau. of Thomas de Pisan, councillor of the
Venetian republic, and astrologer to
Charles V, was a voluminous writer in
prose and verse. A print of the illumination is given in *Works* i. opp. p. 288. It
represents 'Reason, Rectitude & Justice appearing to Christina de Pisan, and promising to assist her in writing *La Cité des
Dames.*' HW procured the drawing through
Mme du Deffand (see her letter to HW 10
Jan. [1780]).

6. John de Montacute or Montagu
(1350?–1400), 3d E. of Salisbury, was sent to
Paris to further negotiations for the marriage of Richard II and the Princess Isabella, where he met Christine de Pisan,
complimented her, and encouraged her in
her literary pursuits. When she tacitly refused him, he offered to educate her son in

his own household. HW printed an entertaining account of the affair in *Postscript
to the Royal and Noble Authors,* SH, 1786
(forty copies), where it will be noted that
the 'amour' did not reach beyond a strictly
Platonic interpretation. It is reprinted in
Works i. 553–61.

7. Cole's note, following his copy of
HW's letter (Add MS 5826, f. 186v): 'A letter more strongly marked with patriotic
despondence and concern on advantages
gained, I never met with: so different from
his lively turns of wit and vivacity in all
his others. When all the friends of the
Constitution are singing *Hallelujah* and
Te Deum, the patriotic Republicans are at
Tenebrae and *De Profundis.*'

1. Cole apparently carried this letter
when he went to Cambridge to dine, and
put it into the post before he received
HW's letter of 27–8 Feb. Either inadvertently or purposely, Cole did not acknowledge that letter, the contents of which
displeased him.

to find that you think it a poor and lean performance, partial and flattering to their own connections. I received it on February 24 and ran it over as to the new articles and additions by the 27 at night, and have made a perfect book of remarks and censures upon it.[2] Political matters are above my reach: matters of doctrine only I took notice of, which are all tending to what offends my orthodoxy, viz., Arianism, Socinianism, Deism and Independency. Your remarks on those selected, viz., Drs Birch, Blackwell and Brown are spirited and most ingenious: true as truth itself. All you say about Dr Brown is most just, yet I can't help having a predilection for his *Estimate* and *Essays on the Characteristics*,[3] as tending to a worthy purpose.

Dr Kippis's threat on your father is already put in execution on yourself. His impatience to show his malice has made him begin his attack sooner than he intended, though in some places he affects to be very civil. That he is a partial writer, I think there needs no better evidence than the long note, pp. 677–8, to Sir George Buck's article. He was introduced[4] to the Antiquarian Society by Mr Gough, and evidently means to cajole the President.[5] Mr Gough it was that desired me to assist him in his work, which I peremptorily refused to have any concern in,[6] though I see with concern my friend Dr Lort[7] held out in the preface, in order to gain themselves credit with a particular set of people, who might be alarmed at such a work's appearing under the sanction of two Anabaptist teachers.[8] I say then, that Dr Kippis is a partial writer, from facts in abundance in both the volumes.[9] That he is a writer of no taste or judgment may be proved from what he says in the note I referred to, for after condemning loosely the *Historic Doubts,* he is not content with mentioning some of Dr Milles's arguments against them, but even condescends to produce 'the learned Mr Masters's *Remarks,*'[10] and concludes by pronouncing Richard to have been an usurper, a tyrant and a mur-

2. Cf. *ante* 5 Feb. 1780, n. 22.

3. *Essays on the Characteristics of the Earl of Shaftsbury*, 1751, in which Brown gave a clear statement of utilitarianism. Kippis says that it 'perhaps may still be regarded as his capital production' (*Biographia Britannica*[2] ii. 655).

4. 'as a friend who was present, told me, Dr Colman' (addition in Cole's copy).

5. Jeremiah Milles.

6. MS reads *any concern it*.

7. 'chaplain to his Grace the Abp of Canterbury' (addition in Cole's copy).

8. According to the title-page of *Biographia Britannica*[2] vol. 2, Kippis was assisted by the 'Rev. Joseph Towers, LL.D.' (1737–99), a Dissenting minister and biographer.

9. MS reads *both the volume*.

10. 'The learned Mr Masters hath also made some Remarks upon Mr Walpole's *Historic Doubts* in general, and hath clearly evinced that his reasonings are far from being in every case decisive' (*Biographia Britannica*[2] ii. 678).

derer. When a man quotes such a wooden performance as Masters's *Remarks*,[11] a disgrace to the directors of the *Archaeologia*, one may fairly conclude that he either had not read them, or was determined at all events to approve of them. He has civilly mentioned me[12] in one place, yet I expect his utmost vengeance when he has a fit opportunity, for my avoiding any communication with him. I always suspect civilities from an inimical quarter.[13] *Timeo Danaos etiam dona ferentes*. Masters made me a present last month of a pair of Scotch Aberdeen gloves: I mean to return them the first time I see him.[14]

I never missed the loss of your *Noble Authors* so much as I do now, to consult the places you refer to. I gave them to Dr Glynn last year after my illness, as he generously refused all fees but them and a medal of Oliver Cromwell, which you likewise gave me.[15] Let not this be looked on as begging meanly another set, which I will not receive if you send, for I know I can get them for sending for,[16] and it is more than probable that your own edition is long ago exhausted, but if I thought you had any guinea-fowls I would beg a cock and hen of you.

I go tomorrow to Cambridge, if well, though today am feverish with a little sore throat, to see a staircase window in the Gothic style and painted glass, which Mr Essex has had made for Mr Gough. The Cambridge glass-painter[17] has mended the old glass in it, and added some arms and ornaments. He has lately done some figures for Mr Tyson, beautifully executed, but I have proof that they will not stand the weather.

I am continually at work, and have been remarkably well all the

11. In spite of the arguments of Buck and HW, Kippis apprehends that Richard III 'must still be regarded as an usurper, a tyrant, and, we fear it must be added, a murderer' (loc. cit.).

12. 'in Cardinal Bourchier's article' (addition in Cole's copy). Cole is referred to as 'the learned Mr. Cole,' and his remarks on the arms of Cardinal Thomas Bourchier (1404?–86) in Bentham's *Ely*[2] (Appendix, pp. 44–5) are quoted at length (op. cit. 439).

13. 'If you recollect, I did so when Sir George Savile seemed the friend of the Roman Catholics: I knew it was a junction unnatural and impossible' (addition in Cole's copy). See *ante* 23 May 1778.

14. 'I should have a conscience in being kept warm by them' (addition in Cole's copy).

15. 'with an illuminated missal and a few things of the virtuoso sort' (addition in Cole's copy). For an account of the medal, see *ante* 29 May, and 13 June 1773. Cole was given the illuminated missal by Lord Montfort in 1769, when the latter had piqued Cole by his unseemly behaviour. The missal was priced £30 when Cole received it, but he later learned that Montfort had paid only £5 for it (see Palmer, *William Cole* 63).

16. That is, Dodsley's London edition, 1759.

17. Charles Freeman.

cold weather. Since the frost has left us for these two or three days, I am not so well: at best can't go out into my garden, which is a great mortification, but I thank God that I am as I am, and not worse.[18]

Dear Sir, I wish you every earthly blessing, and am

Your ever faithful servant,

WM COLE

In my next I will give you a curious blunder of these editors,[19] which the Masters of Benet and Emmanuel, who called here, and looking into the book, found out.

To COLE, Monday 6 March 1780

Add MS 5953, ff. 81–2.

Cole has the following notes on the cover: '*Modern Anecdotes of the antient Family of the Kinkvervankotsdarsprakengotchderns: a Tale for Christmas 1779.* Dedicated to the Hon. Horace Walpole, Esq. Small 8vo. 2s. Printed by Davenhill. *Crit. Rev.* for 1780, p. 122. Pen[nant's] pri[nt]. Far[mer] and Col[man].' For his use of the notes, see *post* 10 March 1780.

Address: To the Reverend Mr Cole at Milton near Cambridge.
Postmark: GC 6 MR.

Berkeley Square, March 6, 1780.

I HAVE this moment received your portrait in glass, dear Sir, and am impatient to thank you for it and tell you how much I value it. It is better executed than I own I expected, and yet I am not quite satisfied with it. The drawing is a little incorrect, the eyes too small in proportion and the mouth exaggerated. In short, it is a strong likeness of your features, but not of your countenance, which is better and more serene. However, I am enough content to place it at Strawberry,[1] amongst all my favourite, brittle, transitory relics,

---

18. 'When I was last in London, five years ago, I walked nine miles or more in London streets, but was ill after it. I used frequently to walk from St James's Church to Bishopsgate Street and back again, but often caught colds and sore throats by heating myself too much, as I hated coach-hire money, which, saved, would buy me

books or prints. My walkings are all at an end' (addition in Cole's copy).
19. Kippis and Towers.

———

1. It does not appear in the Sale Catalogue, and its present whereabouts is not known.

which will soon vanish with their founder—and with his no great unwillingness for himself.

I take it ill that you should think I should suspect you of asking
indirectly for my *Noble Authors*—and much more if you would not
be so free as to ask for them *directly*—a most trifling present surely—
and from you who have made me a thousand! I know I have some
copies in my old house in Arlington Street, I hope of both volumes,
I am sure, of the second—I will soon go thither and look for them.

I have gone through the six little volumes of Leicester.[2] The author is so modest and so humble, that I am quite sorry it is so very
bad a work; the arrangement detestable, the materials trifling, his
reflexions humane but silly. He disposes all under reigns of Roman
emperors and English kings, whether they did anything or nothing
at Leicester—I am sorry I have such predilection for the histories of
particular counties and towns: there certainly does not exist a worse
class of reading.

Dr E.[3] made me a visit last week—He is not at all less vociferous
for his disgrace. I wish I had any guinea-fowls—I can easily get you
some eggs from Lady Ailesbury,[4] and will ask her for some, that you
may have the pleasure of rearing your own chicks—but how can you
bear their noise? They are more discordant and clamorous than pea-
cocks. How shall I convey the eggs?

I smiled at Dr Kippis's bestowing the victory on Dean Milles, and
a sprig on Mr Masters. I regard it as I should if the sexton of Broad
St Gyles's were to make a lower bow to a cheesemonger of his own
parish than to me. They are all three haberdashers of small wares,
and welcome to each other's civilities. When such men are sum-
moned to a jury on one of their own trade, it is natural they should
be partial. They do not reason, but recollect how much themselves
have overcharged some yards of buckram. Adieu!

Yours most cordially,

H. Walpole

2. John Throsby's *Memoirs of the Town
and County of Leicester* (see *ante* 27 Feb.
1780).
3. William Howell Ewin of Cambridge.
For his 'disgrace,' see *ante* 21 Feb. 1777.

4. Caroline Campbell (1721–1803), dau.
of Gen. John Campbell, m. (1) (1739), as
his 3d wife, Charles Bruce (1682–1747), 3d
E. of Ailesbury, and (2) (1747) Hon. Henry
Seymour-Conway.

PS. Mr Pennicott[5] has shown me a most curious and delightful picture. It is Rose,[6] the royal gardener, presenting the first pineapple, raised in England, to Charles II. They are in a garden with a view of a good private house,[7] such as there are several at Sunbury and about London. It is by far the best likeness of the King I ever saw; the countenance cheerful, good-humoured and very sensible. He is in brown lined with orange, and many black ribbons, a large flapped hat, dark wig, not tied up, nor yet bushy, a point cravat, no waistcoat, and a tasselled handkerchief hanging from a low pocket. The whole is of the smaller landscape size, and extremely well coloured with perfect harmony. It was a legacy from London,[8] grandson of him[9] who was partner with Wise.[10]

From COLE, Friday 10 March 1780

VA, Forster MS 110, ff. 231–2. COLE's copy, Add MS 5826, ff. 187v–188v.

Address: Honourable Horace Walpole, Berkeley Square, London.

Postmark: Cambridge 11 MR.

Milton, March 10, 1780, Friday.

Dear Sir,

NEVER, sure, was there a head so clear, penetrating and explicit as yours! My portrait was generally thought very like, but most people said there was a peevishness and dissatisfaction in the countenance that did not always belong to me. You have exquisitely

5. Rev. William Pennicott (1726–1811), of Exeter College, Oxford (B.A. 1746); rector of Long Ditton, Surrey, 1758–1811 (see *Alumni Oxon;* GM March 1811, lxxxi. 294b). Pennicott subsequently presented the picture to HW, who describes it in *Description of SH, Works* ii. 423 (cf. HW to Mason 28 May 1780). It was sold SH xi. 20 to —— Smith for £22.1.0. On 15 July 1920 it was sold at Sotheby's for £620. Pennicott also gave HW a portrait of Henry VIII, which was in the Holbein Chamber at SH (see ibid. ii. 460).

6. John Rose (1619–77), gardener to the Duchess of Somerset, afterwards to the Duchess of Cleveland and Charles II (see Musgrave, *Obituary*). He was the author of

The English Vineyard Vindicated, which was published in 1666, ed. with a preface by 'Philocepos,' i.e., John Evelyn (see *BM Catalogue*).

7. 'The house seems to be Dawny-court near Windsor, the villa of the Duchess of Cleveland. The whole piece is well painted, probably by Danckers' (*Description of SH, Works* ii. 423).

8. Probably Edward London, who died 28 Nov. 1776 at Tottenham (see Musgrave, *Obituary*).

9. George London (d. 1714), gardener to Queen Anne (see ibid.).

10. Henry Wise (1653–1758), gardener to William III, Queen Anne and George I.

débrouillé, if I may use a French for want of a better or more apposite expression, or unravelled the difficulty by distinguishing the features from the countenance. Hundreds have looked at it but found not the error. I am sure I never should. Your 'it is a strong likeness of your features, but not of your countenance, which is more serene' is admirable. I should read with rapture the writers upon virtu and painting if I had, as here, good and just sense and remarks, instead of wordy galimatias. But I stop and say I am ashamed for saying so much about my own picture,[1] which I am glad you accept of, and will [give] an humble place to at Strawberry Hill. I am still more ashamed of my dirty begging another set of your *Noble Authors.* I shall never look at them but with compunction, so will say no more about it.

I am sorry the *History of Leicester*[2] turns out so bad, and much more that you condemn so positively a class of reading as the worst of the sort. Local histories, I own, please me much. It has been the great object of my life. To hear so severe a censure upon them, and from you, whose judgment in most things is with me infallible, mortifies me not a little.

Dr Ewin called on me a few days before he went to London. I said not one word, and never mentioned your name, nay, avoided sending the picture by him, knowing his forwardness to press himself into all sorts of company, sometimes improperly. Dr Lort wrote to me that he called upon him at Lambeth: if he had common sense or modesty, he must know that his visit there could not be agreeable. I don't know that I ever mentioned his affair to you. He told me on Saturday was sennight (I think) that he expected, notwithstanding all possible efforts, that he should be struck out of the commission both for town and county. If he is, God knows what will become of him, for he has no taste for reading or sporting or exercise, but makes an excellent Justice and very useful, and I think will be much missed in that walk. He is now going forthwith to build a picture gallery, under Mr Essex's direction, of fifty feet long and sixteen broad and fourteen high.[3] He has plenty of pictures to furnish it with, which no one ever sees, and a great deal of painted glass—but I

1. 'which was designed originally for you' (addition in Cole's copy).
2. John Throsby's *Memoirs of the Town and County of Leicester.*

3. 'with a large bow window' (addition in Cole's copy).

am too long upon him. I desired him, among a few other commissions, to buy me a cock and hen guinea-fowl. I dare say he has not done it, or I should have heard of it. I am greatly obliged to you for your kind offer to get me a few eggs of Lady Aylesbury. If packed up in hay or wool, I imagine a little basket would convey them safely to me by the Cambridge fly, to be left for me at the Rose Tavern in Cambridge till called for. The fly sets out every morning from the Queen's Head, Gray's Inn Lane.

I told you I would send you a curious double mistake of Dr Kippis. On the last day of February the Masters of Benet and Emmanuel calling in here on their ride, seeing the *Biographia*[4] on the table, on my mentioning something about Bishop Bull,[5] they turned to look at it, and fell upon Eustace Budgell,[6] p. 693, where, seeing the epitaph and epigram (which stand glaringly in view) produced by Dr Kippis as specimens of the fine taste and poetical abilities of Mr Budgell, Dr Farmer read them aloud. After a moment's pausing, he said that the epitaph, he was sure, was the two last lines of that made on Queen Elizabeth, and is on her tomb in Westminster Abbey, recorded by Camden in his *Remains*.[7] This was confoundedly unlucky, but what was more so, Dr Colman averred that the distich or epigram on the bad dancers to good music was by Mr George Jeffries of Trinity College, and published in some miscellaneous poetry[8] which he had by him. I have not the books, but if it should prove true,

4. *Biographia Britannica*[2], vol. 2.

5. George Bull (1634–1710), Bp of St David's 1705–10. His life appears in *Biographia Britannica*[2] ii. 695–708.

6. (1686–1737), miscellaneous writer. His life appears in *Biographia Britannica*[2] ii. 688–93.

7. The lines were the last two of seven written by one Henry Holland, possibly the London divine (d. 1604), on the occasion of Queen Elizabeth's death, and were first printed by Camden in his *Remaines*[2], 1614, pp. 378–9. They were not on her tomb in Westminster Abbey (see John Dart, *Westmonasterium*, 2 vols, [1742?]), but were the last two of eight lines (different from the above except for the last two lines) on a monument to the memory of Queen Elizabeth, erected by James I in the Church of St Mary Le Bow (see Edward Hatton, *A New View of London*, 2 vols, 1708, ii. 371).

The two lines also appeared on a print of the Queen (see *Granger*[5] i. 217).

8. George Jeffreys (1678–1755), poet and dramatist, published by subscription *Miscellanies in Verse and Prose*, 1754, to which Colman was a subscriber. The epigram is there (p. 16) printed as follows:

'Ex tempore; on Sight of a Dance.*
How ill the Motion with the Music suits!
So once play'd *Orpheus;* but so danc'd the Brutes.'

In the preface (pp. vii–viii) Jeffreys states that his Epigram had been 'tossed' about as Mrs Rowe's, Philips's, Welsted's and Budgell's. Kippis, in assigning the epitaph and epigram to Budgell, followed Theophilus Cibber's *Lives of the Poets*, 5 vols, 1753, v. 16.

'* This Epigram has by mistake been ascribed to Mr Ambrose Philips.'

could anything be more unfortunate? The two distichs I will transcribe, as you may have returned the volume:

On a Fine Lady. Epitaph.
She was, she is (what can there more be said?)
On Earth the first, in Heaven the second Maid.

——————

But ill the motion with the music suits:
So Orpheus fiddled, and so danced the Brutes.

Have you seen a book dedicated to you, called *Modern Anecdotes of the Antient Family of the Kinkvervankotsdarsprakengotchderns: a Tale for Christmas 1779.*⁹ Small 8vo. 2s. Printed by Davenhill.¹⁰ It is mentioned in the last *Critical Review,* p. 122, which is all that I know of it. The reviewers have no remarks relating to you.

I have just received Mr Pennant's portrait, engraved by Sherwin¹¹ very elegantly, holding Barrington's *Statutes*¹² in his arms. As I never saw him, I can be no judge whether it resembles him.

I am, dear Sir, in no small hurry,

Your ever faithful and affectionate servant,

WM COLE

To COLE, Monday 13 March 1780

Add MS 5953, ff. 83–4.
Address: [From COLE's copy, Add MS 5826, f. 188v.] Rev Mr Cole at Milton near Cambridge.

Strawberry Hill, March 13, 1780.

YOU compliment me, my good friend, on a sagacity that is surely very common. How frequently do we see portraits that have catched the features, and missed the countenance or character, which is far more difficult to hit. Nor is it unfrequent to hear that remark made.

9. The title should read *Modern Anecdote . . .* The author was Lady Craven, afterwards Margravine of Anspach. The dedication of ten pages, dated 30 Nov. 1779, is extremely flattering to HW.

10. Matthew Davenhill, bookseller of 13 Cornhill.
11. After Gainsborough.
12. Daines Barrington's *Observations on the Statutes,* 1766.

I have confessed to you that I am fond of local histories. It is the general execution of them that I condemn, and that I call *the worst kind of reading*. I cannot comprehend but they might be performed with taste. I did mention this winter the new edition of Atkyns's *Gloucestershire*,[1] as having additional descriptions of situations, that I thought had merit. I have just got another, *A View of Northumberland*[2] in two volumes quarto, with cuts; but I do not devour it fast, for the author's predilection is to Roman antiquities, which, such as are found in this island, are very indifferent, and inspire me with little curiosity. A barbarous country, so remote from the seat of empire, and occupied by a few legions, that very rarely decided any great events, is not very interesting, though one's own country—nor do I care a straw for the stone that preserves the name of a standard-bearer of a cohort, or of a colonel's daughter. Then I have no patience to read the tiresome disputes of antiquaries to settle forgotten names of vanished towns, and to prove that such a village was called something else in Antoninus's *Itinerary*.[3] I do not say that the Gothic antiquities that I like are of more importance; but at least they exist. The site of a Roman camp, of which nothing remains but a bank, gives me not the smallest pleasure. One knows they had square camps—has one a clearer idea from the spot, which is barely distinguishable? How often does it happen that the lumps of earth are so imperfect, that it is never clear, whether they are Roman, Druidic, Danish or Saxon fragments—the moment it is uncertain, it is plain they furnish no specific idea of art or history, and then I neither desire to see or read of them.

I have been diverted too to another work, in which I am personally a little concerned. Yesterday was published an octavo pretending to contain the correspondence of Hackman and Miss Wray, that he murdered.[4] I doubt whether the letters are genuine, and yet

1. Rudder's *New History of Gloucestershire*, which followed the same plan as Atkyns's work (see *ante* 27 Dec. 1779).

2. *A View of Northumberland, with an Excursion to the Abbey of Mailross in Scotland*, 2 vols, Newcastle, 1776–8, by William Hutchinson (1732–1814). HW's copy was sold SH v. 157.

3. '*Antonini Itinerarium*, a valuable register, still extant, of the stations and distances along the various roads of the Roman Empire' (*Encyclopaedia Britannica*,

14th edn). It perhaps belongs to the reign of Marcus Aurelius Antoninus Bassianus Caracalla (186–217 A.D.), Emperor 212–17.

4. *Love and Madness. A Story too true, in a Series of Letters between Parties, whose Names would perhaps be mentioned were they less known or less lamented*, which was published anonymously, Saturday, 11 March 1780 (see *Public Advertiser* 11 March; *Whitehall Evening Post* 9–11 March 1780). It was written by Sir Herbert Croft (1751–1816), 5th Bt, and contained

if fictitious, they are executed well, and enter into his character—hers appear less natural; and yet the editors were certainly more likely to be in possession of hers than of his. It is not probable that Lord Sandwich should have sent what he found in her apartment, to the press. No account is pretended to be given of how they came to light.

You will wonder how *I* should be concerned in this correspondence, who never saw either of the lovers in my days. In fact, my being dragged in, is a reason for my doubting the authenticity; nor can I believe that the long letter in which I am frequently mentioned, could be written by the wretched lunatic.[5] It pretends that Miss Wray desired him to give her a particular account of Chatterton. He does give a most ample one—but is there a glimpse of probability that a being so frantic should have gone to Bristol and sifted Chatterton's sister and others with as much cool curiosity as Mr Lort could do? and at such a moment? Besides he murdered Miss Wray, I think, in March;[6] my printed defence was not at all dispersed before the preceding January or February, nor do I conceive that Hackman could ever see it. There are notes indeed by the editor, who has certainly seen it—but I rather imagine that the editor, whoever he is, composed the whole volume. I am acquitted of being accessory to the lad's death, which is gracious; but much blamed for speaking of his bad character, and for being too hard on his forgeries, though I took so much pains to specify the innocence of them; and for his character, I only quoted the very words of his own editor and panegyrist. I did not repeat what Dr Goldsmith told me at the Royal Academy, where I first heard of his death, that he went by the appellation of *the young villain*—but it is not new to me, as you know, to be blamed by two opposite parties. The editor has in one place confounded me and my uncle, who, he says, as is true, checked Lord Chatham for being too forward a young man in 1740.[7] In that year I was not even come into Parliament; and must have been absurd indeed if I had taunted Lord Chatham with youth, who was at least six or seven years younger than he was—and how could he reply by

some material on Chatterton which Croft acquired on false pretences from Chatterton's relations (see DNB). The letters are generally believed to be fictitious, but see *The Love Letters of Mr. H. & Miss R., 1775–1779*, ed. Gilbert Burgess, 1895, pp. v–xvi.

5. Croft later acknowledged that he was the author of this letter (No. xlix), dated 7 Feb. 1779. The first reference to HW (which exonerates him of Chatterton's death) is at p. 135.

6. On the night of 7 April 1779 (see DNB).

7. Croft, op. cit. 136.

reproaching me with old age, who was then not twenty-three? I shall make no answer to these absurdities, nor to any part of the work. Blunder I see people will, and talk of what they do not understand; and what care I? There is another trifling mistake of still less consequence. The editor supposes that it was Macpherson who communicated Ossian to me.[8] It was Sir David Dalrymple who sent me the first specimens.[9] Macpherson did once come to me—but my credulity was then a little shaken.

Lady Ailesbury has promised me guinea eggs for you, but they have not yet begun to lay.

I am well acquainted with Lady Craven's little tale dedicated to me. It is careless and incorrect, but there are very pretty things in it.

I will stop, for I fear I have written to you too much lately. One you did not mention; I think it was of the 28th of last month.

Yours entirely,

H. WALPOLE

From Cole, Monday 27 March 1780

VA, Forster MS 110, ff. 233–4. Cole kept no copy.

Address: The Honourable Horace Walpole, Berkeley Square, London.
Postmark: Cambridge 28 MR.

Easter Monday, March 27, 1780.

Dear Sir,

I AM extremely ill at this time, yet I would no longer defer my expressing my gratitude for your kind present,[1] which Dr Lort sent to me a week ago. I told him the case, and how ashamed I was at making so mean a request in reality, though possibly only a hint in

---

8. Croft, in a note acknowledged to be by the 'Editor,' refers to HW as 'this patron of Ossian, and rejector of Chatterton' (ibid. 136). Later in the letter (ostensibly by Hackman) is this passage: 'That Chatterton had Walpole and Ossian in some measure present to his mind, is manifest from his fixing upon the same person

(Mr. W.) to introduce Rowley to the world, whom Macpherson chose for Ossian' (ibid. 212).

9. See HW to David Dalrymple 4 April 1760.

---

1. Another copy of *Roy. & Nob. Authors* (cf. *ante* 6 March 1780). This copy was lot

fact, especially as I might have purchased them. 'Yes,' said Dr Lort, 'you might, but you must have given thirty shillings for them,' and mentioned one of his acquaintance who lately did so. Sir, I heartily thank you for them, and pray forget the mode of getting them. If you do, I hardly shall. Dr Lort called on me on Thursday, the only time I saw him, and that only for half an hour. I had been blooded the day before for one of the vilest colds I ever had, and though much broken out about my lips, am still worse and worse.

On Saturday we had a tumult at Cambridge about petitioning,[2] brought forward by an Anabaptist alderman,[3] for the sheriff[4] would not call the county together. It consisted wholly, I may say, of Dissenters of all hues and complexions. They were patronized by the Duke of Rutland[5] (who had a design to recommend his brother, Lord Robert Manners,[6] to be[7] one of the members for the county), the Duke of Manchester, who told the populace that they were the origin of power and law, and that from them alone, he and others in his station, now become so corrupt, must expect protection. Lord Duncannon[8] was in the chair and read the petition, which Mr Crisp Molineux of Lynn,[9] having a better voice, repeated. John Wilkes made several harangues, as did a Mr Daye,[10] who has been much in

1142 in the sale of George Steevens's library, 13 May 1800 and ten following days. It was the 1759 edition. The same copy was lot 341 in the sale of Kirgate's collection, 4 Dec. 1810, where it was bought by Lowndes.

2. The petition, which asked for a reduction of the public expense and the abolition of sinecures, is printed in Cooper, *Annals* iv. 393. It was printed in the *Cambridge Chronicle*, 4 and 11 March 1780, and unanimously agreed to, 9 March. A longer account of the meeting is quoted from Cole's MSS (Add MS 5855, ff. 140–4) in George Warren Gignilliat, Jr., *The Author of Sandford and Merton: A Life of Thomas Day*, New York, 1932, pp. 181–2, 185–6.

3. John Purchas, an eminent brewer, who, 'with all the confidence of a true fanatic, opened to the assembly the occasion of the meeting' (Cole, quoted loc. cit.).

4. Thomas Rumbold Hall (1722–99), of Hildersham, Cambs; High Sheriff of Cambs and Hunts, 1780–1 (see *Alumni Cantab.*; GM July 1799, lxix. 625a).

5. MS reads *Dukes*.

6. (1758–82), 3d son of John Manners (1721–70), M. of Granby; commander of the 'Resolution,' 74 guns; d. 24 April 1782 of wounds received in battle twelve days earlier (see *Annual Register for 1783*, 1785, 'Characters,' pp. 35–40).

7. MS reads *to to*.

8. Frederick Ponsonby (1758–1844), Lord Duncannon, who suc. as 3d E. of Bessborough in 1793; M.P. for Knaresborough, 1780–93.

9. Crisp Molineux (d. 1792), of Garboldisham, Norfolk, later of Thundersley Hall, Essex; High Sheriff of Norfolk, 1767; M.P. for King's Lynn, Norfolk, 1774–90. He died 'at St Kitt's whither he went for the recovery of his health' (GM, *Supplement*, lxii. 1220–1).

10. Thomas Day (1748–89), the author of *Sandford and Merton*, who lived at this time at Stapleford Abbots, near Abridge, Essex. His speech was published under the title of *The Speech of Thomas Day, Esq., on the Necessity of a Reform in Parliament, delivered at Cambridge, March 25,*

way of it in Essex. These were attended by Dr Watson,[11] Regius Professor of Divinity and Archdeacon of Ely, in a lay habit, who spoke not himself, but often prompted them. The two county members, Sir John Cotton and Sir Sampson Gideon, were there *ex officio*, and said all that could be said against it, but the popular dissenting tide was so strong that nothing could stem it. They had adjourned from the town hall, which was too small for the purpose of having the mob introduced, to the Senate-House yard, where the steps and colonnade made a good stage for the actors. They have appointed a committee,[12] and I heard a very extraordinary personage of the clergy[13] is one of it. Not a gentleman of the country appeared there to give it any countenance, yet this will be produced as the voice of the county. We live in sad times. I declare sincerely, fearing the ill tendency of all this mischief brewing, that I hope I shall be out of the way before it is accomplished.

I am wholly of your mind in respect to Roman antiquities among us, but I always thought my little taste for them proceeded from an ignorance of them and their paraphernalia. I am better pleased now about it.

You have so unhinged the hypothesis of Chatterton's letters, or Miss Wray's,[14] that it would spoil the sale of them did the world know as much as I do.

Your letter of the 27 of last month I extremely observed, but as it was on politics, I did not choose to say anything about what I did not comprehend, and I hope and wish I have not explained myself too much in this very letter, which I scribbled on without thinking. Do excuse my zeal, as I do yours.

Adieu! dear Sir, and wishing you every blessing, I am, with the greatest sincerity,

Yours eternally,

WM COLE

1780, London: Printed for D. I. Eaton, [n.d.].

11. Richard Watson (1737–1816), afterwards (1782) Bp of Llandaff; a strong Whig.

12. The committee was appointed 'to carry on a correspondence to restore the freedom of Parliament.' The members of it were the Dukes of Portland, Richmond, Manchester, and Rutland, Earl Spencer, Lord Bessborough, Lord Duncannon, Lord Robert Manners, Hon. William Pitt, Sir Robert Bernard, Sir Gillis Payne, John Wilkes, and others (see Gignilliat, op. cit. 186).

13. Not identified.

14. Cole, who had not seen Croft's *Love and Madness*, misses the point of HW's remarks.

To Cole, Thursday 30 March 1780

Add MS 5953, ff. 85–6.
Address: To the Reverend Mr Cole at Milton near Cambridge.
Postmark: 30 MR.

Berkeley Square, March 30, 1780.

I CANNOT be told that you are extremely ill, and refrain from begging to hear that you are better. Let me have but one line; if it is good, it will satisfy me. If you was not out of order, I would scold you, for again making excuses about the *Noble Authors:* it was not kind to be so formal about a trifle.

We do not differ so much in politics as you think, for when they grow too serious, they are so far from inflaming my zeal, they make me more moderate: and I can as easily discern the faults on my own side as on the other; nor would assist Whigs more than Tories in altering the Constitution. The project of annual Parliaments or of adding an hundred members to the House of Commons would I think be very unwise and will never have my approbation—but a temperate man is not likely to be listened to in turbulent times; and when one has not youth and lungs, or ambition to make oneself attended to, one can only be silent and lament, and preserve oneself blameless of any mischief that is done or attempted.

Yours most sincerely,

H. W.

From Cole, Saturday 1 April 1780

VA, Forster MS 110, f. 235. Cole kept no copy.
Address: The Honourable Horace Walpole, Berkeley Square, London.
Postmark: Cambridge 3 AP.

Milton, Saturday morning, April 1, 1780.

Dear Sir,

YOUR most kind letter obliges me to thank you for it as early as possible, and to tell you that, if I am not better, I am no worse. The contrast of our two constitutions amazes me every time I think of it. You was bred up delicately in cotton, when coarse wool was my lot, yet have I seen you in the dews and damps of November in slippers, without hat or other clothing than within doors, walking your garden at Strawberry Hill. The sitting with your back against an open window, in an east wind last year in the evening for hours,[1] would absolutely have killed me. Your never using greatcoat is to me astonishing. I am told I keep myself too warm. It may be so, but I know not how to avoid it. If I leave off an handkerchief less than usual, a sore throat is the immediate consequence. All this fine weather, with the finest blow of snowdrops, hepaticas and crocuses I ever had, I have, though in general tolerable well, not dared to go into the garden to look at them, nor have been at the farther end of it these six weeks.

I shall think the better of my own, the nearer they draw to <your> politics, but I am free to own that if the present system of committees and associations go on, I dread the consequences, and wish to be out of the way of them. How much is your wise father's peaceable plan to be preferred! He knew the turbulence of the nation, and had no small plague to keep them quiet. No king nor[2] government can long please a people given up to changes of all sorts. If an angel was sent to be viceroy, they would chop off his wings. A boisterous, blustering king is a savage and despotic tyrant: a learned, peaceful king a pedant: a virtuous one shall be abused by Mrs Macaulay for being uxorious and loving his wife too well:[3] a profligate one shall be abused for the very reverse.[4] But I will stop, and wish men would return to their senses and be as moderate and temperate as you are. Good God! that annual Parliaments should be ever thought of! They would not probably be so much brigued,[5] but the drunken scene would never be laid asleep. But we live in an age of projects: I wish they were good ones. I may speak my mind the more freely, as I never was benefited by any government, and never asked favour or preferment from any. All my ambition was to see things

1. See *ante* 2 June 1779.

2. MS reads *nor nor*.

3. Mrs Macaulay says of Charles I: 'His chastity has been called in question . . . and were it allowed, it was tainted by an excess of uxoriousness, which gave it the properties and the consequences of vice' (*History of England*[2], 1769, iv. 395).

4. Cole apparently has in mind another passage from Mrs Macaulay, who says that

Charles II 'encouraged by his practice . . . guilty excesses, in entering into an intrigue, the first night which succeeded this day of triumph [the Restoration], with the wife of Roger Palmer, a Papist' (*History of England*[1], 1772, v. 358).

5. 'Brigue,' an obsolete Scotticism, meant 'solicit by underhand methods; canvass' (OED).

THE REVEREND WILLIAM COLE

pass quietly and regularly, but to be governed by a mob, and under the pretence of Wilkes and Liberty to be enslaved to the vilest and lowest of despotism is galling to a degree not to be resented by, dear Sir,

Your ever faithful and most obliged old friend and servant,

Wm Cole

To Cole, Thursday 11 May 1780

Add MS 5953, ff. 87–8.
Address: To the Reverend Mr Cole at Milton near Cambridge.
Postmark: GC 11 MA.

Berkeley Square, May 11, 1780.

MR Godfrey the engraver[1] told me yesterday that Mr Tyson is dead[2]—I am sorry for it, though he had left me off. A much older friend of mine died yesterday, but of whom I must say the same, George Montagu[3] whom you must remember at Eton and Cambridge. I should have been exceedingly concerned for him a few years ago—but he had dropped me, partly from politics and partly from caprice, for we never had any quarrel—but he was grown an excessive humourist, and had shed almost all his friends as well as me. He had parts and infinite vivacity and originality till of late years—and it grieved me much that he had changed towards me after a friendship of between thirty and forty years.

1. MS reads *Godrey*, but Cole silently corrected the error in his copy, Add MS 5826, f. 190v. Richard Bernard Godfrey (1728–ca 1795), who engraved plates for several antiquarian works (see DNB), was acquainted with Tyson (see LA viii. 639). He engraved, apparently in 1778, ten plates for the 1784 edition of HW's *Description of SH* (see Gough, *British Topography*[2] i. 571*; *post* 19 Dec. 1780).

2. He died 4 May 1780.

3. HW's correspondent. 'George Montagu was Hereditary Ranger of Sawsey [Salcey] Forest in Northamptonshire, and secretary to the Chancellor of the Exchequer' (Cole's note following his copy of HW's letter, Add MS 5826, f. 190v). Another note on this letter appears at f. 193v:

'In the *General Evening Post* of May 18, 1780, was this article: "Mr Montagu who died last week, has left Lord North and his family a reversion of £600 a year after the death of Frederick Montague, Esq."—sufficiently explanatory of Mr Walpole's dislike of Mr Montagu, who was eldest son of Brigadier-General Montagu, only brother to George the second Earl of Halifax.' Cole exaggerates. HW's explanation of his 'coolness' with Montagu minimizes his long-suffering with Montagu's 'humourousness,' which their correspondence clearly shows. Montagu died at his house in Brook Street, London, Tuesday, 9 May (not 10 May as HW's 'yesterday' indicates). See *Public Advertiser* 17 May 1780; GM May 1780, l. 252a.

I am told that a nephew of the Provost of King's has preached and printed a most flaming sermon,[4] which condemns the whole opposition to the stake. Pray who is it, and on what occasion? Mr Bryant has published an answer to Dr Priestley.[5] I bought it, but though I have a great value for the author, the subject is so metaphysical, and so above human decision, I soon laid it aside.

I hope you can send me a good account of yourself, though the spring is so unfavourable.

Yours most sincerely,

H. Walpole

From Cole, Sunday 14 May 1780

VA, Forster MS 110, ff. 236–7. Cole's copy, Add MS 5826, ff. 190v, 191v, 192v. *Address:* To the Honourable Horace Walpole, Berkeley Square, London.

Milton, Whitsunday, May 14, 1780.

Dear Sir,

POOR Mr Tyson was carried off by a violent fever after a week's illness. I am sorry he had left off visiting you. However that may be, I am morally certain he had the sincerest regard for you, and though he had his oddities, yet he was a most valuable and ingenious friend. I have regretted no one so much since the loss of Mr Gray.[1]

I well remember Mr George Montagu, was acquainted with him a little, and either called upon him in Craven or Norfolk Street, or found him at the present Lord Dacre's,[2] for I shall scarce ever forget one of his vivacities at that time. When Mr Gray was with me at Blecheley for a week or fortnight, he left me to go to him in Northamptonshire.[3] I think he met you at Horton[4] when I accompanied you to Burleigh.[5]

---

4. See following letter, nn. 6, 10.

5. Joseph Priestley (1733–1804), theologian and scientist. Bryant's pamphlet was *An Address to Dr. Priestly . . . upon Philosophical Necessity.*

---

1. Cole makes a similar declaration in his letter to Gough 14 May 1780, printed in LA i. 683.

2. Thomas Barrett-Lennard (1717–86), 17th Bn Dacre of the South, friend and occasional correspondent of HW.

3. 'and in a letter to Mr. Gray at my house proposed my attending Mr Gray to him' (addition in Cole's copy). Montagu was then living at Greatworth, near Brackley (see *Country Seats* 51).

4. Or Haughton, Northants, the seat of

It is not a nephew, but a son[6] of Cooke the Provost of King's, who, being a sycophant from assistant at Eton, continues his trade now in a more elevated station:[7] Bishop Keene collated him last week to a prebend in his church at Ely.[8] His son had dedicated about two months before a sermon on *Religious and Moral Liberty* to his Lordship.[9] This was rewarded by a stall to the father. The sermon you allude to is the second part of the same tune, being on *Civil Liberty*.[10] They were both preached at St Mary's extempore, very unusual there, and are the most bombast, pedantical, obscure sermons I ever read, and were much ridiculed at the time of preaching them, and no bad copy of verses against the former appeared in the Cambridge paper, in which he had aimed to throw some discredit on Sir Isaac Newton and his philosophy,[11] than which nothing could be more unpopular, he being the idol of the place. The last[12] is vehement against Dr Watson, the Patriot Divinity Professor. Now I mention Dr Cooke, you will probably be pleased with the following anecdote relating to him. The Master of Benet College has an acquaintance in Dorsetshire, a Mr Hall,[13] who is mentioned by Kippis in the preface to his second volume as one of his assistants. This gen-

Lord Halifax, which HW and Cole visited in July 1763 (see ibid. 52–3).

5. Cole's copy reads: 'I think he met us at Horton, when we took our tour to Drayton and Burleigh.'

6. William Cooke (1749–1824), the younger, Fellow of King's, Professor of Greek at Cambridge, 1780–92, first translated Gray's *Elegy* into Greek verse, 1785 (see LA ix. 154; DNB *sub* his father).

7. 'and is as great a flatterer of Bishop Keene under a pretence of gaining votes for his son, as he used to be to Dr George, in hopes to succeed him' (addition in Cole's copy).

8. Cole seems to be mistaken in the date: 'April 12, 1780, he [William Cooke the elder] was collated by his kind friend, Bishop Keene, to the Third Stall of this [Ely] Cathedral, and on August 9th, the same year, was instituted to the Deanery, and installed Sept. 2d' (Bentham, *Ely*², Addenda, p. 14).

9. *Liberty Moral and Religious. A Sermon preached before the University of Cambridge on February 27th, 1780, at Great St. Mary's Church*, Cambridge, 1780.

The dedication reads: 'To the Right Reverend Edmund, Lord Bishop of Ely, this sermon is most humbly inscribed by his Lordship's most obedient and obliged servant the author.'

10. *Civil Liberty: A Sermon*, Cambridge, 1780.

11. Cooke attacks Sir Isaac Newton indirectly, as the philosopher is not mentioned by name in the sermon.

12. That is, the sermon on *Civil Liberty*.

13. 'The Rev. Mr Hall, rector of Child Okeford, in Dorsetshire' (*Biographia Britannica*² ii. p. viii). Henry Hall (1734–1815), son of Henry Hall of Child Okeford; Exeter College, Oxford (B.A. 1755); rector of Child Okeford 1758–1815; archdeacon of Dorset 1801–15. He died at Child Okeford 'after a residence and faithful discharge of his pastoral duties . . . for more than 50 years,' and was buried in the parish church (see *Alumni Oxon*; John Hutchins, *History and Antiquities of the County of Dorset*, 3d edn, ed. by William Shipp and James W. Hodson, 4 vols, Westminster 1861–70, iv. 82).

tleman, in a letter which the Master left with me to transcribe, has the following long passage, which I shall transcribe, and which I make no doubt refers to Cooke, as the picture is the very likeness of the preaching son, and was very like the father when we were at school, as you may recollect if you have the *Polymetis*.¹⁴ The passage is this:

I have been this week most delightfully engaged in perusing some original letters and MSS of the late Mr Joseph Spence, Mr C. Pitt,¹⁵ Dr Cobden¹⁶ and others. I have really felt myself as free and intimate with them as their friends could ever be to them when living, etc.

As Mr Spence's letters are before me, I will transcribe you an anecdote from one of his letters to Mr C. Pitt, which may be new to you and your Cambridge friends.

'I am glad some of the schoolmasters of your acquaintance are pleased with the grave animal at the end of the 17 Dialogue.¹⁷ There are others, who have been angry at it, though it could not be meant for any man of good sense, and is indeed the representative only of one real blockhead: a gowned ass who, when I offered him some of my receipts, from an old acquaintance with him, said that he could have nothing to do with them,¹⁸ because the book and subject was such as could not be of any use to him in his way. He was master in one of the greatest schools, and had I dedicated my plates, that print should have been consecrated to his name. As it is, it may as well be concealed. What I like most in it is that simple wisdom in the air of the face, which does not at all disagree with the gentleman who sat for it.'

I should be glad to know the name of this curious schoolmaster, and to hear from you very soon.

That it was meant for Cooke there can be no <doubt,> both from the likeness of the figure to him, and the subject of that chapter being on langu<age and gram>mar and a criticism on the Eton method of teaching boys to make Latin verses and get <by rote 600>¹⁹ verses of

14. *Polymetis; or, an Enquiry concerning the Agreement between the Works of the Roman Poets, and the Remains of the Antient Artists*, by Joseph Spence, 1747. HW's copy (G.1.27) was sold SH iv. 79.
15. Christopher Pitt (1699–1748), poet and translator, friend of Pope.
16. Edward Cobden (1684–1764), author of poems and sermons; chaplain to George II, 1730–52.
17. According to the reference in the in-

dex of plates, this plate represents 'An Ass, in the Greek Pallium, teaching: a Gem, in Gorlaeus's *Dact[yliothecae]*, Part 2. No. 507.' A gowned ass is teaching two youths (see *Polymetis*¹, pp. 291, 336). The print was engraved by Louis Peter Boitard. Another plate was substituted in the second edition of the work, 1755.
18. Cooke's name does not appear in the list of subscribers.
19. Supplied from Cole's copy.

Homer and Virgil even when they have no taste for them.[20] I speak experimentally, having been frequently flogged, at this pimping fellow's instigation,[21] for what I conceive was no fault of my industry, but want of a poetical genius. Now to speak the truth, the case to me seems to be this: Mr Spence, a refined and lively coxcomb, offered to get off some of his copies to this formal, solemn, insolent and proud coxcomb, who refused to oblige him. The elegant writer knew no better way to revenge himself than to make the pedant ridiculous among a few friends, for it would not have been decorous to have spoken out. The excuse that Cooke made for his refusal was no doubt extremely absurd, as the book was a treatise on heathen mythology, language and grammar: the only things, I suppose, that Cooke knows much about, and as a schoolmaster was the most useful book he could have subscribed for.

Mr Gough has published his new edition of *British Topography*,[22] in two large quarto volumes. I looked at the indexes to see what mention he made of you, but it is only on the *Aedes Walpolianae*. He sent me the book: an handsome present, and I am sure I never expected it.[23] I had it only last night, with the tombs[24] behind the altar at Westminster Abbey and Sir Joseph Ayloffe's *Dissertation*.[25] I have had no time to look at them.

In the last month's *Gentleman's Magazine,* p. 196, you will find Frederic Prince of Wales, omitted by you as a royal author,[26] for a *chanson à boire* by him there printed; and at p. 179 is an account

20. 'If the general design of our schools should be that of teaching us to understand what the Latin and Greek authors have said in their writings . . . why are we so often obliged to fix hundreds of their lines in order, one after another, in our heads; and taught to repeat whole books of Homer and Virgil, by rote? . . . And why is every boy set to write things, that are called Latin verses; and obliged to endeavour at becoming a poet, in a foreign tongue?' (*Polymetis*[1], p. 289).

21. Cooke was a Præpositor and Cole a Colleger. (For the disciplinary powers of the Præpositors, see Sir Henry C. Maxwell Lyte, *A History of Eton College*, 1911, p. 316.)

22. Cole was mistaken: the work was not published until 5 June 1780 (see *Public Advertiser*, 12, 16, 28 May 1780). Gough sent an advance copy to Cole.

23. 'especially as we have always been rather shy one of the other' (addition in Cole's copy).

24. Cole's copy reads 'the prints of the tombs found . . .'

25. *An Account of Some Ancient Monuments in Westminster Abbey . . . Read at the Society of Antiquaries March 12, 1778*, 1780, by Sir Joseph Ayloffe (1709–81), 6th Bt. The account, with the prints, was incorporated into Kippis's *Vetusta Monumenta*, vol. 2, 1789, published by the Society of Antiquaries.

26. Frederick Louis (1707–51), Prince of Wales, and father of George III. HW added the following brief account of him in *Roy. & Nob. Authors* (*Works* i. 278): 'Wrote French songs, in imitation of the Regent ['Philip Duke of Orleans.'—HW], and did not miscarry solely by writing in a language not his own.'

of a curious picture in King James I's time of a procession to St Paul's, by one John Gipkyn.[27]

My friend Mr Bryant's books are much too elevated for my taste and capacity.

It is incredible the riot, expense and drunkenness going forward all over this county,[28] beyond belief, and what was ever practised before.

I am, dear Sir,

Yours most sincerely and affectionately,

WM COLE

To COLE, Friday 19 May 1780

Add MS 5953, ff. 89–90.

Address: To the Reverend Mr Cole at Milton near Cambridge.

Postmark: GC 20 MA.

Friday night, May 19, 1780.

BY tomorrow's coach you will receive a box of guinea hen's eggs, which Lady Ailesbury sent me today from Park Place. I hope they will arrive safe and all be hatched.

I thank you for the account of the sermon and the portrait of the uncle.[1] They will satisfy me without buying the former. As I knew Mr Jos. Spence, I do not think I should have been so much delighted as Dr Kippis[2] with reading his letters. He was a good-natured harmless little soul, but more like a silver penny than a genius. It was a

27. The account (pp. 179–81) is by Gough (see LA i. 685 n). The picture was painted on board in 1616 by John Gipkyn for Henry Farley, and was sold at auction for two shillings in the parlour of Lambourne parsonage (where Tyson then lived) to 'Dr Webster . . . a surgeon, man-midwife, etc.' The latter offered it for sale for thirty guineas, but sold it for fifteen to 'Edward Bridgen, Treasurer to the Society of Antiquaries, who for the same sum transferred it to that learned body. Grieved am I to add that it is now consigned . . . to a subterranean warehouse!' (John Nichols, *The Progresses . . . of King James the First*, 4 vols, 1828, iv. 597 n; see also LA viii. 664–5.) The assistant Secretary to the Society of Antiquaries, Mr

H. S. Kingsford, writes, 20 March 1935: 'It now adorns the main staircase, where it has been ever since we [The Society of Antiquaries] came to Burlington House in the 70's of the last century. It is on the back of the wing of the picture of Old St. Paul's, so is not visible unless the picture is closed.'

28. In connection with the elections for Parliament. The election for the University took place 9 Sept., and for the county, 14 Sept. 1780 (see Cooper, *Annals* iv. 399).

1. See preceding letter. The 'portrait' was of the 'father,' not the 'uncle.' 'A sermon by the Rev. W. Cooke, 1780,' was sold SH v. 207.

2. HW's mistake for 'Mr Hall.'

neat fiddle-faddle bit of sterling, that had read good books and kept good company, but was too trifling for use, and only fit to please a child.[3]

I hesitate on purchasing Mr Gough's second edition.[4] I do not think there was a guinea's worth of entertainment in the first: how can the additions be worth a guinea and half?

I have been aware of the royal author you tell me of, and have noted him for a future edition—but that will not appear in my own time—because, besides that, it will have the castrations in my original copy, and other additions that I am not impatient to produce. I have been solicited to reprint the work, but do not think it fair to give a very imperfect edition, when I could print it complete, which I do not choose to do, as I have an aversion to literary squabbles. One seems to think oneself too important, when one engages in a controversy on one's writings; and when one does not vindicate them, the answerer passes for victor, as you see Dr Kippis allots the palm to Dr Milles,[5] though, you know, I have so much more to say in defence of my hypothesis. I have actually some hopes of still more, of which I have heard, but till I see it, I shall not reckon upon it as on my side.[6]

Mr Lort told me of King James's Procession to St Paul's, but they ask such a price for it, and I care so little for James I, that I have not been to look at the picture.

Your electioneering will probably be increased immediately. Old Mr Thomas Townshend is at the point of death.[7] The Parliament will probably be dissolved before another session.[8] We wanted nothing but drink to inflame our madness, which I do not confine to politics—but what signifies it to throw out general censures? We old folks are apt to think nobody wise but ourselves—I wish the disgraces of these last two or three years did not justify a little severity more than flows from the peevishness of years!

Yours ever,

H. W.

3. Cf. Mann to HW 21 Aug. 1741.
4. Of *British Topography*.
5. See *ante* 1 March 1780.
6. The meaning of HW's reference is not clear, but, as he did not add a note to *Historic Doubts* in support of his hypothesis, the evidence was probably not on his side.

7. Hon. Thomas Townshend (1701–80), 2d son of Charles Townshend, 2d Vct Townshend; M.P. for Cambridge University 1727–74. HW obviously thought he was M.P. for Cambridge University at this time. He died 21 May 1780 (see GM May 1780, l. 252b).
8. It was dissolved 1 Sept. 1780.

From COLE, Wednesday 24 May 1780

VA, Forster MS 110, ff. 238–9. COLE's copy, Add MS 5826, ff. 192v, 193v.
HW sketched on the cover the coat of arms which he describes in his reply to this letter, as being on the shutters he purchased at Ives's sale.

Address: The Honourable Horace Walpole in Berkeley Square, London.

Postmark: Cambridge 26 MA.

<Dea>r Sir,   Milton, Wednesday morning, May 24, 1780.

I THANK you for your kind attention in procuring me the eggs. They came very safe, and I took them with me from Cambridge on Monday evening, and that night put them under a hen that was ready for them, and hope for better luck than last week, when, after sitting a month full, a dozen eggs I had procured elsewhere, were found to be all addled. Indeed I never much depended on them, as the person who sent them said that the cock bird had been killed by a pointer, but the man who fetched them heard in the kitchen that the dunghill cock trod the hen. I had another interruption, having, after much pains, two months ago procured a cock and hen: the last was not well when she came, moped about the yard for [a] month, and now seems recovered, yet has made no attempts to lay any eggs. I hope <your> bounty will fully satisfy my passion about them. I have so few amusements, and can see these creatures from my study window when I can't stir out of my room, that that must be my excuse for the trouble I have given you on this occasion.

I have got no further than the 234 page of Mr Gough's first volume, having had continual interruptions of one kind [or] another ever since he was so kind to send it to me. I remember when the first edition came out, you seemed well pleased with it.[1] It is certainly a book of great use to an antiquary, and in some articles of this second edition shows more impartiality than I expected from one so much connected with Mr Kippis. In one instance he has failed in regard to you, through forgetfulness, which I may mention in another letter.[2] In this, which was to return my oval thanks[3] only, I cannot, being much taken up, and have hardly time to tell you how sincerely and faithfully I am, dear Sir,

Yours,

WM COLE

1. See *ante* 27 May 1769.
2. Cole does not mention it, and Gough's 'failure' has not been located.

3. That is, thanks for the eggs.

Yesterday I was all day in the severest trial of electioneering I ever saw: such multitudes, such riots, drunkenness,[4] bearishness and heat I never wish to experience and meet with again. Sir Harry Peyton[5] nominated the Duke of Rutland's brother, whom they call here Lord Robert Manners.[5a] Sir Sampson Gideon was nominated by Sir Charles Gould,[6] and who produced the son[7] of the late Mr Charles Yorke I don't know, for I dared not venture into the air of the Castle Hill, but was[8] in an house in the Castle Yard. Mr Thomas Townshend, Senior, long served for the University. The present members are Messrs Croftes[9] and Mansfield. Poor Mr Soame Jenyns was near being trampled to death by the mob: his face was much bruised. He is not made for mixing with a riotous mob. He rejoices at the thoughts of no more entering St Stephen's Chapel.

To COLE, Tuesday 30 May 1780

Add MS 5953, ff. 91–2.

Address: To the Reverend Mr Cole at Milton near Cambridge.
Postmark: GC 30 MA.

Berkeley Square, May 30, 1780.

I HOPE you will bring your eggs to a fair market. At last I have got from Bonus my altar doors which I bought at Mr Ives's.[1] He has repaired them admirably. I would not suffer him to repaint or varnish them. Three are indubitably Duke Humphrey of Gloucester, Cardinal Beaufort and Archbishop Kemp. The fourth I cannot

4. 'of men, women and children' (addition in Cole's copy).

5. Sir Henry Peyton (d. 1789), 1st Bt (n.c.), of Doddington, Cambs; born Dashwood, but took name of Peyton by Act of Parliament on succeeding to the estate of his maternal uncle, Sir Thomas Peyton, 3d Bt, of Doddington, Cambs. He was M.P. for Cambridgeshire, 1782–9.

5a. He was more often called Captain Lord Robert Manners (see *ante* 27 March 1780, n. 6).

6. (1726–1806) Kt (1779); 1st Bt, of Tredegar, Monmouth, 15 Nov. 1792, and on the following day, by royal licence, took the name of Morgan for himself and issue. He was M.P. for Brecon, 1778–87; and for Breconshire, 1787–1806.

7. Philip Yorke (1757–1834), who, in 1790, succeeded his uncle as 3d E. of Hardwicke; M.P. for Cambridgeshire, 1780–90. He was the son of Hon. Charles Yorke (1722–70).

8. 'in my chariot and sometimes' (addition in Cole's copy).

9. Richard Croftes (d. 1783), of West Harling, Norfolk, and Little Saxham, Suffolk; of St. John's College, Cambridge; M.P. for Cambridge University, 1771–80 (see John Gage [Rokewode], *The History and Antiquities of Suffolk. Thingoe Hundred,* 1838, p. 138; Cooper *Annals* iv. 361).

1. See *ante* 20 Feb. 1777.

make out. It is a man in a crimson garment lined with white, and not tonsured. He is in the stable with cattle, and has the air of Joseph— but over his head hangs a large shield with these arms. The Cornish

choughs are sable on or. The other three divisions are gules, on the first of which is a gold crescent.

The second arms have three bulls' heads sable, horned or. The chevron was so changed that Bonus thought it sable, but I think it was gules, and then it would be Bullen or Boleyn. Lord DeFerrers says, the first are the arms of Sir Barthol. Tate, who he finds married a Sanders.[2] Edmonson's new *Dictionary of Heraldry*[3] confirms both arms for Tate and Sanders,[4] except that Sanders bore the chevron ermine[5]—which it may have been. But what I wish to discover is, whether Sir Bartholomew Tate was a benefactor to St Edmundsbury, whence these doors came, or was in any shape a retainer to the Duke of Gloucester or Cardinal Beaufort. The Duke's and Sir Bartholo-

2. Sir Bartholomew Tate (d. 1533) m. Anne, dau. of Lawrence Saunders of Harington, Northants. He purchased the monastery and lands of Delapré Abbey, Northants. His arms were 'per fess or and gules, a pale counterchanged, three cornish choughs proper' (William Flower, *Visitations of the County of Nottingham in the Years 1569–1614*, ed. George William Marshall, *Publications of the Harleian Society* iv (1871). 84; see also Burke, *Landed Gentry*, 2 vols, 1851, *sub* Tate). There is no evidence that he was connected with St Edmundsbury.

3. *A Complete Body of Heraldry*, 2 vols,

1780, by Joseph Edmondson. HW's copy (D.1) was sold SH iv. 12.

4. Edmondson gives for Sanders or Saunders: 'Per chev[ron] ar[gent] and sa[ble] three elephants' heads erased counterchanged' (see Edmondson, op. cit. *sub* Tate and Sanders).

5. The Sanders family that bore for arms 'Sa[ble], a chev[ron] erm[ine] betw[een] three bulls' heads cabossed ar[gent]' was of 'Derbyshire, Staffordshire and of Charwood in Surrey,' and not of Northamptonshire, as was the family to which Sir Bartholomew Tate's wife belonged (see Edmondson, op. cit. *sub* Sanders).

mew's figures were the insides of the doors (which I have had sawed
into four panels) and are painted in a far superior style to the Cardinal and the Archbishop—which are very hard and dry. The two
others are so good that they are in the style of the school of the Caracci. They at least were painted by some Italian; the draperies have
large and bold folds, and one wonders how they could be executed
in the reign of Henry VI. I shall be very glad if you can help me to
any lights, at least about Sir Bartholomew. I intend to place them in
my chapel, as they will aptly accompany the shrine. The Duke and
Archbishop agree perfectly with their portraits in my Marriage of
Henry VI and prove how rightly I guessed. The Cardinal's is rather
a longer and thinner visage—but that he might have in the latter end
of life; and in the Marriage he has the red bonnet on, which shortens
his face. On the door he is represented in the character he ought to
have possessed, a pious contrite look, not the truer resemblance
which Shakespeare drew—'He dies—and makes no sign!'[6]—but An-
nibal Caracci[7] himself could not paint like our Raphael-poet!—Pray
don't venture yourself in any more electioneering riots—you see the
mob do not respect poets,[8] nor, I suppose, antiquaries.

P. S. I am in no haste for an answer to my queries.

From Cole, Thursday 1 June 1780

Cole's copy, Add MS 5826, f. 194v. The original is missing.
Address: To the Hon. Horace Walpole in Berkeley Square, London.

Milton, June 1, 1780.

Dear Sir,

HAVING looked through my *Antiquitates Suffolciences, or an
Account of Ancient Suffolk Families,* by Sir Ric. Gippes,[1] I can
find none of the name of Tate there, nor do I find it in my extracts

---

6. *2 Henry VI* III. iii. 29.
7. Annibale Caracci or Carracci (1560–
1609). He was represented in HW's collection by 'Young Hercules with the Serpents,'
which was in the Tribune at SH, sold SH
xiii. 28; and by 'The Dead Christ,' on black
marble, sold SH xxii. 94.

8. That is, Soame Jenyns (see preceding
letter).

---

1. This was a MS which Cole had transcribed into one of his MS volumes (see
ante 9 June 1775).

from the ledger of Bury Abbey, from whence, I think, I formerly
sent you this entry relating to the Cardinal.[2]

1436. Oct. 4. Litera fraternitatis concessa Henrico Dei gratia titulo Sci'.
Eusebii S. S. Ro' Eccliae' Presb' Cardinali de Anglia vulgariter nuncu-
pato, in qua pater ejus Johes' Dux Lanc' vocatur alter monastii' Sci'
Edmi' fundator. Thomas Dux Exon, vir sanctissimus, Cardinalis dicti
Frater, apud Scum' Edmundum humatus perhibetur.

Neither meet I with any mention of Sir Barth. Tate in Batteley's
History of Bury Abbey,[3] which indeed comes not so low as Henry VI
by a century or two, but the appendix has nothing about him, no
more than the index to Blomefield. If you choose it, I will write to
Sir John Cullum, though I have no acquaintance with him further
than an antiquarian knowledge of him through poor Mr Tyson: he
is more likely than anyone I know to give you the proper information. I will have an eye to your query in my travelling, and if I
should be so happy to meet with anything relating to him, you may
depend upon hearing of it. In my old MS[4] the arms of Tate agree
with your painting, as do those of Sanders of London, *temp*. Elizabeth, except in colours, etc. Yet I can't help thinking but that the
arms belong to Boleyn, an ancient family of those parts. The va-
rieties of colours and bearings in heraldry are so often mistaken in
the same name and even family, both formerly and in our own time,
that I lay no stress upon small differences. I am sorry I can't assist
you in my little way.

I heard last week from Dr Lort, who told me that Mrs Jervis[5] has
a small piece of painted glass that Mr Lombe of Cambridge, an acquaintance of mine, offered 25 guineas for. It ought to be delicate.

I can't help observing one thing: when I had first the honour of
your acquaintance, a boy of fourteen or fifteen years of age, I once
caught you under the hands of Mr Lens[6] at Chelsea, who was teach-

2. Cole had already sent the passage to
HW, in his letter of 23 Feb. 1777. The
Cardinal was Henry Beaufort.

3. *Joannis Battely . . . Opera Posthuma. Viz., Antiquitates Rutupinae et
Antiquitates S. Edmundi Burgi ad Annum
1272 Perductae*, Oxford, 1745.

4. Cf. *ante* 2 March 1779.

5. Probably a mistake for 'Mr Jervis.'
Thomas Jervais, the glass-painter was exhibiting his works at 'Mr Pinchbeck's,

Cock-Spur Street, in the bottom of the
Haymarket. Admittance one shilling.' The
exhibition opened 1 May and closed 17
June 1780 (see *Public Advertiser* 1 May,
14 June 1780).

6. Bernard Lens (1680–1740), 'the incomparable painter in water-colours . . .
whose copies from Rubens, Van Dyck, and
many other great masters, have all the
merit of the originals, except, what they
deserve too, duration. He was drawing-

ing you to draw. His lessons I find you despised, caring not for the mechanical part of a science, the theory of which you are so intimately versed in. You may guess my meaning by your drawing the coat so coarsely.[7] Have you heard of Mr Pegge's book of ancient cookery, from the MS of the master cook of King Richard II?[8] It is printed, but possibly not yet published. Mr Hollis's *Life*[9] no doubt you have seen. I want more to see Davies's *Life of D. Garrick*.[10]

I am,

Yours, etc.,

WM COLE

To COLE, Thursday 15 June 1780

Add MS 5953, ff. 93-4.

Address: To the Reverend Mr Cole at Milton near Cambridge.

Postmark: 15 I[V].

Strawberry Hill, June 15, 1780.

YOU may like to know one is alive, dear Sir, after a massacre and the conflagration of a capital.[1] I was in it both on the Friday

master to the Duke of Cumberland and the Princesses Mary and Louisa, and to one whom nothing but gratitude would excuse my joining with such names, the author of this work: my chief reason for it is, to bear testimony to the virtues and integrity of so good a man, as well as excellent artist' (*Engravers, Works* iv. 107-8; see also DNB). For HW's pictures by Lens, see *Description of SH, Works* ii. 431, 447, 492.

7. Almost certainly this paragraph to this point was not in the letter HW received. HW does not refer to it, and it is the sort of addition Cole reserved for his copy. He wrote a similar note in his copy of *Engravers*[2] (now WSL), p. 128: 'I remember to have seen Mr Lens more than once at Sir Robert Walpole's at Chelsea, when he came to instruct the author of this work, I being then a schoolboy at Eton, and calling, as usual, upon him. But from scratchings in the shape of drawings which I have occasionally received in letters forty or fifty years since, it looks as if the author never took much delight in drawing, or at least had quite forgotten it.'

8. *The Forme of Cury, a roll of ancient English cookery. Compiled about A.D. 1390, by the master-cook of King Richard II, presented afterwards to Queen Elizabeth by Edward, Lord Stafford, and now in the possession of G. Brander.* With notes . . . By an Antiquary [Samuel Pegge], 1780. HW apparently did not have a copy.

9. *Memoirs of Thomas Hollis, Esq.*, 2 vols, 1780. The work was privately printed, and, as HW says, 'not published, but sent as presents to the elect' (to Mason 13 and 17 April 1780). In May, however, the work was published at £4.4.0 (see GM Sept. 1780, l. 425-30; *Public Advertiser* 24 and 25 May 1780, where it is said the work is 'Printed by J. Nichols; and sold by T. Cadell [etc.]'). Presumably Cole had seen this or a similar advertisement. HW's copy 'elegantly bound in green morocco' was sold SH vii. 58.

10. *Memoirs of the Life of David Garrick, Esq., interspersed with characters and anecdotes of his theatrical contemporaries*, 2 vols, 1780, by Thomas Davies (1712?-85). The work was published Saturday, 6 May 1780 (see *Public Advertiser* 1 and 6 May 1780), and reached a second edition in

and on *the Black Wednesday*, the most horrible night I ever beheld, and which for six hours together I expected to end in half the town being reduced to ashes.

I can give you little account of the origin of this shocking affair. Negligence was certainly its nurse, and religion only its godmother. The ostensible author is in the Tower.[2] Twelve or fourteen thousand men have quashed all tumults—and as no bad account is come from the country, except for a moment at Bath,[3] and as eight days have passed, nay more since the commencement, I flatter myself the whole nation is shocked at the scene, and that, if plan there was, it was laid only in and for the metropolis. The lowest and most villainous of the people, and to no great amount, were almost the sole actors.

I hope your electioneering riotry has not nor will mix in these tumults. It would be most absurd, for Lord Rockingham,[4] the Duke of Richmond,[5] Sir George Saville[6] and Mr Burke,[7] the patrons of

July (see ibid. 8 and 22 July 1780). Cf. HW to Mason 14?–19 May 1780. HW's copy, with his MS notes, was sold SH vi. 65.

1. The Gordon riots began on Friday, 2 June, and reached their height on 'Black Wednesday,' 7 June. HW gives a detailed account of them in his letters of this period, and in *Last Journals* ii. 306–13. Much new material was published by J. Paul de Castro in *The Gordon Riots*, 1926.

2. Lord George Gordon (1751–93) was arrested 9 June, and the following day was committed to the Tower on a charge of high treason. He was tried and acquitted 5–6 Feb. 1781 (see de Castro, op. cit., *passim*).

3. 'On Friday night last [9 June] a great riot happened at Bath. Its beginning . . . was accidental. . . . About eight o'clock in the evening some boys were playing on St. James's Parade, near the Romish chapel, when one of them threw a stone, and broke one of the windows. A man who lived in an adjoining house, coming out and reprimanding the boy, a number of people gathered together, took the boy's part, and threw the man over a wall into St. James's churchyard. They then proceeded to demolishing the windows and doors, and entering the chapel, threw everything that was movable into the

street, and burnt them. . . . A party of Bath Volunteers . . . endeavored to disperse the mob; one of them fired, and killed an ostler. This . . . served only to enrage them still more. They immediately set fire to the chapel, which . . . was burnt down, together with six or seven new-built houses adjoining, the property of Roman Catholics. Their numbers were by this time increased to eight or ten thousand. We do not hear that they committed any further mischief' (*Public Advertiser* 13 June 1780). A similar account from a correspondent appears ibid. 14 June 1780.

4. His house in Grosvenor Square, threatened by the rioters, was kept closely guarded (see de Castro, op. cit. 74, 80, 87, 110, 114, 163).

5. He 'and Edmund Burke were particularly threatened by the mob' on the night of 2 June (*Last Journals* ii. 306).

6. He had introduced the bill for the relief of the Roman Catholics, and consequently was obnoxious to the rioters. His house, Savile House in Leicester Fields, was plundered on the night of 4–5 June, but the wreckers were checked before it could be burned (see de Castro, op. cit. 63–4).

7. Edmund Burke (1729–97), while helping to defend Sir George Savile's house, heard that his own house in Charles Street,

toleration, were devoted to destruction as much as the ministers. The rails torn from Sir George's house were the chief weapons and instruments of the mob. For the honour of the nation I should be glad to have it proved that the French were the engineers. You and I have lived too long for our comfort—shall we close our eyes in peace? I will not trouble you more about the arms I sent you; I should like that they were those of the family of Boleyn; and since I cannot be sure they were not, why should not I fancy them so?[8] I revert to the prayer for peace. You and I that can amuse ourselves with our books and papers, feel as much indignation at the turbulent, as they have scorn for us. It is hard at least that they who disturb nobody, can have no asylum in which to pursue their innoxious indolence! Who is secure against Jack Straw and a whirlwind? How I abominate Mr Banks and Dr Solander[9] who routed the poor Otaheitians out of the center of the ocean, and carried our abominable passions amongst them! Not even that poor little speck could escape European restlessness—well! I have seen many tempestuous scenes and outlived them! The present prospect is too thick to see through—it is well Hope never forsakes us! Adieu!

Yours most sincerely,

H. W.

From Cole, Sunday 2 July 1780

Cole's copy, Add MS 5826, ff. 195v, 196v. The original is missing.

Address: To the Honourable Horace Walpole, Strawberry Hill, Twickenham, Middlesex.

Milton, Commencement Sunday, July 2, 1780.

Dear Sir,

I CONGRATULATE your and all honest men's escape from the horrors of the Black Wednesday, which will be a black spot in our

St James's Square, would be destroyed next. He immediately returned to his house, which was soon guarded by a detachment of soldiers. Later his life was openly threatened (ibid. 64–5, 81).

8. HW says in the *Description of SH* that the arms are those of 'Tate, impaling Boleyn or Sanders, for the colour of the chevron is turned black' (*Works* ii. 507).

9. Daniel Charles Solander (1736–82),

Swedish botanist; came to England 1760, and in 1768 was engaged by Banks to accompany him on Cook's voyage in the *Endeavour.* On their return in 1771, he became secretary and librarian to Banks, and in 1773 was made Keeper of the Natural History Department of the British Museum. In connection with this passage, see Edward Smith, *The Life of Sir Joseph Banks,* London and New York, 1911, pp.

annals as long as time will last. How and whence it originated, in my opinion, is no very difficult matter to find out. Pray God we may have seen the worst of it! It is matter of astonishment to me in this enlightened age to observe the intolerant spirit of the Dissenters. I am sure we want no proof that if the Catholics are bigots, the fanatics of this island are on a par with them, as also, which are the peaceable and which the factious, seditious subjects.

Dr Lort, who comes down among us for the last time for the completion of his degree,[1] called here, with Dr Shepherd,[2] Canon of Windsor, yesterday for a few minutes in their way from Ely, where they had been to dine with the Dean.[3] Whether I shall see him any more I cannot say. I promised to let him see a little MS which I had copied for poor Tyson some years ago, and it being in my hand, Mr Gough, who looked over the papers for the widow, thinking it was mine, sent it to me with some other things which I had lent to him, but observing that I had mentioned him in the MS and had tricked out his arms in it, he was desirous to have it, and desired Mr Essex to sound me about it. As he had just before sent me his two new volumes,[4] I was glad of the opportunity of obliging him: and the MS not being half filled, I have completed the volume by writing the lives, in short, of all such antiquaries as have been educated in Benet College.[5] In the course of this work I have had occasion to refer to your MS 'Life of Mr Baker,'[6] but have not mentioned your name, no

173–5, where HW is called 'a representative scoffer.'

1. Of D.D., which he received in this year. Doctors designate were 'created' full doctors 'at the Commencement following their admission' (Denys A. Winstanley, *Unreformed Cambridge*, 1935, p. 78).

2. Antony Shepherd (1721–96), Plumian Professor of Astronomy at Cambridge University, 1760–96; Canon of Windsor, 1777–96; friend of Captain Cook (see DNB). For Cole's account of him and his preferments, see Brydges, *Restituta* iv. 253–4.

3. Hugh Thomas, Dean of Ely. He died 11 July 1780 (Bentham, *Ely*[2] Addenda, p. 14).

4. *British Topography*.

5. This MS, now Add MS 5886, has the following notes in Cole's hand on the first page: 'This book I desire may be given to Mr Gough within a year after my decease.

Wm Cole, 1780.' 'But in case the Hon. Mr Horace Walpole of Strawberry Hill survives me, I desire it may be delivered to him, who will order it to be delivered to Mr Gough after his decease. Wm Cole, Feb. 25, 1782.' 'But on Mr Gough's dining with me at Milton, Sunday, Sept. 8, 1782, and looking over the book with indifference, it may not be worth his acceptance, and therefore let it go with the rest of my MSS. Wm Cole. Sept. 9, 1782.' The MS contains the lives of Thomas Markaunt, Matthew Parker, William Stukeley, Robert Masters, Philip Yorke 2d E. of Hardwicke, Richard Gough, William Colman, James Nasmith, Michael Tyson, Edward Haistwell, John Denne, Frederick Hervey E. of Bristol and Bp of Derry, Brock Rand and George North, several of which were printed in LA.

6. For Cole's reference, see *post* 8 July 1780.

more than in another part of the work which refers to you.[7] The thing has been finished above a month, but as I made you a promise never to show the 'Life' to anyone, I have had a scruple whether I should send it without your seeing it, and how to send it to you I know not, seeing I have, as usual, been as free in speaking out my political principles as if they were certain and truth uncontroverted. If therefore you give me leave, unsight unseen (as we say at school), to send it away, I will do so. If you choose rather to see the MS, I will desire Dr Lort to send it to you after his perusal of it, and from you it must be sent to Mr Gough at Enfield, or rather to Mr Nichols his printer for him, but with these conditions: that if you approve not of the two places where I refer to you, you have full liberty to scratch out with your pen whatever I have written, which is no great deal; also, that, as our political and religious creed somewhat varies, I shall be obliged to you not to convince me of my obstinacy, as I am too old to alter my faith either way. I dare say Mr Gough, as a Dissenter, will be more displeased with me for my observations than your liberal way of thinking will allow you to be.

I have had occasion to correspond this week and the former with our President, Dr Milles, from whom I received a very obliging letter on Wednesday from Sunning Hill. His son[8] is just married to a great heiress, the daughter of Mr Gardener of Pishiobury in Hertfordshire, formerly the seat of Sir Walter Mildmay,[9] the founder of Emmanuel College. This lady was to have been married to the eldest son of Sir John Cotton,[10] who, through an inherent hauteur and pride, has let her slip out of his hands. My friend the Master of Emmanuel had been acquainted with the young lady's father, who had promised to give him the painted glass and arms of the Mildmays,

7. Cole, in his life of the E. of Hardwicke, has the following passage in connection with the second edition of *Letters from and to Sir Dudley Carleton:* 'I received a letter from a friend, who, soon after reading over the second edition, has this reflection: "What signifies raising the dead so often, when they die the next minute?" I have more on this subject which may as well be kept where it is' (Add MS 5886, f. 21). The 'friend' was HW, and the 'reflection' occurs in *ante* 10 Dec. 1775.

8. Jeremiah Milles (1751–97), eld. son of Dean Milles; of Queen's College, Oxford (B.A. 1772) and of Merton (Fellow 1775);

barrister-at-law, Lincoln's Inn, 1776; m. (7 June 1780) Rose Gardiner (1757–1835), dau. and sole heiress of Edward Gardiner (d. 1779), of Pishiobury (see *Alumni Oxon; GM* Feb. 1779, xlix. 103b and June 1780, l. 298a; John Edwin Cussans, *History of Hertfordshire . . . Braughing Hundred,* Hertford, 1870, pp. 81, 95; *Public Advertiser* 9 June 1780).

9. (1520?–89), Chancellor of the Exchequer.

10. John Cotton, who was accidentally killed while hunting, 30 July 1781 (see *post* 5 Aug. 1781; GM Aug. 1781, li. 395a).

had actually had them taken out of the windows and packed up ready to be sent, when he was snatched away, and before he had given proper orders about them, and on the match being concluded last year between the young lady and Major Cotton, the Master thought all was safe, as he had been his pupil. On mentioning this untoward circumstance to me as we were going, about a fortnight ago, to dinner at Sir John Cotton's, I told him how I could still secure the glass to the College. The Dean was under obligations to me, in pressing me, some four or five years ago, when his son stood for the Vinerian Professorship,[11] to influence my curate (Mr Sugden),[12] a Fellow of one of the Colleges, to go thither and vote for him: this he did twice, having failed in his first application. I thought I was entitled to ask for the glass, as I was likely to have no other return. The Dean very politely has promised to send it to the College by the first opportunity.

I hope you continue well this strange variable weather. Thank God, I never have been able to walk so freely, and so free from my other usual complaints, as at this time. May it continue! I use my pen, I am afraid, too freely, being constantly employed one way or other. If I do no good, I do no harm except to myself, for no one sees what I write. Now that I am in a manner freer than usual from bodily complaints, my mental faculties are disturbed with wayward circumstances at Burnham. My total non-residence gives me eternal uneasiness, yet I know not how to avoid it. I applied to our diocesan here two or three years ago to make me an exchange or remove me nearer, but his way is to give nothing but for an equivalent: unluckily I have nothing of the sort. I must finish, though I had more to say besides, than that I am

Yours everlastingly,

WM COLE

11. In 1777, when, on the resignation of Robert (afterward Sir Robert) Chambers (1737–1803), Richard Wooddeson (1745–1822), Fellow of Magdalen, was elected (24 April) Vinerian Professor of Common Law at Oxford.

12. William Sugden (1748?–1820), son of William Sugden, surgeon, of Manchester, Lancs; of Brasenose College, Oxford (B.A. 1768, Fellow 1771); rector of Cottingham, Northants, 1800–15 (see *Alumni Oxon;* GM Jan. 1820, xc. 91b). Some of his letters to Cole are preserved in Add MSS 5833, 5846 and 5992 (see *Index to the Additional Manuscripts . . . in the British Museum . . . acquired . . . 1783–1835,* 1849). He was Cole's curate at Burnham.

The hen sat her full month last Monday, and all her eggs were addled. This is the second attempt of the sort. Luckily my own hen begins to lay, and I have five eggs, but I am afraid it is rather too late to rear the chicks.

To COLE, Tuesday 4 July 1780

Add MS 5953, ff. 95–6.

Cole has the following note on the cover: 'Gent[leman's] Mag[azine] for June 1780, p. 287. Dr Gl[ynn] very angr[y]. V. also p. 290.' The first reference is to a review of Croft's *Love and Madness,* in which HW is severely dealt with (see *post* 13 April 1782); the second to a review of *Biographical Memoirs of Extraordinary Painters,* in which HW is barely mentioned. Cole did not use the notes in his letters to HW.

Address: To the Reverend Mr Cole at Milton near Cambridge.
Postmark: 5 IY.

Strawberry Hill, July 4, 1780.

Dear Sir,

I ANSWER your letter the moment I receive it, to beg you will by no means take any notice, not even indirectly and without my name, of my 'Life of Mr Baker.' I am earnest against its being known to exist. I should be teased to show it. Mr Gough might inquire about it. I do not desire his acquaintance; and above all things I am determined, if I can help it, to have no controversy while I live. You know I have hitherto suppressed my answers to the critics of *Richard III* for that reason—and above all things I hate theologic or political controversy—nor need you fear my disputing with you, though we disagree very considerably indeed about Papists and Presbyterians. I hope you have not yet sent the MS to Mr Lort, and if you have not, do intreat you to efface undecipherably what you have said about my 'Life of Mr Baker.'

I am heartily glad you enjoy health, and am equally sorry you are teased about Burnham. I have, thank God, been better lately than for a year past—but I have some thoughts of going to Malvern for a month or six weeks the end of this month.[1]

I am sorry the eggs failed. If the journey was too long, it is vain to offer you more, though I can procure them next season.

1. He did not go (see *post* 3 Oct. 1780).

Pray satisfy me that no mention of Mr Baker's 'Life' shall appear in print. I can by no means consent to it, and I am sure you will prevent it.

Yours sincerely,

H. W.

From Cole, Saturday 8 July 1780

VA, Forster MS 110, f. 240. Cole kept no copy.

Address: To the Honourable Horace Walpole, Strawberry Hill in Twicken-ham, Middlesex. *Postmark:* Cambridge 10 IY.

Milton, Saturday, July 8, 1780.

<Dea>r Sir,

I RECEIVED your letter last night, and as I am going to Cambridge will leave this for tomorrow's post.

I am very glad I had not sent the MS[1] away, though it has been finished above a month, but having been fully employed by other things, I had no time to put an index to it and send it away; and though I have seen Dr Lort two or three times since he came down, the MS has not once been mentioned to him, though I had wrote to him at Lambeth that I would send it to him. I am very glad I did not, and that he nor no other person whatever has seen, except Mr Essex, to whom I lent it, but with a particular charge to show it to no one, which I suppose he complied with, though when he returned it, he said nothing about it, as I asked him no questions. Indeed, if he did, as your name was not mentioned in any part of it, I much question whether he would know to whom the passage alluded. However, I shall see him today and ask him. I have been so punctual an observer of your prohibition about Mr Baker's 'Life,' that I never have shown it to any mortal, nor indeed, since you completed it, ever mentioned it to anyone. Indeed, while you were so obliging to undertake it, I mentioned it to Mr Beadon and to Dr Penington, both of St John's, who procured me the MS History of that college, and to whom I applied for materials, and to two or three confidential friends, who I daresay never mentioned it again, nor has it ever been

---

1. Cole's 'Some Short Account of the Benedictine Antiquaries of Cambridge,' which he intended for Gough (see *ante* 2 July 1780).

talked of, that I know of. This I mention because of your expression of being earnest 'to have it not known to exist.' Mr Gough does not know there is such a 'Life': possibly he might have guessed had the MS gone to him in its present state, but I will so erase the passage[2] that no traces shall be left, as you 'can by no means consent that any part of Mr Baker's "Life" shall appear in print.' I can be no judge what use Mr Gough may put my little MS to: I dare say never print it. It is only a trifle that I should be as averse to have printed as it would be improper to think of it. I will give you the occasion how I came to mention the 'Life,' and then transcribe the faulty passage, which will be erased.

At p. 13, preface of the new edition of the *Topography*, Mr Gough says, 'Only one college in each University has found an historiographer,' alluding to Dr Savage's *Baliofergus*[3] and Mr Masters's *Benet College*. And at p. 220 of the book Mr Gough further says (no doubt from his friend Masters's information) that Dr Grey's materials for a life of Mr Baker falling into the hands of Mr Masters, that gentleman not thinking them worth publishing by themselves, applied to the late Master of St John's, Dr Powell,[4] for leave to print Mr Baker's history of that society, to which he would have prefixed them, 'but this was declined, as the history, though containing several curious matters, is written under the influence of partiality and resentment.' This is so manifest an injury to the memory of Mr Baker, and so contrary to what you have said about him, that I could not resist the temptation of inserting these six or seven lines of your 'Life' of him, in justification of an abused character, and doing an act of justice which I thought you would not be averse to, in the concealed way I had done it: 'Of his own college he undertook and executed a very valuable history, valuable still less for its accuracy and fidelity than for its author's singular impartiality,' etc., to 'which have no value

---

2. Cole did not do this, as he did not send the MS to Gough (see *ante* 2 July 1780 n. 5).

3. *Balliofergus, or a Commentary upon the Foundation, Founders and Affaires of Balliol Colledge*, Oxford, 1668, by Henry Savage (1604?–72), Master of Balliol College, 1651–72.

4. William Samuel Powell (1717–75), Master of St John's College, Cambridge, 1765–75. Cole calls him 'a most bigoted and violent creature of a Master' (Add MS 5886, f. 18), but in a note added sometime later he says: 'From what I can collect since the republication of Mr Gough's *Topography* in 1780, I beg leave to recant my harsh expressions relating to Dr Powell, who, I am apt to believe, made use of the expressions relating to Mr Baker (whom yet I believe he did not love) rather as a shift and pretence in order to get rid of an importunate solicitation to publish Mr Baker's *History*, by the rector of Landbeche [Masters]' (Add MS 5886, f. 17v).

but that of existence.'[5] I meant to have transcribed the whole that I
had written introductory to it,[6] but I am not well—a little touch of
a sore throat, feverish and vexed that I am to go out to dinner. I
should never make appointments, as it is rarely I am in a condition
to keep them.

I shall hardly send the book to Enfield[7] this month, as two mon-
strous pedigrees, two or three hundred arms in them, all which I
copy as I go on, and other things which require expedition, will
prevent looking at anything else till they are done. If you go to
Malvern, I will give you a letter about an inscription in that church.[8]
I hope the waters will do you good.

I am, dear Sir,

Yours most sincerely,

WM COLE

5. For the entire quotation, see *Works*
ii. 357.

6. Cole introduced the above quotation
in his life of Masters with the following:
'To this just character of Mr Baker, by
Mr Gough, give me leave to subscribe my
feeble attestation, in consequence of having transcribed, and carefully observed (by
the permission of the present worthy Master of St John's College), Mr Baker's
history of that society; which exhibits
throughout a true picture of his own
worthy heart, and where the influences of
partiality and resentment are so totally
banished, that even the Puritans of Queen
Elizabeth's time, and the sectaries of the
next century (averring principles widely
different from those of his own) have so
far from his ill word that they are often the
subjects of his commendation. I assert this
upon my own authority and knowledge: if
better is required, I might produce uncon-
tested, was I at liberty to do so, having the
"Life of Mr Baker" (from materials which
I sent, together with his MS History of the
College) now in my possession, and ready
for the press (but I believe in no hurry to
see the light), drawn up by a gentleman
whose political principles were, *toto caelo,*
different from those of the person whose
life he was so kind to undertake the writing
of, and in many parts of which (according
to my ideas of things) he bears too hard
upon them, agreeable to the latitude of the

present fashionable way of thinking. Yet
this gentleman, eminent in the republic of
letters, after reading Mr Baker's MS History, which I had lent him, from a thorough sense and conviction of the historian's worth, integrity, candour and impartiality, draws towards a conclusion of the
"Life" in these words, which, I hope, without breach of promise, I may here transcribe, in justification of an abused character, and doing an act of justice, which, I
am satisfied, he would not refuse, though
under a promise of not letting this "Life of
Mr Baker," by him, be seen: which possibly he may sometime publish himself.'
The quotation follows, after which Cole remarks: 'Does not this specimen create an
appetite for the whole performance? Yet
to be as impartial in my turn, I must needs
own that I have no eager desire to see it
published. Might I pick and cull such
favorite bits as almost always occur, and
such as I have now produced, it would be
the choicest morsel that I could sit down
to, but there are so many crude parts in
this delicate treat, too hard for my digestion (who am not apt to think as is the
modish way of the times) that, however
relishing and delicious the feast might be
to others, the olio is too high seasoned for
my palate' (Add MS 5886, ff. 18v–19).

7. That is, to Gough at Enfield.

8. Cf. *post* 30 Sept. 1780.

To Cole, Wednesday 27 September 1780

Add MS 5953, ff. 97–8.

Address: To the Reverend Mr Cole at Milton near Cambridge.
Postmark: Isleworth 27 SE.

Strawberry Hill, Sept. 27, 1780.

Dear Sir,

I MUST inquire how you do after all your electioneering agitations,[1] which have growled even round your hermitage. Candidates and their emissaries are like Pope's authors.

They pierce our thickets, through our grots they glide.[2]

However, I have barred my doors; and when I would not go to an election for myself, I would not for anyone else.

Has not a third real summer and so very dry one, assisted your complaints? I have been remarkably well, and better than for these five years. Would I could say the same of all my friends—but alas! I expect every day to hear that I have quite lost my dear old friend Madame du Deffand.[3] She was indeed near eighty-four,[4] but retained all her interior faculties—two days ago the letters from Paris forbade all hopes![5]—so I reckon myself dead as to France, where I have kept up no other connection.

I am going at last to publish my fourth volume of *Painters*,[6] which, though printed so long, I have literally treated by Horace's rule, *Nonumque prematur in annum.*[7] Tell me how I shall send it to you.

Yours as ever,

H. Walpole

1. The general elections occurred in September (see Cooper, *Annals* iv. 399–400). Cole had deplored the extravagant electioneering which began in the previous spring (see *ante* 24 May 1780).

2. Pope, 'Epistle to Dr Arbuthnot,' l. 8.

3. She died at five o'clock, Saturday morning, 23 Sept., but HW did not receive the news until 7 Oct. (see Wiart to HW 27 Sept.; HW to Thomas Walpole 8 Oct. 1780).

4. HW was mistaken: she died two days before her eighty-third birthday.

5. See, for example, Wiart to HW 13, 17 and 20 Sept. 1780. HW probably received letters from Thomas Walpole, and perhaps from others, with the information.

6. It was published 9 Oct. The printing was completed 13 April 1771 (see *Jour. Print. Off.* 16, 19).

7. *De Arte Poetica* l. 388.

From COLE, Saturday 30 September 1780

VA, Forster MS 110, ff. 241–2. COLE's copy, Add MS 5826, ff. 197v, 198v.
Address: Honourable Horace Walpole, Strawberry Hill, Twickenham, Middlesex. *Postmark:* Cambridge 2 OC.

Milton, September 30, 1780.

Dear Sir,

IT was the 4th of July that I received your last letter, except that of yesterday. I thought it a tedious long interval. You mentioned then a design of going to Malvern, where I had thoughts of following you by letter to inquire about the exactness of Tom Hearne or myself, but I did not well know how to direct to you. When I was at Malvern in 1746, I drew a rough sketch of an old coffin-stone for Walcherus Lotharingus,[1] Prior of Malvern in 1135, with his epitaph in six Latin verses engraved on it, very ancient and curious, yet Mr Hearne, in his preface to the *History of Glastonbury*, p. xlvi, says that it is on a brass plate. I don't believe the use of brass plates for monumental inscriptions was introduced so early as the time of Henry I. Perhaps you might observe the old monument if you went into the church, which is a very handsome Gothic structure. But possibly you might not go at all thither, for in my return from a great feast at Cambridge yesterday, where were the Duke of Rutland <and> the victorious electioneers, I met on the road the Master <of> Pembroke, who told me that he saw you at Ramsgate.[2] Wherever you was, I rejoice at the account you give of yourself. The heat of the summer was very unpleasant to me. It occasioned a constant perspiration, which I was never before subject to, yet I believe it did me service, though I have had three slight fits of the g<out> within these two months, but of so slight a nature as not worth mentioning. The last reduced me, a month ago, to my crutch, but was gone without any the least pain in four or five days. Milk[3] and water is and has been for years my only drink,[4] and I flatter myself that so

1. Walcher (d. 1135) of Lorraine, second Prior of Great Malvern Priory. His monument was dug up in 1711, on the site of the cloisters, and now 'lies in the recess of St Ann's Chapel in the Priory Church.' The inscription is not on a brass plate (see James Nott, *Some of the Antiquities of "Moche Malvern,"* Malvern, 1885, pp. 25–

8, where the text of the Latin inscription is given).
2. HW was not there (see following letter).
3. 'Skimmed milk' in Cole's copy.
4. 'at meals, with no supper at all for these thirty years' (addition in Cole's copy).

cooling a beverage and temperate life as I have always led is now of great benefit to me.

No book in the world have I ever longed for so much as your continuance of the *Painters*. Do, be so kind to gratify this rage as soon as you can conveniently, by sending it to the Cambridge fly in Gray's Inn Lane, at the Queen's Head, and to be left for me at the Rose Tavern in Cambridge. Horace's rule[5] may be a very useful one to other folks: I am clear you have no occasion for it, and however prudential motives may have determined you not to publish matters so near our own times, I can conceive no others why the world (which deserves not your labours) should not have been gratified with them nine years before. I say this not from my own judgment, but from all I ever conversed with.

I lament your loss. Such a connection is as irreparable as it is unavoidable.[5a]

I met yesterday at St John's Lodge a gentleman[6] whose carriage was waiting for him at the College Gate, who was going to town to meet the Duchess of Ancaster,[7] Lady Willoughby,[8] Lady Charlotte Bertie[9] and Mr Burrell,[10] to attend them to Paris, and in about a fortnight after to Nice en Provence for the winter, for their healths.

Your last letter of July 4 seemed so anxious about my having hinted only, and that very obliquely and without naming your name, in my little tract intended for Mr Gough, that I determined never to show it, nor even to send it to him, and from that time to this

5. See preceding letter.

5a. That is, 'such a connection is as irreparable as its loss is unavoidable' (see preceding letter).

6. 'Mr Bowyer' (addition in Cole's copy). Possibly the son of Mrs Chevallier (wife of the Master of St John's) whose first husband was a Mr Bowyer of Willoughby, Lincs (GM March 1778, xlviii. 141a).

7. Mary Panton (d. 1793), dau. of Thomas Panton (1697–1782), Master of the King's Running Horses; m. as his 2d wife, Peregrine Bertie (1714–78), 3d D. of Ancaster. 'Lady Willoughby' and 'Lady Charlotte Bertie' were her daughters, and 'Mr Burrell' was her son-in-law.

8. Priscilla Barbara Elizabeth Bertie (1761–1828), eld. dau. of 3d D. of Ancaster by his 2d wife; on the death of her brother

Robert Bertie (1756–79), 4th D. of Ancaster, 8 July 1779, she became, with her sister, Lady Charlotte, his co-heiress, and in March 1780 was declared by patent, *suo jure* Baroness Willoughby of Eresby. She m. 23 Feb. 1779, Peter Burrell (1754–1820), of Langley in Beckenham, Kent, son of Peter Burrell, Commissioner of Excise; Eton and St. John's, Cambridge; M.P. for Haslemere, 1776–80; for Boston, 1782–96; knighted 1781; suc. as 2d Bt of West Grinstead Park, Sussex, in 1787; cr. (1796) Bn Gwydir of Gwydir, co. Carnarvon.

9. Georgiana Charlotte Bertie (1764–1838), 2d dau. of 3d D. of Ancaster by his 2d wife; m. (1791) George James Cholmondeley (1749–1827), 4th E. and afterwards (1815) 1st M. of Cholmondeley.

10. See n. 8 above.

have neither wrote to or heard from him.[11] I must invent some excuse why I do not fulfil my promise, but I had rather lose a new than an old friend, though should be glad to retain both. I beg you will say no more about it, but here it is, and here it shall be.

I have had sad luck with my guinea-fowls. After procuring a cock and hen, they produced six eggs, and the hen fell ill. A hen hatched four: one is since dead. After a time the hen got well again and laid a dozen eggs, when a strange dog killed her on her nest. I thought I was secure with these eggs, and put them under a hen, but this week, after sitting a month, they all turned out addle, so my hopes are in the young family of three, that one will prove a hen. I have had three disappointments of this sort. The first was a present of twelve eggs, but it seems there was no father to them: the next, those you was so kind to send me. They were injured, as I imagine, by the journeyings. These last, I guess, from the ill health of the mother, or perhaps the cock might not tread her. But enough and too much on such a subject, which I hope you'll excuse from, dear Sir,

Yours most cordially and sincerely,

WM COLE

To COLE, Tuesday 3 October 1780

Add MS 5953, ff. 99–100.
Address: To the Reverend Mr Cole at Milton near Cambridge.
Postmark: GC 3 OC.

Berkeley Square, Oct. 3, 1780.

I DID not go to Malvern, and therefore cannot certify you, my good Sir, whether Tom Hearne mistook stone for brass or not, though I dare to say that your criticism is just.

My book,[1] if I can possibly, shall go to the inn tomorrow, or next

---

11. Cole's next letter to Gough is dated 17 Dec. 1780; in it he says: 'The book I promised you was finished near six months ago; nay, I sent it to Mr Essex, who had it a week, and who had a design of sending it to you in a day or two, had not I called before it went off. Some reasons, which may be explained to your satisfaction here-after, prevent my sending it at present: but, such as it is, you shall not be long without it, *for it is your book, and so I have marked it*' (LA i. 687). Cf. *ante* 2 July 1780 n. 5.

---

1. *Anecdotes,* vol. 4.

day at least. You will find a great deal of rubbish in it, with all your partiality—but I shall have done with it.

I cannot thank you enough for your goodness about your notes that you promised Mr Grose[2]—but I cannot possibly be less generous and less disinterested; nor can by any means be the cause of your breaking your word—in short, I insist on your sending your notes to him—and as to my 'Life of Mr Baker,' if it is known to exist, nobody can make me produce it sooner than I please, nor at all if I do not please; so pray send your account, and leave me to be stout with our antiquaries, or curious. I shall not satisfy the latter, and don't care a straw for the former.

The Master of Pembroke (who he is, I don't know) is like the lover who said

Have I not seen thee, where thou hast not been?[3]

I have been in Kent with Mr Barrett,[4] but was not at Ramsgate: the Master, going thither, perhaps saw me. It is a mistake not worth rectifying. I have [no] time for more, being in the midst of the delivery of my books.

Yours ever,

H. W.

To Cole, Saturday 11 November 1780

Add MS 5953, ff. 101–2.
Address: To the Reverend Mr Cole at Milton near Cambridge.
Postmark: 11 NO.

Berkeley Square, Nov. 11, 1780.

I AM afraid you are not well, my good Sir, for you are so obligingly punctual, that I think you would have acknowledged the receipt of my last volume, if you were not out of order.

Lord Dacre lent me the new edition of Mr Gough's *Topography*,[1]

2. HW's mistake for *Gough;* Cole made the correction '[Mr Gough]' in his copy, Add MS 5826, f. 198v.

3. Not located.

4. At Lee, near Canterbury, the seat of Thomas Barrett (1744–1803), HW's friend and correspondent (see GM Jan. 1803, lxxiii. 90–1). For HW's account of his visit to Lee and other seats on this tour, see *Country Seats* 76–7; HW to Lady Ossory 23 Aug. 1780; to Mason 24 and 31 Aug. 1780. He went to Lee on Monday, 28 Aug. and returned 30 Aug.

1. MS reads *Typography*.

and the ancient maps and quantity of additions tempted me to buy it. I have not gone through much above half of the first volume, and find it more entertaining than the first edition. This is no partiality, for I think he seems rather disposed, though civilly, to find cavils with me. Indeed in the passage in which I am most mentioned, he not only gives a very confused but quite a wrong account; as in other places he records some trifles in my possession not worth recording— but I know that we antiquaries are too apt to think that whatever has had the honour of entering our ears is worthy of being laid before the eyes of everybody else. The story I mean is p. xl of the preface.[2] Now the three volumes of drawings and tombs by Mr Lethueillier and Sir Charles Fredericke,[3] for which Mr G. says I refused [to give] £200[4] and are now Lord Bute's—are not Lord Bute's, but mine, and for which I never was asked £200, and for which I gave £60—full enough. The circumstances were much more entertaining than Mr G.'s perplexed account. Bishop Lyttelton told me Sir Charles Fredericke complained of Mr L.'s not bequeathing them to him,[5] as he had been a joint labourer with him; and that Sir Charles wished I would not bid against him for them, as they were to be sold by auction. I said, this was a very reasonable request, and that I was ready to oblige Sir Charles; but that, as I heard others meant to

2. Gough's account is as follows: 'The late Smart Lethieullier, Esq.; of Aldersbrook, Essex, besides three folio volumes of original drawings of churches, monuments, painted windows, Roman pavements, etc., in England, most of them by an eminent private pencil, now in the hands of the Earl of Bute, collected in three more volumes all engraved maps, plans, views, and monuments, that fell under his notice, and are now in the same cabinet.' In a note on the passage, he says of the drawings: 'These were the work of many years' tours about England, on which Sir Charles Frederick had spent near 500l. which, on the death of Mr L. (who had always promised to leave them to Sir Charles, but did not) were offered to him for 200l., who refusing them, Mr Walpole got intelligence of them, but on finding them so valued, and offered, refused them. Meantime, Mr Wortley [Worseley], Surveyor of the Board of Ordnance, was ordered by the King to give that money and

present them to Sir Charles, on which Mr L.'s widow paid the money to the bookseller who had bought them, and took them away, and afterwards sold them as above.'

3. Sir Charles Frederick (1709–85), K.B. (1761); 3d son of Sir Thomas Frederick, Governor of Fort St George, East Indies; F.R.S. and F.A.S., 1731; M.P. He 'was eminently distinguished for his taste in the polite arts, and for his great skill in drawing' (GM Dec. 1785, lv. 1010b). He contributed two articles to *Archaeologia*.

4. Gough did not say this (see n. 2 above).

5. Lethieullier, however, bequeathed to Frederick a portrait of Raphael Urbino, said to have been painted by Leonardo da Vinci, and his choice of Lethieullier's collection of gold, silver, Greek and Roman coins (see C. H. Iyan Chown, 'The Lethieullier Family of Aldersbrook House, Part II,' *Essex Review*, Colchester, 1927, xxxvi. 15).

bid high for the books, I should wish to know how far he would go, and that I would not oppose him—but should the books exceed the price Sir Charles was willing to give, I should like to be at liberty to bid for them against others—However, added I, as Sir Charles (who lived in Berkeley Square as I did then in Arlington Street) passes by my door every time he goes to the House of Commons, if he will call on me, we will make such agreement—you will scarce believe the sequel. The dignity of Sir Charles Fredericke was hurt that I should propose his making me the first visit, though to serve himself—Nothing could be less out of my imagination than the ceremonial of visits; though when he was so simple as to make a point of it, I could not see how in any light I was called on to make him the first visit—and so the treaty ended; and so I bought the books.

There was another work, I think in two volumes, which was their diary of their tour, with a few slight views. Bishop Lyttelton proposed them to me, and engaged to get them for me from Mr Lethieullier's sister[6] for ten guineas. She hesitated, the Bishop died. I thought no more of them, and they may be what Lord Bute has.

There is another assertion in Mr Gough which I can authentically contradict. He says, Sir Matthew Decker[7] first introduced ananas. p. 134. My very curious picture of Rose,[8] the royal gardener, presenting the first ananas to Charles II proves the culture here earlier by several years.

P. 373, he seems to doubt my assertion of Gravelot's making drawings of tombs in Gloucestershire, because he never met with any engravings from them.[9] I took my account from Vertue, who certainly knew what he said.[10] I bought at Vertue's own sale some of Grave-

6. That is, Lethieullier's sister-in-law: Mary Gore, dau. of William Gore of Tring, Herts, who m. Charles Lethieullier (1712–59), barrister and younger brother of Smart Lethieullier. The latter, dying without issue, left most of his estate to his sister-in-law, in trust for her daughter Mary (1747–1813), the wife (m. 1769) of Edward Hulse (1744–1816), afterwards (1800) 3d Bt, of Breamore, Hants. Mrs Lethieullier ordered the sale of her brother-in-law's library (see C. H. Iyan Chown, op. cit. 15–17).

7. (1679–1749), 1st Bt; writer on trade. He was generally, though erroneously, credited with the introduction of 'ananas' or pineapples into England (see DNB;

Thomas Wotton, *The English Baronetage*, 4 vols, 1741, *sub* Decker).

8. See *ante* 6 March 1780 and n. 6.

9. Gough says: 'Mr Walpole ['Catalogue of Engravers,' p. 124] says that Henry Gravelot, a faithful copier of ancient buildings, tombs, and prospects, was for some time employed in drawing churches and antiquities in this county. If he engraved any, it has not been my good fortune to meet with them.' Gough in no way questions HW's statements concerning Gravelot's *drawings;* HW's prejudice against Gough led him to interpret the passage incorrectly.

10. Vertue wrote in one of his note-

lot's drawings of our regal monuments, which Vertue engraved—but, which is stronger, Mr Gough himself a few pages after, viz. in p. 387*, mentions Gravelot's drawings of Tewksbury Church[11]—which being in Gloucestershire Mr G. might have believed me that Gravelot did draw in that county. This is a little like Mr Masters's being angry with me for taking liberties with bishops and chancellors, and then abusing grossly one who had been both bishop and chancellor.[12]

I forgot, that in the note on Sir Charles Fredericke Mr Gough calls Mr Worseley, Wortley.[13]

In p. 354, he says Rooker exhibited a drawing of Waltham Cross to the Royal Academy of Sciences[14]—pray, where is that Academy? I suppose he means that of painting.

I find a few omissions; one very comical; he says Penshurst was celebrated by Ben Jonson[15]—and seems totally in the dark as to how much more fame it owes to Waller.[16] We antiquaries are a little apt to get laughed at for knowing what everybody has forgotten, and for being ignorant of what every child knows. Do not tell him of

books for 1733: 'He [Gravelot] has been lately in Glocestershire [sic], where he was employed to draw ancient monuments in churches and other antiquities' (Vertue Note Books iii. 67, Walpole Society, vol. 22, Oxford, 1934).

11. 'Mr. Lethieullier showed the Antiquary Society 1733, a plan of Tewksbury church and the six chapels . . . taken by Mr. Gravelot 1733.'

12. Masters accuses HW of having 'stigmatised Sir Thomas [More], and taxed his patron Archbishop Morton with violating his allegiance' ('Some Remarks on Mr Walpole's Historic Doubts,' Archaeologia ii. 202), and a few pages below Masters refers to Robert Stillington (d. 1491), Bishop of Bath and Wells and Lord Chancellor, as 'a time-serving prelate, and kept revenge in his mind twenty years, acted the part of a pimp to King Edward . . . and at length died, as he deserved, in prison' (ibid. 206).

13. For the passage in question, see note 2 above. Thomas Worseley (d. 1778), of Hovingham Hall, near Malton, in Yorks; Surveyor-General of the Board of Works (not 'Surveyor of the Board of Ordnance,' as Gough calls him: Sir Charles Frederick was Surveyor-General of the Board of Ordnance); M.P. for Orford, Suffolk, 1761–

8; for Callington, Cornwall, 1768–74 (both Walpole boroughs). He was a friend of Bute (see Musgrave, Obituary; Burke, Commoners iv. 608; HW, Mem. of the Reign of George III i. 29, 331).

14. Michael Rooker (1743–1801), called 'Michael Angelo' Rooker, A.R.A., exhibited 'Waltham Cross; stained drawing,' at the Royal Academy of Arts in 1775 (see Algernon Graves, The Royal Academy of Arts: A Complete Dictionary of Contributors . . . 1769–1904, 8 vols, 1905–6).

15. 'Penshurst, or rather the hospitality of its Lord, has been celebrated in epigrams by Ben Jonson' (British Topography[2] i. 485). Penshurst Place, in Kent, is famous for its connection with the Sidney family, into whose possession it came by grant of Edward VI. Sir Philip and Algernon Sidney were born there. Cf. Works ii. 263 n. Jonson's 'To Penshurst' (more properly a poem than an epigram) was published in The Forest, 1616.

16. Notably in his two poems, 'To My Lord of Leicester' and 'At Penshurst,' with its lines (5–6):

'Embroider'd so with flow'rs where she stood,
That it became a garden of a wood.'

these things, for I do not wish to vex him. I hope I was mistaken, and shall hear that you are well.

Yours ever,

H. W.

From Cole, Monday 13 November 1780

VA, Forster MS 110, ff. 243–4. Cole's copy, Add MS 5826, ff. 200v, 201v.
Address: For the Honourable Horace Walpole in Berkeley Square, London.
Postmark: [Cambridge] 14 NO.

Milton, Monday, Nov. 13, 1780.

<D>ear Sir,

YOU judged very rightly that I was ill, and in no capacity to thank you for your kind and most ingenious and amusing present. It has but one great fault: it is too short. My walk, though ill, into your Garden of Eden[1] was most enchanting, and I believe did me good. I must repeat it, that I was vexed to come to the end of it.

Poor Mr Gough! Woe befall that man that comes under your criticizing eye! There seems little danger of my communicating your remarks to him, for I have never heard from or wrote to him since the beginning of May,[2] when I thanked him for his present, and indeed have not yet gone through 300 pages of his book. I have had so much employment, and, just as your present came, was so hurried in a work that was obliged to be returned before a new Vice-Chancellor came into office,[3] that I believe [it] did me no small injury in my health, for the gout, always ranging about me, fixed in my head,

---

1. HW concludes *Anecdotes*, vol. iv, with his essay 'On Modern Gardening,' which begins with a humorous paragraph on the Garden of Eden. Cole wrote to Gough 23 Dec. 1780: 'Mr Walpole was so kind to send me his last volume before it was published. I am glad you approve of it. I have an exception only to two or three passages' (LA i. 689).

2. This statement is not correct: Cole wrote to Gough 14 May (when he thanked him for *British Topography*), 24 May, 18 June and 24 July 1780 (see LA i. 683–7; viii. 391). His next letter is dated 17 Dec. 1780 (see ibid. i. 687) and is as cordial as the others.

3. Lowther Yates (d. 1798), Master of St Catharine's College, 1779–98, was Vice-Chancellor 4 Nov. 1779 to 4 Nov. 1780 (and again in 1794–5). He was succeeded by John Barker (1727?–1808), Master of Christ's College (see *Alumni Cantab.*). Cole wished to return the MS because he was prejudiced against Barker, a 'warm' Whig (see John Peile, *Biographical Register of Christ's College 1505–1905*, 2 vols, Cambridge, 1910–13. ii. 247). The 'work that was obliged to be returned' was probably the volume of pedigrees mentioned *ante* 8 July 1780; see also Cole to Gough 18 June 1780, LA i. 686.

so that I had no rest for many nights, and about three weeks ago an humour settled in my nose, which was enormously inflamed and swelled, and seemed to threaten my eyes. Thank God, for these last two or three days I am better, my nose reduced to its usual size, and can a little use my pen, which I have not been able to do these five weeks, nor have been over my threshold for that time, nor expect it this winter.

Mr Essex and family dined with me about six weeks ago.[4] Dr Farmer happened to come the same day. He told Mr Essex that Mr Masters was most violently enraged at Mr Gough's calling him a plagiary at p. 251*,[5] that he had wrote to him about it, and was determined to write a pamphlet and expose the many gross mistakes in his book. Dr Farmer, who is much with Mr Masters, and his friend, said at the same time that Mr Gough's book was fuller of mistakes than he had ever met [with in] one of the size. However that may be, I am afraid Robin Masters's book will meet with the same fate that his other did against *Richard III*—that is, never be read. Mr Gough's book may have many mistakes, as a book treating of such multifarious matter is impossible to avoid them, but there is surely great information and much useful knowledge in it. I wish you would communicate to me, for my own use, any other material blemishes in it. He shall never know of them, without your leave, for it is probable that our correspondence, though dropped for so long a time, may revive, for I promised him I would send him what remarks I made on his book, which may get to a third impression before I send them, if I make no more haste in reading his book than I have hitherto done.

I heard a fortnight ago that our President, the Dean of Exeter, had a bad stroke of the palsy, and in a dangerous way.[6]

I have met with your old friend Peter Curtis, or Peers Curtes,[7]

4. Cole's copy reads: 'on Sunday was six weeks, when I was first taken ill.'

5. Gough mentions (*British Topography*[2] i. 251*) ' "Mr. James Essex's letter to his subscribers to the plan and elevation of an intended addition to Corpus Christi College, in Camb. 1748-9." 12mo. Vindicating himself from the plagiarism of the then bursar [Masters].' For Cole's account of this affair, see LA v. 117 n. See also DNB, *sub* Essex, James.

6. Milles was sufficiently recovered on 11 Jan. 1781 to deliver a speech to the Antiquarian Society 'upon their removal to the apartments assigned to them in Somerset House.' In the *Gentleman's Magazine*, the public and the Society were congratulated on his recovery (see GM Feb. 1781, li. 85b). Milles lived until 13 Feb. 1784.

7. HW quoted in *Historic Doubts*[1], pp. 65–7, part of 'the account of Peter Courteys keeper of the great wardrobe' which 'dates from the day of King Edward the Fourth his death, to the Feast of the Puri-

who was mayor of Leicester and served as member of Parliament for that borough 22 Edward IV and 1 Richard III and 4 and 7 Henry VII. Mr Samuel Carte's MS *History of Leicester*[8] was lately lent me: in it I met these circumstances, and he adds that part of the traditionary stone coffin of King Richard III is still preserved at the White Horse Inn there, in which he says 'one may observe some appearance of the hollow fitted for retaining the head and shoulders.'[9] I much doubt whether such sort of stone coffins were in use as late as Henry VII's time: it is more probable a stone coffin from the Austin Friars,[10] belonging to some other person.[11]

I shall tire you as well as myself if I write longer, and shall only add that I am, with great obligations for all your kindnesses to me through life,

Your ever faithful and obliged servant,

WM COLE

Masters had better be quiet with Essex and Gough about plagiarism, for if there was ever one man more guilty of that sin than another, it is Robin Masters. I can prove it in an hundred instances, but, poor man! having but a poor stock of his own, no wonder he ranges into other men's pastures![12]

---

fication in the February of the following year.' This section of *Historic Doubts* was the occasion of Milles's criticisms.

8. Samuel Carte (1653–1740), antiquary, was the author of a MS *History of Leicester* which was used by John Nichols in his *The History and Antiquities of the County of Leicester . . . including also Mr. Burton's Description of the County, published in 1622; and the later Collections of Mr. Staveley, Mr. Carte, Mr. Peck, and Sir Thomas Cave*, 4 vols (in 8 parts), 1795–1815. The passage to which Cole refers (concerning the election of Curteys as mayor and burgess) is quoted by Nichols, vol. 1, pt 2, p. 432; see also p. 451.

9. 'The Rev. Samuel Carte, vicar of St. Martin's in Leicester, says, in 1720, "I know no other evidence that the stone coffin formerly used as a horse-trough was King Richard's, but the constancy of the tradition. There is a little part of it still preserved at the White Horse Inn, in which one may observe some appearance of the hollow, fitted for retaining the head

and shoulders" ' (Nichols, op. cit., vol. 1, pt 2, p. 298). Before 1758 parts of the coffin were used as steps to a cellar in the same inn (ibid. 299).

10. A rich Augustinian monastery, Leicester Abbey, of which only ruins remain. Cardinal Wolsey died there.

11. Nichols quotes in support of Carte's theory, the following passage from 'Baker's *Chronicle*, p. 235': ' " . . . the stone chest wherein his [Richard III's] corpse lay is now made a drinking-trough for horses, at a common inn in Leicester, and retaineth the only memory of this monarch's greatness" ' (op. cit., vol. 1, pt 2, p. 298).

12. GM, March 1784, liv. 195 has the following in a review of Masters's *Life of Thomas Baker:* 'Some disagreeable truths have come out in the second edition of the *British Topography*. Historic verity has recorded something to the discredit of Mr M[asters] in his dispute with a modest and ingenious architect of Cambridge, whose works he had purloined. To his *History of Corpus Christi College* he has annexed a

What a strange affair between our Chancellor[13] and Lord Pomfret! This quarrel of Gough and Masters is the more extraordinary, as they used to be great cronies, and so late as this spring, when Robin carried up his two daughters[14] to see the lions,[15] etc., in their return stayed a day or two at Enfield: at least made a visit there. Indeed I blame Mr Gough, who must do it inadvertently, as there seemed no reason to revive a controversy between Mr Masters and Mr Essex which had been asleep these thirty years, and never regarded when first broached.

To COLE, Friday 24 November 1780

Add MS 5953, ff. 103–4.

Address: To the Reverend Mr Cole at Milton near Cambridge.
Postmark: GC 24 NO.

Berkeley Square, Nov. 24, 1780.

I AM sorry I was so much in the right in guessing that you had been ill—but at our age there is little sagacity in such divination. In my present holidays from the gout, I have a little rheumatism, or some of those accompaniments.

plan of the intended new building, *designed by himself*. Let Mr Cole, who best knew the whole transaction, give an account of it. "This was just as much designed by himself as the drawing of Pythagoras's school was; that is, he had no hand in either. Mr Essex drew the plan of the new college, where *invenit* honestly stands for *found* it, if it relates to the compiler of this book; if to Mr Essex, in its natural sense." ' This appears to have been written by Nichols, who reprints it in LA v. 117.

13. The Duke of Grafton, Chancellor of Cambridge. Lord Pomfret, whom HW calls 'half a madman,' challenged the Duke of Grafton 'for an affront offered to him, he said, when the Duke was minister—you know what an age ago that was' (HW to Mann 2 Nov. 1780). Pomfret was committed to the Tower 6 Nov., and was not freed until 17 Nov., when he made his submission and agreed not to pursue his resentment against the Duke of Grafton or anyone else (see *Last Journals* ii. 334–6; GM Nov. 1780, l. 510–12).

14. Anne and Mary: Anne m. (8 Oct. 1790) the Rev. John Rowland Sproule or Sprowle (1754?–1829) of Oriel College, Oxford (see GM Oct. 1790, lx. 955b; April 1829, xcix. 378a; *Alumni Oxon; History of Westmoreland*, 2 vols, Kendal and London, 1747–8, ii. 6). Mary (1763?–1859) m. (5 Dec. 1797) Thomas Cooke Burroughs (1756?–1821), President of Caius College, 1795–7; rector of Landbeach, 1797–1821 (Masters resigned in his favour) (see John Venn, *Biographical History of Gonville and Caius College, 1349–1897*, 3 vols, 1897–1901, ii. 93 [where Mary is erroneously called the sister of the Rev. Robert Masters]; William Keatinge Clay, *A History of the Parish of Landbeach*, Cambridge, 1861, p. 119).

15. In the Lion Tower of the Tower of London. The animals were transferred to the Zoological Gardens in 1834 and the site of the Lion Tower is now 'a plain refreshment room' (see *The Blue Guides: London and its Environs*, ed. Finlay Muirhead, 3d edn, 1927, p. 298).

I have made several more notes to the new *Topography*,[1] but none of consequence enough to transcribe. It is well it is a book only for the adept, or the scorners would often laugh. Mr Gough speaking of some cross that has been removed, says, there is now *an unmeaning market house* in its place. Saving his reverence and our prejudices, I doubt there is a good deal more *meaning* in a market house than in a cross. They tell me that there are numberless mistakes. Mr Pennant, whom I saw yesterday, says so. *He* is not one of our plodders: rather the other extreme: his *corporal* spirits (for I cannot call them *animal*) do not allow him time to digest anything. He gave a round jump from ornithology to antiquity—and as if they had any relation, thought he understood everything that lay between them. These adventures divert me who am got on shore, and find how sweet it is to look back on those who are toiling in deep waters,[2] whether in ships, or cockboats, or on old rotten planks. I am sorry for the Dean of Exeter. If he dies, I conclude the leaden mace[3] of the Antiquarian Society will be offered to Judge Barrington,[3a]

Et simili frondescet virga metallo.[4]

I endeavoured to give our antiquaries a little wrench towards taste— but it was in vain. Sandby and our engravers of views have lent them a great deal—but there it stops. Capt. Grose's dissertations[5] are as dull and silly as if they were written for the Ostrogoth maps at the beginning of the new *Topography*;[6] and which are so square and so incomprehensible that they look as if they were ichnographies of the New Jerusalem.

I am delighted with having done with the professions of author

---

1. MS reads *Typography*. HW refers to Gough's *British Topography*[2].

2. Suave, mari magno turbantibus
   aequora ventis,
   e terra magnum alterius spectare laborem.
   Lucretius *De Rerum Natura* II. 1–2.

3.   'O murderous slumber,
Lay'est thou thy leaden mace upon my boy
That plays thee music?'
           Julius Caesar IV. iii. 266–8.

3a. 'In 1784, on the demise of Dr Milles, he [Edward King (1735?–1807)] was elected President of the Society of Antiquaries. . . . On St George's day next ensuing, . . . in an unprecedented contest for the chair, Mr King was obliged to resign it in favour of George Lord De Ferrars (afterwards Earl of Leicester and Marquis Townshend).' See LA viii. 58.

4. Virgil, *Aeneid* vi. 144.

5. HW probably has in mind Grose's *Antiquities of England and Wales*, of which he and Cole had very poor opinions (see *ante* 30 Dec. 1779; 5 Jan. 1780).

6. MS reads *Typography*. Professor Pottle suggests that HW wrote *Typography* deliberately to show his contempt for the book. Gough included in his work an historical account of the maps of England and Scotland, and gave eight plates of old maps as illustrations.

and printer, and intend to be most comfortably lazy, I was going to
say, idle (but that would not be new) for the rest of my days. If there
was a peace, I would build my offices—if there is not soon, we shall
be bankrupt—nay, I do not know what may happen as it is—Well!
Mr Grose will have plenty of ruins to engrave! The Royal Academy
will make a fine mass, with what remains of old Somerset House.[7]

Adieu! my good Sir. Let me know you are well. You want nothing
else, for you can always amuse yourself, and do not let the foolish
world disturb you.

Yours most sincerely,

HOR. WALPOLE[8]

From COLE, Monday 27 November 1780

VA, Forster MS 110, ff. 245–6. COLE's copy, Add MS 5826, f. 202v.

Address: The Honourable Horace Walpole, Berkeley Square, London.

Postmark: Cambridge 29 NO.

Monday, Nov. 27, 1780. Milton.

Dear Sir,

I AM the more expeditious in my answer to your kind letter of
yesterday, as my friend Dr Farmer, Master of Emanuel, calling
upon me this morning (as he often has done since I have been ill),
saw your last volume of *Anecdotes* on my table. He told me he had
been with Merrill, our principal bookseller, to get a complete set
for the Library (he being University Librarian,[1] the place that Dr
Middleton held),[2] but that Merrill told him that it was difficult to
get one, and even at an enormous price. He then expressed a wish
that you would be so kind to your old Alma Mater as to give your
works to the Public Library, promising them an eminent place in it.
You have ever been so generous to me in particular, that I am the
worst person that could have been employed on such a begging er-

---

7. The Royal Academy occupied quarters at Somerset House 1771–1837, but the
first exhibition was held there in 1780 (see
The Blue Guides: London 3d edn, p. 197).

8. Cole wrote at the end of HW's letter:
'Mem[orandum:] to ask for his publications for the Univ[ersity] Libr[ary]. Dr
Farmer was here Nov. 27 and told me he
had desired Merrill to get the Anecd[otes]

of *Painting*, but could not get them but
at an extravagant price.' See following
letter.

---

1. Cole's copy reads *Principal Librarian*,
which is correct: Farmer was *Protobibli-
othecarius* 1778–97.

2. Conyers Middleton was *Protobibli-
othecarius* 1721–50.

rand, but my esteem for Dr Farmer, and zeal to have your books in the University Library, give me a confidence and assurance that I should hardly have ventured on without them.

If I take too great a liberty, I hope you will pardon me: I know the value of your books, and how difficult it is to get <the>m: as money will not do, I wish love to the old place may have a better chance. If my request is excessive, say no more of it, and I will be equally silent to Dr Farmer.

Your kind and lively letter gave me spirits. I was sorry, however, to find that you pleased yourself so much with the thoughts of quitting authorship and printership: a circumstance that no one else will be happy in.

I am surprised I have not heard from Mr Pennant, to whom I wrote in March last, and never heard from him since.

As I don't much know Judge Barrington, what think you of Robin Masters having the leaden mace offered to him?[3] O' my conscience I believe there never was a more dull, plodding, heavy-headed fellow in the universe.

I have not wrote to or heard from Dr Lort of these three months. Today I took courage to write to him, though after a bad night, with complaint in my head, from which I have been free for near a fortnight.

I hope things will go better than you augur: pray God they may! I am of your great father's opinion about peace, and we enjoyed the blessing of it under his administration, but if things are so circumstanced that we cannot have it but with disgrace, we must submit to war.

I have been much taken up with transcribing a large folio MS of letters and negotiations of Cardinal Wolsey.[4] They are lent to me by Dr Farmer, and probably came out of Lord Exeter's[5] library. If you have any curiosity to see them, I will send them to you.

I can write no more with ease, and am, dear Sir,

Your ever faithful and most obliged servant,

WM COLE

3. As President of the Society of Antiquaries (see preceding letter).
4. See *ante* 12 Feb. 1780.
5. It is not evident to which Lord Exe-

ter Cole refers, but probably it is to Wolsey's contemporary and opponent, Henry Courtenay (1496?–1538), M. of Exeter and E. of Devonshire.

To Cole, Thursday 30 November 1780

Add MS 5953, ff. 105–6.

Address: To the Reverend Mr Cole at Milton near Cambridge.
Postmark: 30 NO.

Berkeley Square, Nov. 30, 1780.

I AM sorry, my dear Sir, that you should be so humble with me your ancient friend, and to whom you have ever been so liberal, as to make an apology for desiring me to grant the request of another person.[1] I am not less sorry that I shall not, I fear, be able to comply with it; and you must have the patience to hear my reasons. The first edition of the *Anecdotes* was of three hundred, of the two first volumes; and of as many of the third volume and of the volume of *Engravers*.[2] Then there was an edition of three hundred of all four.[3] Unluckily I did not keep any number back of the two first volumes, and literally have none but those I reserved for myself.[3a] Of the other two I have two or three; and I believe I have a first, but without the cuts. If I can, with some odd volumes that I kept for corrections, make out a decent set, the library of the University shall have them; but you must not promise them, lest I should not be able to perform.

Of my new fourth volume I printed six hundred; but as they *can* be had, I believe not a third part is sold. This is a very plain lesson to me, that my editions sell for their curiosity, and not for any merit in them,—and so they would, if I printed Mother Goose's tales, and but a few. As my *Anecdotes of Painting* have been published at such distant periods, and in three divisions, complete sets will be

1. Farmer wished HW to give a set of *Anecdotes* to the Cambridge University Library (see preceding letter). HW did not do so, although he had presented one of the second edition to the Bodleian (see *Jour. Print. Off.* 48).

2. HW's entry in *Jour. Print. Off.*, made at the time he published the first two volumes, gives 600 copies (p. 10). He does not give the number of copies of the third volume or of the *Engravers*, but as he printed 600 copies of the fourth volume (ibid. 19, and note below), and as he gives 600 copies for the first edition of the four volumes in *Description of SH* (*Works* ii. 515), we may put down 300 copies as a characteristic slip.

3. HW does not give the number of copies of the second edition in *Jour. Print. Off.* or in his annotated 1784 *Description of SH*, now WSL.

3a. There are two complete sets of the first edition in SH Cat.: iv. 138, now Sir Thomas Fermor-Hesketh, Bt, Easton Neston, Towcester; iv. 139, now Lord Derby, Knowsley Hall, in the first and second volumes of which set, HW wrote, 'My own copy.' It is profusely extra-illustrated. A complete set of the second edition was sold SH iv. 140 (now WSL). Kirgate, apparently without HW's knowledge, retained several complete sets of both editions, as appears from the sale catalogue of his library, which was sold by King and Lochrée, 3–14 Dec. 1810, and from invoices (now WSL), which show he sold SH imprints after HW's death. See W. S. Lewis, *The Forlorn Printer*, Farmington, 1931.

seldom seen[4]—So, if I am humbled as an author, I may be vain as a printer—and when one has nothing else to be vain of, it is certainly very little worth while to be proud of that.

I will now trust you with a secret, but beg Mr Gough may not know it, for he will print it directly. Though I forgot Alma Mater, I have not forgotten my Almae Nutrices, wet or dry, I mean, Eton and King's. I have laid aside for them, and left them in my will,[5] as complete a set as I could of all I have printed. A few I did give them at first—but I have for neither a perfect set of the *Anecdotes*, I mean not the two first volumes. I should be much obliged to you, if, without naming me, you could inform yourself if I did send to King's those two first volumes;—I believe not.[6]

I will now explain what I said above of Mr Gough. He has learnt, I suppose, from my engravers,[7] that I have had some views of Strawberry Hill engraved—slapdash, down it went, and he has even specified each view in his second volume.[8] This curiosity is a little impertinent—but he has made me some amends by a new blunder, for he says they are engraved for a second edition of my Catalogue. Now I have certainly printed but one edition for which the prints are designed.[9] He says truly, that I printed but a few for use—consequently, I by no means wished the whole world should know it—but he is very silly—and so I will say no more of him.

Dr Lort called on me yesterday, and asked if I had any message to you; but I had written too lately.

4. This has not proved to be so.

5. This bequest does not appear in HW's final will, which was written 15 May 1793, and included seven codicils.

6. He had not sent them (see following letter).

7. Gough apparently had his information from Godfrey (see following note).

8. The passage in question appears in *British Topography*[2] i (not ii, as HW says). 571*: 'Mr Walpole printed in 4to for private use a catalogue of his curious collection drawn up by himself. Ten views of *Strawberry Hill* have been engraved by Godfrey, from drawings by Marlow, for a new edition of this catalogue.

N[orth], S[outh] and S[outh] E[ast] Fronts.
View from the Terrace.
View of the Chapel in the Garden.
View of the Prior's Garden.
View from the Great Bedchamber.
E. View of the Cottage Garden.
Chimney-Piece of the Holbein Chamber.
Library.'

Only eight of the above plates are signed by Godfrey: those of the south and east fronts lack the names of artist and engraver, but, as HW did not deny Gough's statements, Godfrey probably engraved them. Marlow's name appears only on the 'North Front of Strawberry Hill,' and two others; the plates of the 'Library' and the 'Chimney-Piece in the Holbein Chamber,' have no artist's name. Pars made the drawings for the remaining five views.

9. That is, the 1774 edition, which was printed without plates. HW inserted these prints in his own copies of this edition and they were issued with the second, 1784, edition.

Mr Pennant has been, as I think I told you, in town—by this time I conclude he is, as Lady Townly says of fifty pounds, all over the kingdom.[10] When Dr Lort returns, I shall be very glad to read your transcript of Wolsey's letters, *for* in your hand I *can* read them. I will not have them but by some very safe conveyance, and will return them with equal care.

I can have no objection to Robin Masters being Woodenhead of the Antiquarian Society—but I suppose he is not dignified enough for them. I should prefer the Judge,[11] too, because a coif makes him more like an old woman, and I reckon that Society the midwives of superannuated miscarriages.

I am grieved for the return of your headaches—I doubt you write too much.

Yours most sincerely,

H. WALPOLE

PS. It will be civil to tell Dr Farmer that I do not know whether I can obey his commands; but that I will if I can. As to a distinguished place, I beg not to be preferred to much better authors—nay, the more conspicuous, the more likely to be stolen for the reasons I have given you, of there being few complete sets—and true collectors are mighty apt to steal.

From COLE, Sunday 17 December 1780

VA, Forster MS 110, ff. 247–8. COLE's copy, Add MS 5826, f. 204v.
Address: For the Honourable Horace Walpole in Berkeley Square, London.
Postmark: Cambridge 18 DE.

Sunday, Dec. 17, 1780.

Dear Sir,

I WOULD have thanked you for your last obliging letter of Nov. 30 sooner, but that I stayed to get intelligence from King's Col-

10. As Mrs Piozzi noted in her copy of *Letters from the Hon. Horace Walpole to the Rev. William Cole*, 1818 (now WSL), p. 221, 'It was £500, though.' The passage occurs in *The Provok'd Husband; or, A Journey to London*, by Vanbrugh and Cibber, first performed at Drury Lane 10 January 1728, Act V, Scene 2:

'*Lord Town[ly]*. . . . what's become of the last five hundred I gave you?

Lady Town[ly]. Gone.
Lord Town. Gone! what way, Madam?
Lady Town. Half the town over, I believe, by this time.'

HW's jocular reference to Pennant is explained by the latter's propensity to travel, as evidenced by his publication of several *Tours*.

11. Hon. Daines Barrington (see *ante* 24 Nov. 1780).

lege, where I have acquaintance left but Dr Glynn, and him I have not seen these ten months. However, I managed very well by one of the last year's proctors calling on me, whom I commissioned, as from himself, to ask his brother proctor whether they had the two first volumes of your *Anecdotes* in their Library. His answer was, after diligent search, that no such books were in it. This came to me on Friday.

I now heartily thank you for excusing my impertinence in being forward to ask for others what you so liberally have always bestowed on myself, and for your easy compliance with my request.

You need not fear my telling this secret to Mr Gough, with whom I had not corresponded from the time his book came out,[1] when I wrote to thank him for it. However, the correspondence is renewed, for last week I received a letter from him, full of queries. I was vexed when it came, for two reasons: I should be obliged to give myself a great deal of trouble to answer all his questions; and especially as I had that very day got through Cardinal Wolsey's *Negotiations,* which had much tired me, and I wanted rest, and pleased myself with the prospect of it.[2]

Your mentioning the views of Strawberry Hill will make me a further beggar. You was so kind to send me five: if there are any more, I wish you would complete my set. I have two views of the chapel,[3] view from the bedchamber, of t<he> cottage garden, and view from the terrace.

Dr Lort dined here one day, which is all I saw of him. He would readily have taken the book,[4] but I had not finished it when he called, which was the day after he came to Cambridge, when he told me that he should not stay above four or five days. I understand he was very busy in packing up his books and goods, to leave college entirely.[5] He told me a little about Madame du Deffand:[6] I wish you had taken her china.

The Earl of Carlisle has lately sent a picture to King's College for

1. See *ante* 13 Nov. 1780 n. 2.

2. See in this connection, Cole to Gough 17 Dec. 1780, printed in LA i. 687–8.

3. Only one print of the 'View of the Chapel in the Garden' appears in *Description of SH,* 1784, and in *Works.* The other prints were used in both works.

4. Wolsey's *Negotiations.*

5. Lort vacated his fellowship in Trinity

College, Cambridge, on Lady Day, 1781.

6. 'Madame du Deffand's intended generosity to you' (addition in Cole's copy). Although much pressed by her to accept a large bequest, HW consented to take only her MSS and her dog, Tonton (see Du Deffand to HW 15 Feb. 1771 and 25 Jan. 1780).

the altar-piece,[7] which cost him £400. Mr Essex tells me the light will not suit it.

As you do not, I believe, purchase new sermons, a volume just published by a Mr Mainwaring of St John's College,[8] an ingenious man, a passage alludes to you, I suppose, in a dissertation prefixed to them, which I will wholly transcribe, that you may not have the trouble to send for the book. It is at p. 97,[9] where, speaking of the 'fatal jealousy of authorship' that divided Mr Pope and Mr Addison, he thus goes on:

It is more satisfactory to conclude these notes with a striking instance of a contrary kind, and perfectly in point. For the late Mr. Gray [whom he had been speaking of before][10] and his illustrious friend not only excelled greatly as poets, but precisely in the same species of poetry,—a circumstance, which instead of impairing the early affection between them, served only to strengthen and cement it.[11]

I am not very well, and will not tire you or myself any further at present, but by[12] assuring you of my most unfeigned regard and esteem, and am, dear Sir,

Yours eternally,

WM COLE

I will send the volume[13] in a very short time by some friend going to town, and leaving it where you may send for it, if not convenient to leave it at your door.

---

7. The picture was 'The Deposition,' ascribed to Daniele da Volterra (Daniele Ricciarelli, 1509–66) (see following letter). It is now on the north side of the chapel. 'It previously occupied the central position in the woodwork placed there in 1774, and was removed in 1896 when the east window was re-leaded' (W. P. Littlechild, *A Short Account of King's College Chapel*, Cambridge, 1920, p. 16).

8. *Sermons on Several Occasions, preached before the University of Cambridge*, [Cambridge?], by John Mainwaring

(d. 1807). Cole was mistaken in saying that it was 'just published,' as it was published in the preceding May (see *Public Advertiser* 24 May 1780).

9. Cole's copy reads 'p. xcvii,' which is correct.

10. Cole's interpolation.

11. HW notes on this passage: 'Mr Cole mistakes totally: I never excelled in poetry and never wrote odes. Mr Mason is the person meant. H.W.'

12. MS reads 'by by.'

13. Wolsey's *Negotiations*.

To Cole, Tuesday 19 December 1780

Add MS 5953, ff. 107–8.
Address: To the Reverend Mr Cole at Milton near Cambridge.
Postmark: GC 19 DE.

Berkeley Square, Dec. 19, 1780.

I CANNOT leave you for a moment in an error, my good Sir, when you transfer a compliment to me, to which I have not the most slender claim; and defraud another of it, to whom it is due. The friend of Mr Gray in whom authorship caused no jealousy, or variance, as Mr Mainwaring says truly, is Mr Mason.[1] *I* certainly never excelled in poetry, and never attempted the species of poetry alluded to, odes.

Dr L. I suppose is removing to a living or prebend[2]—at least, I hope so. He may run a risk, if he carries his books to Lambeth.[3] *Sono sonate le venti tre e mezza,* as Alexander VIII said to his nephew, when he was chosen Pope in extreme old age.[4] My Lord of Canterbury's[5] is not extreme, but very tottering.

I found in Mr Gough's new edition, that in the Pepysian Library is a view of the theatre in Dorset Gardens,[6] and views of four or five other ancient great mansions.[7] Do the folk of Magdalen ever suffer copies of such things to be taken? and if they would, is there anybody at Cambridge who could execute them, and reasonably? Answer me quite at your leisure; and also, what and by whom the altarpiece is that Lord Carlisle has given to King's.[8] I did not know he had been of our college.[9]

I have two or three plates of Strawberry more than those you men-

1. Cole's note on the original: 'Why "illustrious"? Is Mr Mason so?' (See following letter.) Cole did not like Mason (see *ante* 9 April 1775).

2. Lort was collated to the prebendal stall of Tottenhall in St Paul's Cathedral, 11 April 1780. HW apparently was not aware of the appointment.

3. Lort ran the risk of losing his position as domestic chaplain to the Archbishop of Canterbury when the latter died (see n. 5 below).

4. Cf. *ante* 14 June 1769.

5. Frederick Cornwallis, Abp of Canterbury, who was sixty-seven at this time. Lort resigned his position as the Archbishop's domestic chaplain, 31 Oct. 1782, and the

Abp d. 19 March 1783 (see *post* 30 Oct. 1782).

6. ' "A Description of the Playhouse in Dorset Gardens, A Poem," in one sheet folio, 1706. A view of it in the Pepysian Library' (*British Topography*[2] i. 688).

7. Gough mentions numerous prints that fit this description, but HW possibly refers to the following passage: 'In the Pepysian Library are Hollar's drawings of Suffolk, York, Durham, Salisbury, Worcester, and Somerset houses' (ibid. i. 780).

8. Cole's note on the original: 'Daniele de Volterra.'

9. The E. of Carlisle was admitted as fellow commoner at King's, 1764, but he left without taking a degree.

tion, but my collections are so numerous, and from various causes, my prints have been in such confusion, that at present I neither know where the plates or proofs are. I intend next summer to set about completing my plan of the *Catalogue* and its prints: and when I have found any of the plates or proofs, you shall certainly have those you want. There are the two large views of the house, one of the cottage, one of the library, one of the front of the road, and the chimney-piece in the Holbein Room. I think these are all that are finished—oh! yes, and I believe, the Prior's Garden;[10] but I have not seen them these two years. I was so ill the summer before last, that I attended to nothing; the little I thought of in that way last summer, was to get out my last volume of the *Anecdotes*—now I have nothing to trouble myself about as an editor, and that not publicly, but to finish my *Catalogue*—and that will be awkwardly enough, for so many articles have been added to my collection since the *Description* was made, that I must add them in the appendix, or reprint it— and what is more inconvenient, the positions of many of the pictures have been changed; so it will be a lame piece of work. Adieu, my dear Sir,

Yours most cordially,

H. W.

From Cole, Saturday 3 February 1781

VA, Forster MS 110, ff. 249–50. Cole kept no copy.
Address: Honourable Horace Walpole, Berkeley Square, London.
Postmark: [Cambridge] 5 FE.

<D>ear Sir,   Milton, February 3, 1781. Saturday morning.

YOU must conclude me to be extremely ill-mannered, or very much indisposed, that I have not answered your kind letter of 19 December. I wish I don't stand guilty of both: one certainly may excuse me, for these six weeks I have been more than ordinarily incommoded with gouty complaints, for a month confined to my

10. According to Gough's list (see *ante* 30 Nov. 1780), Godfrey had completed three additional prints: View from the Terrace, the Chapel, and the View from the Great Bedchamber.

chamber. Thank God I am got downstairs, but have the gout slightly in both feet, and far from well. Thus much for apology.

You certainly are right in respect to Mr Mainwaring. But why the *illustrious Mr Mason?* I did not know or think that title belonged to him: it was *that* which led me astray.

In answer to your queries about Magdalen Library and the King's College altar-piece, I send you Mr Kerrich's letter.[1] At the same time I send you, as the opportunity offers, my last letter from Mr Gough,[2] as perhaps you have not visited the new Antiquarian apartments or heard of the solemnity of the members' admission into them. They may both be kept, burnt or returned in the way they came, as you like, for I have no use for them.

I shall be obliged to you for completing my set of the Strawberry Hill plates at your leisure, but God knows that *sono sonate le venti tre hore e mezza,* which makes me careless about everything. I hope Dr Lort will have a long half-hour and replete with good things. He has been much out of order since Christmas, and I am the same delinquent towards him as to you, but I fear nothing from either, as I know the candour of you both, yet I have had daily compunctions on my mind, and indeed should have wrote, had not a friend,[3] a fortnight ago, undertaken to convey my fifty-ninth volume[4] of rubbish to you in a day or two. He called again yesterday to tell me that he would send it on Monday, so you may expect to have it left at your house in a day or two. The Master of Emmanuel offered me to send you the original:[5] I don't think it worth troubling you with: mine is a faithful transcript, and keep it at your leisure. I wish you don't find here and there something of the old leaven that may vex you, and which is irradicable in my constitution, yet I rely on your candour and generosity, which I am assured is equal to my perversity.[5a]

I have just seen the *Antiquarian Repertory.*[6] In vol. 2, p. 238, Sir

1. This letter, dated 27 Dec. 1780, is in LI vi. 821–2. It answers HW's queries regarding the views in Magdalene College Library, and the picture given to King's College Chapel by Lord Carlisle.
2. Missing.
3. Unidentified.
4. That is, the volume containing Wolsey's *Negotiations,* now Add MS 5860.
5. Farmer's MS was itself a copy of the original.

5a. Cole refers to his political differences with HW. Before a similar loan of one of his MS volumes to Gough, he wrote (10 Aug. 1781): 'Mr Walpole and myself are as opposite in political matters as possible; yet we continue friends. Your political and religious opinions possibly may be as dissimilar; yet I hope we shall all meet in a better world and be happy' (LA i. 693).
6. Four vols, 1775–84, ed. Francis Grose, Thomas Astle and others.

John Cullum has a letter with a description of Little Saxham Church in Suffolk, in which is a monument of William Lord Crofts,[7] well executed by Story,[8] an artist omitted, he thinks, by you. I rather doubted whether the mistake is not his own, and that it means Stone or his son,[9] famous artists and statuaries for monuments, if the time will allow it, for Lord Crofts died so late as 1677.

Adieu, my dear Sir, and God bless you.

Yours most sincerely,

WM COLE

I hear poor Mr Pennant is *un peu dérangé*.[10] Have you heard anything of it, or know anything about it? He had too many things in his head to keep it cool and sedate.

May I beg the favour of you to let your servant put the three letters[11] into the post: that to Dr Lort into the Penny Post.

To COLE, Wednesday 7 February 1781

Add MS 5953, ff. 109–10.

Cole wrote the following notes on the cover: 'M[r] Rob. Adame, A. M., inst[ituted] to the V[icarage] of Haslingfield 17 Oct. 1473. V. 25, p. 201. Rob. Ippeswell Clare made Justice of the Peace for the Isle [of Ely] by Bishop Alcok in 1487. V. 26, p. 7. He was Rector of Newton or Master of the Hospital there and died in 1495. V. 26, p. 39.' These notes have nothing to do with Cole's correspondence with HW. Cole probably jotted them down for another friend. The references, apparently, are to his own MS volumes.

Address: To the Reverend Mr Cole at Milton near Cambridge.
Postmark: 8 FE.

Berkeley Square, Feb. 7, 1781.

Dear Sir,

I WILL not leave you a moment in suspense about the safety of your very valuable volume,[1] which you have so kindly sent me, and which I have just received, with the enclosed letters, and your

---

7. William Crofts (1611?–77), Bn Crofts of Saxham. Sir John Cullum says: 'In a chapel on the N. side of the church is a handsome monument for William Lord Crofts, and the Lady Elizabeth his wife, with their figures, large as life, in marble, well executed by Story, an artist omitted, I believe, by Mr. Walpole.'

8. He is not mentioned in *Anecdotes*,

nor, apparently, in any dictionary of artists. Rev. H. I. Kilner, rector of Little Saxham Church in 1887, says the monument 'was executed by Story,' but he gives no further information (*Proceedings of the Suffolk Institute of Archaeology and Natural History*, Ipswich, 1888, vi. p. xlvii).

9. Nicholas Stone the elder died in 1647, and his three sons, Henry, John and

other yesterday. I have not time to add a word more at present, being full of business, having the night before last received an account of Lady Orford's death at Pisa, and a copy of her will,[2] which obliges me to write several letters, and to see my relations. She has left everything in her power to her *friend* Cavalier Mozzi[3] at Florence; but her son comes into a large estate, besides her great jointure. You may imagine how I lament that he had not patience to wait sixteen months, before he sold his pictures!

I am very sorry you have been at all indisposed. I will take the utmost care of your fifty-ninth volume (for which I give you this receipt) and will restore it the instant I have had time to go through it,[4]

Witness my hand,

Hor. Walpole

To Cole, Friday 9 February 1781

Add MS 5953, ff. 111–12.

Cole wrote the following notes (which he did not use) on the cover: 'Though Bishop Tanner quotes Bishop Bourchier's Register for the Priory being granted to Pembroke Hall in 1450, yet by the same Register, my vol. 25, p. 3, it appears that Pembroke Hall was in possession of it in 1444, and by this deed in 1439, 18 Henry VI.

'Probably procured for them by Duke of Somerset.

'Joane, daughter of Charles King of Navarre, and second wife of King [Henry] IV, died at Havering in the Bower in Essex, *sans* issue, 10 July 1437, and buried at Canterbury. [She did have issue by her first husband, John IV (d. 1399), D. of Brittany.]

'Humfrey, Duke of Gloucester, son of Henry IV, and died 1447.

'The Priory of All Saints in Fulburn was given by Alcon Earl of Richmond to

Nicholas all died before 1677 (see DNB). Obviously Cole's suggestion is untenable. See also *The Walpole Society*, vol. vii, which contains *The Note-Book and Account Book of Nicholas Stone*, by Walter Lewis Spiers.

10. This report was unfounded (see *post* 29 March 1781).

11. They were sent with Cole's MS volume (see following letter).

1. This was apparently the first time that Cole had ever loaned one of his MS volumes to another; he wrote to Gough 10 Aug. 1781: 'I am going to do what I never yet did to anyone except Mr Walpole—entrust you with one of my volumes' (LA i. 693).

2. In Mann's letter of 16 January 1781.

3. Italian savant. (See HW's correspondence with Mann.)

4. Cole received the volume 7 March 1781 (see *post* that date).

Bon Repos Abbey, who leased it to the Abbey of Scutre in Hunts. Vide my vol. 19, p. 14.

'Tho. Bourchier Bishop of Worcester, translated to Ely, 1443, and translated to Canterbury 1554 [1454].'

Address: The Reverend Mr Cole at Milton near Cambridge.

Postmark: GC 9 FE.

[Berkeley Square,] Feb. 9, 1781.

I HAD not had time, dear Sir, when I wrote last, to answer your letter, nor do more than cast an eye on your MS. To say the truth, my patience is not tough enough to go through Wolsey's *Negotiations.* I see that *your* perseverance was forced to make the utmost efforts to transcribe them. They are immeasurably verbose; not to mention the blunders of the first copyist. As I read only for amusement, I cannot so late in my life purchase information on what I do not much care about, at the price of a great deal of ennui. The old wills at the end of your volume diverted me much more than the obsolete politics. I shall say nothing about what you call *your old leaven.* Everybody must judge for himself in those matters; nor are you or I of an age to change long-formed opinions, as neither of us is governed by self-interest.

Pray tell me how I may most safely return your volume. I value all your MSS so much, that I should never forgive myself if a single one came to any accident by your so obligingly lending them to me. They are great treasures, and contain something or other that must suit most tastes: not to mention your amazing industry, neatness, and legibility, with notes, arms, etc. I know no such repositories. You will receive with your MS Mr Kerrich's and Mr Gough's letters.[1] The former is very kind.[2] The inauguration of the *Antiquated* Society is burlesque, and so is their dearth of materials for another volume:[3] can they ever want such rubbish as compose their preceding annals?

I think it probable that *Story* should be *Stone*—however, I never piqued myself on recording every mason. I have preserved but too many that did not deserve[4] to be mentioned. I dare to say that when I am gone, many more such will be added to my volumes.

1. See *ante* 3 Feb. 1781.
2. Kerrich offered to make drawings of the prints and views HW wanted, as they were not allowed out of the library (see Kerrich to Cole 27 Dec. 1780, printed in LI vi. 821–2).

3. Probably allusions to information in Gough's missing letter.
4. MS reads *deserved.*

I had not heard of poor Mr Pennant's misfortune. I am very sorry for it, for I believe him an honest good-natured man. He certainly was too lively for his proportion of understanding, and too impetuous to make the best use of what he had. However, it is a credit to us antiquaries to have one of our class disordered by vivacity.

I hope your goutiness is dissipated, and that this last fine week has set you on your feet again.

Yours most sincerely and gratefully,

H. W.

PS. Your letters were all put into the post.

From COLE, Monday 12 February 1781

VA, Forster MS 110, f. 251. Cole kept no copy.

Address: Honourable Horace Walpole, Berkeley Square, London.
Postmark: Cambridge 13 FE.

Milton, Feb. 12, 1781.

<D>ear Sir,

I RECEIVED both your obliging letters of the 7th and 9th of this instant. I judged the *Negotiations* would hardly please you, except you had a mind to examine the Cardinal's[1] chicanery and manner of treating with the Pope[2] and Emperor.[3] I wish, however, that you would look into the index, which will point out to you an original letter of Mr Pope to Mr Broome[4] in Suffolk, giving an account of Mr Elijah Fenton and his death, which to a biographer I esteem curious. There is also a short note by Mr Grey,[5] with his sentiments of the MS.

If you will be so kind to keep the MS till I have a fair opportunity of someone's calling for it, or I should have no doubt of its coming safe by Mr Salmon's wagon at the Green Dragon in Bishopsgate Street, and left for me at Cambridge at Mr Salmon's, only it is such a journey from Berkeley Square. However, I shall send for it soon, if

---

1. Wolsey's.
2. Clement VII (Giuliano de' Medici) (d. 1534), who refused to grant Henry VIII a divorce from Catherine of Aragon.
3. Charles V (1500–58).
4. William Broome (1689–1745), collaborator of Pope and Fenton in translating the *Odyssey*, 1722–6. Pope's letter to him 29 Aug. 1730 was printed in Johnson's 'Life of Fenton' (see LA i. 662–3, vi. 181, viii. 388–9; Pope's *Works*, ed. Elwin and Courthope, viii. 164–5).
5. For Gray's note to Richard Farmer, see *Gray's Corr.* iii. 1119–20.

it comes not by the wagon, as the Colne MS[6] is left unfinished, and I shall be glad to return the original, and not keep it, as Mr Gough did, for two years.

I see by the papers that Lady Orford desired to be buried in Italy. I suppose, therefore, she conformed to the religion of the country where she spent her days.[7]

I have been worse since I wrote, with a fresh attack of the gout in my feet, but I am glad to have it there rather than marauding about here and there and everywhere.

I most sincerely wish you health and every enjoyment, and am, dear Sir,

Your ever faithful and obliged servant,

WM COLE

To COLE, Friday 2 March 1781

Add MS 5953, ff. 113–14.
Address: To the Reverend Mr Cole at Milton near Cambridge.
Postmark: GC 2 MR.

Berkeley Square, March 2, 1781.

Dear Sir,

AS you have not lighted on a trusty person to fetch your MS, I am unwilling to detain it longer from you, and therefore shall send my printer with it tomorrow morning to the Green Dragon, according to your directions; though I should not have ventured it in that manner, unless you yourself had warranted me. I do not know on what day the wagon sets out; but I have ordered the book to be left at Mr Salmon's at Cambridge,[1] till called for.

My Lady Orford ordered herself to be buried at Leghorn, the only place in Tuscany where Protestants have burial. Therefore I suppose she did not affect to change. On the contrary I believe she had no preference for any *sect*, but rather laughed at all.

I know nothing new, neither in novelty nor antiquity. I have had

6. See *ante* 14 Nov. 1779.
7. See following letter.

———

1. 'Salmon's wagons set out from the foot of the Great Bridge on Mondays and Tuesdays, inn at the Black Bull in Bishopsgate Street, and return from thence on Wednesdays, Thursdays, and Fridays' (Cooper, *Annals* iv. 332).

no gout this winter, and therefore call it my *leap* year. I am sorry it is not yours too. It is an age since I saw Dr Lort. I hope illness is not the cause.

You will be diverted with hearing that I am chosen an honorary member of the new Antiquarian Society at Edinburgh.[2] I accepted for two reasons. First, because it is a feather that does not demand my flying thither; and secondly, to show contempt for our own old fools. To me it will be a perfect sinecure, for I have moulted all my pen-feathers, and shall have no ambition of nestling into their printed transactions. Adieu! my good Sir,

Your much obliged,

H. WALPOLE

From COLE, Sunday 4 March 1781

VA, Forster MS 110, f. 252. Cole kept no copy.

Address: Honourable Horace Walpole, Berkeley Square, London.
Postmark: [Cambridge] 5 MR.

Milton, March 4, 1781. Sunday noon.

Dear Sir,

I HAVE just now an opportunity of letting you know where to send my book, which has given you little amusement and much trouble. I did not choose to write till I could inform you, and when I have received it will inform you further.

I am glad you escape gout and all complaints. I am like a tree in the same position:[1] tolerably well on one day and pay for it the next.

I hear Lord Hardwick has printed a small parcel of *Walpoliana.* I desire not to know your sentiments about it, as a friend[1a] has de-

2. See HW to Mason 9 Feb. 1781; to Buchan 10 Feb. 1781. HW was elected an honorary member of the Society of Antiquaries of Scotland 29 Jan. 1781 (see *Account of the Institution and Progress of the Society of the Antiquaries of Scotland,* Pt 3, Edinburgh, 1831, p. 16).

1. Cole wrote to his half-brother, Dr Stephen Apthorp (5 Aug. 1782): 'The inanimate life I lead, fixed like a tree to its soil, or I to my chair . . .' (Palmer, *William Cole* 25; Add MS 5855, f. 55).

1a. Michael Lort, who wrote to Cole 17 Feb. 1781: 'Lord Hardwicke has printed what he calls *Walpoliana; or a few Anecdotes of Sir Robert Walpole.* Not many copies are printed; and these distributed only to particular people. I really do not know whether he has sent Mr W. a copy; but I believe not. However, you may take an opportunity of asking this question of

sired me to write to you, and tell him your opinion of it.[2] I long to see the book, and hope to get a sight of it by a person[3] to whom he generally gives them. I will, indeed can, say no more, as I have company.

I am sorry to give you so much trouble, but must beg you to send the MS to Mr Anderson's, a woollen draper's in Grace Church Street,[4] as soon as may be, who will be in Cambridge on the beginning of the week, and if you choose to see any more old wills, I have a large volume of that sort just fresh from the anvil.

    I am, dear Sir,

Yours most cordially,

Wm Cole

To Cole, Monday 5 March 1781

Add MS 5953, ff. 115–16.

Address: To the Reverend Mr Cole at Milton near Cambridge.
Postmark: 5 MR.

[Berkeley Square,] March 5, 1781.

YOU will have found by a letter that I thought you would receive yesterday, that I sent your MS, dear Sir, to the Green Dragon in Bishopsgate Street, and I shall be very glad to hear that you have received it safe.

I do not in the least guess or imagine what you mean by Lord Hardwicke's publication of a *Walpoliana*. Naturally it should mean a collection of sayings or anecdotes of my father, according to the

that gentleman when you shall next write to him, without mentioning to him from whence you have your intelligence; and if he should make any particular reply, and you be under no injunction of secrecy, I shall be glad to know what it is' (Brydges, *Restituta* iv. 370). Lort's description of *Walpoliana* is inaccurate, and has been followed in DNB and Halkett and Laing, *Dictionary of Anonymous . . . Literature,* 1882–8. The title is merely *Walpoliana.* The first edition, 1781, was 16 pp., 4to. The second edition, 1783, was 17 pp., 4to; a supplement of 3 pp. has been pasted into Thomas Astle's copy, which is now WSL. Astle has noted that there were only 50

copies of this edition. HW's copy of the 1781 edition, with many MS notes, was sold in the Rosebery Sale, 30 June 1933, lot 1310, to Mr Hugh Walpole. Hardwicke's copy of the 1783 edition, now WSL, is annotated throughout by Hardwicke in answer to HW's strictures.

2. That is, Cole wished to avoid the possible consequences of retailing gossip.

3. Probably Robert Plumptre, Master of Queens' College (see *post* 7 March 1781).

4. William Anderson, of 42 Gracechurch Street, a member of the Merchant Taylors Company (see *List of the Whole Body of Liverymen of London . . . to . . . 1792,* 1792).

French *anas,* which began I think with those of Ménage.¹ Or is it a collection of letters and state papers during his administration? I own I am curious to know at least what this piece contains. I had not heard a word of it—and were it not for the name, I should have very little inquisitiveness about it, for nothing upon earth ever was duller than the three heavy tomes his Lordship printed of Sir Dudley Carleton's *Negotiations* and of what he called *State Papers.* Pray send me an answer as soon as you can, at least of as much as you have heard about this thing.

I shall be obliged to you for the sight of the old wills you mention, but not just yet, as I should not have time to read them now, and might detain them too long.

Your MS went to the Green Dragon on Friday night, and they said the wagon would set out the next day.

Yours ever,

H. W.

From Cole, Wednesday 7 March 1781

VA, Forster MS 110, f. 253. Cole's copy, Add MS 5826, f. 53v.
Address: The Honourable Horace Walpole, Berkeley Square, London.
Postmark: [Cambridge] 10 MR.

Milton, Wednesday morning, 9 o'clock, March 7, 1781.

Dear Sir,

I WROTE to you last Sunday, and I this moment received from the most punctual and careful person living my MS, by a person whom I sent to Cambridge this morning, and that you may have nothing on your mind about it, I write immediately, though possibly I may not be able to send it today.

I wrote last week, and, I repeat it, I don't want to know your opinion or sentiments about the *Walpoliana,* or anecdotes about

---

1. 'Le Ménagiana, qu'on regarde avec raison comme un des meilleurs recueils en ce genre qui aient encore paru, fut d'abord publié en un seul vol. in-12 sous le titre de *Ménagiana, sive excerpta ex ore Aegidii Menagii,* à Paris, . . . 1693' (Jacques-

Charles Brunet, *Manuel du Libraire,* 6 vols, Paris, 1860–5). HW's copy (F.6.55), *Ménagiana, ou les bons mots et remarques critiques, historiques, morales, etc., de Ménage,* 4 vols, Paris, 1729, was sold SH ii. 135.

your father, which, if not shown to you before publication, I must think it one of the grossest pieces[1] of ill manners I ever heard of. I a little suspect that the desire to know your opinion about them through my medium may come from a quarter not quite right honourable.[2] As the motion was made to me by a particular friend[3] who has the honour of your acquaintance, it will be better to take no notice of this my information. However, of this I am uncertain.

Dr Lort has been extremely ill, but is got well again through the care of Dr Heberden. Perhaps that might occasion his not calling.

I give you joy of your Scotch honour: they owed it you for your panegyric in the *Noble Authors*.[4] I am only sorry we have lost one of our most learned, ingenious and most creditable members, to ornament the Society in the North. Indeed we deserved it, through the absurdity and indecency of a few bungling members.[4a]

When I wrote last, I was tolerable, and could manage to hobble about without a stick. The gout came on a sudden, in an hour's time, into one of my feet on Monday, and may it keep there, for when <it> is roaming about, one is never well, and may perhaps fix in a worse part. I <con>gratulate you sincerely on your leap year:[5] I have had none these six or seven years.

Thus far I had written[6] in hopes to get a conveyance to the post today, but had none. Your letter came this moment (five o'clock), and am surprised to find you have not heard of the book,[7] for on my mentioning it to a particular friend,[8] since my receipt of the inquisitive letter, he mentioned it to a late member of Parliament,[9] who said that his Lordship had shown him the MS some four or five years ago. As I have wrote to my inquisitive friend,[10] and meant to send it with your letter, and have told him that I had mentioned the book to you, but had received no intelligence from you about it (which was literally fact), and I wanted to shift the argument, I will venture now to say that I received a letter from you and that you

1. MS reads *piece*.
2. That is, from the author, Lord Hardwicke.
3. Michael Lort (see *ante* 4 March 1781).
4. See *ante* 14 May 1768.
4a. That most of the members of the Society of Antiquaries regretted HW's resignation from it may be deduced from Tyson's letter to Gough, 21 Jan. 1773, that 'Masters's strictures on Walpole are much disliked here [at Cambridge], and all seem to wish that they were not to have a place in the Society's book' (LA viii. 602).
5. See *ante* 2 March 1781.
6. 'this morning' (addition in Cole's copy).
7. *Walpoliana*.
8. 'Dr Farmer' (addition in Cole's copy).
9. 'Sir John Cotton' (addition in Cole's copy).
10. Lort.

had not heard of the book or its publication, and I hope that will stop all future improper inquiries of this sort. When I first was informed of it a fortnight ago, the Master of Queens' son[11] dined here with two of his nephews and mine also, viz., the Master's nephews.[12] As I knew Lord Hardwicke gave his publications to him, I inquired whether one was come to his father: he said not. I begged to have a sight of it when one came. No doubt, on inquiry, you will be able to get a sight of one from the few that are given to his friends, for I cannot conceive that he will send one to you, after not making you acquainted with his design. But some people, though *titolati*, have nothing nobly liberal or ingenuous in them.[13]

Adieu, dear Sir, I can write no more, being feverish.

WM COLE

To COLE, Thursday 29 March 1781

Add MS 5953, ff. 117–18.
Address: To the Reverend Mr Cole at Milton near Cambridge.
Postmark: GC 29 MR.

Berkeley Square, March 29, 1781.

YOU are so good-natured, that I am sure you will be glad to be told that the report of Mr Pennant being disordered, is not true. He is come to town, has been with me, and at least is as composed as ever I saw him. He is going to publish another part of his *Welsh Tour*,[1] which he can well afford, though I believe he does not

11. Joseph Plumptre, son of Robert Plumptre, Master of Queens' College (see *ante* 7 April 1779).

12. Richard and George William Newcome, 2d and 3d sons of Henry Newcome by Cole's niece, Mary Mawdsley, and therefore Cole's great-nephews. Richard Newcome entered Queens' College, 1779 (B.A. 1783, Fellow 1786), was afterwards Master of the school at Hackney, and retired to Burcot near Wells, Somerset. George William Newcome (1763–1833) entered Queens' in 1780, but did not graduate, and was afterwards in the Comptroller's Office, Whitehall. He died in Upper Wimpole Street, London, 6 Feb. 1833 (see Add MS 5825, f. 167v; Palmer, *Monumental Inscriptions* 276; GM Feb. 1833, ciii.

187a; *Familiae Minorum Gentium*, ed. John W. Clay, in *Publications of the Harleian Society*, 4 vols, 1894–6, iii. 1045).

13. 'In no instance is it more conspicuous, and his appearance is more that of a tailor than a senator' (addition in Cole's copy).

———

1. *The Journey to Snowdon*, 1781, which was published 1 May 1781 (see *London Chronicle* 17–19, 19–21 April, 1–3 May 1781). According to Pennant's note in the Advertisement, p. i, 'This journey is the continuation of my *Tour in Wales*.' It forms the first part of the second volume: the second and concluding part was published in 1784.

lose by his works. An aunt[2] is dead exceedingly rich, who had given some thousands to him and his daughter[3]—but suddenly changed her mind and left all to his sister,[4] who has most nobly given him all that had been destined in the cancelled will.

Dr Nash has just published the first volume of his *Worcestershire*.[5] It is a folio of prodigious corpulence, and yet dry enough—but then it is finely dressed, and has many heads and views.

Dr Lort was with me yesterday, and I never saw him better, nor has he been much out of order. I hope your gout has left you—but here are winds bitter enough to give one anything.

Yours ever,

H. W.

From Cole, Friday 30 March 1781

VA, Forster MS 110, f. 254. Cole kept no copy.
Address: To the Honourable Horace Walpole, Berkeley Square, London.

Milton, Friday evening, March 30, 1781.

Dear Sir,

I HAVE been extremely uneasy this fortnight that I did not hear from you, and now I have received your letter this afternoon I am more so, as by it I think I am confirmed in my suspicion that my letter to you on March 7, giving you what account I could pick up concerning the *Walpoliana*, was never put into the post office, when I sent last Saturday to inquire about it, but the answer was that if it was ever carried thither, it would certainly go as directed. I am the more concerned about it as I took freedom with L[ord] H[ard-wicke]'s character that might be improper. The case was this: Captain Ward and his wife[1] dined with me Thursday, March 8, and as

2. Not identified.
3. Arabella Pennant (d. 1828), Pennant's dau. by his 1st wife, Elizabeth Falconer (d. 1764), dau. of James Falconer, Esq., of Chester; she m. Edward Hanmer (4th son of Sir Walden Hanmer, who d. in 1783), barrister-at-law of Stockgrove, Bucks (see Burke, *Landed Gentry*, 2 vols, 1851, ii. 1024; William Betham, *Baronetage*, 5 vols, Ipswich and London, 1801–5, iii. 432).

4. Catharine Pennant (1729–97) (see Burke, *Commoners* iii. 34).
5. Cf. *ante* 7 April 1779. The first volume was advertised 'This day was published' in *The St James's Chronicle* 24–7 and 27–9 March 1781. HW's copy (A.1) was sold SH i. 73.

———

1. See *ante* 26 Jan. 1779 n. 1.

I had wrote my letter to you the evening before, and one to Dr Lort, I desired Mr Ward, as he passed by the post office, to put both these letters into the office. He took them and promised to put them both in that evening, but it was too late before they left me, for the letters to go forward till Friday, the next day. I sent to them this week to know if they had not forgotten them: they assured me they were delivered safely. As I know your punctuality in answering letters, it has made me uneasy, and especially as I see nothing in your letter that relieves me, or seems to point to anything I said in my last.

I am sincerely glad to find my intelligence relating to Mr <Penna>nt was without foundation, and also that his finances are repaired by a bountiful sister.

I have been extremely ill since I wrote last, and despair of ever being better.

I have had no answer from Dr Lort, which also adds to my perplexity.

The weather is now colder than at any time in Christmas: such sudden transitions from great heat of ten days ago to such freezing blasts as we now experience is too sensibly felt by such a valetudinarian as is, dear Sir,

Yours most faithfully,

WM COLE

To COLE, Tuesday 3 April 1781

Add MS 5953, f. 119.

Cole wrote the following notes on the cover of this letter: 'See *Monthly Review* for 1781, pp. 187–8, 196.' The passages to which Cole refers occur in a review of *Anecdotes* iv. In the first reference, the reviewer points out slight errors in HW's account of Hogarth; in the second, he expresses a wish that living artists 'may have their merits estimated by a writer of talents, taste, and industry, equal to those of Mr Walpole.' The complete review of the work appears in *Monthly Review* lxiv. 129–37, 182–96.

The second note: 'Dr Farmer going to London about the middle of April 1781, I gave him an introductory letter to Mr Walpole, in which I told him that I was glad to introduce the Master to one of the chiefest characters of the age. The Master's affairs obliged him to return with[out] delivering my letter, which he gave to me again, and I sent it by the post: this occasioned the letter on the other side, which I gave to a friend.' Cole's 'introductory letter' is missing (see following letter). The 'letter on the other side' is Cole's copy of HW's letter of 4 May 1781.

Address: To the Reverend Mr Cole at Milton near Cambridge.
Postmark: 3 AP.

[Berkeley Square,] April 3, 1781.

I AM very sorry, dear Sir, that in my last letter but one I took no notice of what you had said about Lord Hardwicke. The truth was, I am perfectly indifferent about what he prints or publishes. There is generally a little indirect malice, but so much more dullness, that the latter soon suffocates the former. This is telling you that I could not be offended at anything you said of him—nor am I likely to suspect a sincere friend of having the smallest intention of disobliging me. You have proved the direct contrary for above forty years. I have not time to say more, but am,

Ever most truly yours,

H. Walpole

PS. I am very sorry you have been indisposed again.

To Cole, Friday 4 May 1781

Cole's copy, Add MS 5953, f. 120; collated with Cole's second copy, Add MS 5826, ff. 54v, 55v. Cole gave the original to Farmer (see next paragraph), and inserted the first copy in its proper place among HW's original letters.

Cole noted at the end of his second copy of the letter: 'The occasion of this letter was this: Dr Farmer going to London about the middle of April 1781, I gave him an introductory letter to Mr Walpole, in which I told him that I was glad to introduce my friend to one of the chiefest characters of the age. The Master's affairs obliged him to return without delivering my letter, which he gave to me again, and I sent it by the post. The original letter [of HW's] I gave to Dr Farmer. My letter to Mr Walpole I kept no copy of.' HW apparently burned Cole's letter (see below). Cf. introductory note to preceding letter.

Address: To the Rev. Mr Cole at Milton near Cambridge.

Berkeley Square, May 4, 1781.[1]

I SHALL not only be ready to show Strawberry Hill, at any time he chooses, to Dr Farmer, as your friend,[2] but to be honoured with his acquaintance, though I am very shy now of contracting new.

1. Cole's second copy reads 'April [May 4] 1781,' that is, Cole corrected HW's mistake.   2. This phrase is omitted in Cole's second copy.

I have great respect for his character and abilities and judicious taste; and am very clear that he has elucidated Shakespeare[3] in a more reasonable and satisfactory manner than any of his affected commentators, who only complimented him with learning that he had not, in order to display their own. Pray give me timely notice whenever I am likely to see Dr Farmer, that I may not be out of the way when I can have an opportunity of showing attention to a friend of yours, and pay a small part of your gratitude to him. There shall be a bed at his service; for you know Strawberry cannot be seen in a moment, nor are Englishmen so *liants* as to get acquainted in the time they are walking through a house.

But now, my good Sir, how could you suffer your prejudiced partiality to me to run away with you so extravagantly, as to call me one of the greatest characters of the age? You are too honest to flatter, too much a hermit to be interested, and I am too powerless and insignificant to be an object of court, were you capable of paying it, from mercenary views. I know then that[4] could proceed from nothing but the warmth of your heart. But if you are blind towards me, I am not so to myself. I know not how others feel on such occasions, but if anyone happens to praise me, all my faults gush into my face, and make me turn my eyes inward and outward with horror. What am I but a poor old skeleton, tottering towards the grave, and conscious of ten thousand weaknesses, follies, and worse! And for talents, what are mine, but trifling and superficial; and, compared with those of men of real genius, most diminutive! Mine a great character! Mercy on me! I am a composition of Anthony Wood and Madame Danois,[4a] and I know not what trumpery writers. This is the least I can say to refute your panegyric, which I shall burn presently;[5] for I will not have such an encomiastic letter found in my possession, lest I should seem to have been pleased with it. I enjoin you, as a penance, not to contradict one tittle I have said here; for I am not begging more compliments, and shall take it seriously ill if you ever pay me another. We have been friends above forty years; I am satisfied of your sincerity and affection—but does it become us, at past threescore each, to be saying fine things to one another? Consider how soon we shall both be nothing!

3. In his *Essay on the Learning of Shakespeare*, 1767.
4. Cole's second copy reads 'I know then it.'
4a. HW's favourite writer of fairy tales.
5. As the letter is missing, it is almost certain that HW destroyed it.

I assure you, with great truth, I am at this present[6] very sick of my little vapour of fame. My tragedy has wandered into the hands of some banditti booksellers, and I am forced to publish it myself to prevent piracy. All I can do is to condemn it myself, and that I shall.[7]

I am reading Mr Pennant's new *Welsh Tour;* he has pleased me by making very handsome mention of you[8]—but I will not do what I have been blaming.

My poor dear Madame du Deffand's little dog[9] is arrived. She made me promise to take care of it the last time I saw her.[10] That I will most religiously, and make it as happy as is possible.[11]

I have not much curiosity to see your Cambridge Raphael,[12] but great desire to see you, and will certainly this summer accept your invitation, which I take much kinder than your *great character*— though both flowed from the same friendship. Mine for you is exactly what it has been ever since you knew (and few men can boast so uninterrupted a friendship as yours and that of)

Hor. Walpole

PS. I have seen the *Monthly Review.*[13]

From Cole, Monday 7 May 1781

VA, Forster MS 110, f. 255. Cole's copy, Add MS 5826, ff. 55v, 56v.
Address: The Honourable Horace Walpole, Berkeley Square, London.
Postmark: Cambridge 10 MA.

<Dea>r Sir,   Milton, Monday, May 7, 1781.

YOUR kind letter I received last night, and am infinitely obliged to you for every part of it, even for that wherein I am called to

6. Cole's second copy reads 'at this instant.'

7. *The Mysterious Mother* was published by Dodsley, 1781. HW's introductory explanation and condemnation is dated 'April 29, 1781.' HW heard of the banditti (not identified) from John Henderson (see HW to him 16 April 1781).

8. Pennant acknowledges that 'an old drawing' of a tomb, 'and some other ancient Welsh monuments were most obligingly presented to me by that excellent antiquary, the Rev. Mr William Cole, of

Milton near Cambridge; a gentleman to whom I have been frequently indebted for variety of useful information' (*Journey to Snowdon* 20 n).

9. Tonton.

10. 'should I survive her' (addition in Cole's second copy).

11. Cole's second copy reads 'as it is possible.'

12. Possibly Charles Freeman.

13. Cole obviously had mentioned the review of HW's *Anecdotes* in that magazine (see introductory note, 3 April 1781).

account for I know not what. You don't believe that I would tell a barefaced lie, and if I said what I conceived to be truth, neither you have cause to be offended nor I to be ashamed. It might be coarse and indelicate to say so much to your face, but I wrote in a great hurry, and this is all the submission I am willing to make about a trifle which seems to affect you too seriously.

Dr Farmer went to town on College business, and meant to have dined at St George's Feast.[1] However, he was, through much business, disappointed in both going among the Antiquaries and delivering my letter to you, which he returned the day after his arrival at Cambridge. When I see him next, I will communicate the contents of your most kind and friendly letter to him.[2] When he goes next to town I will inform you of it, and no doubt he will embrace your most kind invitation.

I am quite sorry that your tragedy has been purloined, and that it gives you so much uneasiness.

I have not seen Mr Pennant's book, nor did I know that he had mentioned me till your letter informed me of it.

I congratulate the little Parisian dog that he has fallen into the hands of so humane a master. I have a little dog,[3] full as great a favourite, and never out of my lap. I have already, in case of an accident, insured it a refuge from starvation and ill usage. It is the least one can do for poor, harmless, shiftless, pampered animals that have amused us and we have spoiled.

<Your ki>nd intention of seeing me this summer is highly flattering, but God knows whether I shall be able to get through it and reap the advantage of it. For the first time since 13 October I went to Cambridge on Friday last, and got home again by five.[4] The next day I was seized with the gout in one foot. Sunday it was gone in a manner, but today a little troublesome. This is the fourth attack since Christmas, so that it will be necessary to give me notice of your coming, lest I should receive you in my bedchamber.

I have within this fortnight entered into a new correspondence with Mr Nichols the printer, for whom I am now writing out[5] the

1. That is, the annual dinner of the Society of Antiquaries, 23 April.

2. Cole gave the original of HW's letter to Farmer (see introductory note to preceding letter).

3. Cole's copy reads 'a little diminutive dog, *Busy*.'

4. 'You know I never drink anything stronger than small beer and eat moderately, yet the next day . . .' (addition in Cole's copy).

5. 'with the assistance of my servant' (addition in Cole's copy).

oration of Sir Thomas Higgons at the funeral of the Countess of Essex, his wife.[6] I hope his next number of the *Bibliotheca Topographica Britannica* will be more amusing than his first,[7] than which nothing can be more discouraging to subscribers. I could not have been employed at a worse time than when my hand can hardly subscribe myself, though my heart most affectionately does, dear Sir,

Your most obliged and faithful servant,

Wm Cole

To Cole, Saturday 16 June 1781

Add MS 5953, ff. 121–2.

HW dated the letter 'May 16, 1781,' but Cole corrected it to 'June 16, 1781,' and in his copy (Add MS 5826, f. 56v) he wrote *'June* it should be.' See also the postmark below. It is printed 'May 16' in Toynbee.

Address: To the Reverend Mr Cole at Milton near Cambridge.
Postmark: Isleworth 16 IV.

Strawberry Hill, June 16, 1781.

YOUR last account of yourself was so indifferent, that I am impatient for a better; pray send me a much better.

I know little in your way but that Sir Richard Worseley has just published a *History of the Isle of Wight,* with many views poorly

6. *A Funerall Oration spoken over the Grave of ye Lady Elizabeth, Countess of Essex, by her husband Mr. Higgons, at her interment in ye Cathedrall church of Winchester Sept. 16th, 1656. Imprinted at London, 1656.* Cole's copy of the oration (which is extremely rare in printed form) is in Add MS 5830, f. 122 ff. Nichols acknowledged the copy which Cole sent to him, in the following words: 'By the favour of the Rev. Mr Cole of Milton, I have a transcript of the very curious *Oration* of Sir Thomas Higgons, which may perhaps be communicated to the public' (*Select Collection of Poems,* 8 vols, 1780–2, viii. 281). Apparently Nichols never printed the oration. It was reprinted in *Miscellanies of the Philobiblon Society,* vol. 3, 1856–7.

Elizabeth Paulet (d. 1656), dau. of Sir William Paulet, and widow of Robert Devereux (d. 1646), E. of Essex (from

whom she had been separated soon after marriage), m. (1647 or 1648) Thomas Higgons (1624–91), of Grewell Manor, Hants, diplomatist and author, who was knighted in 1663.

7. Nichols published *Bibliotheca Topographica Britannica,* 8 vols, 1780–90, and *Miscellaneous Antiquities, in continuation of the Bibliotheca Topographica Britannica,* 4 vols [1774–1819]. The first number contained 'Queries for the better illustrating the Antiquities and Natural History of Great Britain and Ireland,' and 'The History and Antiquities of Tunstall in Kent. By the late Mr Edward Rowe Mores.' After he had read this number, Cole wrote to Nichols 4 April 1781, and again 14 April and 6 May 1781 (see LA i. 661–4), offering additions and corrections. This was the beginning of a correspondence that lasted until Cole's death.

done enough.[1] Mr Bull is honouring me, at least my *Anecdotes of Painting*, exceedingly. He has let every page into a pompous sheet, and is adding every print of portrait, building, etc., that I mention and that he can get, and specimens of all our engravers. It will make eight magnificent folios, and be a most valuable body of our arts.[2]

Nichols the printer has published a new *Life of Hogarth*[3] of near 200 pages—many more in truth than it required—chiefly it is *the life* of his works, containing all the variations, and notices of any persons whom he had in view. I cannot say there are discoveries of many prints which I have not mentioned, though I hear Mr Gulston says he has fifteen such—but I suppose he only fancies so. Mr Nichols says our print-sellers are already adding Hogarth's name to several spurious. Mr Stevens,[4] I hear, has been allowed to ransack Mrs Hogarth's[5] house for obsolete and unfinished plates, which are to be completed and published. Though she was not pleased with my account of her husband,[6] and seems by these transactions to have encouraged the second,[7] I assure you I have much more reason to be satisfied than she has, the editor or editors being much civiller to living me than to dead Hogarth—yet I should not have complained. Everybody has the same right to speak their sentiments. Nay, in general I have gentler treatment than I expected, and I think the world and I part good friends.

1. Sir Richard Worsley (1751–1805), 7th Bt, Governor of the Isle of Wight, published *The History of the Isle of Wight*, 1781. The dedication to the King is dated 4 June 1781. Most of the views were engraved by Richard Bernard Godfrey and Thomas Vivares 'in so miserable a style, that they are far below the recompense of so munificent a patron as . . . the . . . editor' (GM Aug. 1781, li. 372a). One plate by William Watts and another by Peter Mazell are better.

2. The copy of HW's *Anecdotes*, enlarged to 14 vols imperial folio, descended to the poet Swinburne, through his grandmother, Lady Swinburne, granddaughter of Bull's wife by her first marriage. This copy of *Anecdotes* was sold at Sotheby's 29 April–1 May 1880 for £1,800. The library was described (without Bull's name) as 'collected, and many of the books tastefully illustrated, by an intimate friend of Horace Walpole, Earl of Orford' (W. P. Courtney, 'Richard Bull,' N&Q 1 March 1913, 11th Ser. vii. 171).

3. *Biographical Anecdotes of William Hogarth, and a Catalogue of his Works chronologically arranged; with occasional Remarks*, 1781. Pp. 157. HW's copy, with several MS notes, is now WSL. Nichols was largely indebted to HW's account, as he fully acknowledged.

4. George Steevens (1736–1800), commentator on Shakespeare, friend of Johnson and Cole, and acquaintance of HW.

5. Jane Thornhill (1709?–89), only dau. of Sir James Thornhill, m. (1729) William Hogarth (1697–1764). Her house was in Leicester Fields (see John Nichols, *Biographical Anecdotes of William Hogarth*, 3d edn, 1785, p. xix).

6. Cf. HW to Mrs Hogarth 4 October 1780.

7. That is, Nichols's *Biographical Anecdotes*.

I am now setting about the completion of my *Aedes Strawber-rianae.* A painter[8] is to come hither on Monday to make a drawing of the Tribune and finish T. Sandby's fine view of the Gallery, to which I could never get him to put the last hand. They will then be engraved with a few of the chimneypieces,[9] which will complete the plates. I must add an appendix of curiosities purchased or acquired since the *Catalogue* was printed. This will be awkward, but I cannot afford to throw away an hundred copies.[10] I shall take care, if I can, that Mr Gough does not get fresh intelligence from my engravers, or he will advertise my supplement before the book appears.[11] I do not think it was very civil to publish such private intelligence, to which he had no right, without my leave—but everybody seems to think he may do what is good in his own eyes. I saw the other day in a collection of prints of seats[12] (exquisitely engraved) a very rude insult on the Duke of Devonshire. The designer went to draw a view of Chiswick,[13] without asking leave, and was—not hindered, for he has given it, but he says he was treated *illiberally,* the house not being shown without tickets, which he not only censures, but calls a singularity, though a frequent practice in other places, and practised *there* to my knowledge for these thirty years[14]—So

8. Edward Edwards (1736–1806), A.R.A. He was much employed at SH 1781–3, and wrote *Anecdotes of Painters who have resided or been born in England . . . Intended as a continuation to the Anecdotes of Painting by the late Horace Earl of Orford,* 1808. HW pasted the drawings of the Tribune and Gallery in his extra-illustrated copy of the 1784 *Description of SH,* now WSL. Both of these drawings were engraved by Thomas Morris (fl. 1780–1800) for the *Description of SH.*

9. Prints of the chimneys of the Great Parlour, China Room, Yellow Bedchamber, Blue Bedchamber, Round Room, and the Screen of the Holbein Chamber appeared in the 1784 *Description of SH.* All except those of the China Room and the Round Room are signed 'T. Morris,' and they are in his style.

10. HW changed his plan and in 1784 printed a new edition with additions.

11. See *ante* 30 Nov. 1780.

12. *The Seats of the Nobility and Gentry, in a Collection of the most interesting & picturesque Views, engraved by W. Watts. From Drawings by the most eminent Artists. With Descriptions of each View. Published by W. Watts.* The book appeared in parts, Chelsea, 1779–86. HW's copy was sold SH vii. 134 (London 926).

13. Chiswick House, Middlesex, the seat of the Duke of Devonshire. This is Plate XXX, and is dated May 1781.

14. Watts concludes his description: 'It is somewhat remarkable that no persons are admitted to see this place without tickets for that purpose, a ceremony, we believe, not observed at any other seat in the kingdom; and that upon admission you are prohibited from making any drawings. The author of this publication, unacquainted with these particulars, met with very disagreeable treatment, in consequence of having taken some sketches of the building. This illiberal injunction is the more extraordinary, as plans and elevations of the house have been published many years since by Kent.'

THE OAKEN HEAD OF HENRY III

everybody is to come into your house, if he pleases, draw it, whether you please or not, and by the same rule, I suppose, put anything into his pocket that he likes. I do know by experience what a grievance it is to have a house worth being seen, and though I submit in consequence to great inconveniences, they do not save me from many rudenesses. Mr Southcote[15] was forced to shut up his garden, for the savages, who came as connoisseurs, scribbled a thousand brutalities, in the buildings, upon his religion. I myself at Canons[16] saw a beautiful table of Oriental alabaster that had been split in two by a buck in boots jumping up backwards to sit upon it.

I have placed the oaken head of Henry III over the middle arch of the Armory.[17] Pray tell me what the Church of Barnwell near Oundle was, which his Majesty endowed, and whence his head came.

Yours most sincerely,

H. W.

15. 'Philip Southcote, Esq., a Roman Catholic gentleman, second husband of Anne Pulteney, Duchess Dowager of Cleveland, . . . was the first designer of the *ferme ornée*. . . . Wooburn Farm near Weybridge in Surrey, where Mr Southcote displayed his peculiar style with happiness and taste, is the habitation of such nymphs and shepherds as are represented in landscapes and novels, but do not exist in real life' (HW's note, in *Satirical Poems published anonymously by William Mason with Notes by Horace Walpole*, ed. Paget Toynbee, Oxford, 1926, pp. 39–40). Southcote died 25 Sept. 1758 (see Musgrave, *Obituary*). His seat had the reputation of being 'one of the most charming retreats in the neighbourhood of London' (*Oxford Magazine*, Aug. 1772, ix. 66).

16. The magnificent seat of James Brydges (1673–1744), 1st D. of Chandos, near Edgware, Middlesex, built ca 1712 at an estimated cost of £200,000 or £250,000 and sold by auction in 1747 for the materials, which were largely bought by William Hallett, the cabinetmaker, who erected a new house on the site (see DNB). Pope's *Epistle to Lord Burlington*, 1731, contains the famous description of Timon's villa, which was immediately identified with Canons in spite of Pope's denial.

17. 'over the middle arcade [on the staircase at SH] is a curious ancient head of Henry III carved in alto-rilievo on oak, from the Church of Barnwell near Oundle in Northamptonshire, which he endowed. This head is very like to the effigies on his tomb, and to that in painted glass in the Chapel here at Strawberry Hill' (*Description of SH, Works* ii. 439). The Church of Barnwell St Andrew was built during the last half of the thirteenth century, which would explain the presence of Henry III's head there, but apparently no record exists of his endowment of it (see *The Victoria History of the County of Northampton*, ed. Wm Page, vol. 3, 1930, p. 74). The head was drawn by John Carter (see illustration) and is now WSL. See also Lort to HW 23 Dec. 1780. A print of it appears in Carter's *Specimens of the Ancient Sculpture and Painting now remaining in England*, new edn, 1838, plate lxxviii, p. 108. Below this drawing HW has pasted a second drawing, probably also by Carter, which shows where the head was found forty years before in the church. An inscription explains how it came to a Dr Palmer of Peterborough, from whom HW probably bought it. It was sold SH xix. 84 to Lord Lilford.

From COLE, Saturday 30 June 1781

VA, Forster MS 110, ff. 256–7. COLE's copy, Add MS 5826, f. 57v.

The letter was not posted until a week after Cole began it (see postmark below).

Address: To the Honourable Horace Walpole at Strawberry Hill in Twickenham, Middlesex. *Postmark:* Cambridge 7 IY.

Milton, Saturday, June 30, 1781.

Dear Sir,

I HAVE been so ill with a complication of gout, gravel, fever, etc., that I was less desirous of answering your last kind letter than I should otherwise have been. However, I dined yesterday at Cambridge, and find myself today, as usual, worse for my stirring. This hot weather kills me.

I have read Sir Richard Worseley's book, and am delighted that gentlemen of fortune will condescend to turn their minds that way. I should have liked it better had it been more ecclesiastical: no monuments, no epitaphs in churches, no account of successions in parish churches.

Hogarth's Life I have not yet seen, but am amazed that Mrs Hogarth should be offended at your fine and delicate character of her husband. I defy any other pencil to do him such strict and real justice, and at the same time to draw such a finished picture of him. Your apologies for his defects are such encomiums as would rejoice the heart of anyone else.

By this post I write to Mr Gough, from whom I have not heard before these six months, but he and Mr Nichols, I find, will fully employ me if I attend to all their queries: indeed they had fatigued me already. <He> shall not be informed by me of your *Aedes Strawberrianae,* which <I long> to see published; and though you have an hundred copies of the catalogue by you, I think that should not prevent your giving a complete book <of> the curiosities of your Paradise.[1]

I am afraid that I am not well with Dr Lort,[2] from whom I have never heard since I wrote to you and him by the same post,[3] relating

1. Cole's copy reads 'your charmingly singular mansion.'

2. Obliterated in MS; supplied from Cole's copy.

3. See *ante* 7 March 1781.

to the *Walpoliana*. What confirms me in my suspicion is that he has employed a common friend, Dr Collignon,[4] to ask me the price of a large Cotenham cheese I sent to him some time before, and meant as a present, but for which he insists to pay me. I shall be extremely sorry to lose his friendship, as I have received many obligations from him, and always esteemed him an unpolished diamond, but a most virtuous and honest man, yet what I did I should do again. I named him not in my letter to you, and desired you not to give any insinuation that you had received that advertisement from, dear Sir,

Your ever faithful servant,

Wm Cole

I am sorry I can't answer your query about Oundle,[5] but I have consulted Tanner,[6] Camden, Morton,[7] etc. The new *History of Northampton*[8] I have not complete, and so can give no account of it.

Mr Gough says that the large print,[9] companion to the Windsor picture,[10] will be delivered in about a month, and that the sixth volume of the *Archaeologia* is in the press.[11]

Since I wrote this, I received a letter from Lambeth,[12] dated June 30, in which I discover no resentment: and yesterday the gout made an attack on my right foot, which is the [more] troublesome as I have hardly been ever free from it for many months, and had a respite of only three or four days.—Monday, July 2.

Dr Lort says that the Dean of Exeter[13] and Mr Bryant[14] are both

4. Charles Collignon (1725–85), physician; Professor of Anatomy at Cambridge, 1753–85.

5. Cole's copy reads 'Barnwell,' which is correct (see preceding letter).

6. Thomas Tanner (1674–1735), *Notitia Monastica*, Oxford, 1695; 2d edn, ed. John Tanner, 1744.

7. John Morton (1671?–1726), *The Natural History of Northamptonshire; with some Account of the Antiquities*, 1712.

8. *The History and Antiquities of Northamptonshire. Compiled from the manuscript collections of the late . . . John Bridges*, by Peter Whalley, 2 vols, Oxford, [1762–]1791. At this time only the first volume and part of the second had been published (see *ante* 16 May 1762 n. 42).

9. 'The Embarkation of King Henry VIII at Dover, May 31, 1520, preparatory to his interview with the French King Francis I, from the original picture 12 feet and 1 inch in length, and 6 feet 5 inches in height, preserved in the Royal Apartments in Windsor Castle, with an historical description.' It sold for £1.11.6 (see *Archaeologia* vi. 415). It was engraved by J. Basire after a drawing by S. H. Grimm.

10. 'Le Champ de Drap d'Or' (see *ante* 12 Feb. 1773).

11. It bears the date of 1782 on the title-page. It was delivered to the members of the Society of Antiquaries in Nov. 1782, but was not advertised for sale until the beginning of Feb. 1783 (see GM Feb. 1783, liii. 149b).

12. That is, from Lort.

13. Jeremiah Milles, whose edition of *Poems, supposed to have been written at*

engaged in researches to settle Rowley's authenticity, and he seems inclined to be of the same side. I was in hopes that controversy was put a stop to by your pamphlet.[15]

From COLE, Monday 23 July 1781

VA, Forster MS 110, f. 258. COLE's copy, Add MS 5826, ff. 57v, 58v.

Address: For the Honourable Horace Walpole at Strawberry Hill in Twickenham, Middlesex. *Postmark:* Cambridge 25 IY.

Milton, Monday, July 23, 1781.

\<De\>ar Sir,

THOUGH I wrote last, I have no objection to scribble again, having met with a curious passage in Matthew Paris's *Life of Paul Abbot of St Albans*,[1] who was elected to that office *anno* 1077, giving an account of a very early architect, one Robert, who built not only the monastery, for the chiefest part, but also that noble pile the Abbey Church, now existing. I thought it so particular that, if not already apprised of it, you would be glad to have it.

Multa ad Firmam dimisit improvide (viz: Paulus Abbas) non precavens sibi de Fallaciis et Cavillationibus nequam Sæculi subsequentis . . . Tradidit ad Firmam Petro Seniori de Valoniis Silvam quæ dicitur de Northaga, &c. . . .

Concessit etiam Roberto Cementario, et Heredibus suis, pro Artificio suo et Labore (quibus præ omnibus Cæmentariis suo Tempore pollebat) Terram de Syret, et Terram de Wanthonio, et unam Domum in Villa de

---

Bristol in the Fifteenth Century, by *Thomas Rowley* was published in Dec. 1781 (see *St James's Chronicle* 8–11 Dec. 1781), but the title-page is dated 1782.

14. His *Observations upon the Poems of Thomas Rowley: in which the Authenticity of those Poems is ascertained* was published about Dec. 1781 (see *St James's Chronicle*, 29 Nov.–1 Dec., 1–4, 4–6 Dec. 1781).

15. *Letter to the Editor of the Miscellanies of Thomas Chatterton*.

———

1. *Matthaei Paris . . . Historia Major . . . Huic primum editioni accesserunt . . . viginti trium abbatum S. Albani vitae*

. . . ed. William Watts, London, 1640. An edition of this work appeared in Paris, 1644, and another at London, 1684. The source of Cole's text has not been located. It does not agree with that of the first two editions, and as the third edition is practically the same as the first, it is probably not copied from it (see 1st edn 52–3; 2d edn 33; *Gesta Abbatum Monasterii Sancti Albani, a Thomas Walsingham*, ed. Henry Thomas Riley, 3 vols, 1867–9, i. 62–4). The extract is quoted from Cole's letter *verbatim et literatim*. He invariably abbreviates *Sancti* and *Sancto* to *Sci* and *Sco*, the result of long experience in transcribing.

Sco' Albano, solutam et quietam. Hanc nempe Terram de Syret, Uxor Derlewini prius tenuerat, pro qua reddebat unoquoque anno 60 solidos Eccliae' Sci' Albani. Abbas autem Paulus Laborem ejusdem Roberti in Pecunia pacta et taxa persolvisse, sine Ecclesiae' Gravamine, tenebatur. Porro deinde aliquanti Temporis elapso Curriculo, idem Robertus, sibi conscius quod legitimum Ingressum non habuerat (unde Murmur in Conventu personuit) in Infirmitate ultima, qua et mortuus est, Terram præfatam de Syret, solutam et quietam ab omni Calumnia, tam sui, quam Heredum suorum, resignavit coram Hamelino Priore Sci' Albani, ut in Dominico esset Monachorum, sicut antea fuit.

In the most curious Book of St Albans, now lodged in Benet College Library, I formerly, though I had forgotten it, took the following extract.

Rodbertus Cementarius, Tempore Pauli Abbatis, circa Reedificationem hujus Eccliae fideliter laboravit, et singulis annis quamdiu vixit dedit decem Solidos Sco Albano.

His portrait is illuminated, among a vast number of other benefactors to that Abbey, and is the profile of a man in brownish hair. *Vide* my vol. 42,[2] p. 164.

I meant to have wrote more, but a young man of Trinity calling here this morning (July 24), after a most uncomfortable night with the gout in one foot, which came on on Sunday, I was glad of the opportunity of finishing this scrawl and subscribing myself, dear Sir,

Yours most sincerely,

WM COLE

To COLE, Thursday 26 July 1781

Add MS 5953, ff. 125–6.
Address: To the Reverend Mr Cole at Milton near Cambridge.
Postmark: Isleworth 26 IY.

Strawberry Hill, July 26, 1781.

I WILL not delay thanking you, dear Sir, for a second letter, which you wrote out of kindness, though I have time but to say a word, having my house full of company.[1] I think I have somewhere or other mentioned the *Robertus Caementarius* (probably on some

2. Now Add MS 5843.   1. See HW to Lady Ossory 25 July 1781.

former information from you, which you never forget to give me) at least the name sounds familiar to me[2]—but just now I cannot consult my papers or books from the impediment of my guests. As I am actually preparing a new edition of my *Anecdotes*,[3] I shall very soon have occasion to search.

I am sorry to hear you complain of the gout, but trust it will be a short parenthesis.

Yours most gratefully,

Hor. Walpole

From Cole, Sunday 5 August 1781

VA, Forster MS 110, ff. 259–60. Cole's copy, Add MS 5826, ff. 58v, 59v.
Address: For the Honourable Horace Walpole, Strawberry Hill, Twickenham, Middlesex. *Postmark:* Cambridge 6 AV.

Milton, Sunday, August 5, 1781.

Dear Sir,

AN article I saw in one of the London papers yesterday, that the Hon. Horace Walpole was married to Miss Churchill,[1] occasions you this trouble; and as your last letter of July 26 mentions your house being full of company, I was in doubt whether I ought not to congratulate you on the occasion. If it is so (as I don't believe), I do sincerely wish you every blessing of the married state, and every comfort in it. If it is so, it astonishes me, for I thought you as indisposed to be put out of your way as myself, but God disposes everything for the best, and whether married or single, you have my best wishes for your happiness in every department of life.

Poor Mr Cotton, eldest son of Sir John, last Monday morning going out before breakfast to shoot rabbits in the park, by accident the gun went off and shot him through the head.[2] It was so near the

2. HW is thinking of Richard de Gainsborough, whom Cole mentioned in his first letter to HW 16 May 1762. 'Robertus Caementarius' is not mentioned in *Anecdotes*.

3. The 3d edn, with additions, was published by Dodsley, 4 vols, 1782.

———

1. Hon. Horatio Walpole (1752–1822), eld. son of Horatio Walpole, Bn Walpole of Wolterton, afterwards (1806) 1st E. of Orford of the 3d creation. He m. (27 July 1781) Sophia Churchill (d. 1797), 2d dau. of Col. Charles Churchill, of Chalfont, Bucks, by Lady Mary Walpole, HW's half-sister (see following letter).

2. 'by the cheek-bone' (addition in Cole's copy).

house that the ladies[3] heard the report of it. They were uneasy at his not coming to breakfast, for he had shifted his coat and put on his shooting frock. As he did not come to dinner, they sent about to such places as was thought probable he might dine at, and was not found till next day by one of the servants. As Sir John's affairs were much embroiled, and some differences had been between them in point of <set>tlement (insomuch that the father and the three daughters had hired an house at Colchester, whither they were on the point of going, Mr Cotton having agreed to take the estate and to allow his father £600 per annum), it was reported that the son had shot himself, but I was assured by the surgeon, Mr Thackeray,[4] and Dr Pennington, the physician, whom I saw on Friday, who examined the body, that it was accidental. The brewhouse of the Parsons family[5] has been £40,000 detriment to Sir John's estate, and I am told that Lady or Mrs Parsons was in debt when Sir John married the daughter.[6]

I dined at Cambridge on Friday, and had the honour by compulsion of sitting next to the Duke of Rutland, who, though I voted against his brother, Lord Robert Manners, at the late election, was most gracious and civil to me, has promised me an heap of old evidences of his family and of Beauvoir Priory,[7] and invited me to Beauvoir Castle. I told his Grace that he honoured me greatly, but that I was sure never to be able to go out of this county. He said his brother has a great turn for antiquities, and what was more surprising, for the study of divinity. I told his Grace that I rejoiced at the first, but did not tell him that I was so at the second. Divines by profession have so puzzled and perplexed our faith that it is almost fribbled away to nothing, and when young noblemen undertake to

3. That is, his three sisters, Sarah, Anne and Lettice. Anne m., 23 Oct. 1793, at Madingley, Rev. John Oldershaw, fellow and tutor of Emmanuel College, afterwards (1797) Archdeacon of Norfolk and (1798) rector of Redenhall with Harleston (see GM Oct. 1793, lxiii. 957; *Supp.*, 1797, lxvii. 1137b; Sept. 1798, lxviii. 818b).

4. Thomas Thackeray (1736–1806), 4th son of Rev. Thomas Thackeray, headmaster of Harrow; an eminent surgeon at Cambridge. 'In his disposition he was kind and benevolent; in his manners mild and unassuming' (GM Dec. 1806, lxxvi. 1176b; *Eton Coll. Reg. 1698–1752*).

5. Cole's copy reads 'Alderman Parsons.'

6. John Cotton (he did not succeed to the baronetcy until 1752) m., 1 July 1745, Anne Parsons (d. 1769), 2d dau. of Alderman Humphrey Parsons by Sarah Crowley. It was reported that she brought her husband a fortune of £20,000 (see GM July 1745, xv. 388a).

7. Belvoir Priory, near Grantham in Leics, founded in 1077. On the dissolution of the monasteries, Henry VIII granted the lands to the Manners family. Belvoir Castle, the family seat, was rebuilt by James Wyatt in 1808–16 after a fire (Baedeker, *Great Britain*, 1927, p. 304).

write on the subject, their authority and new notions will not probably contribute much to the fixture of it, according to my old orthodox plan.

I do not remember to have mentioned Robertus Caementarius to you, for indeed I just met with it when I sent it to you piping hot: Alanus Strayler and Ricardus de Gainsburg I well remember to have mentioned to you;[8] the last Caementarius.

As you mention in your last a design of a new edition of your *Anecdotes,* perhaps you may not meet with a new catalogue of books by Berry, a bookseller of Norwich, to be sold the seventh of this month,[9] p. 37, in which your four volumes of that work are marked at ten guineas, the prints in them being a choice selection.

I will tease you no longer. Thank God, I have been for near a week better than these ten or eleven months, and am

Most assuredly yours,

WM COLE

To COLE, Tuesday 7 August 1781

Add MS 5953, ff. 123–4.

HW dated the letter 'July 7, 1781,' but the date, as appears from the postmark and from the contents of the letter (which is in answer to Cole's of 5 Aug.), should be *August* 7, 1781.

Address: To the Reverend Mr Cole at Milton near Cambridge.
Postmark: Isleworth 7 AV.

Strawberry Hill, July [August] 7, 1781.

MY good Sir, you forget that I have a cousin, eldest son of Lord Walpole and of a marriageable age, who has the same Christian name as I. The Miss Churchill he has married, is my niece, second daughter of my sister Lady Mary Churchill, so that if I were in

---

8. See *ante* 16 May 1762, 31 July 1762.
9. *A Catalogue of a Numerous and Valuable Collection of Books, many of them extremely rare and in elegant Bindings . . . and will begin to be sold on Tuesday, Aug. 7, 1781. By J*[ohn] *and C*[hristopher] *Berry, Bookseller, in Norwich at the prices marked in the Catalogues, and in the first*

leaf of each book. . . . It was advertised, 'This day was published,' in the *St James's Chronicle* 24–6 and 26–8 July 1781. John Berry died 14 July 1789, when he was succeeded by his brother Christopher [Charles?] and —— Rochester (see LA viii. 467).

my dotage, I must have looked out for another bride—in short, I hope you will have no occasion to wish me joy of any egregious folly. I do congratulate you on your better health, and on the Duke of Rutland's civilities to you. I am a little surprised at his brother, who is a seaman, having a propensity to divinity and wonder you object to it: the Church Navigant would be an extension of its power. As to *orthodoxy;* excuse me, if I think it means nothing at all but every man's own opinion. Were every man to define his faith, I am persuaded that no two men are or ever were exactly of the same opinion in *all* points; and as men are more angry at others for differing with them on a single point, than satisfied with their concurrence in all others, each would deem everybody else a heretic. Old or new opinions are exactly of the same authority, for every opinion must have been new when first started, and no man has or ever had more right than another to dictate, unless inspired. St Peter and St Paul disagreed from the earliest time, and who can be sure which was in the right? And if one of the apostles was in the wrong, who may not be mistaken? When you will tell me which was the orthodox, and which the heterodox apostle, I will allow that you know what orthodoxy is. You and I are perhaps the two persons who agree the best with very different ways of thinking—and perhaps the reason is, that we have a mutual esteem for each other's sincerity, and from an experience of more than forty years are persuaded that neither of us has any interested views. For my own part I confess honestly that I am far from having the same charity for those whom I suspect of mercenary views. If Dr Butler,[1] when a private clergyman, wrote Whig pamphlets, and when Bishop of Oxford preaches Tory sermons, I should not tell him that he does not know what orthodoxy is, but I am convinced that he does not care what it is. The Duke of Rutland seems much more liberal than Butler or I, when he is so civil to you, though you voted against his brother. I am not acquainted with his Grace, but I respect his behaviour: he is above prejudices.

1. John Butler (1717–1802), a popular London preacher; chaplain to George III; Bp of Oxford 1777, and of Hereford 1788. His 'Whig pamphlets' include, notably, *An Address to the Cocoa Tree, from a Whig*, 1762, in which he attacked Bute and the conduct of the ministry after the accession of George III. Later, however, he became a strong Tory, and supported the policy of Lord North. HW, at the request of his brother Sir Edward, recommended Butler to Lord Hertford as chaplain to George III, but after Butler's change of political opinions, HW heartily condemned him (see, e.g., *Last Journals* i. 103, 594; to Mason 25 April 1781).

The story of poor Mr Cotton is shocking whatever way it happened, but most probably it was accident.

I am ashamed at the price of my books, though not my fault—but I have too often been guilty myself of giving ridiculous prices for rarities, though of no intrinsic value, that I must not condemn the same folly in others. Everything tells me how silly I am!—I pretend to reason, and yet am a virtuoso!—Why should I presume that at sixty-four I am too wise to marry?—And was you, who know so many of my weaknesses, in the wrong to suspect me of one more?—Oh! no, my good friend; nor do I see anything in your belief of it, but the kindness with which you wish me felicity on the occasion. I heartily thank you for it, and am

Most cordially yours,

Hor. Walpole

From Cole, Saturday 22 December 1781

VA, Forster MS 110, f. 261. Cole's copy, Add MS 5826, ff. 60v, 61v.
Address: For the Honourable Horace Walpole in Berkeley Square, London.
Postmark: Only a small part of the postmark is visible, but enough to indicate that the letter was posted in London and sent by the Penny Post.

Dear Sir,   Milton, Dec. 22, 1781.

WHEN I look at your last letter it startles me, yet I am not totally without excuse. I was loath to trouble you unnecessarily, and have been confined for three months with a constant indisposition both of mind and body, so that I have had no inclination to write or do anything. About ten days ago this hovering gout fixed itself in one foot, and gives me better spirits and an ability to write. Last year from 13 of October for seven months I never crossed my threshold: how it will fare with me this year, God knows, but it begins awkwardly.

I have not yet seen our President's book.[1] Mr Bryant's[2] was presented to me. He seems, notwithstanding a great appearance of candour, to be very angry, encouraged by some more angry.

---

1. Milles's edition of the Rowley *Poems* (see *ante* 30 June 1781).
2. Dr Glynn gave his *Observations* to

Cole (see Cole to Lort 31 Dec. 1781; la i. 672).

I had a letter about a fortnight or three weeks ago from Mr Gough, with some proof sheets of a new and expensive work[3] he is engaged in, which I think would please you, and if you choose it, I will send it up to you. This is the third or fourth time within these ten years that he has hinted to me how gladly he would gain your favour. In no letter or by word of mouth did I ever give him the least encouragement to think I would endeavour it, for I knew your just exceptions, and besides, he never was a favourite of mine, though I honour his industry. So you may do as you like about it. If I send you his plan, I will take no notice of your approbation or dislike of it. In short, I might have nothing else to do but to write from morning to night, was I to comply with all his wants.

Mr Tyson some years ago passing by Blecheley, I desired him to copy for me a portrait of Mr Browne Willis.[4] It has laid by me these ten years, but having got acquainted within these two years with a most ingenious and polite gentleman, George Steevens,[5] Esq., of Hampstead Heath, he offered to etch me any portrait I chose to have done. I gladly embraced his kind offer, and he struck off fifty copies of Mr Tyson's copy for me, but as the sketch was done negligently, though very like the original, and his was only a facsimile, he did not choose to put his name to it.[6] I beg your acceptance of one of them for your collection, and if you would have more, I will send them.

3. *Sepulchral Monuments in Great Britain*, 2 vols, 1786–96. The work is usually bound in five parts. It does not appear what part of the work was in proof at this time.

Gough to Cole 28 Nov. 1781 (Add MS 5992, ff. 152–3) contains an account of Gough's plans to publish *Sepulchral Monuments*, which the Society of Antiquaries refused to support. Gough continues: 'I know not whether Mr Tyson ever dropped any hint of this to you. He wished me to consult you about it; he wished me also to have a sight of Mr Walpole's beautiful drawings—by your means. Mr W.'s collections and his use of them I look up to with envious reverence. I am afraid I am too active a member of an obnoxious Society and too uncourtly an antiquary to merit his regard. . . .'

4. Cole wrote to Granger 28 Dec. 1770: 'I long to have Mr Browne Willis's portrait engraved. I mentioned it to Mr Tyson near two years ago, when he promised me to

take a copy of a picture of him which I told him of, and do it himself' (Granger, *Correspondence* 343; the original letter is WSL). The portrait was by Michael Dahl (1656–1743).

5. Cole 'met him at dinner, with Dr Farmer, etc., at Dr Lort's chambers in Trinity College, Aug. 9, 1780. He is much of a gentleman, well bred, civil, and obliging' (LA ix. 803). Steevens bought several of Cole's books after his death (see *A Catalogue of the . . . Library of George Steevens, Esq.*, 1800, pp. 69–70 *et passim*).

6. 'The drawing . . . is so incorrect and slight that I could gain no credit by setting my name to the etching from it, which is a mere facsimile of the coarsest kind. The little reputation I may have gained by working on copper with the dry needle I should be sorry to lose by means of my present slovenly performance' (Steevens to Cole 30 Nov. 1781, Add MS 6401, f. 168). For Cole's opinion of the print, see LA vi. 208–9.

Mr Steevens, I know, would be delighted to see your place at Strawberry Hill and drawings. He has not desired me to ask that favour, yet I think, did you know him, that you would not be displeased with his amiable manner and ingenuity. He is quite the reverse of Mr G[ough].

I can write no m<ore th>an to assure you of my inviolable attachment and affectio<n, and> am,

Yours,

WM COLE

To COLE, Sunday 30 December 1781

Add MS 5953, ff. 127–8.

Address: [From COLE's copy, Add MS 5826, f. 61v.] To the Rev. Mr Cole at Milton near Cambridge.

Berkeley Square, Dec. 30, 1781.

WE are both hearty friends, my dear Sir, for I see we have both been reproaching ourselves with silence at the same moment. I am much concerned that you have had cause for yours. I have had less though indisposed too in a part material to correspondence, my right hand, which has been in labour of chalk-stones this whole summer, and at times so nervous as to tremble so much, that except when quite necessary, I have avoided a pen. I have been delivered of such a quantity of chalky matter, that I am not only almost free from pain, but hope to avoid a fit this winter. How there can be a doubt what the gout is, amazes me! What is it, but a concretion of humours, that either stop up the fine vessels, cause pain and inflammation, and pass away only by perspiration; or which discharge themselves into chalk-stones, which sometimes remain in their beds, sometimes make their passage outwardly. I have experienced all three. It may be objected that the sometimes instantaneous removal of pain from one limb to another is too rapid for a current of chalk —true, but not for the humour before coagulated. As there is evidently too a degree of wind mixed with the gout, may not that wind be impregnated with the noxious effluvia, especially as the latter are pent up in the body and may be corrupted!—I hope your present complaint in the foot will clear the rest of your person.

Many thanks for your etching of Mr Browne Willis: I shall value it not only as I am a collector, but because he was your friend.

What shall I say about Mr Gough? He is not a pleasant man, and I doubt will tease me with curiosity about many things, some of which I never cared about, and all which I interest myself very little about now, when I seek to pass my remnant in most indolent tranquillity. He has not been very civil to me, he worships the fools I despise, and I conceive has no genuine taste—yet as to trifling resentments, when the objects have not acted from bad hearts, I can most readily lose them. Please Mr Gough I certainly shall not: I cannot be very grave about such idle studies as his and my own, and am apt to be impatient or to laugh when people imagine I am serious about them. But there is a stronger reason why I shall not satisfy Mr Gough. He is a man to minute down whatever one tells him that he may call information, and whip it into his next publication. However, though I am naturally very frank, I can regulate myself by those I converse with; and as I shall be on my guard, I will not decline visiting Mr Gough, as it would be illiberal or look surly if I refused. You shall have the merit, if you please, of my assent, and shall tell him I shall be glad to see him any morning at eleven o'clock. This will save you the trouble of sending me his new work,[1] as I conclude he will mention it to me.

I more willingly assure you that I shall like to see Mr Steevens and to show him Strawberry. You never sent me a person whom you commended that I did not find deserved it.

You will be surprised when I tell you, that I have only dipped into Mr Bryant's book,[2] and lent the Dean's[3] before I had cut the leaves, though I had peeped into it enough to see that I shall not read it.[4] Both he and Bryant are so diffuse on our antiquated literature, that I had rather believe in Rowley than go through their proofs. Mr Warton[5] and Mr Tyrwhit[6] have more patience and in-

1. Proof sheets of part of the first volume of *Sepulchral Monuments*, which Gough had sent to Cole (see preceding letter).

2. *Observations upon the Poems of Thomas Rowley.* HW's copy is now WSL. It has several MS notes in HW's hand, which will be found in an Appendix to the HW–Chatterton correspondence.

3. Milles's edition of *Poems . . . by Thomas Rowley.* HW's copy is now in the British Museum. It has many MS notes in HW's hand (see Appendix to HW–Chatterton correspondence).

4. He read part of it a few days later and was 'stupefied by Dr Milles's wagon-load of notes on Rowley' (to Mason 3 Jan. 1782).

5. Thomas Warton wrote *An Enquiry into the Authenticity of the Poems attributed to Thomas Rowley. In which the Arguments of the Dean of Exeter, and Mr Bryant, are examined,* 1782. Below the date

tend to answer them—and so the controversy will be two hundred years out of my reach. Mr Bryant I did find begged a vast many questions, which proved to me his own doubts. Dr Glynn's foolish evidence[7] made me laugh—and so did Mr Bryant's sensibility *for me*. He says Chatterton treated me very *cruelly* in one of his writings.[8] I am sure I did not feel it so. I suppose Bryant means under the title of Baron of Otranto, which is written with humour. I must have been the sensitive plant, if anything in that character had hurt me! Mr Bryant too, and the Dean, as I see by extracts in the papers,[9] have decorated Chatterton with sanctimonious honour—think of that young rascal's note, where summing up his gains and losses by writing for and against Beckford,[10] he says, 'Am glad he is dead by 3*l.* 13*s.* 6*d.*'[11] *There* was a lad of too nice honour to be capable of forgery!— and a lad, who, they do not deny, forged the poems in the style of Ossian, and fifty other things. In the parts I did read,[12] Mr Bryant, as I expected, reasons admirably, and staggered me, but when I took up the poems, called Rowley's, again, I protest I cannot see the smallest air of any antiquity but the old words. The whole texture is conceived on ideas of the present century. The liberal manner of think-

---

HW has written in his copy (now wsl) 'March 21st.' It went into a second edition late in June of the same year (see *St James's Chronicle* 27–9 June, 2–4 July 1782).

6. Thomas Tyrwhitt wrote *A Vindication of the Appendix to the Poems, called Rowley's, in reply to the Answers of the Dean of Exeter, Jacob Bryant, Esquire,* 1782. Below the date HW has written in his copy (now wsl) 'August 7th.'

7. His evidence consisted of a dialogue between himself and William Smith, one of Chatterton's friends at Bristol, which Glynn 'wrote down with great accuracy' (see Jacob Bryant, *Observations* 527–34).

8. According to Bryant, Chatterton 'could never forgive those who controverted his assertions. Thus in a treatise, where he has subscribed himself by the title of Harry Wildfire, he falls very cruelly upon an honourable person whose rank and character deserved far greater respect. This gentleman had supposed the poems in question to be spurious; which was sufficient to make him incur the invective of Chatterton' (op. cit. 495–6). In

the passage to which Bryant refers, HW appears as Baron Otranto (see *ante* 17 Aug. 1778 n. 3).

9. Not located.

10. William Beckford (1709–70), Lord Mayor of London. Chatterton was 'perfectly frantic' at his death, as he expected support and favour from the Lord Mayor (see Meyerstein, *Chatterton* 381).

11. HW gives the note in his *Letter to the Editor of the Miscellanies of Thomas Chatterton,* 51–2 (*Works* iv. 231). It is an endorsement in Chatterton's hand on the back of his rejected 'Letter to the Lord Mayor Beckford.' 'Accepted by Bingley, set for and thrown out of the *North Briton,* 21 June, on account of the Lord Mayor's death.

	£	s.	d.
Lost by his death on this essay	1	11	6
Gained in elegies	2	2	0
in essays	3	3	0
Am glad he is dead by	3	13	6'

12. It appears from his marginalia that HW read the first twenty-nine pages, a section of 'References to Ancient Histories,' and the last 175 pages.

ing of a monk so long before the Reformation is as stupendous—and where he met with Ovid's *Metamorphosis,* eclogues and plans of Greek tragedies, when even Caxton, a printer, took Virgil's *Aeneid* for so rare a novelty, are not less incomprehensible—though on these things I speak at random, nor have searched for the era when the Greek and Latin classics came again to light—at present I imagine, long after our Edward IV.

Another thing struck me in my very cursory perusal of Bryant. He asks where Chatterton could find so much knowledge of English events?[13] I could tell him where he *might* by a very natural hypothesis, though merely an hypothesis. It appears by the evidence that Canninge left six chests of MSS, and that Chatterton got possession of some or several. Now what was therein *so probably* as a diary drawn up by Canninge himself or some churchwarden, or wardens, or by a monk or monks? Is anything more natural than for such a person amidst the events at Bristol to set down such other public facts as happened in the rest of the kingdom? Was not such almost all the materials of our ancient story? There is actually such an one, with some curious collateral facts, if I am not mistaken, for I write by memory, in the *History of Furnese* or *Fountain's Abbey,*[14] I forget which—if Chatterton found such an one, did he want the extensive literature on which so much stress is laid? Hypothesis for hypothesis, I am sure this is as rational an one, as the supposition that six chests were filled with poems never else heard of.[15]

These are my indigested thoughts on this matter—not that I ever intend to digest them—for I will not at 64 sail back into the fourteenth and fifteenth centuries, and be drowned in an ocean of monkish writers of those ages or of this!

Yours most sincerely,

H. WALPOLE

13. For Bryant's discussion of this matter, see especially *Observations* 479–80.

14. As no 'History of Fountains Abbey' existed at this time, HW almost certainly refers to *The Antiquities of Furness; or, An Account of the Royal Abbey of St Mary,* published by subscription in 1774, by Thomas West (1720–79), a Jesuit, and the author of *Guide to the Lakes,* 1778.

HW received the book as a present from Lord George Cavendish in 1774 (see HW to Conway 31 Dec. 1774). It contains extracts from the MSS of Thomas Park, High Constable of Furness, 1642–7 (see West, op. cit., pp. li–liii). HW's copy (B.2) was sold SH i. 133.

15. See also HW to Edmond Malone 4 Feb. 1782.

From COLE, Friday 4 January 1782

VA, Forster MS 110, ff. 262–3. COLE's copy, Add MS 5826, ff. 62v, 63v.
Address: To the Honourable Horace Walpole, Berkeley Square, London.
Postmark: [Cambridge 5] IA.

Milton, Jan. 4, 1782.

\<De\>ar Sir,

I COULD never repay a tenth part of my obligations to you, for your unalterable friendship and kindnesses throughout a long life, was I to live to the age of Methusalem. Your politeness last summer in accepting my recommendation of Dr Farmer, who has never been in London since, your present extreme kindness in regard to Mr Gough, but particularly to Mr Steevens, can never be forgotten. I would not have offered to have mentioned the last had I not thought his gentlemanly behaviour would never be troublesome to you. In respect to the other, I had my doubts, and left it to yourself, yet could hardly avoid saying something, his applications had been so frequent. I shall be extremely sorry if he is troublesome, as I a little suspect he may, but you may easily, I hope, if you find him so, seclude him. I a little suspect he is disgusted with the Antiquary Society by a passage in his proposed book.[1] I have a great desire to send you his letter[2] and his proof of his book, and will, if I can meet with a convenient conveyance, as also Mr Steevens's last letter, whose sentiments about Bryant and the Dean are so correspondent to yours.[3]

Since my last, the gout has shifted from my feet into my left hand, and I don't know I ever suffered more pain and sleepless nights than for these ten days. I think, and have said so these two years, that a chalky matter is forming in a joint of my middle finger, on which I have worn a flannel cot for all that time. It is uneasy to write even with my well hand, and how you managed when your right hand was so disordered with chalkstones, I cannot conceive. I think it very

1. That is, in a passage in the proof sheets of *Sepulchral Monuments* (see *ante* 22 Dec. 1781).

2. See *ante* 22 Dec. 1781 n. 3.

3. Steevens to Cole 25 Dec. 1781 (Add MS 6401, f. 170) contains the following passage: 'Neither Bryant nor Mills [*sic*] will gain additional credit by their respective works. Remove misinformation, misinterpretation, a plentiful crop of blunders, and a sufficient degree of ignorance of the ancient English language, and not much will be left for their purpose. Tyrwhitt is preparing to answer them both. Some parts of Mills's performance confute the rest, and much of Glynn's evidence (conveniently enough for his reputation) seems to be suppressed in Bryant's book.'

severe that you and I, temperate men, originally water-drinkers all
our lives, should thus be tormented with so cruel a distemper. But
God's will be done: if we laid upon roses all our lives, the ending of
it would be most miserable to us. These things qualify us to quit it
without so great regret.

Mr Bryant's remark about the Baron of Otranto I don't so well
comprehend, as I never met with the book,[4] but I think his qualified
expression in respect to Chatterton's burning all Rowley's poems, p.
228,[5] might have been spared. Mr Bryant, though my old friend and
acquaintance, I ever looked on to have the greatest share of the pride
of science about him, with a great show of modesty, candour and
condescension, that I ever met with. After your masterly and unan-
swerable narrative, I think you are wise to say no more about a subject that bids fair to be as voluminous as the Bangorian controversy.[6]
I can write no more, but to assure you of the most invariable esteem
and affection of, dear Sir,

Yours most sincerely,

WM COLE

The Earl of Hereford[7] is rather an equivocal addition to your
Noble Authors, as Mr Bryant at last makes him only an encourager
and not the translator of the old poem.

In the *Gentleman's Magazine* for last month, p. 555, etc., you will
see a good letter on Rowley,[8] and at p. 570 a letter from your father
to General Churchill.[9]

4. That is, Chatterton's *Miscellanies,*
1778, which contained 'Memoirs of a Sad
Dog.' Cf. *ante* 17 Aug. 1778 n. 3.

5. 'In short, I [Bryant] am persuaded
that Rowley made a large collection of
obsolete writings, both in prose and verse.
. . . He [Chatterton] would have faithfully produced them to the world. But his
veracity being questioned, and his pride
repeatedly hurt, it produced in him an un-
conquerable resentment, and there is reason to think that he consigned the greater
part of them to the flames. Thus have we
by some very justifiable, but unfortunate,
scruples been deprived of an inestimable
treasure' (*Observations* 227–8).

6. Benjamin Hoadly (1676–1761), Bp of
Bangor 1715–21, by his *Preservative against
Principles and Practices of the Nonjurors,*
1716, and his sermon *The Nature of the*

Kingdom or Church of Christ, 1717, caused
the Bangorian controversy (1717–20) and
the silencing of convocation.

7. 'Humphrey de Bohun' (addition in
Cole's copy). Humphrey de Bohun (1309?–
61), 6th E. of Hereford, is mentioned by
Bryant (ibid. 14–23) in connection with a
MS poem in the Library of King's College.

8. The letter was by Edmond Malone
(it is signed 'Misopiclerus'), and appeared
originally in GM 1781, li. 555–9, 609–15. Dr
R. W. Chapman suggests that 'misopicle-
rus' is a mis-reading for 'myopiclerus'—
Μυωπικληρος. Malone revised and en-
larged it, and published it under the title
*Cursory Observations on the Poems attrib-
uted to Thomas Rowley . . . with some
Remarks on the Commentaries on those
Poems, by the Rev. Dr Jeremiah Milles,
Dean of Exeter, and Jacob Bryant, Esq.;*

To Cole, Sunday 27 January 1782

Add MS 5953, ff. 129–30.
Address: To the Reverend Mr Cole at Milton near Cambridge.
Postmark: 28 IA.

Berkeley Square, Jan. 27, 1782.

FOR these three weeks I have had the gout in my left elbow and hand, and can yet but just bear to lay the latter on the paper while I write with the other. However, this is no complaint; for it is the shortest fit I have had these sixteen years, and with trifling pain: therefore as the fits decrease, it does ample honour to my bootikins, regimen and method. Next to the bootikins, I ascribe much credit to a diet drink[1] of dock roots, of which Dr Turton[2] asked me for the receipt, as the best he had ever seen, and which I will send you if you please. It came from an old physician of Richmond,[3] who did amazing service with it in inveterate scurvies, the parents, or ancestors at least, I believe of all gouts. Your fit I hope is quite gone.

Mr Gough has been with me—I never saw a more dry, or more cold gentleman. He told me his new plan[4] is a series of English monuments. I do like the idea; and offered to lend him drawings for it.[5]

I have seen Mr Stevens too, who is much more flowing. I wish you

and a Salutary Proposal addressed to the Friends of those Gentlemen, 1782. It went into a second edition, 'revised and augmented,' about the middle of Feb. (see St James's Chronicle 14–16 Feb. 1782). HW's copy of the second edition is now wsl (see Appendix to HW–Chatterton correspondence).

9. The letter is dated 24 June 1743. 'General Churchill' was Charles Churchill (d. 1745), natural son of the famous General Charles Churchill (1656–1714). Politically he was long connected with the Walpole family, and his natural son Charles (1721?–1812) m. (1746) Lady Mary Walpole, Sir Robert's natural dau. (see GM May 1745, xv. 276b; DNB, sub Oldfield, Anne, and Churchill, Charles). The original of this letter was sold by the American Art Association–Anderson Galleries 25 Nov. 1936 (lot 1593) to wsl. It has since been inadvertently destroyed. Its first appearance in print seems to be in A Select Collection

of Original Letters by the Most Eminent Persons . . . from the Reign of Henry the Eighth to the Present Times, 2 vols, 1755, ii. 227.

---

1. See *post* 14 Feb. 1782.
2. John Turton (1735–1806), Fellow of the Royal College of Physicians, 1768; physician to George III and the royal family.
3. Not identified.
4. That is, his plan for *Sepulchral Monuments.*
5. Gough acknowledged his indebtedness to HW, who, 'with that readiness of communication which marks his character, indulged me with the free use of a number of drawings by Mr Vertue or Sir Charles Frederick, which he purchased among a vast fund of others at Mr Lethieullier's sale' (*Sepulchral Monuments*, vol. 1, pt 1, Preface, p. 10).

had told me it was the editor of Shakespeare,[6] for on his mentioning Dr Farmer, I launched out and said, he was by much the most rational of Shakespeare's commentators, and had given[7] the only sensible account of the authors our great poet had consulted. I really meant those who wrote before Dr Farmer. Mr Stevens seemed a little surprised, which made me discover the blunder I had made, for which I was very sorry, though I had meant nothing by it—however, don't mention it. I hope he has too much sense to take it ill, as he must have seen that I had no intention of offending him—on the contrary, that my whole behaviour marked a desire of being civil to him as your friend, in which light only you had named him to me. Pray, take no notice of it, though I could not help mentioning it, as it lies on my conscience to have been even undesignedly and indirectly unpolite to anybody you recommend. I should not, I trust, have been so unintentionally to anybody, nor with intention unless provoked to it by great folly or dirtiness. Adieu, my good Sir,

Yours sincerely,

H. W.

From COLE, Thursday 7 February 1782

VA, Forster MS 110, f. 264. Cole kept no copy.
Address: To the Honourable Horace Walpole in Berkeley Square, London.
Postmark: Cambridge 11 FE.

Milton, Feb. 7, 1782.

Dear Sir,

I HAVE been so incommoded with my left hand, into which the gout on Christmas Day entered, and after possession of a month, I thought was going to leave me, but it returned again and put me to some pain, and am afraid my fingers will never recover their right tone. You have more philosophy and patience than I have, and I am satisfied more pain also, yet your natural good spirits bears you up against this cruel distemper. I wish I knew your regimen and method, and shall be greatly obliged to you for the receipt of the

---

6. Steevens and Johnson published an edition of Shakespeare in 10 vols, 1773. The second edition, 'revised and augmented,' appeared in 1778 (see DNB).

7. In his *Essay on the Learning of Shakespeare.*

diet drink. I know the scurvy is at the bottom of all, but yet have no great dependence that anything will eradicate so inveterate an habit in such a shattered carcass as mine.

You are a complete master of your pencil: a more concise and true picture of Mr Gough's dryness and coldness never was taken. I much question, after all your favours and civilities to him, whether he will have the good manners to say, Thank you. I have sent you his three last letters to me, that you may see his eagerness for me to do what I hope I shall have no reason to repent of my acquiescence in.[1] You may send them back, or burn them. I send you also his proof of his intended work, as I find you have not yet seen it, and as I have this opportunity, I enclose an old piece of enamel which was lately given to me as a curiosity. It seems, by its ugliness, to be one of the first attempts, and so far may be worthy of attention: the figures are horrible, and it represents the Last Judgment. If you won't accept of it, return it to me by the same conveyance, though I have no value for it. I likewise enclose Mr Steevens's last letter, in order to convince you, that your conscience may be at rest, in respect to any supposed indelicacy you may have shown him.[2] I thought I had mentioned him as an editor of Shakespeare. He was a fellow-commoner of

1. Cole had lent to Gough his MS collections relating to Croyland Abbey (now Add MS 5845), and had promised to assist Gough in his *History and Antiquities of Croyland Abbey*, 1783 (No. XI of Nichols's *Bibliotheca Topographica Britannica*). See LA i. 693 ff. For Gough's acknowledgment of indebtedness to Cole, see *History and Antiquities of Croyland Abbey*, p. vi. The three letters from Gough are dated 13 Sept., 28 Nov. 1781 (see *ante* 22 Dec. 1781); and 28 Jan. 1782 (Add MS 5992, ff. 172–3, 152–5). In addition to his avowed purpose in sending the letters, Cole doubtless wished HW to see the following paragraphs:

'A variety of engagements put it out of my power to pay my respects to Mr Walpole before last Saturday. I had the most polite and obliging *accueil*, but I had not prepared myself for the probability of his monumental collections being at Strawberry Hill. He has, however, given me a most friendly invitation thither, and you may be sure I shall not decline it.

'As far as he could judge of my plan

without seeing it in black and white, he was pleased to approve it and give me every hope of his hearty concurrence in it' (28 Jan. 1782, Add MS 5992, f. 154).

2. 'On Saturday I paid Mr Walpole a visit. He received me with the utmost politeness, and promised me a future sight of his curiosities at Strawberry Hill. I found him crippled by the gout, but full of that vivacity and good sense that distinguishes all his productions. He is, like the rest of the world, bestowing much attention on the Rowleian controversy, and furnished me with many hints that will be useful hereafter on that popular subject. You know, I imagine, that Tyrwhitt, Tom Warton, Mr Malone and others have taken up their pens in opposition to the books of Bryant and Mills. My friend Dr Johnson says he is sorry for the former, who possesses a very great and deserved reputation; as to the Dean's performance, it is everywhere treated as it deserves, and to its fate he resigns it without concern' (Steevens to Cole 21 Jan. 1782, Add MS 6401, f. 171).

King's College the year after I quitted it.³ He has been so extremely civil to me ever since my acquaintance with him, that I should have been much hurt by any incivility to him, which I know is as far from your nature, as intention to do. You may depend on my not mentioning it.

In the *Gentleman's Magazine* for last December and 'Supplement,' is an admirable answer to the late advocates for Rowley. It is by the hand of a master, and I think I can guess at the writer.⁴

I have sent the parcel to Mr Nichols, printer in Red Lion Court, Fleet Street, to whom I was sending a seal of an old hospital at Leicester,⁵ and desired him to send it to you: and when you have done with the papers, I beg you will be pleased to send them to him, directed for me to be left at the Rose Tavern in Cambridge. He will send it to the fly in Grey's Inn Lane at the Queen's Head.

I have also sent you two more of Mr Willis's heads, to give away to your collecting friends: and am quite tired with writing, dear Sir,

Your most assured and faithful servant,

WM COLE

From COLE, Monday 11 February 1782

VA, Forster MS 110, ff. 265–6. Cole kept no copy.

Address and Postmark: None. The letter apparently was sent with the MS volume, referred to in the letter below.

Dear Sir,   Feb. 11, 1782. Milton.

AS I have employed myself for these last ten days in putting in an index to a MS¹ which I had made a year and half ago, and added a new life² to it, as the book was under my hand, and I had so

3. Steevens was admitted a fellow-commoner at King's 29 March 1753, but left college in 1756 without taking a degree.

4. Cole of course is thinking of HW, but he was mistaken: Malone was the author (see *ante* 4 Jan. 1782, and two following letters).

5. A seal of St Leonard's Hospital at Leicester, 'an impression of which has . . . been kindly conveyed to me by my worthy friend Mr Cole' (John Nichols, *Bibliotheca Topographica Britannica, No. VII, Con-*

taining the History and Antiquities of Hinckley in the County of Leicester, 1782, p. 120). A representation of the seal appears in Plate VII, Fig. 5, and Cole's description of it is quoted from one of his letters to Nichols at p. 9.

1. Cole's 'Short Account of such Antiquaries as received their Education in Corpus Christi College, Cambridge,' now in Add MS 5886 (see *ante* 2 July 1780 n. 5).

2. Apparently the life of George North

fair an opportunity of conveying it to you, I send you the MS which
I meant for Mr Gough, and which was never out of my hands, but
just as it was finished, when I sent it to Mr Essex, to convey it to
him. Luckily he kept it a week before he sent it, during which time
I received a letter from you,[3] in which you wished any mention of
your having wrote Mr Baker's 'Life' might be struck out. I immediately sent to inquire whether the parcel was forwarded, and it has
never been seen by anyone since, and though I promised it to Mr
Gough, who had seen it after Mr Tyson's death at his widow's, and
begged it of me (thinking it was mine, though I had given it to Mr
Tyson, and then containing only the former part, by Dr Stukeley),[4]
yet when Mrs Tyson returned it to me on the same supposition that
it was my property, I added, by way of amusement, to the blank
leaves, the lives of the Benedictine antiquaries. I now send it to you
to see what I had said relating to Mr Baker.[5] Indeed it is probable,
had I sent it, he would have guessed at my meaning, and I have made
excuses in retaining it, which he acquiesces in, for he never mentions it, yet I design it for him, according to my promise, but send
it to you to scratch out whatever may be disagreeable to you: and if
you think the time too early for him to have it (as on the first leaf),[6]
keep it yourself, and make a similar memorandum. You will find my
politics as flaming as ever, but as I never meant that you was to see
this tract, you will excuse the ebullitions of my mind, especially
when you know that I get nothing by them, and are so unfashion-
able.

I was in an error in respect to the writer of the remarks on Dr
Milles and Mr Bryant in the *Gentleman's Magazine*, for I have,
since I wrote last, the *Cursory Observations*, from the author.[7]

Did you write the prologue to the *Count de Narbonne?*[8] I saw it

---

(1710–72), numismatist: it is the last life of
the Corpus antiquaries, and Cole's writing
shows the effects of the last attack of gout.
Cole received most of the materials for it in
a letter from Lort 10 Jan. 1781.

3. See *ante* 4 July 1780.

4. The first part of the volume in question, now Add MS 5886, contains Cole's
copy of an account of the 'Escape of K.
Charles I,' by William Stukeley (1687–
1765), the antiquary.

5. For the passage, see *ante* 8 July
1780 n. 6.

6. At this time there was only one note
on the first leaf (see *ante* 2 July 1780 n. 5).
Cole later added two others.

7. HW's suggestion to Cole 22 Feb. 1782,
that Steevens may have sent Malone's
pamphlet to Cole is probably correct. Apparently Cole was not acquainted with
Malone, but it is possible that Malone sent
his pamphlet to Cole as the result of
HW's reference to Cole in HW to Malone
4 Feb. 1782.

8. *The Count of Narbonne,* by Robert
Jephson (1736–1803), friend and corre-

asserted in one paper that *you was,* and a friend of mine bought the play and lent it to me on that account: since which I have seen it attributed to *another person.*

I don't believe Mr Gough knows to this day that you ever wrote anything relating to Mr Baker.

To COLE, Thursday 14 February 1782

Add MS 5953, ff. 131–2.

Address: To the Reverend Mr Cole at Milton near Cambridge.
Postmark: 14 FE.

Berkeley Square, Feb. 14, 1782.

I HAVE received such treasures[1] from you, dear Sir, through the channel of Mr Nichols, that I neither know how to thank you, nor to find time to peruse them so fast as I am impatient to do. You must complete your kindness by letting me detain them a few days, till I have gone through them, when I will return them most carefully by the same intervention; and particularly the curious piece of enamel; for though you are, as usual, generous enough to offer it to me, I have plundered you too often already—and indeed I have room left for nothing more, nor have that miserly appetite of continuing to hoard what I cannot enjoy nor have much time left to possess.

I have already looked into your beautiful illuminated MS copied from Dr Stukeley's letter, and with anecdotes of the antiquaries of Bennet College; and I have found therein so many charming instances of your candour, humility, and justice, that I grieve to deprive Mr Gough for a minute even, of the possession of so valuable a tract. I will not injure him or it by begging you to cancel what relates to me,[2] as it would rob you of part of your defence of Mr Baker. If I wish to have it detained from Mr Gough till the period affixed

spondent of HW, was first performed 17 Nov. 1781, and was published shortly thereafter (see *St James's Chronicle* 29 Nov.–1 Dec. 1781). It was founded on *The Castle of Otranto* (see HW–Jephson correspondence; Martin Severin Peterson, *Robert Jephson*, Lincoln, Nebraska, 1930, pp. 34–8). The prologue was written by Jephson (see following letter). HW's copy is in the Merritt–Walpole Collection in the Harvard College Library.

1. Cole's MS volume, now Add MS 5886, a piece of old enamel, three letters from Gough to Cole, one from Steevens to Cole, and two prints of Browne Willis (see two preceding letters).

2. See *ante* 8 July 1780 n. 2.

in the first leaf, or rather to my death,[3] which will probably precede yours, it is for this reason only; Mr Gough is apt, as we antiquaries are, to be impatient to tell the world all he knows, which unluckily is much more than the world is at all impatient of knowing. For what you call *your flaming zeal* I do not in the least object to it. We have agreed to tolerate each other, and certainly are neither of us infallible. I think, on what we differ most, is, your calling *my* opinions *fashionable*—they were when we took them up—I doubt it is yours, that are most in fashion now, at least in this country. The Emperor[4] seems to be of *our* party[5]—but if I like his notions, I do not admire his judgment, which is too precipitate to *be* judgment.

I smiled at Mr Gough's idea of my declining his acquaintance as a member of that *obnoxious* Society of Antiquaries[6]—it is their folly alone that is obnoxious to me—and can they help that?—I shall very cheerfully assist him.

I am glad you are undeceived about the controversial piece in the *Gentleman's Magazine,* which I should have assured you, as you now know, that it was not mine. I declared *in my defence* that I would publish nothing more about that question. I have not, nor intend it. Neither was it I that wrote the prologue to the *Count of Narbonne,* but Mr Jephson himself.

On the opposite page I will add the receipt for the diet drink—As to my regimen, I shall not specify it. Not only you would not adopt it, but I should tremble to have you. In fact I never do prescribe it, as I am persuaded it would kill the strongest man in England, who was not exactly of the same temperament with me, and who had not embraced it early. It consists, in temperance in quantity, as to eating—I do not mind the quality; but I am persuaded that great abstinence with the gout is dangerous: for if one does not take nutriment enough, there cannot be strength sufficient to fling out the gout, and then it deviates to palsies. But my great nostrum is the use of cold water inwardly and outwardly on all occasions, and total disregard of precaution against catching cold. A hat you know I never wear, my breast I never button, nor wear greatcoats, etc. I have often had the gout in my face (as last week) and eyes, and instantly dip my head in a pail of cold water, which always cures it,

---

3. Cole, in accordance with this wish, added a note to the MS when he received it from HW 25 Feb. 1782 (see *ante* 2 July 1780 n. 5).

4. Joseph II (1741–90).
5. HW explains his meaning to Cole 22 Feb. 1782.
6. See *ante* 22 Dec. 1781 n. 3.

and does not send it anywhere else. All this I dare do, because I
have done so these forty years, weak as I look—but Milo would not
have lived a week if he had played such pranks. My diet drink is not
at all of so Quixote a disposition, and any of the faculty will tell you
how innocent it is at least. In a few days, for I am a rapid reader
when I like my matter, I will return all your papers and letters, and
in the meantime thank you most sincerely for the use of them, and
am,

Your ever obliged,

H. Walpole

PS. My old friend and your acquaintance Mr Dodd[7] died last Sunday—not of cold water. He and I were born on the very same day,
but took to different elements.[8] I doubt he had hurt his fortune as
well as health.

Diet Drink[9]

℞   Rad. Bardanæ
     Rad. Lapathi acut: aa ʒvj.
     Fol. Menyanth: ♍j. Coque in aquæ
     fontanæ lb ii ad lb i.   Cola et adde
     Succor. Becabungæ   ⎫
     "   " Cochlear: ⎬ commist.
     "   " Trifol. aquat. ⎭
     quantitatem dimid. scilicet lbs ad lbj
     decoctionis.   Deinde adde
     Spir. Cochlear. ʒij. M. F. Apoz.

7. John Dodd (1714–82), of Swallowfield,
Berks, M.P. for Reading, 1740–1, 1755–82.
Cole says of him: 'Mr Dodd was my fel-
low-collegian and school-fellow at Eton;
a man universally beloved; lively, generous, and sensible. I think his father kept
an inn at Chester; but a Judge Dodd, of
that county, related to him, left him his
large fortune. He had a wretched tutor at
college, John Whaley, who would have
ruined most other people; but Mr Dodd's
natural good sense got the better of his
vile example. Mr Walpole and Mr Dodd,
while at college, were united in the strictest friendship' (LI viii. 575).

8. In Sept. 1736, Sneyd Davies (1709–
69), Eton, and Fellow of Kings, wrote
verses, 'On Two Friends Born on the Same
Day,' addressed to HW and Dodd. Part of
the second stanza reads:

'The one of Nature easy and compos'd,
Untoss'd by Passion, and in Arts repos'd;
T'other of eager and impetuous Soul,
Starting in Honour's Race, and stretching
   to the Goal.
One calm, like Theodosius, to desire,
The other glowing with Varrane's Fire,
This pleas'd to wander in Pierian Glades,
Where the Rill murmurs, and the Laurel
   shades;
That warm'd and rous'd by what his Soul
   approves,
The Sport, the Mistress, or the Friend he
   loves.'

(First printed in John Whalley's *Poems*,
1745, dedicated to HW; reprinted in LI,
with several alterations, i. 591.)

9. For an analysis of the diet drink, see
Appendix 4.

I take a full wine-glass about noon and another at night—and have done so above this twelvemonth, and have found vast benefit. I had tried twenty other medicines in vain.

TO COLE, Friday 15 February 1782

Add MS 5953, ff. 133–4.

Address: [From COLE's copy, Add MS 5826, f. 65v.] To the Rev. Mr Cole at Milton near Cambridge. Free T. Caswall.

[Berkeley Square,] Feb. 15, 1782.

I WAS so impatient to peruse all the literary stores you sent me, dear Sir, that I stayed at home on purpose to give up a whole evening to them. I have gone through all, your own MS, which I envy Mr Gough, his specimen, and the four letters to you from the latter and Mr Steevens.[1] I am glad they were both satisfied with my reception. In truth, you know, I am neither formal nor austere, nor have any grave aversion to our antiquaries, though I do now and then divert myself with their solemnity about errant trifles—yet perhaps we owe much to their thinking those trifles of importance, or the Lord knows how they would have patience to investigate them so indefatigably. Mr Steevens seemed pleasant, but I doubt I shall never be demure enough to conciliate Mr Gough. Then I have a wicked quality in an antiquary, nay one that annihilates the essence; that is, I cannot bring myself to a habit of minute accuracy about very indifferent points. I do not doubt but there is a swarm of diminutive inaccuracies in my *Anecdotes*—well! if there is, I bequeath free leave of correction to the microscopic intellects of my continuators. I took dates and facts from the sedulous and faithful Vertue, and piqued myself on little but on giving an idea of the spirit of the times with regard to the arts at the different periods.

The specimen you sent me of Mr Gough's Detail of our Monuments is very differently treated; proves vast industry, and shows most circumstantial fidelity. It extends too much farther than I expected, for it seems to embrace the whole mass of our monuments, nay, of some that are vanished. It is not what I thought, an inten-

1. Cole's account of the antiquaries educated at Corpus Christi College, Cambridge, now in Add MS 5886, and the letters mentioned *ante* 7 Feb. 1782.

tion of representing the succession of our modes of dress from figures on monuments, but rather a history of our tombs. It is fortunate, though he may not think so, that so many of the more ancient are destroyed, since for three or four centuries they were clumsy, rude and ugly—I know I am but a fragment of an antiquary, for I abhor all Saxon doings, and whatever did not exhibit some taste, grace or elegance, and some ability in the artists. Nay, if I may say so to you, I do not care a straw for archbishops, bishops, mitred abbots and cross-legged knights. When you have seen one of a sort, you have seen all. However, even to so superficial a *student in antiquity* as I am, Mr Gough's work is not unentertaining. It has frequently anecdotes and circumstances of kings, queens and historic personages that interest me, though I care not a straw about a series of bishops who had only Christian names, or were removed from one old church to a newer. Still I shall assist Mr Gough with whatever he wants in my possession. I believe he is a very worthy man, and I should be a churl not to oblige any man who is so innocently employed. I have felt the selfish, the proud avarice of those who hoard literary curiosities for themselves alone, as other misers do money.

I observed in your account of the Count-Bishop Hervey, that you call one of his dedicators Martin Sherlock Esq., p. 53.[2] That Mr Sherlock is an Irish clergyman: I am acquainted with him. He is a very amiable good-natured man, and wants judgment not parts. He is a little damaged by aiming at Sterne's capricious pertness, which the original wore out: and which having been admired and cried up to the skies by foreign writers of reviews,[3] was on the contrary too severely treated by our own. That injustice shocked Mr Sherlock, who has a good heart and much simplicity, and sent him in dudgeon last year to Ireland, determined to write no more—yet I am persuaded he will, so strong is his propensity to being an author —and if he does, correction may make him more attentive to what

---

2. Martin Sherlock (d. 1797), traveller, chaplain to Frederick Augustus Hervey, 4th E. of Bristol and Bp of Derry (see DNB). Cole mistakenly refers to him as 'The Rev. Martin Shelvock' (see *post* 24 Feb. 1782). Cole writes: 'The Rev. Martin Shelvock, in his *Letters from an English Traveller: translated from the French Original, printed at Geneva, with notes*, 4to, 1779, dedicates his work to the Bishop of Derry,'

etc. etc. (Add MS 5886, f. 29). Cole's remarks closely follow the words of the review of Sherlock's book in GM Dec. 1779, xlix. 601–3, from whence Cole almost certainly took it, and not from the book itself.

3. See the extravagant praise of French and Italian reviewers, printed in Sherlock's *Letters from an English Traveller*, new edn, revised and corrected, 1780, pp. 175–90.

he says and writes. He has no gall; on the contrary too much benevolence in his indiscriminate praise—but he has made many very ingenious criticisms. He is a just, a due enthusiast to Shakespeare[4]—but alas! he scarce likes Richardson less!

Pray would it be possible to get a print of Mr Cowper[5] by Mr Tyson, mentioned in your MS, p. 45—Beware!—Do not plunge into your natural generosity and say, 'I have *one* at your service.'—You have put me on my guard against your bountiful spirit. I vow solemnly I will not accept *an only one;* nor without that vow would I have named it.

There is another favour I am inclined to ask, but upon conditions too that you refuse if you have the least objection. I have a curiosity to see what the Count-Bishop and Wilkes wrote in an album you mention in p. 52.[6] It is merely a curiosity to *see* them. I give you my honour I will return your transcript without transcribing it. Yet decline my request, if it is not agreeable to you.

The first minute I can spare a servant to send into the city, all your papers written and printed and the enamel shall be conveyed

---

4. See Sherlock, op. cit., Letter XXI, pp. 134–46. It is possible that HW is recalling a conversation with Sherlock.

5. John Cowper (1737–70), younger brother of William Cowper, the poet. For an account of him, see Wm Cowper, *The Task*, Book II, ll. 780–7, and Henry P. Stokes, *Cowper Memorials*, Olney, 1904. Cole wrote, in his life of Tyson (Add MS 5886, f. 25): 'Mr Tyson has often told me that he owed much to the friendship and acquaintance of Mr John Cowper . . . who gave him a thorough knowledge and insight into the Greek language, of which he was in a manner ignorant when he left school. . . . Mr Tyson, out of gratitude to his memory, has etched a drawing of him, which is very like him, and which will be a curiosity, as so few copies were taken from the plate.'

6. The passage in Cole's MS reads: 'I would wish to suppress any mention of his Lordship's [the 4th E. of Bristol's] visits to the Grande Chartreuse, especially as a visit by John Wilkes some little time before contrasts too favourably in his regard, with that of his Lordship. What each wrote in the album of that convent will astonish mankind, when we consider one

as a nobleman, a bishop, a man of politeness and character, and the other as an abandoned profligate and the tool of a faction, and then observe the difference of style and behaviour of these two persons. They will not bear an examination, and therefore I will say no more about this subject' (Add MS 5886, f. 28v). Wilkes's remarks are printed in an unidentified newspaper cutting, dated Feb. 1791, pasted into George Daniel's copy of Mason's *Gray:* 'I had the happiness of passing the entire day of July 24th, 1765, in this romantic place, with the good fathers of the Grande Chatreuse, and I reckon it amongst the most agreeable of my life. I was charmed with the hospitality and politeness I met with, and edified by the conversation of the Père Général, and the Père Coadjuteur. The astonishing height of the mountain, the savageness of the rocks, the gloom of the woods, and the perfect solitude, conspire to make the mind pensive, and lull to rest all the turbulent, guilty passions of a vain, wicked world. I felt much regret at leaving the place, and the good fathers, but I carry with me the liveliest sense of their goodness. John Wilkes.' Cf. *post* 24 Feb. 1782.

to Mr Nichols, everything but the two prints of Mr Browne Willis for which I thank you. Mr Nichols has been with me himself—he is a very modest intelligent man. Now I have done with writing, I am pretty sick of both the world and the great world, I have less objection to amusing myself with writers. They divert me, when I have nothing to read, especially as I have little else to do. Adieu!

Yours most sincerely,

H. W.

PS. Saturday 16th.—The parcel for you will go this evening to Mr Nichols so you will inquire for it at the Rose next week.

From Cole, Sunday 17 February 1782

VA, Forster MS 110, f. 267. Cole's copy, Add MS 5826, f. 65v.
Address: For the Honourable Horace Walpole in Berkeley Square, London.
Postmark: Cambridge 18 FE.

[Milton,] Sunday, Feb. 17, 1782.
Dear Sir,

I WRITE this merely to inform you that I am in no hurry about the return of the packet, which you may keep as long as you please. That you are a rapid reader, and writer, too, I need no other proof than your having read the MS from one end to the other, with the letters: now I know you could not receive the parcel till the afternoon of Thursday, and then wrote a long letter, for which I heartily thank you, as also for the receipt, which I shall infallibly follow, for I know the scurvy is the foundation of my gout, yet in such a crazy carcass as mine there can be little prospect of success.

I am sorry for poor Mr Dodd, for whose open, frank and ingenuous disposition I ever had an esteem, and it was well his good sense got the better of a vile tutorage. Death, this last week, seems to make more than ordinary havoc: a particular acquaintance of mine[1] died

1. 'Mrs Serocold, of Cherry Hinton, whose son returned the same week from the East Indies' (addition in Cole's copy). 'Mrs Serocold' was Mrs Walter Serocold (Mary Richardson), dau. of Gilbert Richardson *alias* Marshall. Her son, Walter Serocold (1758–94), afterwards a captain in the navy, was killed in action at the siege of Calvi in Corsica (see GM July 1800, lxx. 632b; Burke, *Landed Gentry*, 1851).

in the neighborhood, Bishop [of Bristol] and Dean of London,[2] Prebendary of Canterbury[3] (which last surely must go to Dr Farmer),[4] two fellows of King's of my standing.[5] Yet we all think, very happily too, that our own exit is at a distance. Come when it will, so that it is easy, I shall be content. Your constitution is athletic, whatever may be the outward cover of it, and I pray God may you enjoy a long life, and every blessing attending it.

The MS I chiefly sent that you might see what I had said on the first leaf,[6] but supposing, reasonably enough, that the period might be too short, I rather chose to put it into your hands, to keep or return it, as seemed best to you, and if you don't choose to enter such a paragraph in your own hand under what I have already written, if you return it, I will make such an entry as you wish, with an order that, in case of my death, it may be sent to you.

Some time ago Mr Essex told me that Sir Harry Inglefeild[7] had called on him, on his return from a tour in the North, where he had taken views of old abbeys and other antiquities: Mr Essex showed him King's Chapel and his draughts of it, with which he seemed much pleased.[8] He said further that he was going to be married to a daughter of Lord Cadogan.[9] I was surprised at such a connection,

2. Thomas Newton (1704–82), Bp of Bristol 1761–82, and Dean of St Paul's, 1768–82, died Thursday 14 Feb. 1782. George III wished to make him Bishop of London in 1768, but the ministry successfully opposed him (see DNB).

3. Rev. William Tatton (1720–82), Prebendary of Canterbury and York; rector of Rotherfield in Sussex, and of St Dionis Backchurch, London. He died 11 Feb. (see GM Feb. 1782, lii. 95a).

4. Farmer was installed Prebendary of Canterbury 5 March of this year (see Le Neve, *Fasti Ecclesiae Anglicanae* i. 58).

5. '(Chafey and Plumptre), though not of my acquaintance' (addition in Cole's copy). Rev. John Chafy (1720–82), Fellow of King's, 1741–52; Prebendary of Salisbury, 1780–2; d. at Salisbury, 8 Feb. 1782 (see GM Feb. 1782, lii. 95a; *Eton Coll. Reg. 1698–1752*). The Rev. Septimius Plumptre (1717–82), Fellow of King's, 1740–52; d. at Mansfield, 12 Feb. (see GM Feb. 1782, lii. 95b; *Eton Coll. Reg. 1698–1752*).

6. See *ante* 2 July 1780 n. 5.

7. Sir Henry Charles Englefield (1752–

1822), 7th and last Bt, of White Knights, Berks; antiquary, astronomer and scientific writer; Vice-President of the Society of Antiquaries. He never married.

8. Essex wrote to Gough 31 Jan. 1781: 'Sir H. Englefield called upon me some time before Christmas, and pressed me much to publish my drawings and observations on King's Chapel' (LI vi. 292–3).

9. 'or his sister to a son of that nobleman, who, I think, has six sons and only one daughter' (addition in Cole's copy). Lord Cadogan had no daughter of marriageable age, and Sir Harry Englefield never married (see following letter, and note 7 above). Teresa Ann Englefield (d. 1810), Sir Harry's only surviving sister at this time, m. 27 May 1782, Francis Cholmeley, Esq., of Brandsby, Yorks (see GM May 1782, lii. 262a; Burke, *Landed Gentry*, 1851). It is possible, however, that a marriage between her and one of the three eldest sons of Lord Cadogan may have been considered (see Collins, *Peerage*, 1812, v. 419–20).

except Sir Harry is as indifferent about his religion as the Emperor, who, by the way, I do not much admire or ever did: his connections with[10] France boded no good, but what he has lately done, I know not, seeing no other paper but the weekly *Cambridge Chronicle*.[11]

I will trouble you no farther than to assure you of the unalterable esteem and regard of, dear Sir,

Your most faithful and obliged servant,

WM COLE

To COLE, Friday 22 February 1782

Add MS 5953, ff. 135–6.
Address: To the Reverend Mr Cole at Milton near Cambridge.
Postmark: GC 22 FE.

[Berkeley Square,] Feb. 22, 1782.

I DOUBT you are again in error, my good Sir, about the letter in the *Gentleman's Magazine* against the Rowleians, unless Mr Malone sent it to you, for he is the author, and not Mr Steevens, from whom I imagine you received it. There is a report that proof of some part of Chatterton's forgery is to be produced from an accomplice[1]—but this I do not answer for, nor know the circumstances. I have scarce seen a person who is not persuaded, that the *fashion* of the poems was Chatterton's own, though he might have found some old stuff to work upon, which very likely was the case; but now that the poems have been so much examined, nobody (that has an ear) can get over the modernity of the modulation, and the recent cast of the ideas and phraseology, corroborated by such palpable pillage of

10. 'and stay in' (addition in Cole's copy). Joseph II travelled in France under the name of Count Falkenstein, April–July 1777.

11. 'for I was quite tired with the lies and contradictory falsehoods in every other paper, and indeed this is as bad, but it tells one a little news of the county' (addition in Cole's copy).

---

1. The 'accomplice' was John Rudhall, an apprentice to an apothecary at Bristol at the time Chatterton was fabricating the Rowley poems, who had seen Chatterton blacken a piece of parchment. For a résumé of his testimony, see Meyerstein, *Chatterton* 119–20. Warton (in *An Enquiry* 113–21) quotes a letter from Herbert Croft (the author of *Love and Madness*) to Steevens, dated 5 Feb. 1782, which contains Croft's remarks on some paragraphs in Milles's edition of the Rowley Poems, pp. 436–7, but offers no information concerning the person who furnished the parchment to Chatterton. Warton's surmise is that 'his [Chatterton's] master's office might have supplied blank slips of refuse or neglected parchment' (*An Enquiry* 112; see also HW to Mason 14–15 Feb. 1782).

Pope and Dryden. Still the boy remains a prodigy, by whatever means he procured or produced the edifice he erected—and still it will be inexplicable how he found time or materials for operating such miracles.

You are in another error about Sir Harry Englefield, who cannot be going to marry a daughter of Lord Cadogan, unless he has a natural one, of whom I never heard. Lord Cadogan had no daughter by his first wife,[2] and his eldest girl by my niece[3] is not five years old.

The act of the Emperor, to which I alluded, is the general destruction of convents in Flanders, and I suppose, in his German dominions too. The Pope[4] suppressed the Carnival, as mourning, and proposes a journey to Vienna to implore mercy. This is a little different from the time when the pontiffs trod on the necks of emperors, and called it trampling *super aspidem et draconem.*

I hope you have received your cargo[5] back undamaged: I was much obliged to you, and am,

Yours ever,

H. W.

From Cole, Sunday 24 February 1782

VA, Forster MS 110, ff. 268–9. Cole kept no copy.
Address: For the Honourable Horace Walpole, Berkeley Square, London.
Postmark: Cambridge 25 FE.

<De>ar Sir,   Milton, Sunday morning, Feb. 24, 1782.

I WAS impatient to give you an account of the safe arrival of your packet, which Mr Nichols did not send to the fly till Thursday, and I did not receive till last night, and I was unwilling to write be-

2. His 1st wife was Hon. Frances Bromley (d. 1768), dau. of Henry Bromley, 1st Bn Montfort, by whom he had six sons and no daughters (see Collins, *Peerage,* 1812, v. 419).

3. HW's niece, Mary Churchill (b. 1750), dau. of Charles Churchill by Lady Mary Walpole; m., 7 Aug. 1777, Charles Sloane Cadogan, 3d Bn (afterwards, 1800, 1st E.) Cadogan, from whom she was divorced in 1796 for criminal conversation with the Rev. Mr Cooper (see GEC). Her eld. dau. was Lady Emily Mary Cadogan (1778–1839), who m. (2 June 1802) the Hon. and

Rev. Gerald Valerian Wellesley (1770–1848), next younger brother to the 1st D. of Wellington (see Collins, *Peerage,* 1812, v. 420; *Publications of the Harleian Society,* vol. 23: *Registers of the Cathedral Church . . . at Durham,* ed. George J. Armytage, 1897, p. 145).

4. Pius VI (Giovanni Angelo Braschi) (1717–99). He paid an unsuccessful visit to Joseph II at Vienna, 22 March 1782 (see GM April 1782, lii. 202b).

5. Of MSS, which Cole received Saturday 23 Feb. (see following letter).

fore I could satisfy you of their safety, which I knew you would be anxious about.

I am, and was before I sent it, totally of opinion with you about Mr Gough's plan, in respect to its deficiency relating to habits and dress: a work like Father Montfaucon's[1] would be the thing. I remember you told me many years ago such a design was forming by Lord Bute and you,[2] both of whom might amply contribute to enlarge and amend Mr Gough's plan, and I wish you would give him an hint of it when he calls again.[3]

I thank you for your correction of Sherlock: I observe you call him three several times by that name (Sherlock), though in my book it is Shelvock, which I suppose is a misnomer.

It grieves me that I can give you no satisfactory answer to your two requests. Mr Tyson gave me one copy of his friend Mr Cowper, and told me he had destroyed the plate, though very like the person, after taking a very few impressions, in order to enhance their value. This went with my collection to Mr Gulston <for Lord> Mount-Steward. I was in hopes the present Master of Benet, con-<nected> with both, might have a duplicate. He told me that Tyson gave <him onl>y one, and afterwards wanted to filch that from him. Last year I <had occ>asion to write to Mr Tyson's widow, and desired her to give me copies <of such> duplicates as she had of her husband's etching, and she sent me <onl>y one of the noted Mrs Lagden who kept the inn at Bournbridge turnpike. So that I am afraid it will be difficult to get one.

The verses wrote by Bishop Hervey in the album of the Grande Chartreuse I never was in possession of. Dr Lort showed them to me some ten or twelve years ago, with *those* by Wilkes, but would not suffer me, though much importuned (being somewhat of a literary miser) to take a copy of them. No doubt he would let you have them now, as the novelty is over, and probably me also, and if you don't choose to ask, I will in my next letter, if you have no objection, without or with mentioning for whom I request them.

Mr Malone is the author of the pamphlet and what is in the *Gentleman's Magazine,* etc.

1. That is, *Les Monumens de la Monarchie Françoise* (see *ante* 14 May 1768).

2. See *ante* 14 May 1768 n. 14.

3. HW evidently did, for the preface of *Sepulchral Monuments* commences with an allusion to Montfaucon, and at p. 3 Gough says: 'It would not be altogether impossible to draw up a list of pictures, including those enumerated by Mr Walpole in his *Anecdotes of Painting,* relating to the history and antiquities of England, in the manner of Montfaucon, from the Conquest to the present time.'

No doubt you have seen the 'Great Harry' from the Society, and Mr Topham's dissertation on it.[4] I hate ships and shipping, consequently the print, though expensive,[5] does not suit my taste.

I am surprised at Mr Nichols's calling upon you with my parcel, as I had sent money (in the box I had sent him of the Leicester seal) to pay the porterage to you. No doubt he had a mind to introduce himself to you. I am sure it was without any kind of encouragement from me, but this is a tax you must pay for eminence.

Excuse my saying more from, dear Sir,

Your ever faithful and affectionate servant,

WM COLE

From COLE, Tuesday 5 March 1782

VA, Forster MS 110, f. 270. Cole kept no copy.
Address: For the Honourable Horace Walpole, Berkeley Square, London.

Milton, Tuesday, March 5, 1782.

Dear Sir,

HAVING an opportunity of sending this under a cover, which might be a double letter[1] if the paper in it was discovered, I am glad to send you a print of Mr Tyson's etching of his friend Mr Cowper. I had in my last letter to Mr Gough (returning his plan of his *Monuments*), made a request to him that, if he had a duplicate, he would spare me one. Luckily, as Mr Cowper was his great friend, he had two, and sent me the enclosed. I did not tell him for whom I begged it.

I hope Dr Farmer, who has been gone to be installed a Canon of Canterbury,[2] will call on you, who gave him so kind an invitation, though I have not seen him of above a month.

4. *A Description of an Antient Picture in Windsor Castle, representing the Embarkation of King Henry VIII at Dover, May 31, 1520: preparatory to his Interview with the French King Francis I*, by John Topham. The paper was read before the Society of Antiquaries 21 June 1781, and published in that year. It appeared also in *Archaeologia* vi. 179–220. John Topham (1746–1803), antiquary and editor, deputy-keeper of state papers, 1781, became treasurer of the Society of Antiquaries, 1787.

5. It sold for £1.11.6 (see *Archaeologia* vi. 422).

———

1. See *ante* 6 June 1769 n. 25.
2. Farmer was installed 5 March, the date of this letter (see *ante* 17 Feb. 1782 n. 4).

It grieves me to my heart to see the apostasy of the great support of the Catholic cause, the son[3] of the apostolical Mary Teresa: for I include the cause of Christianity in that of the Church of Rome, let it be true or otherwise. I may say now fairly my *Nunc Dimittis*, for if the Emperor and other princes are become disciples of Voltaire, adieu to Christianity and its doctrine. Excuse the groaning and sorrow on this occasion of, dear Sir,

Your most affectionate and faithful servant,

Wm Cole

To Cole, Saturday 9 March 1782

Add MS 5953, ff. 137–8.
Address: To the Reverend Mr Cole at Milton near Cambridge.
Postmark: 9 MR.

Berkeley Square, March 9, 1782.

THOUGH I have scarce time, I must write a line to thank you for the print of Mr Cowper, and to tell you how ashamed I am that you should have so much attention to me on the slightest wish that I express, when I fear my gratitude is not half so active, though it ought to exceed obligations.

Dr Farmer has been with me, and though it was but a short visit, he pleased me so much by his easy simplicity and good sense that I wish for more acquaintance with him.

I do not know whether the Emperor will atone to you for demolishing the Cross by attacking the Crescent. The papers say he has declared war with the Turks.[1] He seems to me to be a mountebank who professes curing all diseases. As power is his only panacea, the remedy methinks is worse than the disease. Whether Christianity will be laid aside, I cannot say. As nothing of the spirit is left, the forms I think signify very little. Surely it is not an age of morality and principles: does it import whether profligacy is baptized or not? I look to motives, not to professions. I do not approve of convents: but if Caesar wants to make soldiers of monks, I detest his Reformation, and think that men had better not procreate than commit murder—nay, I believe that monks get more children than soldiers

3. Joseph II.   1. This report was not true.

do—but what avail abstracted speculations? Human passions wear
the dresses of the times, and carry on the same views but in different
habits. Ambition and interest set up religions or pull them down,
as fashion presents a handle, and the conscientious must be content,
when the mode favours their wishes, or sigh when it does not.[2]

Yours most sincerely,

H. W.

From Cole, Friday 12 April 1782

VA, Forster MS 110, ff. 271–2. Cole's copy, Add MS 5826, ff. 71v, 72v.
Address: For the Honourable Horace Walpole, Berkeley Square, London.
Postmark: Cambridge 13 AP.

Milton, Friday, April 12, 1782.

Dear Sir,

I WON'T trouble you with my complaints, which have been very
uneasy since I wrote last, nor will I talk of politics, which would
be absurd for me to enter in, as I am going out of the world and
know not much of them, and especially as your cousin-german[1] was
a principal promoter of the late revolution,[2] yet I lament, sincerely
lament, the fate of poor Mr Chamberlayne,[3] with whom I am told
you was acquainted,[4] and who is universally lamented. If you know
any particulars of him, I wish you would communicate them. But to
deal ingenuously, as I hope I have done through life, I would not

2. 'This was in consequence of what I
had said of the Emperor and my lament-
ing the fate of convents and Christianity'
(Cole's note, at the end of his copy of HW's
letter, Add MS 5826, f. 68v).

1. '(General Conway),' addition in Cole's
copy.
2. That is, the fall of Lord North's ministry, 20 March 1782, and the formation of
another under the Marquis of Rockingham, 27 March 1782. General Conway was
made Commander-in-Chief. HW gives an
account of Conway's part in the proceedings in *Last Journals* ii. 406 ff.
3. Edward Chamberlayne (1741–82), son
of Rev. Edward Chamberlayne, rector of

Great Cressingham, Norfolk; of King's
College (B.A. 1763, Fellow 1761–76); F.S.A.;
one of the joint-secretaries to the treasury
in the Rockingham ministry. He died 6
April 1782 from a fracture of his skull, sustained when he jumped from a window.
'The melancholy accident . . . took its rise
from an excess of diffidence attending his
recent appointment. . . . He was one of
the best scholars of the age, equally pro-
ficient in erudition and taste, at once profound in literature, and polite. The loss of
such a man is therefore to be considered as
a public loss' (GM April 1782, lii. 206b; *Eton
Coll. Reg. 1753–90*).
4. See following letter.

deceive you, as I have a particular reason to be thus inquisitive,[5] which I may communicate to you hereafter, yet I should not have troubled you on that occasion had it not been for the following circumstance.

Mr Essex drank tea here yesterday, and brought me a compliment from the mayor of Cambridge,[6] who ignorantly thinks that I am a better scholar than I ever pretended to be, for God knows my Latinity was[7] never upon par, and now, through the weakness of my intellects, worse than par. It was to compose a short inscription, which the Corporation have a mind to be a corner stone, and hid in the foundation of a new Town Hall, which they are erecting this year, under the direction of Mr Essex,[8] and mean to put a few coins under it. My Latin I know is very feeble and bald, and, as you have applied to me for trumpery, I now request you to look over what I wrote before breakfast, and you will do me a particular favour to scratch out all, polish and amend the Latinity and style, and replace it with anything you think more proper, for I look up to you as the *arbiter elegantiarum,* and the best judge of this and every other matter in the literary way. I really don't know whether *architecto* or *architecta* is proper.[9] Excuse this freedom from, dear Sir,

Your most obliged and faithful servant,

WM COLE

I say nothing about Rowley, yet the *Archaeological Epistle*[10] would tempt one to expatiate, and especially as I am persuaded I know the *poet,* which is perhaps no better title than *etymologist* or *dictionary-*

5. See *post* 13 May 1782.

6. John Merrill (1731–1801), brother of Joseph Merrill, Cole's bookseller; alderman and mayor of Cambridge (see LA ix. 647).

7. Cole's copy reads: 'my Latinity and Grecacity were.'

8. For an account of the new building, which was erected at a cost of £2,500, see Thomas Dinham Atkinson and John Willis Clark, *Cambridge Described and Illustrated,* London and Cambridge, 1897, pp. 86–7. The Town Hall is thought to have been Essex's last work: it was opened 25 May 1784, and Essex died 14 Sept. following (loc. cit.).

9. MS reads 'is is proper.'

10. *An Archaeological Epistle, to the Reverend and Worshipful Jeremiah Milles,* published anonymously in the latter part of March, 1782 (see *St James's Chronicle* 23–6 March 1782, in which the work is advertised 'This day was published'). The author was William Mason (see HW–Mason correspondence for this year and John W. Draper, *William Mason,* New York, 1924, pp. 10, 338). Leslie Stephen in DNB, led astray by LA viii. 113, attributes the poem to John Baynes (1758–87) through whose hands it apparently passed to the press (see DNB, *sub* Baynes). Mason's authorship is stated in LA viii. 569.

writer.[11] People are apt to forget themselves when they are at the head of their profession: all three[12] rose to eminence by their parts, and it is a scandal to see abuse thrown out, like Billingsgate women, only for a difference in politics, or jealousy of preeminence. If one got a pension for Toryism, the other probably got his for his preferment for opposite principles.[13]

Faxit Deus
ut hæc nova Gilda Aula
Communitatis Villæ
Cantabrigiæ,
in ipsissimo loco
veteris jam perantiquæ
et ruinosæ,
posita,
resurgat in honorem
hujus venerandi Municipii
et
prosperitatem.
Reædificata autem fuit
hæc Domus Communis,
sive Gilda Aula,
per Communitatem Villæ,
amicis faventibus,
Joanne Merrill,
tunc Majore Villæ
Cantabrigiæ,
Anno Regni Regis Georgii 3tii 22°.
Annoque Domini
1782.
Jacobo Essex, Architecto.[14]

I only send this to show the plan they are upon. That you had any hand in it shall be a secret, but I am loath such rough and false rub-

11. Cole refers of course to Dr Johnson, but he cannot have read the *Archaeological Epistle,* in which Johnson is attacked both in the preface and in the body of the work. Probably Cole had seen extracts of it in the newspapers.

12. Cole's copy reads (correctly) 'both': that is, Johnson and Milles.

13. As Milles never received a pension, this passage probably should read: 'got his preferment for opposite principles.' Cole

added, above the line, 'preferment for,' and then, presumably, forgot to strike out the words 'for his.'

14. It appears from a copy of the inscription, printed in Cooper's *Annals* iv. 403 n, from the Corporation Cross Book, that Cole made a few changes: in accordance with HW's criticism (see following letter), he changed *perantiquæ et ruinosæ* to *periclitantis et minosæ,* and *Georgii 3tii 22o* to *Georgii tertii 22do.*

bish should have a chance to fall before the greatest of all mortal pedants, Cooke,[15] or indeed, thus crude to descend to posterity: as either of them would reasonably conclude that it was the production of one of the aldermen or of the town clerk.

To COLE, Saturday 13 April 1782

Add MS 5953, ff. 139–40.

Address: To the Reverend Mr Cole at Milton near Cambridge.
Postmark: GC.

[Berkeley Square,] April 13, 1782.

YOUR partiality to me, my good Sir, is much overseen, if you think me fit to correct your Latin. Alas! I have not skimmed ten pages of Latin these dozen years. I have dealt in nothing but English, French and a little Italian, and do not think, if my life depended on it, that I could write four lines of pure Latin. I have had occasion once or twice to speak that language, and soon found that all my verbs were Italian with Roman terminations. I would not on any account draw you into a scrape by depending on my skill in what I have half forgotten. But you are in the metropolis of Latium. If you distrust your own knowledge, which I do not, especially from the specimen you have sent me, surely you must have good critics at your elbow to consult. In truth I do not love Roman inscriptions, in lieu of our own language, though, if anywhere, proper in an university—neither can I approve writing what the Romans themselves would not understand. What does it avail to give a Latin tail to a guild hall? Though the word used by us moderns, would *major* convey to Cicero the idea of a mayor? *Architectus,* I believe, is the right word—but I doubt whether *veteris jam perantiquae* is classic for a dilapidated building—but do not depend on me; consult some better judge.

Though I am glad of the late *revolution,* a word for which I have infinite reverence, I shall certainly not dispute with you thereon. I abhor exultation. If the change produces peace, I shall make a bonfire in my heart. Personal interest I have none; you and I shall certainly never profit by the politics to which we are attached.

15. William Cooke (1711–97), D.D.; Headmaster of Eton, 1743–5; Provost of King's College, Cambridge, 1772; Dean of Ely, 1780. For Cole's opinion of him see *ante* 14 May 1780.

The *Archaeologic Epistle* I admire exceedingly, though sorry it attacks Mr Bryant[1] whom I love and respect. The Dean is so absurd and obstinate an oaf, that he deserved to be ridiculed! Is anything more hyperbolic than his tedious preferences of Rowley to Homer, Shakespeare and Milton. Whether Rowley or Chatterton was the writer, are the poems in any degree comparable to those authors? Is not a ridiculous author an object of ridicule? I do not even guess at your meaning in your conclusive paragraph on that subject. Dictionary-writer I suppose alludes to Johnson, but surely you do not equal a compiler of a dictionary to a genuine poet! Is a brickmaker on a level with Mr Essex? Nor can I hold that exquisite wit and satire are Billingsgate. If they were, Milles and Johnson would be able to write an answer to the *Epistle*. I do as little guess whom you mean that got a pension by Toryism—if Johnson too, he got a pension for having abused pensioners, and yet took one himself—which was contemptible enough. Still less know I who preferred opposition to principles—which is not a very common case. Whoever it was, as Pope says,

> The way he took was strangely round about.[2]

With Mr Chamberlayne, I was very little acquainted, nor ever saw him six times in my life. It was with Lord Walpole's branch he was intimate, and to whose elder son Mr Chamberlayne's father[3] had been tutor. This poor gentleman had an excellent character universally, and has been more feelingly regretted than almost any man I ever knew. This is all I am able to tell you.

I forgot to say that I am also in the dark as to the person you guess for the author of the *Epistle*: it cannot be the same person to whom it is generally attributed,[4] who certainly neither has a pension nor has deserted his principles, nor has reason to be jealous of those he laughs at, for their abilities are far below his. I do not mean that it

---

1. Bryant is treated very gently in comparison with Milles and Johnson: he is referred to in the preface as 'a most profound etymologist' who 'has lately proved that a writer must know his own meaning,' and is noticed in the note to stanza XIV.

2. 'The way they take is strangely round about' ('Epilogue to the Satires, Dialogue II,' l. 125).

3. Rev. Edward Chamberlayne (1699?–1773), of Christ's College, Cambridge, rector of Great Cressingham, Norfolk, 1730–73; held other benefices (see *Alumni Cantab.*); tutor to Horatio Walpole (1752–1822), 2d E. of Orford of the 3d creation.

4. That is, Mason.

is his, but is attributed to him. It was sent to me, nor did I ever see a line of it till I read it in print.[5] In one respect it is most credible to be his, for there are not two such inimitable poets in England. I smiled on reading it, and said to myself, 'Dr Glynn is well off to have escaped.'[6]—His language indeed about me has been Billingsgate—but peace be to his and the *manes* of Rowley, if they have ghosts who never existed. The *Epistle* has put an end to that controversy,[7] which was grown so tiresome. I rejoice at having kept my resolution of not writing a word more on that subject. The Dean had swollen it to an enormous bladder: the archaeologic poet pricked it with a pin, a sharp one indeed, and it burst.

Pray send me a better account of yourself if you can.

Yours most sincerely,

H. W.

From Cole, Monday 13 May 1782

VA, Forster MS 110, f. 273. Cole's copy, Add MS 5826, f. 73v.
Address: For the Honourable Horace Walpole, Berkeley Square, London.
Postmark: Cambridge 14 MA.

Milton, Monday, May 13, 1782.

Dear Sir,

ALTHOUGH I am in the greatest affliction for the unfortunate death of my poor niece Miss Apthorp,[1] who was to have been

5. HW's statement is literally true, but he was aware that Mason was writing the *Archaeological Epistle* as early as February (see Mason to HW 9 Feb. 1782; HW to Mason 14 Feb. 1782, etc.). HW received a copy of it from the printer on the night of 14 March 1782, and wrote a letter to Mason on the following day, in which he refers to the *Epistle* as 'your present of an old Cheshire cheese.'

6. He is not mentioned in the *Epistle*. HW doubtless alludes to Glynn's abusive mention of him in his review of *Love and Madness* in GM June 1780, p. 287 (see *ante* 4 July 1780, introductory note). It is not clear how HW knew this review was by Glynn, for Cole did not tell him. Glynn attacked HW again on the Chatterton affair in 1792 (see HW to Lady Ossory 17 July 1792; *Cambridge Chronicle* 16 June 1792; *European Magazine* June 1792, xxii. 433; *Works* iv. 241 n).

7. HW was too optimistic: the controversy was enriched by several pamphlets before the end of the year, and the battle continued in the columns of the *St James's Chronicle* and other newspapers.

—

1. Anne Apthorpe, only child of Cole's half brother, Dr Stephen Apthorpe. As

married to Mr Chamberlaine, Fellow of Eton, last month,[2] had it not been for the unfortunate accident of his brother[3] at the Treasury, and although my hand is so weak as hardly to hold the pen, yet I am necessitated to trouble you, as I received a letter last night from Miss Cotton,[4] eldest daughter of Sir John Hynde Cotton, to beg me to use my interest with you to see Strawberry Hill. I had lent her this winter, under charge not to let it go out of her hands, your catalogue of that villa, and she is eager to see it, with two or three friends, perhaps her two sisters.[5] She says she goes to Fulham either this week or next, and should be glad of the opportunity, while there, to see your house. If you will be so kind to send me a ticket for her, you will greatly oblige me and the lady, who is very sensible and composed, and thoroughly sensible of the antiquity of her family. Perhaps it may be less trouble to you, than to write the ticket, to give orders to your housekeeper to let ladies of that name see your place. As she is a draughtswoman, the Digby miniatures will enchant her.

For these last three or four weeks I have been more indisposed than ordinary, and hearing of the sad accident on Saturday night has[6] so fluttered my spirits that I had not a wink of sleep. Thank God, I fully recruited last night and made up for that loss.

I hope you continue well, which will ever be a pleasure to hear to, dear Sir,

Your most affectionate and faithful servant,

WM COLE

---

she was returning from the theatre, 9 May 1782, in a coach with her relatives, Mr and Mrs Henry Newcome of Hackney, and their daughter, the coach overturned on a bank in the road between Shoreditch and Hackney, 'by which means Miss Apthorpe was unfortunately killed upon the spot. Mr and Mrs Newcombe were terribly bruised, and their daughter so much hurt, that her recovery is doubtful. She now lies at the Nag's Head, as well as the deceased. What adds to this melancholy accident, is that Miss Apthorpe was to have been married on Monday' (*London Chronicle* 9–11 May 1782; cf. Cole to Gough 20 May 1782, LA i. 696). Mrs Newcome probably died of

injuries sustained in the accident (see *post* 29 June 1782).

2. Rev. Thomas Chamberlayne (1743–1801), Eton and King's (B.A. 1766, Fellow of King's 1765, and of Eton 1772); m. (14 Sept. 1789) Catherine Tunstall, dau. of Rev. James Tunstall. She m. (28 July 1806) as his 2d wife, Horatio Walpole, 2d E. of Orford of the 3d creation (see *Eton Coll. Reg. 1753–90*).

3. Edward Chamberlayne (see *ante* 12 April 1782 n. 3).

4. Sarah Cotton.

5. Anne and Lettice.

6. MS reads 'is.'

To Cole, Tuesday 14 May 1782

Add MS 5953, ff. 141–2.
Address: To the Reverend Mr Cole at Milton near Cambridge.
Postmark: 14 MA.

Berkeley Square, May 14, 1782.

I AM very sorry for the shock you have had in the loss of your niece, dear Sir; and so I am for my old friend Dr Apthorpe. I would say more, but as I am confined with an uncommon complaint for me, a violent cold, cough and tightness on my breast, for which I have been blooded two days together with all possible success, yet as my arm is bound up, it is rather awkward to write—however I could not help telling you how sincerely I partake of whatever affects you, nor defer complying with your request. I prefer sending a card, lest Margaret, who is no scholar but by rote, should make any mistake in giving her, verbal or written orders—to which she is less accustomed than to cards.

I hope you will soon recover your indisposition and flurry, and am,

Ever yours,

H. W.

From Cole, Thursday 16 May 1782

VA, Forster MS 110, f. 274. Cole kept no copy.
Address: For the Honourable Horace Walpole, Berkeley Square, London.
Postmark: Cambridge 17 MA.

Thursday, May 16, 1782. Milton.

Dear Sir,

I WRITE immediately, first to thank you for your kind letter and ready compliance with my request, and above all to recommend to you, in your complaint of a cough, to take ass's milk as soon as possible: it will do you more good than any medicine. I experience it at this instant for catching a bad cold near a month ago, going out for an airing in that detestable east wind which has been the bane of animals and vegetables. It was soon followed by a violent cough. As my gouty habit would not allow me to bleed, I took ass's milk, and it is in a manner gone.

I received by the same post which brought yours last night, a letter from Mr Gough, from whom I had not heard these two months. He concludes thus: 'Mr Walpole has permitted his pamphlet on Chatterton to be printed at large in the *Gentleman's Magazine*.[1] He has, methinks, taken a great deal more pains about it than the subject deserved.' Surely Mr Gough was not aware that your narrative was prin<ted> some years ago, when you was publicly called upon, and accused as being accessory to the death of that imposture. Had not such an incident fallen out, it is more than probable that you would not have troubled yourself about it. As it was, it seemed necessary.[2]

I am sorry your health deprives you of the pleasure of lilac, jonquil and hyacinth season at Strawberry Hill, yet I hope this soft weather and proper applications will soon remove all your complaints. My hand will only permit me to subscribe myself, dear Sir,

Your ever obliged and faithful servant,

WM COLE

To COLE, Friday 24 May 1782

Add MS 5953, ff. 143–4.

Address: [In Kirgate's hand.] To the Reverend Mr Cole at Milton near Cambridge. *Postmark:* GC 24 MA.

Berkeley Square, May 24, 1782.

YOU are always kind to me, dear Sir, in all respects—but I have been forced to recur to a rougher prescription than ass's milk. The pain and oppression on my breast obliged me to be blooded two days together which removed my cold and fever, but as I foresaw, left me the gout in their room. I have had it in my left foot and hand for a week, but it is going. This cold is very epidemic; I have at least half a dozen nieces and great-nieces confined with it, but it is not dangerous nor lasting.[1]

1. It was reprinted in GM April–July 1782, lii. 189–95, 247–50, 300, 347–8. Cf. HW to John Nichols April 1782.

2. Cole wrote to Gough 20 May 1782: 'How can you think that Mr Walpole has taken more pains about the Rowley business than the subject deserved? It is probable he would not have entered into it at all, had he not been called upon publicly as the murderer of Chatterton. Surely it became him to justify his own conduct, and to expose an imposture' (LA i. 696).

1. For a full account of 'The Epidemic Catarrh of 1782' see *Annals of Influenza . . . in Great Britain from 1510 to 1837*, ed. Theophilus Thompson, 1853, pp. 117–99.

I shall send you within this day or two the new edition of my *Anecdotes of Painting*.[2] You will find very little new. It is a cheap edition for the use of artists, and that at least they who really want the book, and not the curiosity, may have it, without being forced to give the outrageous price at which the Strawberry edition sells, merely because it is rare.

I could assure Mr Gough that, the letter on Chatterton cost me very small pains. I had nothing to do but recollect and relate the exact truth. There has been published another piece on it,[3] which I cannot tell whether meant to praise or blame me; so wretchedly is it written; and I have received another anonymous one,[4] dated Oxford (which may be to disguise Cambridge) and which professes to treat me very severely, though stuffed with fulsome compliments. It abuses me for speaking modestly of myself—a fault I hope I shall never mend; and avows agreeing with me on the supposition of the poems, which may be a lie, for it is not uncharitable to conclude that an anonymous writer is a liar—acquits me of being at all accessory to the poor lad's catastrophe; and then with most sensitive nerves is shocked to death, and finds me guilty of it, for having, after it happened, dropped, that if he had lived, he might have fallen into more serious forgeries, though, I declare I never heard that he did. To be sure, no Irishman ever blundered more, than to accuse one of an *ex post facto* murder! If this Hibernian casuist is smitten enough with his own miscarriage to preserve it in a magazine-phial, I shall certainly not answer it, not even by this couplet which it suggested;

So fulsome, yet so captious too, to tell you much it grieves me,
That though your flattery makes me sick, your peevishness relieves me.

Adieu! my good Sir—pray inquire for your books, if you do not receive them. They go by the Cambridge fly.

Yours ever,

H. WALPOLE

2. This, the third, edition was published in five volumes, including *Anecdotes* and *Engravers*, at 15s. It was advertised, 'In a few days will be published,' in the *St James's Chronicle* 16–18 May 1782, and 'This day were published,' in the same newspaper 28–30 May 1782.

3. HW's description fits *Strictures upon a Pamphlet intituled, Cursory Observations . . . With a Postscript on Mr. Thomas Warton's Enquiry into the same*

Subject, 1782, by Edward Burnaby Greene, but published anonymously. HW added no notes to his copy, which is now WSL. The pamphlet was reviewed in GM June 1782, lii. 342a.

4. This was an anonymous letter, not a printed 'piece.' (See HW to Lort 12 Nov. 1788.) It may have been the letter printed in the *European Magazine*, April 1782, i. 260–2, but that is not dated Oxford, and is signed 'H.I.' See also *post* 30 Oct. 1782.

From COLE, Monday 27 May 1782

VA, Forster MS 110, ff. 275–6. COLE's copy, Add MS 5826, ff. 74v, 75v.
Address: For the Honourable Horace Walpole, Berkeley Square, London.
Postmark: Cambridge 31 MA.

Milton, Monday, May 27, 1782.

Dear Sir,

IF I had not heard from you yesterday, I should have wrote today.
But first I thank you for your kind present, which I shall send
after tomorrow. I am sorry to find you still so indisposed. We are in
May at the end, and as cold as November. I remember at Blecheley
some twenty years ago such a fall of snow on 29 May as broke down
the largest branches of the poplars near my garden, which suffered
also greatly: the gooseberry trees being all in full leaf, were almost
all demolished.[1] Yet I hate hot weather so much, I can hardly, though
the fruits of the earth want it, wish for it. Surely ass's milk would be
of service, even for gout, fever and cold: now is the time for it: but
everyone knows what is best for himself. I continue it, and know it
has done me service, but for the same reason which you foresaw,
have not dared to be blooded, though I have an almost uninterrupted feverette upon me.

Your anonymous writer may write and write and be always wrong,
so long as your narrative is in being. Your couplet pleases me wonderfully. The best way is what you pursue, to answer none of them.

Last week I accomplished what I have been in pursuit of for these
two or three years. I have got possession of Elizabeth of York.[2] <I>
always had my eye for you in getting it, and mentioned it to you
<about> that time, when I first saw it. It came from my Lord Bris-
tol's,[3] and an acquaintance of mine[4] bought it at Bury, probably when
the last Earl[5] died and left everything away from the present.[6] The

1. 'from the weight of the snow: I never saw such destruction' (addition in Cole's copy).

2. Cole had mentioned this portrait to HW 26 March 1776.

3. That is, from Ickworth Lodge, the seat of George William Hervey (1721–75), 2d E. of Bristol, whom Cole refers to as 'the ambassador.' From him, the picture apparently went to his uncle, Hon. Felton Hervey, who died later in the same year, and, according to Cole, the picture was bought at the latter's sale (see loc. cit.).

4. Richard Reynolds, Butler of Caius College (see *ante* 26 March 1776).

5. Augustus John Hervey (1724–79), 3d E. of Bristol.

6. This account does not agree with that given *ante* 26 March 1776. The earlier account is probably correct, as Cole mentions the purchase of the picture three years before 'the last Earl died and left everything away from the present.'

ambassador,[7] I have been told, was a man of virtu: his name, in black lead, is at the back. It seems a tolerable picture, small, on wood, a white rose in her hand, and, for the age, in good preservation in a large gilt and carved frame. She was always a favourite of mine, as her husband used her not well, yet her beauty seemed to deserve better treatment. You are welcome to this picture,[8] which came to me on Saturday. I don't mean to make a good bargain for myself, as I know you give more than you receive, but shall be content without any exchange or with any offal picture in your rubbish room, to hang up in the place of two ordinary old pictures I gave for it, with some painted glass which you sent me. Maybe you are full and surfeited with York and Lancastrian portraits, yet I believe one of Elizabeth of York[9] is not very common. I have one old one of her father, certainly done in his time, though not handsome, and another good one of her granddaughter Queen Mary,[10] which I have had these forty years. If you are not surfeited, shall I send you Elizabeth? and if you don't like it, I shall be glad to have it again, and so no harm will be done.

My hand is so weak that I can't talk to you of *Bishop Newton's Life*,[11] where your father and Mr Pulteney are mentioned at large,[12] with other interesting matters, and if the old Bishop gets not heartily flogged by the Monthly Reviewers, I shall wonder. Mr Cumberland fell under their lash last month very severely, not so much for what he deserved, his affectation, but for his opinions about fanatics.[13] He has mentioned you,[14] which had as well have been left

7. That is, the 2d E. of Bristol (see n. 3 above). He was envoy extraordinary to Turin 1755–8, and ambassador at Madrid 1758–61.

8. As HW refused the picture, it remained in Cole's possession until his death, when it was bought by Richard Farmer. At Farmer's sale (7 May 1798 etc.) it was bought by Dallaway for £2.2.0 (36th day, lot 33 of the pictures).

9. Cole's copy reads 'one of Edward IV's daughters.'

10. Mary I (1516–58). This portrait also came into Farmer's possession after Cole's death, and was sold at Farmer's sale (36th day, lot 16), with another of Queen Elizabeth, to Bulmer for 8s.

11. *The Works of . . . Thomas Newton; with some Account of his Life, and*

Anecdotes of several of his Friends, written by himself, 3 vols, 1782.

12. When Pulteney was created Earl of Bath in 1742, he made Newton his chaplain. The latter, as he enjoyed the confidence of his patron in political matters, was therefore in a position to know Pulteney's part in the overthrow of Sir Robert Walpole.

13. Cole cannot refer to the *Monthly Review*, as Cumberland's *Anecdotes of Eminent Painters in Spain, during the Sixteenth and Seventeenth Centuries; with cursory Remarks upon the present State of Arts in that Kingdom*, 2 vols, 1782, was not reviewed there until July 1782. Cole probably refers to the *European Magazine* for April 1782, which contains a review of Cumberland's work (i. 284–6), and in

alone, for I don't see that you are answerable for all that Mr Vertue has alleged, if it be his: if not, not worth a note.

I can get no further, and am, dear Sir,

Yours most cordially,

WM COLE

Yesterday I received a letter from Mr Pennant, who concludes thus:

I shall be glad if you would explain to me the word *Acciliator*. It is mentioned among the persons who compose a garrison. After the words *Decem balistarii, unus capellanus,* and after *Acciliator,*[15] *unus carpentarius.*

Can you make anything of it? It is beyond my skill.

I had a print t'other day sent me to ridicule the author of *The Circassian,*[16] a new play. Pray, who is the author? A lady is divided in two, six inches between her body and haunches.[17] I suspect Mr Cumberland.

To COLE, Saturday 1 June 1782

Add MS 5953, ff. 145–6.

Cole noted at the top of the first page of this letter: '*Marianne, 11 Partie.* Mr Gough has collection about the Oxford family.' (See *post* 18 June 1782.)

Address: To the Reverend Mr Cole at Milton near Cambridge.

Postmark: 1 IV.

Berkeley Square, June 1, 1782.

I THANK you much, dear Sir, for your kind intention about Elizabeth of York, but it would be gluttony and rapacity to accept her. I have her already in the picture of her marriage[1] that was Lady

---

which a passage containing his views on fanatics is quoted.

14. 'in his book on Spanish painters' (addition in Cole's copy). See *post* 18 June 1782.

15. Possibly an error for *anciliator* < *ancile,* 'a small shield.'

16. *The Fair Circassian, A Tragedy,* was first performed at Drury Lane, 27 Nov. 1781, and was published in the same year. The author was Samuel Jackson Pratt (1749–1814), a voluminous writer of prose

and verse. The play is based on *Almoran and Hamet, an Oriental Tale,* 2 vols, 1761, by John Hawkesworth (1715?–73).

17. See Mary Dorothy George, *Catalogue of Political and Personal Satires . . . in the British Museum, 1771–83,* 1935, v. 785. The print ridicules the extravagance of Act V, Scenes 7–8.

——

1. The 'Marriage of Henry VII' (see *ante* 13 Nov. 1762).

Pomfret's;[2] besides Vertue's print of her with her husband, son and daughter-in-law.[3] In truth I have not room for any more pictures anywhere—yet without plundering you, or without impoverishing myself, I have supernumerary pictures, with which I can refurnish your vacancies—but I must get well first to look them out—as yet I cannot walk alone, and my posture, as you see, makes me write ill. It is impossible to recover in such weather—never was such a sickly June.

I have not yet seen Bishop Newton's *Life*. I will not give three guineas for what I would not give three pence, his *Works*—his *Life* I conclude will be borrowed by all the magazines. There I shall see it.

I know nothing of *Acciliator*—I have forgotten some of my good Latin, and happily never knew any bad: having always detested monkish barbarism. I have just finished Mr Pennant's new volume,[4] parts of which amused me though I knew every syllable that was worth knowing before, for there is not a word of novelty; and it is tiresome his giving such long extracts out of Dugdale[5] and other common books, and telling one long stories about all the most celebrated characters in the English history: besides panegyrics on all who showed him their houses—but the prints are charming[6]—though I cannot conceive why he gave one of the Countess of Cumberland,[7] who never did anything worth memory, but recording the very night on which she conceived.[8]

The Fair Circassian was written by a Mr Pratt, who has published

2. Henrietta Louisa Jeffreys (d. 1761), m. (1720) Thomas Fermor, 2d Bn Leominster, afterwards (1721) 1st E. of Pomfret. She paid £200 for the picture (see *Anecdotes, Works* iii. 50, and *ante* 13 Nov. 1762).

3. Under Vertue's 'Historic Prints,' HW lists 'Henry VII and his Queen; Henry VIII and Jane Seymour' (*Engravers, Works* iv. 147). 'A magnificent cartoon' of this picture, 'somewhat worn and defaced' is in the possession of the Duke of Devonshire (see DNB, *sub* Henry VIII).

4. *The Journey from Chester to London*, 1782. It was published Saturday 1 June, the date of HW's letter (see *St. James's Chronicle* 23–5 May 1782, for the advertisement, 'Saturday June 1 will be published').

5. Pennant quotes freely from Dugdale's

Baronage and *Monasticon* (see op. cit., *passim*).

6. The work contains twenty-two plates, not including the frontispiece, executed by various artists.

7. Margaret Russell (1560–1616), youngest daughter of Francis Russell, 3d E. of Bedford; m. (1577) George Clifford, 2d E. of Cumberland, by whom she was the mother of the famous Anne Clifford (1590–1676), Countess of Dorset, Pembroke and Montgomery. The portrait was engraved in Pennant's work, Plate XIII, opp. p. 246, by James Caldwall (b. 1739).

8. Pennant 'cannot help relating two of the minutiae of her journal,' 'which,' he says, 'is preserved in manuscript.' 'She relates that Anne Clifford was begot on her the first of May 1589, in Channel Row

several works under the name of Courtney Melmoth. The play might have been written by Cumberland, it is bad enough. I did read the latter's coxcombical *Anecdotes,* but saw nothing on myself except mention of my *Painters.*[9] Pray what is the passage you mean, on me or Vertue?[10] Do not write on purpose to answer this; it is not worth while.

I have just bought a most curious old picture; a portrait of one of whom I never saw a head. It is Robert Vere, Duke of Ireland,[11] the great favourite of Richard II. It is evidently very ancient, being only part of a larger piece on board—behind the head is this remnant of an inscription, which being defective and thence unintelligible, shows it is not an imposition—I mean not a modern cheat, though perhaps not a genuine portrait—here is what remains

Rob*ert*	The syllables under which I	Robertus Verus
Dux	have drawn a line are evidently	Dux Hiberniæ
Dubl*in*	more recent, and not on the	Dubliniae Marchio
Oxon	same piece of board. I imagine	Oxoniæ Comes
Baro*n*	the part wanting might be as I	Baro—
Rari	have supplied it on the right	
Bula	hand	
Nebo		
ob. 1393		

but I can make nothing of the three last pieces of words, which might be parts of Irish baronies. Will you be so good as to look into Collins's *House of Vere,*[12] or Dugdale,[13] etc., for I have no books in

House, hard by the River Thames; and in Skipton Castle, on Bardon Tower, she felt a child stir in her belly' (op. cit. 246–7). The child was born at Skipton Castle, 30 Jan. 1590.

9. 'the painters who distinguished themselves in England, have by happy fortune found a biographer whose entertaining talents will secure to them a reception with posterity' (Richard Cumberland, *Anecdotes of Eminent Painters in Spain,* 2 vols, 1782, i. 4–5).

10. See following letter.

11. Robert de Vere (1362–92), 9th E. of Oxford and Duke of Ireland (see DNB). HW describes it, 'A head in profile of Robert Vere, Earl of Oxford and Duke of Ireland,

favourite of Richard II, from Mr Scott's collection' (*Description of SH, Works* ii. 493). It was sold SH xx. 116. 'Mr. Scott,' from whose collection the picture came, was George Scott (1721–80), of Wolston Hall, Essex (see LA ix. 606–7).

12. *Historical Collections of the Noble Families of Cavendishe, Holles, Vere, Harley and Ogle,* by Arthur Collins, 1752. HW's copy (E.1.22), with MS notes by him, was sold SH ii. 99, and is now in the British Museum. The account of the Duke of Ireland appears at pp. 242–5. As Cole misunderstood HW's reference (see following letter), he probably did not own a copy of the work.

13. That is, Dugdale's *Baronage.*

town. Let this too be at your leisure, for I am in no hurry—except to hear that you are better. Adieu!

From Cole, Tuesday 18 June 1782

VA, Forster MS 110, ff. 277–8. Cole's copy, Add MS 5826, ff. 76v, 77v.
Address: For the Honourable Horace Walpole, Berkeley Square, London.
Postmark: Cambridge 20 IV.

Milton, Tuesday, June 18, 1782.

Dear Sir,

I DID not write before for fear of fatiguing you with writing an answer, when you might not have been at ease to have done it. I pray God you may be recovered now, though the extremity of heat we are got into may possibly be of as bad consequence as the other excesses. I am sure it is so to me. If you are not quite well, I beg I may not hear from you.

I am sorry I can give you no help about your picture of the Duke of Ireland: no doubt the remainder were Irish titles, Tiperary perhaps one of them, but I have not Dugdale's *Baronage* nor Collins's pedigree of the Earls of Oxford, who were extinct before my edition of 1735.[1] Mr Gough, who threatens you a visit at Strawberry Hill (as by a letter of June 4), has collections relating to the Vere family. I will ask him about it if you choose, but no doubt you will show him your picture, which I long to see, for I look upon it as a most valuable acquisition and great curiosity.

Mr Pennant sent me his book. I am totally of your mind in relation to it: he is a mere book-maker. I do not thus write of him because I am offended with him for a slight expression in relation to my patron Browne Willis,[2] where he has made <me> an accessory, for however ridiculous he might have been, it did not become me to speak slightingly of him, and I am positive I ne<ver did so>:[3] it was

---

1. Cole refers to Collins's *Peerage,* and not his 'House of Vere' (see preceding letter).

2. 'The chapel [of Fenny Stratford] which is in the parish of Blecheley, was rebuilt and endowed at the expense of Mr Brown Willis and his friends. His residence was near the church of Blecheley; but, having a great predilection for the works of his own hands, he entrusted to the Reverend Mr William Cole, then rector of the parish, the following inscription; which Mr Cole was requested to cause to be inscribed on a white marble stone veneered with black, to be laid over him in this chapel' (*Journey from Chester to London,* 1782, p. 212).

3. Supplied from Cole's copy.

foisted in by someone who had the care of the press, and indeed, in
<a former>³ letter a month ago, he seemed to prepare me for it.
That I never could have given him that information is evident from
his saying that Mr Willis lived near the church: he never at any period lived there, but at Whaddon Hall, three or four miles off,
though he had built a mansion near the church, but never slept in it.⁴
But when people write post-haste (as you once expressed it),⁵ no wonder one meets contradictions. He had better have stuck to his zo-
ology.⁶

Mr Cumberland's book I have lent to Mr Essex, and cannot recur
to the page, but I think it is at the beginning of the second volume,
where he gives Rubens's life. He there says, 'Mr Walpole is mistaken,
etc., for saying he was in Spain at such a time.'⁷ I thought it rough
and ungentle, nothing more: it might have been expressed more
politely.

I can't use my pen as I was wont, therefore have recourse to old
and new books in my possession. One pleases me much, and I often
re-read it, though full of Marivauxisms: it is the *Life of Marianne*.⁸ I
have only eleven parts: I should be glad to know whether there are
any more, for it leaves off in a very interesting part. Excuse this nonsense.

The picture of Elizabeth of York in my possession exactly answers
your description of 'a buxom well-looking damsel.' I look upon it as
your own, and you may have it whenever you please. Your kind offer
of supernumeraries greatly obliges me: you know my collection, such
as it is, was picked up in Moorfields, etc. I pretend to no taste or
choice: any offal will satisfy me.

I most heartily thank you for your late edition of the *Anecdotes*,
which came safe.

I can write no more, and only subscribe myself, dear Sir,

Your ever faithful and most obliged servant,

WM COLE

4. Cole's copy reads 'never, as I have
been told, slept in it.'

5. See *ante* 28 May 1774, 28 July 1776.

6. Cole's copy reads 'I wish he had stuck
to his zoology and natural history.'

7. 'Mr Horace Walpole is mistaken in
thinking Rubens was in Spain during the
administration of the Duke of Lerma.
This was not so' (op. cit. i. 170).

8. *La Vie de Marianne, ou les Avantures
[sic] de madame la comtesse de * * **, in
eleven parts, Paris and The Hague, 1731–
41, by Pierre-Carlet de Chamblain de Marivaux (1688–1763). Marivaux left it unfinished, but see following letter.

To Cole, Friday 21 June 1782

Add MS 5953, ff. 147–8.

Cole noted on the cover: 'Nichols's eternal publications. C. of Ess—. D[uke] of Gl[oucester's] Chapl[ain].' The meaning of the second note is not clear, but the first and third are notes for his reply to HW.

Address: To the Reverend Mr Cole at Milton near Cambridge.
Postmark: GC 21 IV.

Berkeley Square, June 21, 1782.

IT is no trouble, my good Sir, to write to you, for I am as well recovered as I generally do. I am very sorry you do not, and especially in your hands, as your pleasure and comfort so much depends on them. Age is by no means a burden while it does not subject one to depend on others—when it does, it reconciles one to quitting everything—at least I believe you and I think so, who do not look on solitude as a calamity.

I shall go to Strawberry Hill tomorrow and will, as I might have thought of doing, consult Dugdale and Collins for the Duke of Ireland's inferior titles. Mr Gough I shall be glad of seeing when I am settled there, which will not be this fortnight.

I think there are but eleven parts of *Marianne,*[1] and that it breaks off in the Nun's Story which promised to be very interesting. Marivaux never finished *Marianne* nor the *Paysan Parvenu*[2] (which was the case too of the younger Crébillon with *Les Égaremens*).[3] I have seen two bad conclusions of *Marianne* by other hands.[4]

Elizabeth of York I beg you will keep, I really have not a place for it—but I shall send you by Monday's fly four very indifferent pictures, which will not deserve the smallest thanks: I shall be content if one of them will serve to fill your vacancy, and if the others will be of any use to you. If they are not, I assure you they are not worth returning, though I bought them all at Mr Sheldon's[5] in lots with

1. HW's copy, 2 vols, Paris, 1742 (F.6.13–4), was sold SH ii. 138.

2. *Le Paysan Parvenu*, in five parts, Paris, 1735. The three parts usually added to the novel are not Marivaux's (see Gustave Larroumet, *Marivaux*, new edn, Paris, 1894, pp. 75, 514). HW's copy, Frankfort, 1737 (G.6.45) was sold SH iv. 37.

3. *Les Égaremens du Coeur et de l'Esprit, ou Mémoires de M. de Meilcour*, 3 vols, Paris, etc., 1736–8. HW's copy, The Hague, 1736 (F.6.33), was sold SH ii. 131.

4. Mme Marie-Jeanne Laboras de Mé-zières Riccoboni wrote a *Suite de Marianne*, as did an anonymous writer. Mme Riccoboni's continuation, which was written with Marivaux's consent, appeared as early as 1745 (see *Catalogue Général des Livres Imprimés de la Bibliothèque Nationale*).

5. William Sheldon (d. 1780), of Weston in Warwickshire (see Burke, *Landed Gentry*, 1851). His collection was sold by Messrs Christie and Ansell, Monday 27 Aug. 1781 and fourteen days following (see *St James's Chronicle* 11–14, 23–5 Aug. 1781).

other articles: one is a portrait of Selden;[6] the three others are an altar-piece and doors,[7] with arms, which by the flourishing sort of mantle round them, seem to be Flemish or Dutch.

Mr Cumberland's brusquerie is not worth notice, nor did I remember it. Mr Pennant's impetuosity you must overlook too, though I love your delicacy about your friend's[8] memory. Nobody that knows you will suspect you of wanting it—but in the ocean of books that overflows every day, who will recollect a thousandth part of what is in most of them? By the number of writers one should naturally suppose there were multitudes of readers; but if there are, which I doubt, the latter only read the productions of the day. Indeed if they did read former publications, they would have no occasion to read the modern, which, like Mr Pennant's, are but borrowed wholesale from the more ancient—it is sad to say, that the borrowers add little new but mistakes. I have just been turning over Mr Nichols's eight volumes of *Select Poems*,[9] which he has swelled unreasonably with large collops of old authors, most of whom little deserved revivifying. I bought them for the biographic notes, in which I have found both inaccuracies and blunders. For instance one that made me laugh; in Lord Lansdown's *Beauties*[10] he celebrates a Lady or Mrs Vaughan. Mr Nichols turns to the peerage of that time and finds that a Duke of Bolton married a Lady Anne Vaughan;[11] he instantly sets her down for the lady in question and

6. John Selden (1584–1654), the jurist. After Cole's death the portrait came into possession of Richard Farmer, and was sold at the latter's sale in 1798 (36th day, lot 5 of the pictures), with four other pictures, to Heber, for 7s.

7. These three pictures likewise came into Farmer's possession, and were sold at his sale (36th day, lot 56 of the pictures) to Basire for 13s. They are described in the sale catalogue as 'the Wise-Men Offering, and 2 side pieces, formerly an altar-piece, and presented by the late Earl of Orford to Mr Cole.'

8. Browne Willis's.

9. *A Select Collection of Poems: with Notes, Biographical and Historical*, ed. John Nichols, 8 vols, 1780–2. HW's copy (B.7) was sold SH i. 79. It is now in the Dyce collection, Victoria and Albert Museum. It has many notes in HW's hand.

10. George Granville or Grenville (1667–1735), 1st Bn Lansdowne, was the author of poems and plays, but he is not the author of the poem to which HW refers. 'The Celebrated Beauties: Occasioned by the Author's being suspected of writing "The British Court," ' which Nichols expressly says is 'anonymous: from Dryden's Collection,' follows several of Lord Lansdowne's poems. HW probably confused this poem with Lansdowne's 'The Court Beauties,' which Nichols prints v. 277–80; 'The Celebrated Beauties' follows at 282–97.

11. Charles Paulet or Powlett (1685–1754), 3d D. of Bolton m. (1713), Lady Anne Vaughan (d. 1751), dau. and heiress of John Vaughan, 3d E. of Carbery. As HW says, however, they soon separated (see GEC).

introduces her to posterity as a beauty. Unluckily she was a monster
—so ugly that the Duke, then Marquis of Winchester, being forced
by his father[12] to marry her for her great fortune, was believed never
to have consummated, and parted from her as soon as his father
died—but if our predecessors are exposed to these misrepresenta-
tions, what shall we be, when not only all private history is detailed
in our newspapers, but scarce ever with tolerable fidelity! I have
long said, that if a paragraph in a newspaper contains a word of
truth, it is sure to be accompanied with two or three blunders—yet
who will believe that papers published in the face of the whole town
should be nothing but magazines of lies, every one of which fifty
persons could contradict and disprove? Yet so it certainly is, and
future history will probably be ten times falser than all preceding.
Adieu!

Yours most sincerely,

HOR. WALPOLE

From COLE, Saturday 29 June 1782

VA, Forster MS 110, f. 279. COLE's copy, Add MS 5826, f. 78v.
Address: For the Honourable Horace Walpole, Berkeley Square, London.
Postmark: Cambridge 1 IY.

Milton, Saturday, June 29, 1782.

Dear Sir,

I JUST now received the pictures. I sent for them on Monday, but
they did not come till the next day, and I have been so ill, so dis-
composed by the death of my niece Newcome,[1] in whose coach my
poor niece Apthorp was killed, and Mrs Newcome much hurt, and
probably might be the occasion of her death.[2] The old altar-piece
seems to be the work of an able hand, and will suit a place I have
for it. Mr Selden I should have known had not his name been on it.
I am much obliged to you for them, and will give them their niches
in a few days. I still continue in the same state, and am sincerely glad

---

12. Sir Charles Paulet or Powlett (1661–
1722), 2d D. of Bolton.

1. Mrs Henry Newcome (see *ante* 13
May 1782).

2. 'though I [have] not yet heard particulars, that I had no heart to write'
(addition in Cole's copy).

so valuable a life as yours is, is protracted, and may it be so for years, till you are as much tired of it as I am of mine.

Dr Farmer calling here yesterday mentioned a mistake in your *Anecdotes*, yet it is not in your edition of 1771,[3] pp. 95, 99, which I consulted when he was gone. He says the statue of Sir Isaac Newton in Trinity College ante-chapel is by Roubiliac,[4] and those of King George[5] and the Duke of Somerset[6] in the Senate House by Rysbrach.[7] You will possibly recur to the place in question.[8] He told me Mr Pennant is made a knight.[9] Was he High Sheriff?[10]

Mr Nichols is so quick in his publications that he hardly gives one time to read one before another pops upon you: they are very expensive, and some not worth publication. In a letter last week, he tells me that he is going to publish a new edition of Hogarth's *Life*.[11] I bought his last not two years ago, and now shall be at the expense of another: this is sad pickpocket work! His mistake about Mrs Vaughan is really pleasant.[12] Your observations on the deluge of books, and lies propagated in periodical papers, are too just, and in the last case infamously scandalous. I have a magazine with your print and Mrs Clive's and history.[13] Should such practices be allowed in any civilized country? It is carrying the liberty of the press to such

3. That is, *Anecdotes*[1] iv. 95, 99, referred to HW's accounts of Rysbrach and Roubiliac.

4. Louis François Roubiliac (1695–1762), sculptor, who gained the patronage of HW's brother, Sir Edward (see Katharine A. Esdaile, *The Life and Works of Louis François Roubiliac*, Oxford, 1928).

5. 'George II' in Cole's copy, but should be George I (see n. 8 below).

6. Charles Seymour (1662–1748), 6th D. of Somerset, known as 'the proud Duke.' He was Chancellor of Cambridge University 1689–1748.

7. John Michael Rysbrack (1693?–1770), sculptor.

8. Farmer's comment applies to the following passage in HW's account of Roubiliac, which he added to the 1782 edition: 'His statue of George I in the Senate House at Cambridge is well executed, and so is that of their Chancellor, Charles Duke of Somerset. . . . His statue of Sir Isaac Newton in the chapel of Trinity College is the best of the three' (iv. 213).

The passage remained unchanged in *Works* iii. 480, but Farmer was correct: the statues of George I (now in the University Library, Cambridge) and of the D. of Somerset (in the Senate House) are by Rysbrack (see Esdaile, op. cit. 205).

9. Farmer was mistaken: Pennant was never knighted.

10. Pennant was High Sheriff of Flintshire in 1761.

11. The second edition was published in this year.

12. Cole's copy reads 'truly laughable.'

13. *The Town and Country Magazine*, Dec. 1769, i. 617–20, contains a 'Tête-à-Tête' of HW and Mrs Clive, with prints of them, under the titles of 'Baron Otranto' and 'Mrs Heidelburgh.' The 'Tête-à-Tête' was probably suggested by HW's 'Epilogue spoken by Mrs Clive, on her quitting the Stage, April 24, 1769,' and it may have been written by Chatterton (see W. S. Lewis, HW's *Fugitive Verses* 69; Meyerstein, *Chatterton* 272).

an <excess> that it disquiets private families, and turns the head of the people.

An acquaintance of mine[14] is gone chaplain with the Duke and Duchess of Gloucester abroad. I hope the distance he will be kept at will prevent his showing his infinite coxcombicalness.

We are now in the height of the Commencement. The Bishop of Ely[15] preached the Hospital Sermon,[16] and was much applauded. His brother[17] is president of it,[18] and attended. The next day the oratorio of *Sampson*,[19] by the Jewish Miss Abrahams[20] and others, was performed at St Mary's. You may well imagine I was not there, nor have been able these eight or ten years.

I am, dear Sir,

Your most obliged and faithful servant,

WM COLE

To COLE, Tuesday 23 July 1782

Add MS 5953, ff. 149–50.
Address: To the Reverend Mr Cole at Cambridge.
Postmark: Isleworth 23 IY.

Strawberry Hill, July 23, 1782.

I HAVE been more dilatory than usual, dear Sir, in replying to your last, but it called for no particular answer, nor have I now anything worth telling you. Mr Gough and Mr Nichols dined with me on Saturday last. I lent the former three and twenty drawings of monuments out of Mr Lethuillier's books, for his large work, which will be a magnificent one. Mr Nichols is, as you say, a very rapid

14. Not identified.

15. Hon. James Yorke (1730–1808), 5th son of the 1st E. of Hardwicke; Bp of St David's 1774–9, of Gloucester 1779–81, and of Ely 1781–1808 (see *Alumni Cantab.;* Bentham, *Ely*[2], Addenda, pp. 12–13).

16. 'on Thursday' (addition to Cole's copy). An annual sermon was preached at Great St Mary's on the occasion of the meeting of the governors and contributors to Addenbrooke's Hospital, and a collection for the benefit of the hospital was taken at the door.

17. Philip Yorke, 2d E. of Hardwicke.

18. Addenbrooke's Hospital.

19. By Handel (cf. *ante* 9 July 1772).

20. Cole's copy reads 'the two Judaical Miss Abrahams.' Harriet Abrams (1760–ca 1825), soprano, and her sister Theodosia, afterwards Mrs Garrow (1766–1834?), contralto (see Sir George Grove, *Dictionary of Music and Musicians,* 3d edn, ed. H. C. Colles, 6 vols, 1927–8; James D. Brown and Stephen S. Stratton, *British Musical Biography,* Birmingham, 1897).

editor, and I must commend him for being a very accurate one. I scarce ever saw a book so correct as his *Life of Mr Bowyer*.[1] I wish it deserved the pains he has bestowed on it every way, and that he would not dub so many men *great*. I have known several of his heroes, who were very *little* men. Dr Meade[2] had nothing but pretensions, and Philip Carteret Webbe[3] was a sorry knave, with still less foundations. To what a slender total do those shrink who are the idols of their own age![3a] How very few are known at all at the end of the next century! But there is a chapter in Voltaire[4] that would cure anybody of being a great man even in his own eyes—it is the chapter in which a Chinese goes into a bookseller's shop and marvels at not finding any of his own country's classics. It is a chapter that ought never to be out of the sight of any vain author.

I have just got the new *Catalogue of the MSS in the Museum*.[5] It is every way piteously dear[6]—the method is extremely puzzling, and the contents chiefly rubbish. Who would give a rush for Dr Birch's correspondence? Many of the pieces are in print. In truth I set little store by a collection of MSS. A work must be of little value that could never get into print, I mean, if it has existed half a century. The articles that diverted me most were an absolute novelty; I knew Henry VIII was a *royal author*, but not a royal quack. There are several receipts of his own, and this delectable one amongst others; 'The King's Grace's oyntement made at St James's, to coole, and dry and comfort the member.' Another, to the same purpose, was devised at *Cawoode*[7]—was not that an episcopal palace? How devoutly was the head of the Church employed!

1. *Biographical and Literary Anecdotes of William Bowyer*, 1782.

2. Richard Mead (1673–1754), whom Nichols calls 'this great' and 'eminent physician' (ibid. 251–3).

3. Philip Carteret Webb (1700–70), antiquary and politician. Nichols calls him 'this distinguished antiquary,' 'learned' and 'able' (ibid. 297).

3a. Nichols quotes this passage, beginning at 'Mr Nichols,' with the comment: 'The late Lord Orford was a good critic, but not always a sincere man. The following . . . may be considered as his real opinion; which I am proud to preserve, though the latter part is somewhat severe. The date of it, compared with that of my Preface [11 June 1782], shows the eager-

ness with which he read the book' (LA iv. 708).

4. 'Entretien avec un Chinois,' in his *Dictionnaire Philosophique*, under 'Gloire, Glorieux,' Section III (Voltaire, *Oeuvres Complètes*, nouvelle édn, 52 vols, Paris, 1877–85, xix. 267–70).

5. *A Catalogue of the Manuscripts preserved in the British Museum hitherto undescribed*, by Samuel Ayscough, 2 vols, 1782. Ayscough (1745–1804) became assistant librarian of the British Museum about 1785, and published several catalogues and indexes.

6. It sold for two guineas in boards. Only 250 copies were printed (see *Lloyd's Evening Post* 5–7 June 1782).

7. 'An oyntement devised by the King's

I hope you have recovered your spirits, and that summer, which is arrived at last, will make a great amendment in you.

Yours most sincerely,

H. W.

From Cole, Thursday 25 July 1782

Cole's copy, Add MS 5826, ff. 79v, 8ov. The original is missing.
Address: For the Honourable Horace Walpole, Strawberry Hill, Twickenham, Middlesex.

Milton, July 25, 1782.

Dear Sir,

I DARE say you made Mr Gough completely happy, both in the sight of Strawberry Hill[1] and its treasures, and by your kind communicativeness in lending him so many of Mr Lethieullier's drawings. I have not yet sent for *Mr Bowyer's Life,* but shall immediately, as you speak so well of Mr Nichols's accuracy, and long to see the chapter of Voltaire you allude to: but alas! though within sight of so many libraries, I dare say I shall not meet with his works. I have only a few detached pieces, and am indeed re-reading at this instant his *Histoire Générale,*[2] which you somewhere call 'a charming bird's-eye view of the world,'[3] and so it is indeed with all its imperfections. What a loss had I in poor dear Mr Gray! He had every new, as well as curious, publication, foreign and English, and lent me to his death all that I wanted, and I never was so happy. I am sorry to say it, but it is inconceivable the trouble one has to get a book from a library.

Majestie at Cawoode, to dry excoriations and comfort the member, called the sweet oyntment' (both recipes are given in Ayscough, op. cit. ii. 627). At Cawood, in Yorkshire, about nine miles from York, was formerly a palace belonging to the Archbishop of York. Cardinal Wolsey was arrested there in 1530.

1. Gough had seen SH once before, in 1775, when HW was in Paris (see LA viii. 671).

2. Voltaire's *Essai sur l'Histoire Générale et sur les Moeurs et l'Esprit des Nations, depuis Charlemagne jusqu'a nos Jours,* 7 vols, Geneva, 1756, contained works published earlier: *Abrégé de l'Histoire universelle . . .,* 2 vols, The Hague, 1753, and *Essai sur l'Histoire universelle . . .,* Leipzig and Dresden, 1754. HW's copy of the *Abrégé . . .,* 2 vols, London, 1753 (G.4.46–7), was sold SH iv. 47.

3. HW refers to Voltaire as the 'author of that beautiful essay on universal history, . . . a most charming bird's-eye landscape, where one views the whole in picturesque confusion, and imagines the objects more delightful than they are in reality, and when examined separately' (*Roy. & Nob. Authors, Works* i. 421).

I have long left off sending for any. They have treasures on treasures, and know not the value of what they enjoy, and like literary misers they will neither use them themselves or suffer others to do so.

I think your character of Mr Webbe as a sorry knave would suit Mr West also. Mr Ayscough's *Catalogue of MSS* I have been running over, but have not yet got to thirty pages. Your stricture is most just: though a catalogue-maker, he does not seem to be acquainted with books. What a delightful anecdote of his Royal Grace and his ointment! Surely he was very curious about the part, as he exhibited it so often and took such care of it! That on the pendulum at Strawberry[4] may be depended on: the other at the Tower may be more doubtful. Cawode belongs to the Archbishop of York. Thank God, my spirits are tolerable, but this hot weather overpowers and oppresses me so that I can hardly hold a pen to subscribe myself, dear Sir,

Your ever faithful servant,

WM COLE

From COLE, Wednesday 30 October 1782

VA, Forster MS 110, ff. 280–1. COLE's copy, Add MS 5826, ff. 80v, 81v.

Address: For the Hon. Horace Walpole at Strawberry Hill, Twickenham, Middlesex. *Postmark:* 4 NO. [Name of post office illegible, but the letter was sent from London through the Penny Post. Steevens probably posted it there; see below.]

Milton, Oct. 30, 1782.

Dear Sir,

IT is so long since I had the pleasure of hearing from you, that a line from you to inform me of your disposition and health will give me great satisfaction. I should have wrote long before now had my health permitted it, and indeed was unwilling to fill my paper with my distresses. All the year has been most uncomfortable, but for the last three months I never had the least expectation of reaching to the end of October: not only every old complaint, except the gout,

---

4. Cole refers to the pendulum of the clock which Henry VIII presented to Anne Boleyn on their marriage. The clock, which was a present to HW from Lady Elizabeth Germaine, was in the Library at SH (see *Description of SH, Works* ii. 444–5). It was sold SH xvii. 48 to Queen Victoria, and now stands in the Royal Library at Windsor. A woodcut of it appears in the SH Sale Catalogue, p. xiv.

which plague I have often wished for, but for above two months have been under the surgeon's[1] hands for a tumour withinside my thigh, occasioned by a bad fall in my chamber. Thank God, I have had no slashings or cuttings, and hope no other ill effect than common in such cases. It was the first surgeon I ever employed. I was also forced to call in the physician,[2] for the first time also. God knows how it will end, but I am resigned, and it is no great sacrifice, with such days and such nights, to wish for a remove. I will here end my complaints.

No doubt you have seen the *European Magazine*.[3] In one of the first numbers, I think, there is something coarse about you.[4] I made a memorandum of it, with a design to have sent it, but could not write, and have mislaid it.

Dr Lort quits the Archbishop's service tomorrow, and report says that he is on the brink of matrimony.[5] It is certain that he has hired an house in Saville Row.

Have you seen a quarto pamphlet, just published, against Mr Warton's *History of English Poetry?*[6] It is cruelly severe and pointed against many of his blunders. The writer is said to be one Ritson of Gray's Inn, and though Mr Warton may deserve to be lashed for his presumption, dogmaticalness and mistakes, yet few people surely will commend his bitter sarcasms, both on him and the Bishop of Dromore, who is spared as little as Mr Warton, and more especially his printing Marlowe's infidelity.[7]

Mr Gough has been here since I wrote last,[8] and stayed a day with me. Mr Steevens has been here, viz., at Cambridge, and often over here, for two full months: he leaves us on Saturday. I had very nearly commenced, if not author, at least editor, had not he deterred me, from its being too much for me at this time, though Mr Gough un-

1. Not identified.

2. Not identified.

3. *The European Magazine and London Review*, the first number of which was for Jan. 1782.

4. 'except it is in Maty's *Review*' (addition in Cole's copy). Paul Henry Maty (1745–87) started *A New Review; with Literary Curiosities, and Literary Intelligence* in Feb. 1782. Cole, however, refers to the letter in *The European Magazine*, April 1782 (i. 260–2), signed 'H. I.,' which attacked HW about Chatterton (see *ante* 24 May 1782 n. 3).

5. Lort m. (19 May 1783) Susannah Norfolk (1742–92) dau. of Alderman Norfolk of Cambridge (see GM May 1783, liii. 451b).

6. *Observations on the Three First Volumes of the History of English Poetry. In a Familiar Letter to the Author*, 1782. The author was Joseph Ritson (1752–1803), antiquary and bibliographer, who attacked Johnson, Steevens, Reed and Malone as well as Warton and Percy.

7. Ritson's account of Marlowe is at pp. 39–42.

8. Gough visited Cole 8 Sept. 1782 (see *ante* 2 July 1780 n. 5).

dertook kindly to correct the press, and Mr Nichols to give me no trouble or put me to expense, yet my fears of the fatigue of writing, now I can so ill do so, have made me lay all thoughts of it aside. Do you guess that I had you in my eye for the dedication or inscription? It is a work by Mr Willis, which he put into my hands three weeks before he died, with a desire that I would methodize and put into order a thousand detached and separate papers relating to two of the hundreds of Buckinghamshire. This I did with great labour when in Buckinghamshire,[9] but was always afraid of the trouble of publishing, and now I am least qualified for it, Mr Gough, when he was lately here, pressed me to have it printed.[10]

You will excuse my writing more, as I am fatigued, and remain, dear Sir,

Your most faithful and obliged servant,

WM COLE

To COLE, Tuesday 5 November 1782

Add MS 5953, ff. 151–2.
Address: To the Reverend Mr Cole at Milton near Cambridge.
Postmark: Isleworth 5 NO.

Strawberry Hill, Nov. 5, 1782.

I HAD begun a letter in answer to another person,[1] which I have broken off on receiving yours, dear Sir. I am exceedingly concerned at the bad account you give of yourself, and yet on weighing it, I flatter myself that you are not only out of all danger, but have had a fortunate crisis which I hope will prolong your life. A boil surmounted is a present from Nature to us who are not boys—and though you speak as weary of life from sufferings, and yet with proper resignation and philosophy, it does not frighten me, as I know that any tumour and gathering even in the gum, is strangely dispiriting.

9. Cole's copy reads 'while at Blecheley.'
10. For the correspondence between Cole, Gough and Nichols on the subject of the proposed publication, see LA i. 667–8, vi. 199–202. Cole's ill health prevented his undertaking such a task, and the work,

'History and Antiquities of Hundreds of Newport and Cotslow,' remains in MS in Add MSS 5839–40.

1. The only other letter of this date which has been located is to Lady Ossory.

I do not write merely from sympathizing friendship, but to beg that if your boil is not closed or healing, you will let me know, for the bark is essential, yet very difficult to have genuine. My apothecary here I believe has some very good, and I will send you some directly.

I will thank you but not trouble you with an account of myself. I have had no fit of gout, nor any new complaint; but it is with the utmost difficulty that I keep the humour from laming me entirely, especially in my hands, which are a mine of chalk-stones, but as they discharge themselves, I flatter myself they prevent heavier attacks.

I do take in the *European Magazine*,[2] and think it in general one of the best. I forget what was said of me[3]—sometimes I am corrected, sometimes flattered—and care for neither. I have not seen the answer to Mr Warton, but will send for it.

I shall not be sorry on my own account if Dr Lort quits Lambeth and comes to Saville Row, which is my neighbourhood—but I did not think a wife was the stall where he would set up his staff.

You have given me the only reason why I cannot be quite sorry that you do not print what you had prepared for the press. No kind intention towards me from you surprises me—but then I want no new proofs. My wish for whatever shall be the remainder of my life is to be quiet and forgotten. Were my course to recommence, and could one think in youth as one does at sixty-five, I have no notion that I should have courage to appear as an author. Do you know too that I look on fame now as the idlest of all visions?—but this theme would lead me too far.

I collect a new comfort from your letter. The *writing* is much better than in most of your latest letters. If your pain were not ceased, you could not have formed your letters so firmly and distinctly. I will not say more lest I should draw you into greater fatigue. Let me have but a single line in answer.

Yours most cordially,

H. W.

2. HW continued his subscription as long as he lived; 28 volumes were sold SH v. 4.

3. See note 4 to preceding letter.

From COLE, Thursday 7 November 1782

VA, Forster MS 110, f. 282. Cole kept no copy.

Address: For the Hon. Horace Walpole, Strawberry Hill in Twickenham, Middlesex. *Postmark:* 9 NO. [The letter was sent by the Penny Post, but the stamp is blurred.]

Milton, Nov. 7, 1782. Thursday morning.

Dear Sir,

YOUR letter does me more good than physicians and surgeons: the former absolutely seem to know little of one's complaints, only formalize and say a few hard words, and are glad to take leave.

I am infinitely obliged to you for your concern. Thank God, my tumour is quite gone, but the surgeon advised me to make use of it, at its leaving me, as an issue, so, though I tak<e as> much bark as most people, it would be cheating you <to> accept of your exceeding kind offer. Warm, foggy, rainy w<ea>ther is my bane: these two days' cold have set me up, and last night I had such a sound sleep as surprised me and revived me; such an one as I have not had these twelve months. I attribute it to have taken thirty drops of laudanum the two preceding nights, the first without any effect. Possibly the virtue of it might remain in me, and unite to compose me so well.

I am glad to hear you are free from gout, yet Dr Glynn some two years ago, when Rowley had not divided us, and I mentioned having taken the bark, exclaimed, 'What! Bark and gout!' His remedy he gave not.

I wonder I did not hear yesterday from Mr Nichols, to whom I had wrote about the book,[1] and he was to come down this week, but Mr Steevens, who carried my letter, told me he would represent to him how troublesome and inconvenient it would be to me to undertake it, and stop his coming.

I most heartily wish you the continuance of your health and use of your hands: you are too prudent to neglect any caution about them. My fingers are so numbed with cold, with the little snow we had last night, that I can hardly subscribe myself, dear Sir,

Your ever faithful and most obliged servant,

WM COLE[2]

1. Cole to Nichols 29 Oct. 1782 is printed in LA vi. 201–2. 'The book' was Willis's 'History and Antiquities of Hundreds of Newport and Cotslow' (see *ante* 30 Oct. 1782).

2. Cole died 16 Dec. 1782.

APPENDICES

APPENDIX 1

Cole's Unsent Letter of Thursday 28 May 1778

Cole's copy, Add MS 5824, ff. 130v, 131v, 147v–154v.

Cole's note: 'The letter I wrote to Mr Walpole May 28, and never sent, was this.' See *ante* 14 June 1778.

Thursday, May 28, 1778. Milton.

Dear Sir,

THE new edition of the *Biographia* has Mr Baker's life drawn up by the editors at pp. 518–25, in which are very few things, indeed none, but what will be found in my papers, except one: which is, that Mr Prior allowed Mr Baker the profits of his Fellowship after he was ejected from it. Of this assertion I much doubt, and shall hesitate till I have better authority than is given for it. We know Mr Prior was a man of no original fortune, and that his offices of secretary and ambassador did not so enrich him, but that on his quitting them he was obliged to the bounty of the Earl of Oxford for the house he lived in:[1] that he solicited, or his friends for him, subscriptions for an edition of his *Poems;* and that he left the Society of St John's College a set of books to the value of £200, with the Earl of Jersey's and his own picture,[2] as an acknowledgment for his retaining the Fellowship during his life. Had he really allowed Mr Baker the profits of it, it seems very odd, not to say ungrateful, to the memory of Mr Prior, that he should not have mentioned it or taken some notice of it. His own declaration at the conclusion of his preface to *Bishop Fisher's Sermon* seems to say the contrary, and that he was quite independent. Besides, if he held his Fellowship till 1717, it is less probable at that time that Mr Prior was in a situation to have been so generous, who died in 1721. It is much more probable that the patron of Mr Prior was also so of Mr Baker. I mean the Earl of Oxford, to whom Mr B. gave the chiefest part of his MSS. This marginal note is added as a proof of the assertion:

This curious fact was communicated to the Rev. Mr Rob. Robinson of Chester-

---

1. Down Hall, near Harlow, Essex, which was bought in 1714 by Prior and Lord Harley (afterwards 2nd E. of Oxford), with reversion to Harley after Prior's death (see Leopold G. Wickham Legg, *Matthew Prior,* Cambridge, 1912, p. 264).

2. 'He . . . left to the College Hyacinthe Rigaud's portrait of his patron, Edward, Earl of Jersey, and his own portrait by Alexis-Simon Belle, familiar in Vertue's engraving' (DNB: Austin Dobson). Edward Villiers (1656?–1711), 1st E. of Jersey, was envoy to The Hague and Paris 1695–9, and Secretary of State, 1700–1. He was Prior's friend and patron, as well as his associate in diplomatic affairs.

ton, by the Rev. Dr Goddard, Master of Clare Hall. The Doctor remembers Mr Baker well, and says he was one of the best men in his moral conduct.

The editor sets out with a small mistake in making Dr Ashton,[3] the founder of the Fellowship which Mr Baker enjoyed, Dean of York; whereas he was only Archdeacon of York, but never Dean.

He is also at some pains to justify Dr Jortin's strictures upon Mr Baker for having censured LeClerc,[4] and on the same principle depreciates Mr Baker's *Reflections upon Learning*. But the design of Mr Baker was consistent with his profession, that of a Christian divine, and not that of a modern philosopher. He meant to show the weakness of human understanding and learning in order to evince the necessity of revelation. And if he has not done it, perhaps it may be some time before such a desideratum will be given us, as we are informed by the editor that it 'would almost require the genius and comprehension of a Lord Verulam to execute it in a proper manner.' These are the thanks that Mr Baker is to expect from the philosophers of the present age for his labours and studies to improve mankind! Dr Jortin and Mr LeClerc hold the more fashionable opinions.

I had the volume[5] sent to me from Cambridge, but allowed so little time to keep it that I could not attempt to write the whole, being near four folio pages in a small letter, though the chief is an unnecessary catalogue of the contents of all Mr Baker's MS volumes, as they are already printed in the *Catalogue of the Harleian Manuscripts*. I hope it will be easy for you to get a sight of it in town. It is inscribed to the Earl of Hardwick, the earliest patron of the work, as Dr Kippis tells him.

In the preface, p. xiii, is this further account of Mr Baker, after mentioning Anthony Wood.

It was once hoped we should have had like attention shown towards the learned men educated at Cambridge; and had the work been executed as it was designed, by the late Rev. and excellent Mr Baker, it must have been a masterly performance; since, with all the care and industry of Wood, he had a fine genius, a piercing understanding, and wrote a correct style, equally removed from the starched setness of a sententious writer and from that luxuriancy of language that produces long and languid periods. But besides all these, he had still greater qualities, such as calmness of mind, candour of heart, and a most unsuspected integrity. We may justly, therefore, regret the loss of such a work from such a man. But as his collections are still preserved, we may yet hope to see their contents by some lucky accident or other.

3. Hugh Ashton (d. 1522), Archdeacon of York 1516–22.

4. Jean LeClerc (1657–1736), French critic, who visited England in 1682; au- thor of *Ars Critica*, 1696, and other scholarly works.

5. *Biographia Britannica*,[2] vol. 1.

At p. 203 is a note respecting yourself which will oblige you to send for the volume.[6]

Erasmus Lewis, in a letter to Dean Swift, dated London, Jan. 12, 1716–7, the very month that Mr Baker was ejected from his Fellowship, confirms my conjecture of the utter improbability and inability of Mr Prior to serve Mr Baker, had his intentions been ever so disposed, thus:

Our friend Prior, says he, not having had the vicissitude of human things before his eyes, is likely to end his days in as forlorn a state as any other poet has done before him, if his friends do not take more care of him than he did of himself. Therefore, to prevent the evil, which we see is coming on very fast, we have a project of printing his *Solomon* and other poetical works by subscription: one guinea to be paid in hand and the other at the delivery of the book. He, Arbuthnot, Pope and Gay are now with me, and remember you. It is our joint request that you will endeavour to procure some subscriptions. You will give your receipts for the money you receive, and when you return it hither, you shall have others in lieu. There are no papers printed here, nor any advertisements to be published, for the whole matter is to be managed by friends in such a manner as shall be least shocking to the dignity of a plenipotentiary. (*Swift's Letters from 1703 to 1740*, 3 vols, 8vo, vol. 2, pp. 50–1, published by Dr Hawksworth at London, 1766.)

I think I need no other proof that the information was not well founded. Mr Prior was exactly in the same situation, and at the same time, with Mr Baker; therefore in no capacity to show his generosity. Before this time, Mr Baker's income was more than sufficient for a man of his retired and secluded state of life, as evidently appears by the expressions he makes use of in his will, where he says that his temporal goods were such as all men might be contented with, being neither poverty nor riches, and which all that knew him were satisfied that he was contented with. I remember him perfectly well, but had no personal acquaintance with him; yet I had a most intimate and familiar one with his particular friend Dr Middleton, whom I have often heard him express himself on Mr Baker's subject, and I think I should have heard somewhat of Mr Prior's generosity to him had there been the least foundation for it. It is of the same fabrication with Bishop Burnet's generosity to him. Mr Baker was a deserving man, and deprived of his maintenance for his loyalty to King James; it is no wonder, therefore, that persons of an humane and candid turn of mind would be contriving to furnish him with a competency. They did not reflect that Mr Baker's method of life would be satisfied with a very moderate income: such he had from his own family and private fortune, and, I believe, an annuity from his great patron the Earl of Oxford. *Vide* p. 147.

6. See *ante* 14 June 1778.

The editors, therefore, seem to be equally ignorant of this circumstance when they assert, at the place before cited, that Mr Prior, who had no scruples about taking the oaths in 1716, and was of ability to assist Mr Baker, who wanted assistance and could not swear, was assisted in this manner. The words in the *Biographia* are these (*Vide* p. 131):

After his ejectment Mr Baker still kept his chamber in St John's College, and resided there as a Commoner-Master during the remainder of his life. But though he lost his fellowship, it appears that this was in part made up to him by the generosity of a friend. The celebrated Matthew Prior, not scrupling the oaths or needing the profits of a Fellowship, took the oaths, kept his Fellowship, and gave Mr Baker the profits of it.

The period is prettily wound up, and only wants truth to give it a free reception. Mr Prior's inability to assist Mr Baker is fully ascertained by a letter from Lord Bolingbrook to Dr Swift, dated Jan. 1, 1721–2, in the same collection and volume, p. 123. It further is demonstrable by a letter to Mrs Johnson, dated so early as 1711–2, from the Dean, who acquaints her that Mr Prior had suffered by the failure of Mr Stafford: 'He can ill afford,' says he, 'to lose money.' Sufficient evidence that both before and after his great offices in the State, it was not in his power to help Mr Baker, had he stood in need of such assistance.

Hearing that my friend Mr George Ashby,[7] rector of Barrow near Newmarket, was at St John's College, of which he had been lately President, on May 6, 1778, I sent a note to him to beg him to inform me whether he had never heard of Mr Baker's having been chaplain to Bishop Crew, and dismissed from his service by that versatile prelate for not praying for King James in his chapel when it was illegal for him to do so. I thought that I had heard such a circumstance from Dr Middleton formerly, but could not recollect the particulars. (*Vide* my vol. 20, p. 83 for Mr Ashby's letter.) Mr Ashby could not recollect the fact at that time, but going to London next day and mentioning my query to Dr Ross,[8] Bishop of Exeter, he assured him that something of this sort did really happen, and referred him to a volume of *Gazettes* in the College Library. On the margins of two of them Mr Baker had entered the following passages, and which Mr Ashby on his return into Suffolk found that he had made a memorandum of, which he communicated to me on the last of that month. On Friday, June 5, I dined at Cambridge, when Dr Pennington of St John's very obligingly accommodated me with the volume out of his College Library. The circumstances are very particular, and fully confirm the account Mr Whiston gives of Mr Baker, and at the

7. (1724–1808), antiquary; Westminster, Eton and St John's; President of St John's, 1769–75.

8. John Ross or Rosse (1719–92), Bp of Exeter 1778–92; of St John's College (B.A. 1741; D.D. 1756; Fellow 1744–70).

same time shows Mr Baker's moderation in respect to the Revolution. His zeal for the Church of England, which he thought to be in danger on the birth of a Prince who would be educated in principles repugnant and hostile to it, staggered his ideas of passive obedience and almost made him a Whig in politics. Archbishop Sancroft and many other virtuous and conscientious Non-jurors had sufficiently shown their dislike to King James's infatuated measures, but could not digest the abjuring a Prince to whom they had sworn fidelity. On the first blank leaf of this collection of *London Gazettes*, from Feb. 28, 1686, to March 18, 1707, Mr Baker has entered this: 'This volume contains *Gazettes* for the year 1688 (*Annus Mirabilis*) and several other years, as follows.' In the *London Gazette*, July 5, 1688, No. 2361, being full of addresses and rejoicings for the birth of a Prince of Wales, is this article from Durham, on the side of which Mr Baker has entered in his own hand the following marginal observation, which sufficiently evinces his political principles at that very critical juncture, and for which he seems afterwards, when he more coolly reflected on its consequences, to have somewhat repented.

Durham, July 2. Yesterday, being the day of thanksgiving for the birth of the Prince, was solemnized here in the following manner. About nine of the clock in the morning, the Deputy-Lieutenants, Justices of the Peace, and divers of the gentry, with the Mayor, Aldermen and Common Council came up to the Lord Bishop of Durham's Palace, and from thence they all attended his Lordship to the Cathedral, where the Sub-Dean (the Dean being absent) and the Prebendaries, with all belonging to the choir, were ready to receive his Lordship at his entrance into the Church; then they sung *Te Deum* in solemn procession, and conducted his Lordship up to his Great Seat. Afterwards the form of prayer and thanksgiving was read by the Prebendaries, and the Lord Bishop preached a very excellent sermon, exhorting all to loyalty and obedience to the King, which was highly approved by a numerous auditory. Then the said company attended his Lordship back again to his Palace, where he entertained them all very much to their satisfaction in his Great Hall. After evening prayers a great bonfire was lighted upon the Palace Green, where their Majesties' healths, and the young Prince's, were drank, with great acclamations. From thence all the gentlemen went to the Town Hall, where Mr Mayor performed his part very well towards all the company, in repeating the same ceremonies, the city conduit running with wine all the while; and bonfires all over the town concluded the solemnity. The next day the Mayor, Aldermen and Common Council signed an address unanimously congratulating their Majesties upon this joyful occasion.

Mr Baker's marginal note is this:

This account was drawn up by the Bishop, as his secretary, Mr Peters, told me. I was present at the solemnity. If I did not rejoice as I ought, pardon me, O God, that sin.

In the same *Gazette* is an account from Whitehall, July 6, of the several removes of the judges, with the names of those who succeeded them, together with the alteration of the judges for the summer assizes; at which time the Lord Chief Justice Wright and Mr Justice Jenner went the Northern Circuit. On the margin by it is entered in Mr Baker's hand this note:

At Durham I preached before the judges (three commissioners then present). I could easily observe the sermon gave offense (and indeed justly), and yet it passed without censure. I have since burned it, as I have done the rest.

The three ecclesiastical commissioners were the Bishop and probably the two Judges.

But the principal passage is this, on the margin of the *Gazette* for Aug. 23, 1688, No. 2375, where [is] his Majesty's ecclesiastical commissioners' order for an account to be returned to them of the names of all such clergy as refused to read his Majesty's declaration of the 7 of April, for liberty of conscience. It is this:

I was ordered by the Bishop of Durham (a commissioner) to attend the Archdeacon, Dr Granvile,9 for the execution of this order, which I readily did, knowing it to be enjoined me as a penance for my former disobedience, having refused to read the declaration in his chapel, and forbid my curate to read it at my living. The good man's [the Archdeacon's] answer was that he would obey the King and the Bishop, and the first man he returned should be the Archdeacon, his curate not having read it in his absence, but had he been present, he would have read it himself. Not long after, he and I were both of us deprived for disobedience of another kind, and the commanding Bishop saved himself by his usual compliance.

Dean Denis Grenvile was also Archdeacon of Durham; he was deprived for not taking the oaths to the new government. What the name of Mr Baker's living was, and how he held it with his Fellowship, is more than I know. This note, however, fully proves my conjecture, as it does the versatility of Bishop Crew's character, and Bishop Burnet's account of him in some particulars.

I have heard Bishop Gooch often lament that Mr Baker's MSS were so divided, and say, while they were in part in Dover Street, that he would endeavour to get copies of all those in Lord Oxford's possession for the University, and let his Lordship's library be enriched with copies of those in our University Library, for the mutual benefit of both. But this useful project never took effect.

In a note at p. 3726 of the *Biographia Britannica* it is said that he held

9. Denis Grenville (1637–1703), of Exeter College, Oxford (D.D. 1671); Archdeacon of Durham 1662–91; Dean of Durham 1684–91; lived in France 1691–1703.

his Fellowship till the accession of King George I, some few years before which time Dr Jenkin,[10] who had been a Non-juror, was elected Master of the College: Mr Baker, therefore, and some other Non-jurors, who had been connived at and suffered to retain their Fellowships, had reasonable expectations that, under a Master of their own complexion, they might have continued in the quiet enjoyment of them to their deaths, and probably they would have done so had not the death of the Queen made it necessary to call upon all denominations to take the oaths to the new family. As he could not do this with quiet to his conscience, he was, together with nine others, ejected from his Fellowship, and Mr Whitley Heald[11] elected in his place on 21 Jan. 1716–7. As this was done in consequence of an Act of Parliament, it seems singular that he should bear a resentment against Dr Jenkin for an act that was none of his, yet a marginal note at p. 3726 of vol. 6 of *Biographia Britannica* intimates as much in this manner:

He always bore a quick resentment of his ejection, and would never believe but that the Master, Dr Jenkin, might have screened him, by connivance, as he had done in the preceding reign. This he expressed particularly by writing in the blank leaves of all the books which he gave to the College himself, *Socius ejectus.*

I rather think another reason might have been more probably assigned for his so signing himself.

In the introductory preface to the first volume of the *Archaeologia* of the Antiquarian Society, p. xxiv, the writer, whoever he was, probably Dean Milles, gives an account of the progress of the Society from its first institution under Queen Elizabeth to the present times, and occasionally enumerates the eminent writers on the subject of antiquities during that period, and thus mentions Mr Baker: 'Mr Thomas Baker, whom death only prevented from digesting his immense valuable collections for the Sister University.' As this follows his eulogia of Twyne,[12] Wood and Hearne, one must conclude that he meant an history of the University of Cambridge. But I am not enough acquainted with Mr Baker's MSS to judge how forward he was in such a design. Sure enough, a person who died at the age of 84 can hardly be said to be prevented in the execution of a project that I do not certainly know he meant to execute. That he

10. Robert Jenkin (1656–1727), Master of St John's College, Cambridge 1711–27; Lady Margaret Professor of Divinity 1711–27; author of theological works.

11. (1694?–1736), Fellow of St John's 1717–32; vicar of North Stoke, Oxon, 1730–6 (*Alumni Cantab.*).

12. Brian Twyne (1579?–1644), Oxford antiquary; author of *Antiquitatis Academiae Oxoniensis Apologia,* 1608, and *Account of the Musterings of the University of Oxford,* not published until 1733; made valuable collections for the history and antiquities of Oxford.

meant to write an history of his own college, and also to publish it, is well known; and that he made great and most valuable collections for an history of the University is equally known, but I believe that latterly he had no thoughts of proceeding farther. His MS notes and additions to Wood's *Athenae* are very numerous: I may venture to say equal to an hundred folio pages of my writing.[12a]

The writers of the *Biographia Britannica,* vol. 1, p. 532, note A, sufficiently bear witness of his indefatigable industry in researches of all kinds relating to antiquity and biography. Their testimony (vol. 6, p. 3726) respecting Bishop Burnet's allowing him an annuity must have further authority before I can credit it. That the second Lord Oxford of the Harley family did so is out of all doubt. Mr Baker gratefully acknowledges his Lordship's kindness. They were friends *ex animo,* and his Lordship could better afford it than Bishop Burnet, whose friendship to Mr Baker, as well as Bishop Kennet's,[13] would reflect as much honour and credit to either of their characters as their correspondence could upon Mr Baker, who very gratefully acknowledges their favours, in sending him their books, in his last will; as well as the singular kindness of Archbishop Wake, to whom he had been useful in his work on *The State of the Church (Biographia Britannica,* vol. 6, p. 4096), and who generously, in return, made him an offer of a living of £200 per annum for any friend of his that he should recommend, as he could not take it himself. This offer Mr Baker as politely declined, requesting that his Grace's favour might center in himself only, by a present of the said work. This was acting as became both their characters. From what I can judge of that of Mr Baker, it seems probable that he would no more have accepted a pension from Bishop Burnet, had it been offered, than he would readily have accepted one from Lord Oxford, at whose house at Wimpole he was a most welcome guest, and whose liberal disposition to men of virtue and merit is well known.

So that, however positive the assertion of the writers of the *Biographia* may be, that Burnet allowed Mr Baker an annuity, I must beg leave to have my doubts, as I have already observed. Whoever reads the very cool and forced acknowledgment that Bishop makes to Mr Baker for his assistance, or rather corrections, on his book, sufficiently marks no great intimacy and less predilection. His mention of Mr Strype for the same assistance is in a much more warm and cordial style: their sentiments were indeed more congenial; yet I suppose their talents and abilities would bear no comparison. The acknowledgments to both, and both their as-

12a. Baker's hand is remarkably similar to Cole's.

13. White Kennett (1660–1728), Bp of Peterborough 1718–28; historian, antiquary, topographer and philologist.

sistances, may be seen in the third volume of the *History of the Reformation*. Mr Baker had sent him large corrections of his two former volumes, which are printed at p. 399 to p. 414 of the third volume. What he says of the corrector is as follows, at p. vii of the introduction, and p. x of the preface:

A very worthy person in one of the Universities has sent me a copious collection of remarks on both my former volumes, but upon condition not to name him, which I will observe religiously, because I have promised it; though it is not easy to myself, since I may not own to whom I owe so great an obligation. But I suppress none of them, and give them entirely as he offered them to me.

The fourth paper is a large collection of many mistakes (descending even to literal ones) in both the volumes of my *History,* and in the records published in them, which a learned and worthy person has read with more exactness than either my amanuensis or myself had done. I publish these sheets as that unknown person sent them to me, whom I never saw, as far as I remember, and who will not suffer me to give any other account of him but that he lives in one of the Universities. In several particulars I do not perfectly agree with these corrections, but I set them down as they were sent me without any remarks on them; and I give my hearty thanks in the fullest manner I can to him who was first at the pains to make this collection, and then had the goodness to communicate it to me in so obliging a manner. For he gave me a much greater power over these papers than I have thought fit to assume.

This was the Bishop's last farewell, for the work he dedicates to King George I, and his Lordship died in March 1714–5; and now let anyone judge whether Mr Baker was a pensioner to Bishop Burnet.

Mr Baker assisted Mr Strype in his various works relating to the Reformation and Establishment of this Church (V. Appendix to his *Annals,* vol. 1, pp. 86, 103, and vol. 2, after the table of contents, p. 494, Appendix, p. 70), who, being attacked by an adversary who accused him of errors and mistakes, Mr Strype, to justify his character to the world, appeals in his preface to his third volume of *Annals* to the testimony and good opinion entertained of him and his writings, to Mr Nic. Batteley[14] of Kent, and Mr Baker of St John's, as of two persons whose testimony was not to be reprobated or withstood (Appendix to vol. 3 of *Annals*, pp. 187, 248).

I was told (1777 by Dr Ewin), who heard it at the Bishop of Ely's table last year at Ely, when Mr Baker's MSS were mentioned as an authority for something that was then advanced in conversation, that the Bishop should say that they were of no credit, and that he was a most credulous person, and put down all he heard, whether true or false. You, who have

14. Nicholas Batteley (1648–1704), author of *Antiquities of Canterbury,* 1703.

perused his *History* of his College, must have observed with what caution, even equal to what you remark of Mr Vertue, he advances any fact. The same scrupulosity he observed in sending materials to Tom Hearne, where his nicety in this matter is notorious and particular. People who advance such characters at random are very injurious to those they criticize. One would suspect that they never looked into his MS or printed writings, the character is so utterly unlike his constant and unvaried method, even to the spelling of a person's name.

Mr Gough, in his *Topography*, pp. 102–3, very judiciously animadverts on the reflection upon Mr Baker by the writer of the article of Anthony Wood in the *Biographia Britannica*, vol. 6, part 2, p. 4325, though Mr Gough talks of Dr Zach. Grey as then living, whereas he died Nov. 25, 1766, aged 79 years, two years before Mr Gough's work appeared (V. my vol. 33, p. 118).

You will please to observe that I write my notes to you in no method, but as I am referred to them by my MS Index. I shall, for your convenience, write only on one side of the paper, that you may make use of the other.

Vide Dr Phil. Williams's[15] letters to Dr Grey, 1740, in my vol. –, p. –, and vol. 31, p. 24.

Vide letter from Dr Warren[16] to Dr Grey, 1740, in my vol. –, p. –.

Mr Baker was born at Crooke in the parish of Lanchester near Durham, Sept. 14, 1656, and died Wednesday, July 2, 1740, in his chambers in St John's College.

Vide his will in my vol. –, p. –, and vol. 30, p. 188 for the extract from the foreign journal and printed in *CCCC*,[17] p. 84 of Appendix. What he has added in crotchets (*Plura occurrunt, sed haec satis*) seems to be Mr Baker's own insertion, and spoken contemptuously, after the account given to the inquirer of Mr Baker's design of writing an history of the University. I never heard that Mr Baker professedly undertook to write such an history; that he collected materials for such an history is evident and certain.

Vide Bishop Burnet's letter to Mr Baker, which I copied from the original, vol. 30, p. 154, and is printed by Dr Grey in his *Review of Neal's History*, pp. 62–3, and wrote a few weeks before the Bishop's death: [it] fully evinces that he was no pensioner to him.

---

15. Philip Williams (1695?–1749), rector of Barrow, Suffolk 1740–9 (*Alumni Cantab.*).

16. William Warren (1683–1745), antiquary and historian (see *Alumni Cantab.*). Cole's copy of the letter in question, dated 4 July 1740, is in Add MS 5831, f. 185 (see *Index to the Additional Manuscripts . . . in the British Museum . . . acquired in the Years 1783–1835*, 1849).

17. Robert Masters, *History of Corpus Christi College, Cambridge*, 1753–5.

In 1688 Mr Baker and Mr Orchard,[18] another Fellow of St John's College, stood godfather to one of my uncles, of the name of Tuer. *Vide* my vol. 18, p. 191.

Vide Mr Baker's additions to Gunton, in my vol. —, p. —.

Vide Bishop Kennet's letter to Mr Baker, in my vol. 30, pp. 158–9.

In all the books left to St John's College by Mr Baker is this printed inscription pasted:

Ex Dono
Viri Reverendi Thomæ Baker S. T. B.
qui olim fuerat hujus Collegii Socius:
Postea vero, ex Senatus Consulto ejectus,
in his Aedibus Hospes consenuit;
Vitæ Integritate et Fama,
quam ex Antiquitatis Studio consecutus est,
celeberrimus.

Vide my vol. 32, pp. 193–4 for my account of his funeral.

Mr Baker was a great assistant to my worthy patron, Mr Browne Willis, in all his publications. In his prefatory epistle, p. vi, to Bishop Tanner, of his second volume of his *History of Abbeys,* he acknowledges his obligations to him. Indeed Mr Baker made innumerable additions to his volume of that work, and, having inserted them in the margins, left the book to Mr Willis, which I have seen, and copied all the additions into my vol. —, p. —. This very book Mr Willis sent to me, with a box full of other curious old books, with a desire I would give them, in his name, to Buckingham, as he used always to call Magdalen College, after having inserted his name in each of them. When I received them, I was going out of college, and Mr Masters being then busy about his *History,* and I much with him or he with me, he being desirous of looking into these books, I inadvertently left them with him with a desire to give them to the Master or Bursar of Magdalen College, as directed, when he had done with them. In 1768, to my no small surprise, I saw in his study at Landbeche the very volume in question. I told him of it, and he seemed to be in no great concern about it. I afterwards told Dr Sandby, the Master, of it, and mentioned it to Mr Hey.[19] Query, whether all the rest were punctually delivered? A man that would secrete one would 20.

One thing I used to remark in Mr Baker's dress (which was a gown, cassock and square cap), and marks the progress of the fashion of the present pudding-sleeve gown, as it is called, to distinguish it from the

18. Arthur Orchard (1640?–1706), rector of Hardwick, Cambs, 1679–1707 (*Alumni Cantab.*).

19. Cf. *ante* 23 May 1778 n. 8.

Master-of-Arts gown. His sleeves were buttoned at the wristband, as a Bishop wears his lawn sleeves, and not tucked up to the middle of the arm, as now universally worn. Neither was there a lining to it in front, under the band, as now worn, but it was buttoned there with a single button so that the cassock was rarely seen. This was the old fashion, and he continued it to the last. I think Mr Strype's print by Vertue, and Mr Flamsted's[20] are so represented. I have never observed anyone to wear it so since. The sleeve you may observe to be so worn in several prints, but the return back, or lining of the opening before, was the fashion in King Charles I's time.

By your account in the life of Mr Vertue, p. 8 of *Engravers*, it seems that Lord Oxford (whom you call Robert, whereas Edward was the second Earl, and his patron, as at pp. 3–4 of Vertue's *Works*) engaged him to go to Cambridge, and there privately, and by stealth, to take Mr Baker's likeness.

Dr Knight, in his *Life of Erasmus*, introduction, p. xvi, pays his acknowledgments to his learned friend Mr Baker for his assistance in that work, and further adds that Mr Baker has judiciously confuted the little critical remarks and mistakes which LeClerc had endeavoured to fasten upon Erasmus. Yet Dr Jortin has since, in his *Life* of that great scholar, pp. 550–1, in his free way, thus censured Mr Baker upon the same score, probably (*tantum Relligio potuit*) because Mr Baker happened to think differently, both in religion and politics, from the more illuminated and (shall I say?) more time-serving (I will say more favoring) Dr Jortin, whose capital favourite, M. LeClerc, had been attacked by Mr Baker, who, in his preface to his *Reflections on Learning*, however, apologizes for his zeal against LeClerc, which [it] would have been candid in Jortin to have taken notice of, when he attacks him in this ungentle manner:

LeClerc hath also observed that Erasmus had neglected to make himself master of geography. Baker, in his *Reflections upon Learning*, defended Erasmus, and attacked LeClerc with a virulence which one would not have expected from a man who, as I remember, was accounted, and who desired to be accounted, a candid, genteel and polite person. But party zeal guided his pen: *Tantum Relligio potuit!* LeClerc gave him a short answer in the index to the fourth edition of the *Ars Critica*, under the word *Erasmus*. Baker hath one chapter upon metaphysics, in which he hath made no mention of Locke, just as if a man should write the lives of the Greek and Latin poets, and only omit Homer and Virgil! He observed, Chap. 16, that there was little or nothing left for the sagacity and industry of modern critics, and thereby he showed that he was no critic himself, and not at all acquainted with the true state of classical books, and particularly of Greek authors.

20. John Flamsteed (1646–1719), first Astronomer Royal. The print was engraved by Vertue, 1721, after the portrait by T. Gibson (EBP).

If party zeal guided Mr Baker's pen, a furious zeal and rancour against monkery and popery guided his own, where no opportunity is omitted to expose the faults of the popish clergy, and an equal ardor to vindicate his beloved Waldenses; or, in short, anyone who acts with liberty and spirit, as he calls it, against the Establishment. Foul names are by no means spared on these occasions. Mr Baker manfully wrote against Mr LeClerc in his lifetime, and it would have been more ingenuous in Jortin to have attacked Mr Baker about his omission of his metaphysician when he could have given his reasons for it.

I am pleased that the writers of the *Biographia Britannica*, vol. 6, p. 3726, have made the same reflections on Dr Jortin which I have done. I had not seen them till I fell upon them in looking after another matter. The new biographers, I see, have vindicated Jortin, and fallen foul on poor Mr Baker for endeavouring to seize out of the hands of LeClerc the fame of the great Erasmus, and are equally unobserving of Mr Baker's candour and humanity in apologizing for his attack on that general criticizer.

You see I send you all my notes just as I have entered them in my books, without order or method.

You have Mr Baker's preface to *Bishop Fisher's Sermon. Vide* pp. 54–8, 60–1, for what relates to himself.

I do not know his noble patron in King James II's time.

Vide Gent's *History of Hull*,[21] pp. 23–4, for an epitaph he put up for his uncle Sir George Baker.[22]

Mr Baker has a letter to Mr Hilkiah Bedford,[23] the author of *Hereditary Right*, in his translation of an answer to Fontenelle's *History of Oracles (Biographia Britannica*, vol. 6, p. 3733).

I copied from the originals in the family numbers of Mr Baker's letters to Bishop Watson, the deprived Bishop of St David's. They were written during the troubles of that Bishop for simony, but as Mr Baker had a very bad method of never dating his letters, many others of whose writing I have seen, the exact time they were sent is difficult to be found out. However, there is no loss in these, as none of them contain public matters, and relate wholly to his private concerns at Wilbraham in Cambridgeshire (*vide* my vol. —, p. —).

The following MS note was entered by Mr Baker in his copy of Wood's *Athenae*, which he left by will to Dr Middleton, who lent it to me, and is

21. *Annales Regioduni Hullini, or the History of the royal and beautiful Town of Kingston-upon-Hull*, York, 1735, by Thomas Gent (1693–1778), printer and topographer.

22. (d. 1667), Kt, of Crook Hall, Durham.

23. (1663–1724), nonconformist divine, author of religious works.

now in the University Library, in vol. 2, p. 230 of the *Fasti,* among the incorporations:

Tho. Baker, A. M., Coll. Jo. Cant., was incorporated this year (1687) at the Act at Oxford, with Mr Smith,[24] A. M., and Fellow of Trinity College in Cambridge. I was presented as Fellow of St John Baptist's College in Cambridge. How it happened that I was not registered, I cannot say. It was done in haste, and I upon a journey. T. B.

In 1708 Mr Baker lent Dr Davies[25] a copy of Tully's *Tusculan Questions,* when he was about publishing a new edition of that work.

He assisted Dr Walker[26] in his *Sufferings of the Clergy,* preface, pp. xxiii–xxiv.

Vide Memoirs of Dr Clarke by William Whiston,[27] 3rd edn, p. 25. Query, ——.

Vide Memoirs of William Whiston by himself, p. 32, vol. 1.

Mr Baker wrote the epitaph on Dr John Smith,[28] Prebendary of Durham, and editor of Bede's *Works,* his relation, printed in LeNeve's *Monumenta Anglicana,* vol. 2, p. 266.

Vide Carter's *History of Cambridge,*[29] pp. 258–261.

Vide preface to Dr Richardson's edition of Goodwin *De Praesulibus.*[30]

Vide preface to Cooke's *Plautus,* p. viii.[31]

The plate of Mr Baker's head, by Simon,[32] was in the possession of the late James West, Esq., President of the Royal Society, and probably pilfered, with many other curiosities, from the library of the Earl of Oxford. It was sold by auction of his prints, drawings, etc., Jan. 19, 1773.

Probably Mr Granger had collected some materials for Mr Baker's life, as that would have made part of his next volume.

24. Jonathan Smith (fl. 1673–93), vicar of Bottisham, Cambs (*Alumni Cantab.*).

25. John Davies (1679–1732), President of Queens' College; editor of numerous classical works, including Cicero's *Tusculanarum disputationum libri quinque,* Cambridge, 1709.

26. John Walker (1674–1747), ecclesiastical historian, author of *An Attempt towards recovering an Account of the Numbers and Sufferings of the Clergy of the Church of England,* 1714.

27. *Historical Memoirs . . . of Dr Samuel Clarke* (1st edn 1730), by William Whiston (1667–1752).

28. John Smith (1659–1715), Prebendary of Durham 1695–1715; editor of *Historiae Ecclesiasticae Gentis Anglorum Libri Quinque, auctore Venerabili Baeda,* Cambridge, 1722; the work was brought out by his son, George Smith (1693–1756).

29. Edmund Carter, topographer and schoolmaster, published (1753) histories of Cambridgeshire and of Cambridge University.

30. William Richardson (1698–1775), edited (1743) *De Praesulibus Angliae Commentarii,* by Francis Godwin (1562–1633), Bp of Llandaff and Hereford.

31. Thomas Cooke (1703–56), commonly called Hesiod Cooke, published (1754) the first and only volume—a translation of *Amphitruo*—of a long-promised edition of Plautus.

32. John Simon (1675?–1751), engraver; Huguenot refugee (EBP).

Professor Ward[33] of Gresham College, in his preface, p. 1, honourably mentions him.

He assisted Mr Fiddes[34] in his *Life of Cardinal Wolsey*.

Dr Middleton, in his *Dissertation on Printing*,[35] calls him his 'worthy and learned friend,' and in another place: 'Mr Baker, who of all men is the most able, as well as the most willing, to give information in every point of curious and uncommon history.'

As I do not recollect that you have all Tom Hearne's books in your curious and extensive library, I shall send you extracts from mine, as I have them all, relating to Mr Baker, who helped him in most of his publications.

Textus Roffensis, preface, p. xli, p. 394.—Nothing material.

The History and Antiquities of Glastonbury, preface, pp. lxv, lxxx. If Tom Hearne had had occasion to have mentioned Sir Isaac Newton or the Duke of Marlborough, he would have been at a loss to have found more lofty expressions.

Heming's *Chartulary,* pp. 672–3.

Tho. de Elmham—Mr Baker sent him many curious materials concerning John Somerset, physician to King Henry VI (*vide* preface, p. xxv and p. 350, etc.).

Walteri Hemingford Historia, preface, pp. 17, 21, 29, 41, 90, and pp. 557, 734.

Historia Regni et Vitae Ricardi II, pp. 390, 393, 397, 400–1.

Duo Rerum Anglicarum Scriptores veteres, viz., Tho. Otterburn, etc., preface, pp. 50, 84, 87, 130.

Johannis de Trokelowe Annales—preface, p. 13; appendix, pp. 273, 292, 426. *Nil.*

Gul. Roperi Vita D. Thomae Mori, preface, pp. 9, 18–20.

Rob. of Glocester's Chronicle, preface, pp. 19, 23, 26, 61, 81; appendix, pp. 584, 609, 677. *Nil.*

Benedictus Abbas Petroburgensis, appendix to preface, p. 29, and p. 53.

Thomae Caii Vindiciae, preface, pp. 13, 48, 54–5, 98; vol. 2, pp. 606, 645, 804, 809. In many parts of this book the great caution in respect to truth and accuracy in what he transmitted to Hearne is observable; and in this and other of Hearne's books is as remarkable [as] his generosity in giving very freely many curious books and MSS to Thomas, which he thought would be agreeable to him.

33. John Ward (1679?–1758), Professor of Rhetoric of Gresham College, London, 1720–58. Cole refers to his *Lives of the Professors of Gresham College,* 1740.

34. Richard Fiddes (1671–1725), divine and historian, author of *Life of Cardinal Wolsey,* 1724.

35. *A Dissertation concerning the Origin of Printing in England,* 1734–5, by Conyers Middleton.

Leland's *Itinerary*, vol. 2, 2nd edn, p. 122.

Johannis Rossi Antiquarii Historia, preface, pp. 4, 6; and p. 233. One would think that Master Thomas, by conversing so long with the meek and candid Mr Baker had caught some of his moderation; for in his zeal about the antiquity he is equally foolish and zealously outrageous. It is at p. vi. Perhaps he thought he had said sufficient already to establish the priority.

Si rogetur, quid de auctoris verbis ad utramque Academiam spectantibus sentiam, illud repono, me controversiam de utriusque antiquitate in medium denuo proferre in animo non habere. Valeant Oxoniensium argumenta quantam valere possunt. Suam itidem vim habeant Cantabrigiensium ratiocinia. Optandum est, ut Cl' Bakerus sua quoque Collectanea de Antiquitatibus Cantabrigiensibus juris faciat publici, quippe qui eruditione summa judicioque acri et subacto polleat.

Johannis Glastoniensis Chronica, preface, p. 53; p. 640.

Peter Langtoft's *Chronicle*, preface, pp. 13, 43; p. 534.

Liber Niger Scaccarii, edit. 1771, p. 190, he says Mr Baker gave him two old maps of Cambridge and Oxford, taken in Queen Elizabeth's time, and wishes a new edition of them was undertaken. I have one by Ric. Lyne,[36] very perfect, lent to me by the Master of Emmanuel. Mr Essex is at this time busy about a map of Cambridge as it was before her time, authenticated by old deeds mentioning the streets before the present colleges occupied their places. In which design I mean to assist him: pp. 474, 542, 666–7, etc.

Chronicon de Dunstaple, preface, p. 49; appendix, p. 729.

Roberti de Avesbury Historia, preface, p. 4. *Nil.*

A Collection of Curious Discourses, p. 300.

Gul. Camdeni Annales, preface, p. 6.

Thomae Sprotti Chronicon, preface, pp. 35–6; pp. 246, 249, etc.

Thus I have given you all the remarkable extracts from Hearne's books relating to Mr Baker. In the six last, from *, I have not so minutely examined the references, and there are a few in which I have not looked at all.

Mr Bedford,[37] in his edition of *Symeonis Monachi Dunelmensis Libellus*, printed in 1732, mentions his helps in that work from Mr Baker.

I am of opinion that the book alluded to in Bishop Burnet's letter of Jan. 29, 1714–5, to Mr Baker, is *The Hereditary Right of the Crown of England Asserted*, printed in folio, 1713, which goes under the name of

36. Richard Lyne, painter and engraver, published an engraved map of the University of Cambridge in 1574.

37. Thomas Bedford (d. 1773), 2d son of Hilkiah Bedford; Nonjuror and church historian; edited *Symeonis monachi Dunhelmensis libellus de exordio atque procursu Dunhelmensis ecclesiae*, 1732.

Mr Hilkiah Bedford,[38] formerly Fellow of St John's, and a relation of Mr Baker, but was really the work of Mr George Harbin,[39] formerly of Emmanuel College, and chaplain to Bishop Kenn.[40] Mr Bedford, who was the editor of it, underwent some difficulties about it, as the book had made a great noise, and given offence at the latter end of the Queen's reign; insomuch that in a letter from a person in England to Mr de Bothmar,[41] the Elector of Hanover's minister, dated May 25, 1714, published in Mr Macpherson's *Original Papers*, vol. 2, p. 619, is this passage:

The pardon which the Queen granted to Dr Bedford, author of the book on *Hereditary Right*, is the greatest affront which her Majesty could offer to the Electoral family.

At p. 202 of this book, the author, with great gravity and decency, mentions Bishop Burnet as reviving an old calumny in respect to the legitimacy of the House of Suffolk, which makes it probable this was the book in question. That Mr Bedford was the editor only is evident from this MS note of the late James West, Esq., entered into his copy of the book, and printed in the catalogue of his books, which were sold by auction in April 1773, where at p. 179, No. 3533, is this article:

The Hereditary Right of the Crown of England Asserted (commonly called Bedford's), with MS notes by Bishop Kennett, 1713. The true author of this book was Mr Harbin, chaplain to Bishop Ken, as himself acknowledged to Mr West, whose note is very curious. 'Upon showing the above notes, wrote by Bishop Kennett, to Mr Harbin, he told me he was the author of the annexed book, and immediately produced the original copy of the same, together with three large volumes of original documents, from whence the same was compiled. He was chaplain to Ken, Bishop of Bath and Wells, and was head of the clergy of the Non-juring persuasion at that time, 1742. A man of infinite knowledge and reading, but of a weak, prejudiced and bigoted judgment.—J. W.'

It is probable the original copy and three volumes of documents here mentioned might have been in Lord Oxford's library, where Mr West might meet Mr Harbin; for, I suppose, it is not unknown that Mr West had free access to that collection.

Etc.,

WM COLE

38. (1663–1724), Nonjuring divine, who was fined 1,000 marks and imprisoned three years for writing the book mentioned above; the real author, however, was George Harbin, as stated in Cole's account (cf. DNB).

39. (d. 1744). See *Alumni Cantab.*

40. Thomas Ken or Kenn (1637–1711), Bp of Bath and Wells 1684–91.

41. Hans Caspar von Bothmer (1656–1732), German diplomat, became Hanoverian envoy to the Court of St James in 1710 and 'was more directly . . . instrumental than any other man in bringing about the Hanoverian Succession' (*Cambridge Modern History*, 1909, vi. 12: A. W. Ward; *Allgemeine Deutsche Biographie*).

APPENDIX 2

Cole's Unsent Letter of Friday 29 January 1779

Cole's copy, Add MS 5850, ff. 224v, 225.
See *ante* 4, 7 Feb. 1779.
Address: For the Honourable Horace Walpole in Arlington Street, Piccadilly, London.

Milton, Friday noon, Jan. 29, 1779.

Dear Sir,

GIVE me leave to recall my letter of Jan. 26 at night, which I wrote in an hurry immediately upon reading hastily the 'Life,'[1] in order to send it to the post time enough to certify you of my receipt of it, and that it was safe. I have since read it over, in my transcribing it, with attention, and, though it may offend, it must take its chance. I beg leave to have my former letter as unsaid and unwritten, and should be very glad to have that letter returned, for I hardly know what I was tempted to say in it, the chief part of the work pleasing me so much that I little attended to what was in other parts of it. In return, I will send you an original letter of Mr Baker to Mr Strype, the historian, and as staunch a Protestant and Whig as any could desire, in full proof of above half the arguments you are pleased to make use of in Mr Baker's favour: a letter that will amply make amends for my retractations, which, whatever be the consequence, I must repeat. The original I speak of may serve also to correct the account, p. 14, of his agreeing with, or approving, the notions of genealogic succession. There are many other specimens of the same cast which I could easily send, if you thought them worth having, for I have lately met with a large collection of his original letters, all written to the same person, and which fully confirm your character of his humanity and other virtues.

In a former letter you desired me severely to criticize the account you was about to oblige me with. It is a liberty I beg to be excused taking. What I have excepted to, I have already, in the course of my transcribing, remitted into the same book on the opposite page. However, I shall so far use your indulgence as to mention a few things which I conceive may be taken notice of with less offence, and may correct a mistake or two in the 'Life,' and this I shall do with the utmost reluctance, fearing it may occasion a debate, which, of all things, I abhor, and which, at my time of

1. HW's 'Life of Baker' (*Works* ii. 341–62).

life, can be of no other consequence than speculation; and to prevent any other consequence, I am determined this shall be my last letter on the subject. If you please to have the last word, I can have no objections; but I hope you will not be offended if I do not reply to it. If I had not made some to what you have advanced, it might have seemed contemptuous. We are said to live in a free country: I am as fully satisfied with my opinions as a better reasoner may be with his; therefore, debates of this nature can answer no other purpose than setting friends at variance. My attachment to old-fashioned opinions in Church or State is never like to promote my interest, no more than my zeal for the Establishment in either, which I never got a farthing by, and is therefore probably disinterested. However, I give you a great deal of thanks for the trouble you have put yourself to on this subject, which you undertook with great courtesy, and which, though not finished in all points according to my mind, is yet most ingenious, and deserves my most grateful acknowledgments.

Whatever poor honeys Archbishop Sancroft and Mr Baker may have been, for being led astray by their conscience against their judgment, the argument may in one instance, perhaps, prove more than was intended, and draw Archbishop Tillotson into the vortex; at least, it is certain, by his letter, 1683, to Lord Russell,[2] that he thought, at that period of his life, resistance to be a sin; and however artfully Dr Birch may have managed this transaction, it is evident such were his thoughts, and such were his words some six years before his acceptance of Archbishop Sancroft's mitre, which was so notorious, notwithstanding the palliatives and glosses put upon it, that the rigid Republican, and probably sour, honest man, Samuel, alias Julian Johnson,[3] a great crony of Lord Russel, Tillotson and Burnet, thought the principles of the letter so much the writer's own, and so injurious to his principles, that he would never afterwards forgive either the one for writing the letter or Burnet for his message directing what to write (Kettlewell's *Life*, p. 334).[4] The letter and dissertation by Dr Birch are in Tillotson's *Life*,[5] from p. 108 to 124. Archbishop Tillotson, I sincerely believe, though a nephew to Oliver Cromwell by marriage, was an honest man and of great worth and integrity; as to the

2. William Russell (1639–83), Lord Russell, 'the patriot,' son of William 1st D. of Bedford. He was convicted of high treason in the Rye House plot and executed.

3. Samuel Johnson (1649–1703), domestic chaplain to Lord Russell; he was imprisoned and fined in 1683 for his *Julian the Apostate*, a tract against the Duke of York.

4. *Memoirs of the Life of Mr John Kettlewell, . . . from the Collections of Dr*

George Hickes and Robert Nelson, 1718. Kettlewell (1653–95) was a Nonjuror and devotional writer. For Bishop Burnet's message to Johnson, see Samuel Johnson, *Notes upon the Phoenix Edition of the Pastoral Letter*, 1694, pp. 91–2.

5. *The Life of . . . Dr John Tillotson*, by Thomas Birch, 1752; Cole refers to the second edition (1753), 'corrected and enlarged.'

other, the less I say of him, I am satisfied, will be the surer way not to offend. But whatever be their destiny, which I sincerely pray God may be
the best, I shall never cease saying, 'Let my soul be with those of Archbishop Sancroft and Mr Baker.'

The note erased, relating to Dr Zach. Grey,[6] I owe to your politeness
and tenderness, as you knew my friendship with him, by his original letter which I had sent you with the other loose papers. The writer of that
note cannot be offended with me for defending one of the Most High
Church, 'tis true, but one of the most humane, benevolent, communica-
tive, good-tempered and friendly men I ever was acquainted with, which
was the more extraordinary, however you may stare, as he always took me
to be of a contrary party, both from my connections and from my never
entering into politics: I say he will not take it ill, because I know not the
hand, nor can give any guess at the writer of it. I am well aware that
should an angel give a new edition of *Hudibras*,[7] with explanatory notes,
however well or ill executed, it would hardly be pardoned at this time
of day, from the nature of the subject. The subscription, indeed, was a
most remarkable one,[8] which seemed rather a partiality to the editor,
with a desire to know more of the allusions in the poem than was commonly understood, and which no one was better qualified to develop
than Dr Grey; and had he not crowded it so much as to be surfeiting, it
would have met with a more general good reception. He was both editor
and author of *Remarks upon Neal's History of the Puritans*, for he was
concerned with the late Dr Madox,[9] bred a Dissenter and afterwards
Bishop of Worcester, who undertook to answer the first volume, with the
assistance of Dr Grey, and has executed it in so masterly a manner,
though without his name, as would be worth your or any impartial gentleman's perusal. I am apt to think, its being anonymous and going with
Dr Grey's other volumes, that it is hardly known to be his, and therefore
neglected and not so much known as it deserves. The other three volumes
fell to the share of Dr Grey, whose work suffers by coming after the
former, which is finished in a style and method equally out of the power
and manner of my worthy friend, who had zeal and a thorough insight

6. Zachary Grey (1688–1766), rector of
Houghton Conquest, Beds, 1725.

7. Dr Grey published *Hudibras . . .
corrected and amended, with large annotations and a preface*, with cuts by Hogarth, 1744 (supplement, 1752).

8. HW was a subscriber to a 'Royal Paper copy' (K. 4. 30), which was sold SH
iii. 164; it is now WSL.

9. Isaac Maddox (1697–1759), Bp of St
Asaph 1736, and of Worcester 1743–59.

Cole refers to the work by which Maddox
is best known: *A Vindication of the Government, Doctrine, and Worship of the
Church of England*, 1733, written as a reply to the first volume (1732) of Daniel
Neal's *History of the Puritans*. Dr Grey
answered the second volume of Neal's
work with *An Impartial Examination . . .*,
1736; and his replies to the third and
fourth volumes appeared in 1737 and
1739, respectively.

of the people he had to deal with, but little art to knit his materials together.

Is not Mr Prior's supposed bounty to Mr Baker talked of as if done before a lawyer, and in form? I apprehend the cession of his Fellowship meant no more than the emoluments of it, and that the reporter only meant to say that Mr Prior ordered the Bursar to pay Mr Baker his dividend (p. 18).

Can the *Reflections upon Learning* be justly said to have drawn Mr Baker into a controversy? Indeed, in them he took occasion to vindicate Erasmus from the scurrility of LeClerc, who retorted with great freedom and ill-nature, of which Mr Baker, I believe, never took the least notice (p. 26).

It is probable I led you into an error, if it is one, that he was always a welcome guest at Wimpole, p. 21. It might be so; but I have no authority for saying so. I am rather inclined to believe he never went out anywhere. Had he been a guest at Wimpole, Lord Oxford would hardly have sent Mr Vertue to Cambridge to catch his likeness, as you have mentioned, but rather have given the painter a better opportunity to have studied his visage at Wimpole. But I remember, in a letter of his about Queen Anne's time, he mentions that he had not been at Ely for between 20 and 30 years.

I write this in no small hurry, as I finished your transcript but this morning, and am in expectations Mr Lort will call today (as by letter he seems to say) to carry it with him to town tomorrow. If he does not call, I will send my servant to College with it, and the MS, that it may be in safe hands, and get safely to you.

If you print it, as you seem to promise at p. 30, I wish there was a neat print of Mr Baker prefixed, from the mezzotinto, which, though badly executed, is extremely like him.

I am, Sir, with true esteem and respect,

Your ever obliged and faithful servant,

WM COLE

As I finished your letter, the postman came with another from you,[10] which perhaps is the only one I did not rejoice to receive. Indeed, I wished not to hear from you till this had reached you, and though I am fearful it may give offence, I cannot but send it.

If I mentioned the word *cautious*, it must be in another sense than you seem to take it.

10. See *ante* 28 Jan. 1779.

Mr Lort is not come, so I send this to him, notwithstanding your kind offer of letting the MS stay longer. I dare say he thought it probable such an heavenly day would have brought me to the Rose Tavern to our County Club, which I never miss if I am well, but the gout has formally taken possession of one leg.

APPENDIX 3

WALPOLE's Unsent Letter of Sunday 26 March 1780

In the possession of the Earl of Derby, K.G., Knowsley Hall, Lancs. Now first published, with Lord Derby's permission.

This letter was sold SH vi. 126, with 'A portfolio containing original letters, deeds, extracts, etc., on the subject of the *Historic Doubts on the Life of Richard III*.' It was not sent to Cole, probably because HW wished to keep his notes on the Court of Henry VII.

Endorsed by HW: To the Rev. Mr Cole.

Strawberry Hill, March 26, 1780.

I HAVE been looking over the miscellaneous papers published by Mr Ives, and dedicated to me, which I never knew till he was dead, for he never sent them to me, and I fear thought me very ungrateful in never thanking him. They have set me on amusing myself with studying the state of the court in the beginning of the reign of Henry VII whose coronation and his Queen's[1] are described there. It was natural enough for me considering my *Historic Doubts:* and this review has farther opened Henry's spite to his wife's branch. Her next sister, the Princess Cicely,[1a] whom for security he married to his mother's near relation Lord Wells, was old enough to be present at those ceremonies, yet he made her take place after the Duchess of Bedford,[2] who was not of blood royal, but widow of the Duke of Buckingham, who was a distant Prince, and then married [in two years after her husband's execution][2a] to his Majesty's own uncle Jasper Tudor Duke of Bedford[3]—I suppose he pretended his uncle's wife and Cicely's own aunt, for the Duchess of Bedford was Catherine Widville, sister of Queen Elizabeth Widville, ought to precede her niece, though a King's daughter, which is very different from our ideas. He made the same duchess precede another princess too, the Duchess of Suffolk, sister of Edward IV. This last lady, if she had any feeling, must have been tolerably agitated on those occasions. The King's mother, Margaret of Richmond, preceded everybody but the Queen, while her Maj-

---

1. Henry VII was crowned 30 Oct. 1485; his Queen, 25 Nov. 1487.

1a. See *ante* 16 June 1771 n. 10.

2. Katharine Widville (b. ca 1458), m. (1) Henry Stafford, 2d D. of Buckingham; (2) (ca 1485) Jasper Tudor, 3d D. of Bedford; (3) (1492) Sir Richard Wingfield.

2a. The brackets are HW's.

3. Jasper Tudor (1430?–1495), E. of Pembroke and D. of Bedford, uncle of Henry VII.

esty's own grandmother and the Duchess of Suffolk's mother, Cicely Duchess of York,[4] is not mentioned, though she was certainly living. I hope, as her son Richard III was just killed, [not to mention the havoc of others of her race][4a] it made her desire to be excused—and so I should think might her daughter have done—whose own son too, the Earl of Lincoln, who had been declared heir to the Crown by his uncle Richard, was in banishment.[5] I cannot find when this duchess died;[6] but her husband John Delapool was certainly alive when his son landed and was killed at the battle of Stoke; and lived at least three years after that.[7]

But in that scene of blood and faction most of the actors at those coronations must have been in grief or in dread; and they had so intermarried that none were uninterested spectators. There was present a Duchess of Norfolk, who, I suppose, must have been Elizabeth Talbot[8] widow of the last Mowbray,[9] and mother of the young duchess[10] that was betrothed to Richard Duke of York, son of Edward IV, for as John Howard, Richard the Third's Duke, was just killed and attainted,[11] I conclude his widow, Margaret Chedworth,[12] was scarce invited to the coronation.

At one of the festivals was a Lady Margaret Pole,[13] who does precede baronesses, but walks after countesses; and yet I believe she too was a princess of the royal blood of York, for I take her to be the good unhappy Margaret Countess of Salisbury, daughter of George Duke of Clarence. As she was seventy at her execution, she was sixteen at the coronation of Elizabeth of York; and I do not doubt but Henry had married her to the insignificant Sir Richard Pole,[14] who is called a Welsh Knight, and I suppose was found out for her by Jasper Tudor the King's uncle, while her poor brother[15] was shut up in the Tower—another affliction for his grandmother Duchess Cicely!

4. Lady Cicely Neville (1415–95), m. (1424) Richard, D. of York.

4a. The brackets are HW's.

5. John de la Pole (ca 1462–87), E. of Lincoln, nephew of Richard III, was declared heir apparent about May 1485. He was apparently at Henry VII's coronation, but was killed at Stoke (20 June 1487) before the Queen was crowned (see GEC).

6. It is not yet determined.

7. John de la Pole (1442–1491), 2d D. of Suffolk.

8. Elizabeth Talbot (d. 1507), Duchess of Norfolk.

9. John de Mowbray (1444–76), 6th D. of Norfolk.

10. Lady Anne de Mowbray (1472–81), Countess of Norfolk, m. Richard, D. of York.

11. John Howard (ca 1430–85), 8th D. of Norfolk, killed at Bosworth.

12. Margaret Chedworth (d. 1494), m. John Howard, D. of Norfolk.

13. Lady Margaret Plantagenet (1474–1541), m. (1494) Sir Richard Pole; Countess of Salisbury (1513). As she was only 67 at her execution, she was 13 at the Queen's coronation, where she would have walked as Lady Margaret Plantagenet.

14. Sir Richard Pole (d. 1504), K.G., son of Sir Geoffrey Pole of Medmenham, Bucks, and Edith St John, half-sister of Henry's mother, Margaret Beaufort. Henry gave him important offices in Wales.

15. Edward Plantagenet (1475–99), 18th E. of Warwick, nephew of Richard III. Executed for complicity with Perkin Warbeck.

I have found another widow of a beheaded Lord, Mary Fitz Lewis, widow of my favourite Anthony Earl of Rivers,[16] brother of the Queen Dowager, and she too walked at the coronation.

In short I have made myself quite master of that ceremony, and think it must have been as dismal a scene of suppressed passions, as ever was exhibited.

The Countesses of Rivers and Oxford[17] knelt and at certain times held a kerchief before her Grace (the Queen)—at Anne Boleyn's coronation two gentlewomen did the same, and it is said it was for her to spit—methinks it was a little humiliating for her Aunt Lady Rivers to execute that office. In short, I have been gossiping amongst the old nobility like Brantome;[18] but yet such inquiries make one taste history ten times more, than if one only reads a bederoll of names. How one should like to have overheard the conversation of Duchess Cicely and her daughter Suffolk, the first time they met after the coronation! The latter must have been in sweet temper, if she had as much of the spirit of the white rose as her sisters, Margaret Duchess of Burgundy, and Anne Duchess of Exeter, who insisted on being divorced from her husband on his taking up arms for the House of Lancaster.[19]

There are two other incidents in the Queen's coronation which show that Henry VII observed no rules, no, not his own; for though he gave precedence to his Uncle Jasper over the Duke of Suffolk, an elder Duke, he did not give like precedence to his father-in-law the Earl of Derby,[20] nor to another uncle, Lord Wells, his mother's uterine brother, except over the Viscount Lisle.[21]

One error I think there must be in the list of the temporal peers; at least I cannot discover that the Earls of Ormond[22] and Wiltshire[23] were different persons—Stay, I have found, that the first was a Butler, and the second a Stafford.

There is another point that I cannot solve—it does not relate to the period of which I have been talking, but a preceding. In Sandford's genealogic history of our Kings,[24] p. 252, is a plate of Eliz. Duchess of

---

16. Mary FitzLewes, dau. of Sir Henry FitzLewes, of Horndon, Essex, and Lady Elizabeth Beaufort, m., as his 2d wife, Anthony Widville (1442–83), E. Rivers.

17. Margaret Neville (d. after 1488), m. (ca 1465), John de Vere, 13th E. of Oxford.

18. Pierre de Bourdeille (1535–1614), Seigneur and Abbé de Brantome.

19. In 1472.

20. Thomas Stanley (ca 1435–1504), 10th E. of Derby, m. (1482) Margaret of Richmond, mother of Henry VII.

21. Edward Grey (d. 1492), 3d Vct Lisle,

son of Edward, Bn Ferrers of Groby; m. Elizabeth Talbot.

22. Thomas Butler (ca 1424–1515), 7th E. of Ormond.

23. Edward Stafford (1469–99), 4th E. of Wiltshire.

24. *A Genealogical History of the Kings of England* . . ., 1677, was published by Francis Sandford (1630–94), herald and genealogist. The engraving, by Wenceslaus Hollar (1607–77), is a copy of a window formerly in Ampthill Church, Beds (see Thomas Dingley, *History from Marble*, 2

Exeter,[25] sister of Hen. IV and of her second husband Sir John Cornwall Lord Fanhope.[26] They are inclosed by two staves wreathed with labels, on which are repeated this strange word, *Lestaredirie*.[27] Can you tell what it means? If one should propose it to the Antiquarian Society, I believe it would produce such a blundering answer as would amount to *éstourderie* —but perhaps I have confounded you with names and genealogies, and you may not choose to hunt after riddles, as I do, who you see when I am here alone, as I am for four or five days, can divert myself with obsolete history, and prefer it to Committees and Associations.

PS.

Yesterday's papers say Dr Greene the Dean of Salisbury is dead. I saw him a little month ago at Gloucester House. We compared notes on gout; I found his spirits and intellects on the decay, but had no notion of his going off so soon and that it was the last time I should see him. He was with us at Cambridge, but I believe a little older.[28]

vols, 1867–8, ii. 117, cccxiii). The plate also appears as the third in *Collections . . . for Bedfordshire*, 1812, by Thomas Fisher; and see EBP.

25. Elizabeth of Lancaster (d. 1426), sister of Henry IV; m. (1) John Holland, D. of Exeter; (2) Sir John Cornwall.

26. Sir John Cornwall (d. 1443); cr. 1432 Bn of Fanhope and 1442 Bn of Milbroke (GEC *sub* Fanhope).

27. The legend, *lestare dirie*, is repeated eight times on the 'labels.' Dr R. T. Hill, Yale University, suggests the following explanation: 'Rejoice on the Day of Judgment,' i.e., *laetare die irae* > *letare di*

ire > *lestare diire* > *lestare dirie*. The transposition of *i* and *r* may have been due to the craftsman's ignorance; or the phrase may have been quoted from a medieval Latin chant in which the last syllable, of *dīre* was slurred. 'Masses for the Dead' in the *Dominican Missal* frequently juxtapose the ideas of rejoicing and final doom.

Dr Robert C. Bates, Yale University: 'History will tell,' i.e., *lestore dire* > *l'histoire dira*.

28. He was Fellow of Corpus 1732–5 (*Alumni Cantab.*).

APPENDIX 4

WALPOLE'S DIET DRINK

See *ante* 14 February 1782.

℞[1]

Radices bardanæ

Radices lapathi acuti: āā ʒvj

Folias menyanthæ: ♏j

Coque in aquæ fontanæ lbsij ad lbj.

Cola et adde:

Succor [succus] beccabungæ ⎱

Succor cochleariæ ⎬ commistim,

Succor trifolii aquatici ⎰

quantitatem dimidiam, scilicet semi-libram ad lbj decoctionis. Deinde
adde spiritus cochleariæ, ʒij, misce, fiat apozema.

TAKE:

roots of burdock ⎱ amount of

roots of sharp-pointed dock ⎰ each, 6 drachms.

leaves of buckbean, 1 minim.

Boil down in spring water, 2 pounds to 1 pound [1 pound = 12 ounces].

Strain and add:

juice of brooklime ⎱

juice of scurvy-grass ⎬ mixed,

juice of marsh trefoil, or buckbean ⎰

in a quantity equal to one-half that of the decoction, i.e., ½ pound to
1 pound.

Then add spirits of scurvy-grass, 2 ounces; mix and make the apozem.

1. For pharmaceutical terms in this recipe, see John Quincy, *Pharmacopoeia Officinalis & Extemporanea: or, A Compleat English Dispensatory*, 1749, and *Pharmacopoeia Collegii Regalis*, 1788. In the interpretation of this 'diet drink' we have been aided by Mr Charles Noyes, New Haven, Conn., and Mr E. S. Peck, Cambridge, England.

APPENDIX 5

Cole's Account of his Visit to Strawberry Hill 30 Oct. 1762

Add MS 5841, ff. 87–8.

Cole describes Pope's monument in the Twickenham Church (Add MS 5841, ff. 86–7) and continues:

SIR WILLIAM STANHOPE,[1] brother to the Earl of Chesterfield, now lives in Mr Pope's house on the banks of the Thames; you pass over his grotto, immediately under the common highway,[2] as you come from the town of Twickenham to Mr Walpole's house of Strawberry Hill. Next to it is the house belonging to the late Earl of Radnor,[3] which is the last house on the Thames bank next to Strawberry Hill, a road going by the Thames-side to Kingston Bridge, being between the river and Mr Walpole's garden, which, however, is within a furlong or two of the river, and his own meadows go quite down to the banks of it, and nothing to obstruct the view of that most beautifying fluid, which makes everything handsome that is within its influence. From the garden you discover the elegant Chinese Temple, being the last building on the bank of the Thames, and close to my Lord Radnor's house or garden wall[4]—though the house belonging to it is on the other side of the road, and is the last house on that side next to Strawberry Hill, and is an handsome new square building—I say, from this garden of Mr Walpole you discover the Chinese summer house in which, about last August, Mr Isaac Fernandez Nunez,[5] a Jew, shot himself through the head, on the loss of the *Hermione*, a rich French ship[6] which he had insured, and by that means ruined his fortune and family. His house and furniture were sold by auction while I was at Strawberry Hill, and I was at the sale for a few minutes. From Mr Walpole's garden and house you have the most beautiful

1. (1702–72), 2d son of Philip, 3d E. of Chesterfield (Collins, *Peerage*, 1812, iii. 426–7). HW did not approve of Stanhope's changes in Pope's villa (HW to Mann 20 June 1760).

2. It is still there, only about a quarter of a mile from SH.

3. John Robartes (1686?–1757), 4th E. of Radnor; F.R.S. He was buried at Twickenham 23 July 1757. HW called the house 'Mabland.'

4. HW calls it a 'Chinese summer-house'

(see HW to Mann 12 June 1753 and illustration).

5. Not further identified.

6. The *Hermione*, a Spanish register-ship bound from Lima to Cadiz, was captured 21 May 1762 by the English frigates *Active* and *Favorite* with a cargo valued at £500,000; the prize reached England 27 July (Wm Laird Clowes, *The Royal Navy* 1897–1903, 7 vols, iii. 308; *London Chronicle* 6–8 July 1762; *Lloyd's Evening Post* 26–8 July).

and charming prospect of Richmond, with variety of fine villas and gardens on the banks of the Thames, which river alone would sufficiently recommend any situation; though when I was there last, viz., in October and the beginning of November, 1762, the excessive rains which had lately fell had so swelled the river that it caused such inundations as were never known in the memory of man; insomuch that during my stay there, two islands just before the garden were totally covered by the waters and could not be seen. The floods did infinite mischief all over England, and particularly in Essex. At Cambridge it was within six inches of the highest flood ever known or recorded there, of which a mark is cut in the wall of King's College Senior Fellows Garden, on the river's bank; and the waters came into the cellars of Queens' College in such a torrent that the butler had not time to go in to stop up the vessels, they having just newly filled their cellars for the year; by which means the water got in, and spoiled all their beer.

APPENDIX 6

COLE's Account of his Visit to Strawberry Hill 29–31 Oct. 1774

Add MS 5847, ff. 205v–207.

SATURDAY, Oct. 29. Very rainy day. I set out after breakfast, and went at the back of the town, through Padington, and through Hyde Park, and got to Twickenham by noon. Before dinner Mr Walpole walked with me into the garden to show me his newly erected Chapel,[1] as he calls it, with the shrine in it from the Church of Santa Maria Maggiore at Rome, where it was erected in 1256, by Gio. Giacomo Capoccio and Vinia, his wife, over the bodies of the holy martyrs, Simplicius, Faustina, and Beatrice, and was executed by Pietro Cavalini, who made the shrine of Edward the Confessor in Westminster Abbey.[2] It is a very curious monument of white marble, standing on twisted pillars, and inlaid with other rich marbles; but altered from what it was when standing in San Mary Maggiore at Rome.[3] It is also mended and completed by the ingenious artist who erected the beautiful marble chimney-piece in the circular drawing room at the end of the gallery.[4] This occupies the whole end of the chapel, the great and only window to which is filled with painted glass from Bexhill in Sussex.[5] There are besides a strange jumble of crucifixes and profane ornaments.[6] It is so small that half a dozen people will fill it. The front is exquisitely performed in the truest Gothic taste.[7]

1. HW's Chapel was begun in 1772 by Thomas Gayfere (1720–1812), master mason to Westminster Abbey ('Genesis of SH' 83). It was not completed until May 1774 (see SH Accounts 151–4).

2. That Cavallini (ca 1259–1344) made the shrine is open to conjecture (see Anecdotes, ed. Wornum, i. 17, n. 1).

3. See illustration.

4. This chimney piece, inspired by the tomb of Edward the Confessor, in Westminster, was 'improved by Mr Adam [1728–92], and beautifully executed in white marble inlaid with scagliola, by Richter' (Description of SH, Works ii. 468). This is probably John Augustus Richter (fl. 1772–1809), 'artist, engraver and scagliolist,' who went to London from Saxony before 1772; he executed several public works in imitation of marble, among them the columns at the Greenwich Hospital (John Lewis Roget, A History of the 'Old Water-Colour' Society, 1891, 2 vols, i. 384; DNB sub Henry J. Richter; Allgemeines Lexicon der Bildenden Künstler, Leipzig, 1907–).

5. See ante 23 Oct. 1771, n. 4.

6. These included a bronze incense-burner, four Etruscan vases, Indian arrows, and a number of Roman urns or ossuaria, in marble, and were sold SH xxiv. 87–99, passim.

7. The façade of the Chapel, of Portland stone, was designed by Chute after the tomb of Edmund Audley, Bp of Salisbury in Salisbury Cathedral ('Genesis of SH' 83 and fig. 30; Description of SH, Works ii. 507).

After dinner, when the lady was withdrawn, Mr Walpole asked me whether I recollected any person to whom that lady was like. I said, she resembled his father and elder brother. He then told me a long history of her, which, as well as I can recollect (November 7, 1774, Burnham) is as follows. She is the natural daughter of Sir Robert Walpole, first Earl of Orford, and that she might not be left destitute when her father was no more, [he] bought a living for £600, and proposed marrying her to Mr Keene,[8] brother to Benjamin Keene, then, or after, Ambassador at the Court of Spain;[9] to both of whom it was proposed, and gladly accepted of. Accordingly, Mr Keene was put into possession of this living,[10] and enjoyed it as his first preferment for some time. In the interim Lord Orford dies, and when the lady was marriageable, it was proposed to Mr Keene to fulfil his engagement; but as he had by this time made other connections,[11] and the lady, I suppose, not over-tempting, though of this Mr Walpole said not a word; and I only judge so from her present squab, short, gummy appearance, though by no means deformed or misshaped, but rather undersized and snub-faced, which probably might have been better when she was younger. When this was determined on, the lady had nothing to do but to retire and live as well as she could with her mother in a starving condition, as no further provision was made for her, and the family knew nothing about her. Nor did Mr Walpole ever hear anything of her, 'till within this year, or two, Mr Trevigar, Canon of Chichester, and formerly Fellow of Clare Hall,[12] where he was my tutor, jointly with Mr Nichols,[13] and whom I have not seen since he left college, called one morning upon him, and told him, 'that he had a very near relation in the utmost distress and necessity, and of whom, he presumed, he was an entire stranger.' Upon this information Mr Walpole immediately sent for her up to town, and took her, as a sister, into his own house, where she lives with him half the year,[14] and chooses to spend the other half in the country with her mother. What country this is, I was not curious to inquire. But I

8. Edmund Keene (1714–81), Bp of Chester 1752–71, and of Ely 1771–81.

9. Sir Benjamin Keene (1697–1757), K.B., ambassador at Madrid 1727–39 and 1748–57.

10. Keene held the rectory of Stanhope in Durham from 1740 to 1770; in 1752, HW stated that the living was worth £700 a year (HW to Mann 11 Dec. 1752).

11. In May 1753, he married Mary Andrews (1728–76), only daughter and heiress of Lancelot Andrews, of Edmonton, formerly a linen-draper in Cheapside; with her, Keene received a large fortune.

12. Luke Trevigar (d. 1772), Fellow of Clare Hall 1728–38; rector of Hurstmonceux, Sussex 1743–72; Canon of Chichester 1753–72 (Alumni Cantab.; GM April 1772, xlii. 199b).

13. Nicholas Nichols (d. 1772), Fellow of Clare Hall 1724–34; vicar of Great and Little Abington, Cambs 1732–6; rector of Patrington, Yorks 1734–72 (Alumni Cantab.).

14. Mrs Daye died at SH of 'asthma and dropsy' in October 1775 (HW to Lady Ossory 3 Aug., 21 Oct. 1775).

guess it to be Sussex, and near Chichester,[15] where Mr Trevigar was beneficed, and as she seemed to be acquainted with the Guilford Road,
whither I was going, about which she gave me instructions, as I was unacquainted with the way. He called her by the name of Mrs Day, which
was, probably, her mother's name. On her coming to town, and being informed of the story, she was instructed to apply to the Bishop, who was
not disposed to lend a favourable ear to it; upon which, he drew up a letter for her,[16] and omitted no circumstance to alarm the Bishop, who was
well aware, as Mr Walpole said to me, that a bishop in his hands would
meet with but little quarter; when, therefore, she was directed to add, by
way of postscript, to direct his answer to her at Mr Horace Walpole's in
Arlington Street, it had its effect. And the Bishop proposed to give her the
£600 or interest for that sum; and, accordingly, he contrived meanly, as
Mr Walpole expressed it, to send her the interest the very day before
quarter day, and by that means defrauded her of about £5, as well as I
remember. This, Mr Walpole said, he was glad of, as the Bishop by so doing either cheated her, or owes her that sum to this day. Now I have related the story, as well as I can recollect it, I must needs add this caution
about it. Mr Walpole is one of the most sanguine friends or enemies that
I know. He has had a long pique, I well know, against the Bishop;[17] and
indeed his being a bishop is a sufficient reason for his spleen and satire. I
love to hear both sides of the question. No doubt Bishop Keene had his
reasons, right or wrong, for his acting in the manner he did. Mr Walpole
added that he often met the Bishop, now his house is building in Dover
Street,[18] but that he always avoided looking at him and constantly held
down his head. Mr Walpole best knows what occasions of goodness or shyness there may be between them. The Bishop, I allow, is as much puffed
up with his dignities and fortune as any on the bench; and I believe Mr
Walpole to be as likely to throw out contemptuous behaviour occasionally
on those whom he supposes not to acknowledge his merit, or deserve his
disregard, as any person living. They are both my friends, and I can see
the blemishes in each. The Bishop was ever esteemed a most cheerful,
generous, and good-tempered man. Great fortune with a wife and great
dignity in the church often make the wisest men forget themselves. Mr
Walpole is one of the best writers, an admirable poet, one of the most
lively, ingenious, and witty persons of the age; but a great share of vanity,
eagerness of adulation, as Mr Gray observed to me, a violence and
warmth in party matters, and lately even to enthusiasm, abates, and takes

15. She lived at Chichester (HW to
Lady Ossory 3 Aug. 1775).
16. Missing.
17. For his opinion of Keene, see HW to
Mann 11 Dec. 1752.

18. Ely House, at 37 Dover Street, became the London residence of the Bishops
of Ely (Henry B. Wheatley, *London Past
and Present*, 1891, i. 517).

off from, many of his shining qualitie<s. I> have given the story as it was related to me, without reserves or cautio<n what>ever. I mean to take notice of it to no one;[19] though I make no doubt but Mr Walpole, as he told it to me, has done the same to others.[20] His zeal against churchmen and the church carries him to such lengths as is scarcely consistent with a wise and ingenuous heart.

On a secretaire, as it is called, or upright writing-stand or desk, in the breakfasting room, which commands a delicious prospect across the Thames up to Richmond Hill, is a most delicate and elegant small statue of Cupid sitting, winged, and holding up one hand, in the Seve or St Cloud manufacture, in white; and on a cartouche in front is this inscription. Cupid sits on a bank or hillock ornamented with roses.

> Quique tu sois, voici ton maître:
> Il le fut, il l'est, ou doit l'être.[21]

Mrs Clive, the celebrated actress and comedian, has a little box, contiguous to Mr Walpole's garden, and close almost to the Chapel. Here she lives retired, and her brother, Mr Raftor,[22] with her. He called at Mr Walpole's while I was with him with a message from his sister, to spend the evening with her; but he was not disposed to stir out. Mr Franks, the Jew,[23] also called on Sunday morning to ask him to a concert, where his daughter,[24] who is an incomparable hand, was to be the chief performer. He also mentioned with raptures his Jewish neighbours, Mr and Mrs Prado,[25] as the most accomplished persons he was acquainted with. This

19. 'I never opened my lips to any mortal about Bishop Keene['s] affair. But Dr Glynn and Mr Jacob Bryant calling here (at Milton the morning July 8, 1779, Thursday) occasionally talking about the Bishop, whom they both agreed was a kiss mine A— fellow (that was their expression) and said it belonged to him with propriety, they mentioned the story about Miss Day. Mr Bryant added that he was well assured that the late Mr Hetherington [d. 1 Dec. 1778; see end of note] left several legacies to people of whom he had no opinion, but merely to show that he died in Christian charity with them and to show that he was as much above resenting their ill behaviour as theirs was below that of a gentleman; and mentioned the £200 left to Bishop Keene as one of them' (addition in margin of MS). William Hetherington (1699–1778), son of Humphrey, of London; M.A. at Peterhouse, Cambridge, 1723; rector of Dry Drayton, Cambs, 1728–53, and of Farnham Royal,

Bucks, 1753–78; founder of the Hetherington Charity for the blind (*Alumni Cantab.*; see also Cole's account of him, Add MS 5848, f. 92, quoted in N&Q June 1917, Ser. XII, iii. 319–23).

20. HW had told Mann of the affair (HW to Mann 11 Dec. 1752).

21. The statue of Cupid was sold SH xi. 87 to J. P. Bevan for £22.1.0.

22. James Raftor (d. 1790), an actor (GM Sept. 1790, lx. 861a).

23. Moses Franks (1718–89) had houses at Richmond and Isleworth; he died at Teddington (GM April 1789, lix. 374; Alfred Rubens, *Anglo-Jewish Portraits*, 1935, p. 33).

24. Not identified.

25. Abraham Prado (d. 1782), of Twickenham (GM Aug. 1782, lii. 406a). He was famous for his knowledge of gardening (Edward Ironside, *History and Antiquities of Twickenham*, 1797, p. 107). Mrs Prado was still alive in 1785 (see HW to Lady Browne 14 Dec. 1785).

puts me in mind of a singular visit he paid for an hour one Sunday afternoon, while I was with him, about ten years ago.[26] It was when the present Bishop of London was Bishop of Peterborough, and then Minister of Twickenham;[27] the visit was to a Jew,[28] where was a Roman Catholic family, the Bishop of Peterborough, and some Dissenters. I remember not the names; but this I remember because it struck me. The Bishop possibly might have assumed some airs, which Mr Walpole might think did not become one who was a lord only by accident, and not by birth or creation; in order therefore to lower and humble the pride of the prelate, who has enough of it about him, I remember Mr Walpole told me on his return, for I did not attend him, that he called him frequently Mr and Doctor Terrick, in order to mortify him. Surely this was not right or proper. The laws of the land and custom unalterable have fixed such and such titles to such and such dignities and offices; and whoever disregards them acts like a clown, and improperly. I presume no one loves titles better than himself, as will be evident to anyone who looks over the description of the Villa of Strawberry Hill, where is a most fulsome enumeration, on every occasion, of the most minute titles of all the Walpole family and its most distant alliances. It would have been thought coarse, unbred behaviour in Bishop Terrick to have addressed Lady Walpole without the title of ladyship. To judge impartially, therefore, to omit giving the due title to a bishop cannot be justified in any light.

While I was at Strawberry Hill, I saw on the table a scrap of paper with the following verses on Mrs Clive, which I took a copy of, though I had no leave from Mr Walpole for so doing. Yet as they laid publicly for anyone to see them, I thought it no breach of honour to copy them. They seemed to me, from the blotting and alterations of the writing, to have been lately composed, probably the evening before, while Mrs Clive <was> present, and meant as a sportive and innocent amusement, and to divert <the t>ime. They were written by way of epitaph, and on a supposition that Mrs Clive was dead. They are as follows:

Epitaph on the Death of Mrs Clive

Ye smiles and jests still hover round!
This is mirth's consecrated ground.
Here liv'd the laughter-loving dame;
A matchless actress, Clive by name.
The comic muse with her retir'd;
The comic wept when she expir'd.[29]

26. Probably 30 Oct. 1762; see Appendix 5.

27. Richard Terrick (1710–77), vicar of Twickenham, 1749–64; Bp of Peterborough, 1757–64 and of London 1764–77.

28. Not identified.

29. These verses were cut on a pedestal supporting an 'urn erected in the garden

For the Cascade

Lull the sweet nymph's repose, ye falling streams,
And murmur sounds of love to soothe her dreams.

On Sunday, Mr Lort, Fellow of Trinity College, came over, as we had agreed, to dinner, and stayed the evening, and next morning, before breakfast, Monday, Oct. 31, I quitted Strawberry Hill.

at Cliveden near Twickenham, 1792' (HW's note on the original drawing of it, pasted into his extra-illustrated copy of the *Description of SH*, 1784, now wsl). The verses appeared, without the couplet 'For the Cascade,' in *Works* iv. 400. An answer was written by 'Peter Pindar' (John Wolcot): 'To Mr Horace Walpole' [etc. *Fugitive Verses* 87]. Both sets of verses have been frequently reprinted. The present appearance of the pedestal (which alone survives) in the garden of SH is given by P. J. Crean, N&Q April 1932, clxii. 272–3. HW's drawing of the urn and pedestal is the frontispiece to *Fugitive Verses*.

APPENDIX 7

A Check-List of Works to Which COLE Contributed

Baker, Thomas, *History of the College of St John the Evangelist, Cambridge,* ed. John E. B. Mayor, Cambridge, 2 vols, 1869. This contains copious extracts from Cole's MSS; see index.

Bentham, James, *History of Ely Cathedral,*[1,2] 2 vols, 1812–17. Cole's help is acknowledged on p. 3; see also pp. 42*–7* *et passim* in the second edition; see LA i. 659 n.

Cole, William, 'Corrections of Sir J. Hawkins's *History of Music*' (GM May, 1777, xlvii. 219).

Cole, William (Palæophilus), 'Origin of Old Nick' (GM March, 1777, xlvii. 119).

Cole, William, 'Saint Whose Emblems Are Naked Boys in a Tub' (GM April, 1777, xlvii. 157).

Cole, William, 'Some Observations on the Horns given by Henry I to the Cathedral of Carlisle' (*Archaeologia*, 1779, v. 340–5).

Cole, William, 'Specimens of the Writings of Mr Cole,' with excerpts from his 'Account of the Inquisition' and his 'Life of Weseham' (GM May, 1784, liv. 333).

Davis, William, *An Olio of Bibliographical and Literary Anecdotes . . . including Mr Cole's unpublished notes on the Rev. Jas. Bentham's History . . . of Ely,* 1814.

Ducarel, Andrew Coltee, *Account of Doctors' Commons.* The MS of this was prepared for the press, but not published; Cole sent Ducarel 52 folio pages of material (LA ii. 687); see also ibid. 686–93.

Ducarel, Andrew Coltee, *A Tour through Normandy,* 1754. The extent of Cole's help in this work is not clear; Ducarel printed no acknowledgment, but see Cole's letters in LA ii. 687, 691.

Gough, Richard, *British Topography,*[2] 2 vols, 1780. Cole's corrections and additions are *passim;* cf. LA ii. 694–5.

Gough, Richard (ed.), *Camden's Britannia,* 3 vols, 1789. Gough used Cole's account of Sir Horatio Palavicini without acknowledgment in vol. ii. 138; he also used the account in his *Short Genealogical View of the Family of Oliver Cromwell,* 1785 (Appendix vi, 44–5). Cf. LA i. 676.

Gough, Richard, *History and Antiquities of Croyland Abbey,* 1783 (*Bibliotheca Topographica Britannica,* ed. John Nichols, vol. 3). Gough acknowledges the use of Cole's transcript of the abbey register (p. vi; see LA i. 693–4, 697).

Gough, Richard, *Sepulchral Monuments,* 3 vols, 1786–99. Cole contributed scattered remarks (LA i. 660).

Granger, James, *A Biographical History of England,*[2] 4 vols, 1775. Granger acknowledges Cole's help (i. sig. A2).

Grey, Zachary (ed.), *Hudibras . . . corrected and amended,* 2 vols, 1744; *Supplement,* 1752. Cole contributed a 'few notes' (LA i. 561; ii. 541–2 n).

Grose, Francis, *Antiquities of England and Wales,* 4 vols, 1773–87. Cole wrote the 'Account of Pythagoras's School at Cambridge' (LA i. 659).

Kippis, Andrew (ed.), *Biographia Britannica,*[2] 5 vols, 1778–93; part of vol. 6, 1795. Cole's additions and corrections are *passim.*

Nichols, John (ed.), *A Select Collection of Miscellaneous Poems,* 8 vols, 1782. For Cole's corrections see viii. 308 *et passim* in the last four volumes; cf. LA i. 661–3.

Nichols, John (ed.), *Biographical Anecdotes of William Hogarth,* 1781. See Cole to Nichols 6 May 1781 (LA i. 663).

Nichols, John, *Biographical and Literary Anecdotes of William Bowyer,* 1782. Cole's assistance is acknowledged in LA i. p. xi.

Nichols, John, *History and Antiquities of Hinckley, in the County of Leicester,* 1782 (*Bibliotheca Topographica Britannica,* vol. 7). For Cole's contributions see LA i. 665–6.

Nichols, John (ed.), *Some Account of the Gentlemen's Society at Spalding,* 1784 (*Bibliotheca Topographica Britannica,* vol. 3). Cole 'supplied several anecdotes of the early members' (LA i. 660).

Roundell, H., *Memoir of Browne Willis, LL.D.,* Aylesbury, 1857.

Tyson, Michael, 'An Account of an Illuminated Manuscript in the Library of Corpus Christi College, Cambridge, 1772 (*Archaeologia,* 1773, ii. 194–7). Cole may have been the author of this paper; see DNB *sub* Tyson.

Walpole, Horace, *Anecdotes of Painting in England.* See Cole to HW 16 May 1762 *et passim.*

Walpole, Horace (ed.), *Copies of Seven Original Letters from King Edward VI to Barnaby Fitz-patrick,* SH, 1772. The letters were transcribed for the press by Cole (HW to Cole 29 May 1771).

Walpole, Horace (ed.), *Miscellaneous Antiquities,* No. 2, 1772. See Cole to HW 22 June 1772.

Walpole, Horace, 'The Life of Mr Thomas Baker' (*Works* ii. 341). HW acknowledges Cole's help in obtaining 'the few notices that I am able to impart' (*Works* ii. 343; see also the index to this correspondence *sub* Thomas Baker).

APPENDIX 8

Cole's Epitaph

'My own Epitaph, in due time, when it pleases God, after taking me out of this world, to make it proper for me.

"Underneath
lyeth the body of
W. C. A. M. and F. A. S.
the son of W. C. of Baberham, in the County
of Cambridge, gent.
lord of the Manor of Halls, in this parish,
by Catharine his wife,
daughter of Theophilus Tuer,
of Cambridge, Merchant.
He was educated in the College of Eton,
and from thence removed to Clare Hall
in the University of Cambridge.
In the former part of his life, and while he
resided in the University,
(which he did for 20 years,)
he was in the Commission of the Peace for the
County of Cambridge,
and acted for many years in that capacity;
and one of his Majesty's Deputy-lieutenants
for the said County;
and was afterwards Justice of the Peace for the
Borough of Cambridge.
On his going into holy orders, he was
first collated by Thomas Sherlock, Bp of London,
to the Rectory of Hornsey in Middlesex;
then by that industrious Antiquary, Browne Willis,
Esq. to the Rectory of Blecheley in Buckinghamshire;
and lastly presented by Eton College to the
Vicarage of Burnham near Windsor.
He departed this life
. . . . in the . . . . . . year of his age.
Memento, homo, quia pulvis es,
et in pulverem reverteris.
Miserere mei, Deus, secundum multitudinem
misericordiarum tuarum.
O Christe, Soter & Judex,
mihi Gulielmo Cole, peccatorum maximo
misericors & propitius esto" ' (LA i. 668–9).

Cole's actual Epitaph is in a niche in the south side of the tower of St Clement's Church: "In / a Tomb / in the center of this Steeple / (erected pursuant to his will and / with money left by him for that purpose) / Are deposited the remains / of the Rev. W. Cole, A. M. / formerly of Clare Hall in this / University. / He was vicar of Burnham / in the County of Buckingham / but resided chiefly at Milton in the County of Cambridge / of which he was a Magistrate / and deputy Lieutenant for many years.

"He died on the 16th day of December, 1782 / in the 68th year of his age.—"

In an elongated lozenge on the north side of the tower is this inscription: "The / first Stone of / this steeple was laid / by Mr Granado Pigott of Ely / the legal representative of the late / Revd Wm Cole of Milton, on the 6th day of June / 1821" (Palmer, *William Cole* 26).

INDEX

References in bold-face type indicate biographical notes.

Franklin, Benjamin II, 84